WOMEN IN ISLAM

WOMEN IN ISLAM

By

Iqbal Mullick

2008

CYBER TECH PUBLICATIONS
4264/3, Ansari Road, Daryaganj, New Delhi-110002 (India)
Ph.: 011-23244078. Fax: 011-23280028
E-Mail: cyberpublicationsdelhi@yahoo.com

WOMEN IN ISLAM

Iqbal Mullick

First Edition 2008

Published by :

G.S. Rawat for **Cyber Tech Publications**
4264/3, Ansari Road, Daryaganj, New Delhi-110002 (India)
Ph.: 011-23244078. Fax: 011-23280028
E-Mail: cyberpublicationsdelhi@yahoo.com

Printed at : **Amit Enterprises**, Maujpur, Delhi, (9810878184)

Preface

Islam is one of the well known and well observed religions of the world. However this religion came into being after all ancient religions of the world but it spread all over the world in very less time. Islam is a religion of lans. There are a number of laws and code of conduct in Islam and the observers of Islam are hoped to abide by these laws. The book is about the status of women in Islam because for women there are also a number of laws in Islam and all Muslim women are expected to abide by these rules and laws.

The book discusses about the social status of Muslim women, setup of Islamic world, marriage and divorce system and family system etc.

All the relating laws and rules are discussed in this book under different headings. The book will be really knowledgeable to the readers is the sincere hope of the undersigned.

Every possible effort has been made but still same facts may remain unnoticed readers are requested to give their suggestions regarding the same and the author will be very thankful to them.

—Author

Contents

1

Social Status of Muslim Women

MERITS OF WOMEN

Farid Wajadi Afandi in his famous book entitled *Al-Mirat ul-Muslima* has discussed the habits and temperaments of women. Maulana Azad has translated this book into Urdu and added footnotes to it. In this book the author writes quoting references from the Encyclopaedia: It is a fact that the construction of the female body resembles that of a child. Due to this reason the woman is sensitive like a child and is readily affected by external impressions. It is the habit of a child that he begins to cry over a painful sight and leaps up with joy over a cheerful thing. The same is the case with the women, who are easily carried away by all sorts of sentiments than men. Experience shows that women are generally hardworking and self-contented. They love their husbands from the core of their hearts, bring up their children with the uvmost care and are the best household managers. They are sincere and loyal. There are more virtues and less weaknesses in them. The laborious and hardworking nature of a woman can be judged at the time of difficulty.

Modern research has proved this fact. The great scholar Lumbrose has written: Just imagine the hardships and tribulations a woman has to go through during pregnancy and at the time of delivery, otherwise the accomplishment of this delicate and difficult task of multiplication of the human race would not be possible.

No doubt woman is a delicate creature. She has a weak and delicate heart. Coquettishness is in her"nature. She is of buoyant and jovial nature. She is also easily annoyed and flares up at trifling matters. A man should adopt some reasonable attitude taking into consideration all these things. In the verses pertaining to divorce, men have been admonished not to commit tyranny and aggression.

Prohibition : It has been said in the Holy Quran:

Retain them not to their hurt so that ye transgress (the limits). He who doeth that hath wronged his spul. Make not the revelations of Allah a laughing stock. *(2:231)*

In the above verse men have been forbidden from tyranny and oppression; but the miraculous style of the verse is very comprehensive. Allah, the Exalted, forbids men from persecuting women. The Holy Prophet (peace and blessings of Allah be upon him) has observed: No one of you should beat a woman like a servant and then next day go to her for sgxual gratification. *(Bukhari)*

The Holy Prophet (peace and blessings of Allah be upon him) has prohibited the beating of woman. The Holy Prophet (peace and blessings of Allah be upon him) said: Do not beat your wife like a maid servant. *(Mishkat)*

Once the Holy Prophet (peace and blessings of Allah be upon him) was questioned about the rights of women over men. He answered: When you dine, dine with them and when you dress, dress with them. Do not beat them on their face, nor rebuke them nor separate them. If you do so, do in the house. *(Mishkat)*

The Holy Prophet (peace and blessings of Allah be upon him) has issued the above commandment as men have the right to admonish women under special circumstances but it is not permissible to admonish them publicly.

The kind and benevolent treatment of the Holy Prophet (peace and blessings of Allah be upon him) towards his wives is a practical example for all the believers. He never even thought of giving physical punishment to his wives.

However, the Holy Quran has allowed the infliction of physical punishment on women in special situations:

As for those from whom ye fear rebellion, admonish them and banish them to beds apart; and beat them. Then if they obey you, seek not a way from them. *(4:34)*

But this prerogative should be applied very rarely when it is absolutely necessary. According to the Holy Quran, if the woman is stubborn and persistent in her behaviour, man should try to convince her by argument. If he does not succeed to bring her round, he should separate his bed. Even then if he does not succeed, he is allowed to beat her. But what could be the nature of beating? In this connection, the Holy Prophet (peace and blessings of Allah be upon him) has said: Give them a light beating. This implies light punishment or rebuke.

Holy Prophet's Instructions : The Messenger of Allah (peace and blessings of Allah be upon him) in his famous historical address observed, besides speaking on other important points:

> *Instruct each other to do good to your womenfolk for they are assigned to you and have no control over anything by themselves and if they are guilty of immodesty, you are allowed to beat them without leaving (serious) injury. But if they repent you must treat them better. Lo! you have your rights against your wives and they have theirs against you. It is their duty to observe chastity and to avoid immorality and their right against you is that you must feed and clothe them with fairness.* *(Tirmidhi)*

It is evident from the above Hadith that the permission for the beating of women granted by the Holy Quran may be utilized very sparingly, only in the case of manifest immodesty. Every word of the above extract of the speech of the Messenger of Allah (peace and blessings of Allah be upon him) is full of profound insight and wisdom regarding the mutual relations of husband and wife.

In order to ensure discipline and stability in domestic life men have been given power over women. If both were vested with equal power, it would have ruined the peace and harmony of the domes tic life as two kings cannot rule over one state. Secondly, men have been given permission to rebuke or to avoid sexual intercourse or to beat, not causing any serious injury, if the woman is found guilty of manifest immodesty. Then the rights of husbands against their wives and those of wives against their husbands have been ezplained. The husband has been instructed to feed and clothe his wife with fairness. He must not take undue advantage of the power vested in him and do what he wishes; but it is his duty to fulfil the needs tastes and interests of his wife as she is dependent on him. Experience shows that if any person is dependent on the other in a certain sphere of life and the latter does not care for his sentiments and tastes, the former's feelings are injured and he feels disgusted.

Before the advent of Islam there was no restriction on the Arab men and women meeting and talking with each other just like the modern western people of today.

Islam put an end to these practices of the Days of Ignorance. The second duty of women is that they should ask the permission of their husbands before they allow any man (Mahram or Ghair

Mahram) to enter their houses and should not let such men enter their houses whom their husbands do not like.

Holy Prophet's Treatment with His Wives : *The Holy Prophet (peace and blessings of Allah be upon him) has taught that a Mumin should be an embodiment of virtues and of excellent moral conduct and behaviour and that the best of you in this respect are the kindest of you to their wives. The Messenger of Allah (peace and blessings of Allah be upon him) has observed: The most perfect of the believers in faith is the best of them in moral excellence, and the best of you are the kindest of you to their wives.*
(Tirmidhi)

According to the above Hadith, the sign of the most perfect and best believer in faith is that he is the kindest to his wife. The husbands should, therefore, be kind and benevolent to their wives and should always try to fulfil their lawful needs and desires to please them. He whose treatment with his wife is the best possesses the most excellent virtues among us. During a short meeting, a person may pose excellent behaviour and manners; but the permanent and lasting company of his wife exposes his real character and temperament. The wife is the real test of his natural and inherent qualities.

Once the Messenger of Allah (peace and blessing of Allah be upon him) said: Avoid beating the living creatures of Allah. In Arabia the women were treated no better than animals. They were entirely at the mercy of men. Men had the right to take the life of a woman or to beat her as an ordinary thing. But with the advent of Islam, the persecution of women ended and they heaved a sigh of relief.

The result of the emancipation of this downtrodden humanity began to be felt in society as is evident from this Hadith. One day Hadrat Umar (Allah be pleased with him) came to the Messenger of Allah (peace and blessings of Allah be upon him) and said: Women have become daring to their husbands. Hearing this the Messenger of Allah (peace and blessings of Allah be upon him) said that the above instructions may not be observed strictly; but the husbands took an undue advantage of the 'relaxation' and complaints began to pour in. Thereupon the Messenger of Allah (peace and blessings of Allah be upon him) said: Many a woman surrounded the family of Muhammad and complained that their husbands were not good people.
(Riyad Al-Salihin)

Who could bear to listen to the complaint from the tongue of the Messenger of Allah (peace and blessings of Allah be upon him)? The result was that there came a moderation in the men's behaviour.

One main aim and object of the Messenger of Allah (peace and blessings of Allah be upon him) in calling for the meeting of the Ummahat-ul-Muminin (mothers of the believers) in Medina, eight or nine years before his death was, besides other things, to give a practical lesson that mutual love and harmony should exist between husband and wife. He used to say: The best of you is the kindest of you to his family and I am the kindest of you all to my family. And when your wife dies pray for her. (Mishkat)

It is evident that pious and good behaviour does not mean temporary posing; but your treatment of your wife and children should fully reflect these virtues. The Messenger of Allah (peace and blessings of Allah be upon him) not only instructed the people to be good and kind to their wives, but also acted upon this principle in his practical life. He used to say: The most perfect of the believers in faith is the best of them in moral excellence and the kindest of them to his wife and children. (Mishkat)

The Messenger of Allah (peace and blessings of Allah be upon him) used to do what he said. There are a number of Ahadith that the Messenger of Allah (peace and blessings of Allah be upon him) did not forget Hadrat Khadijah (Allah be pleased with her) after her death and remembered her frequently. Not only did he talk of her often, but he used to treat her female friends kindly. It has been said by Hadrat Aishah (Allah be pleased with her): Never was I jealous of the Prophet's wives. Although I never saw her, but he remembered her so often (that she was not a stranger to me). His love and devotion for his first wife can be judged from the fact that whenever a goat was slaughtered in the house, he remembered her and distributed a portion of the meat among her female friends. (Mishkat)

Hadrat Aishah (Allah be pleased with her) once asked him (Allah's Messenger) if she had been the only woman worthy of his love? He used to say: Khadijah bore me children and she was such a pious and faithful lady.

Companions' Treatment with their Wives : Due to the above practical teachings of Islam, the Prophet's Companions also moulded their lives accordingly. They had sincere love and devotion for their wives. An illustrious Companion of the Holy Prophet (peace and blessings of Allah be upon him) Hadrat Abdullah bin Umar (Allah be pleased with him) was returning from Jihad. On the way someone told him that his wife was ill. He was perturbed to hear this news. He hastened to reach home and see his wife. On this occasion he offered his Maghrib (evening) and 'Isha (night) prayers consecutively.

It has been reported about Hadrat Abdullah bin Umar (Allah be pleased with him) that his father asked him to divorce his wife for certain reasons. He was in a strange fix. On the one hand, he could not disobey his father's command and on the other hand, love for his wife stood in his way. He was on the horn of a dilemma and almost refused to divorce her. His father (Hadrat Umar) presented this matter to the Messenger of Allah (peace and blessings of Allah be upon him) who decided that he (Abdullah bin Umar) should obey his father. Then he divorced his wife (Uswa Sahaba). Hadrat Imam Hasan (Allah be pleased with him) the son of Hadrat Fatima (Allah be pleased with her) divorced his wife for certain reasons and paid her dowry. When the news of the divorce reached her she was dumbfounded and began to weep. When the Messenger came back and told him about the pathetic condition of his wife, he also burst into tears and said: Had I not pronounced irrevocable talaq (divorce), I would have affected a reconciliation.

A similar incident of Hadrat Abu Bakr's son has been reported. He loved his wife so dearly that he did not proceed on Jihad on several occasions and stayed in the house, thus depriving himself of Allah's blessings and rewards. When Hadrat Abu Bakr (Allah be pleased with him) heard this he asked his son to divorce his wife. The son tried his best to put off this matter, but when his father insisted he was compelled to divorce his wife. But the flame of love continued to burn in his heart and he began to recite painful couplets. When Hadrat Abu Bakr (Allah be pleased with him) came to know about this, he called his son and asked him to re-establish marital relations as the divorce had not yet become irrevocable.

The love story of Hadrat Buraira and Mughith has been narrated in Ahadith. Hadrat Buraira who was a maid-servant was married to Mughith. When she became free, she had the right to live with her first husband or not. Hadrat Buraira decided not to live with Mughith. When he came to know of her decision, he could not bear the pangs of separation and loitered about in the streets of Medina weeping and crying.

The excellence of the rules and regulations promulgated by Islam in the past have raised the prestige and honour of downtrodden humanity. It has given women their due rights and ample opportunities to show their worth and capabilities.

Importance of Wives' Rights : *Worship and prayer etc., are very significant things; but Islam does not allow that a person should remain always busy in 'Ibadat (acts of devotion), and deprive his wives of their legal rights. It discourages the monastic way of life. The Messenger of Allah (peace and blessings of Allah be upon him), showed his displeasure over the action of some of his Companions who spent the whole night in 'Ibadat (worship, prayers etc.) and were heedless of their conjugal duties. The Messenger of Allah (peace and blessings of Allah be upon him) called them and instructed them: Verily, your wife has right against you.* *(Bukhari)*

In order to prove himself to be a good husband a man should not only try his utmost to fulfil his wife's needs and please her; but also act upon the following instructions of the Messenger of Allah (peace and blessings of Allah be upon him).

The husband should be dressed neat and clean so that his wife should be pleased to see him and admire in her heart his aesthetic sense, polished manners and the excellent style of his dress. He should not be dirty, ugly looking or rough or shabbily dressed. If the husband wants that his wife should be neat and good looking, it is also the desire of the wife that her husband should be handsome looking and of cheerful disposition. Islam does not allow a person to wear ugly looks. The Messenger of Allah (peace and blessings of Allah be upon him) led a scrupulously neat and clean life. He had a smiling, cheerful countenance. He always was careful of his personal cleanliness. While he was in the house or on a journey, he did not forget to keep a mirror, a comb and a box for holding collyrium and other toiletries. The Messenger of Allah (peace and blessings of Allah be upon him) did not like people to remain dirty. Hadrat Ata bin Yassar (Allah be pleased with him) reported that the Messenger of Allah (peace and blessings of Allah be upon him) was sitting in the mosque when a person, the hair of whose beard and head was shabby and dishevelled entered. The Messenger of Allah (peace and blessings of Allah be upon him) asked him to arrange his hair. He got his hair arranged. When he turned his face and the

Messenger of Allah (peace and blessings of Allah be upon him) saw him in a good condition he observed: Is this condition not better than the former which was like a devil? There is another Hadith: Verily, Allah is good and likes goodness. He is clean and likes cleanliness. (Mishkat)

It is evident from the above Ahadith that both the husband and wife should pay special attention to their personal cleanliness. It is the duty of the husband to provide such articles as will enable his wife to keep herself neat and clean. It is the duty of the husband to provide such things as a comb, oil, soap, etc., according to the practice in vogue, and perfume whereby she can make herself sweet smelling. It is also his duty to provide water for washing the clothes and body. (Alamgiri)

It has been stated in the Hadith that at the time of return from a journey the husband should try to inform his wife before hand. It is necessary because women often do not take much care for their personal appearance in the absence of their husbands. So that the woman may remove her dirt and remove the hidden (superfluous) hair. (Bukhari)

Sympathizing with Woman : It is the moral responsibility of the husband to be good and kind to his wife. If any misfortune befalls her, he should not withdraw his love and favour; but in the difficult time his treatment should be more kind and sympathetic. If she happens to fall ill, he should take her to the doctor. If she is in difficulty, an attempt should be made to solve her problem. If her face becomes uglier due to illness, indifferent and harsh treatment should not be adopted with her; but every effort should be made to console her. If he would not sympathise with her, her feelings would be injured and her jovial and buoyant face would become dejected. The indifferent attitude of her husband would rend her heart with frustration.

Just imagine, you bring a beautiful, fascinating lady and are ready to sacrifice everything for her. You have purchased the best wedding dress and ornaments just to please her. But by chance she falls ill, and smallpox makes her face ugly or snatches away the light of her eyes. When she looks into the mirror, her eyes become wet with tears or if she becomes blind, the whole world plunges into darkness for her. She weeps bitterly day and night. To add to her calamities, you threaten to turn her out. She is tortured for no fault of her own. Where has her husband's love gone? How has spring turned into winter? All these are the vicissitudes of fortune. Just think, is it proper or human? Is this not a disgrace to love and sheer injustice? It must also be kept in mind that the painful sighs and tears of a helpless and downtrodden woman do not go waste. Islam does not permit this terrible attitude and hard-heartedness. The Prophet (peace and blessings of Allah be upon him) said: He who does not make mercy, Allah will not make mercy on him. *(Riyad AI-Salihin)*

What has been said above is only to give an understanding of the problem. It is the duty of the husband to try his utmost to win the heart of his wife. He must have full regard for her feelings and sentiments. There is a well known story that one night while Hadrat Umar (Allah be pleased with him) was on patrol, he heard the voice of painful songs from a house. Hadrat Umar (Allah be pleased with him) asked the reason for this. He was told that the husband of this woman had proceeded on Jihad. He was deeply moved at her sincere love for her husband and asked Hadrat Hafsa (Allah be pleased with her) how long a woman can bear her husband's separation. Her answer was: For four months. Thereupon he issued the following order to his Commanders: A married person should not remain away from his wife for more than four months. *(Durr-e-Mukhtar)*

It is evident from the above historical incident that it is also among the duties of the husband that he should not be indifferent to the feelings, sentiments and the natural sexual urge of the wife. If he was to stay in a foreign country for long, he should keep his wife and children with him. This fact has also been explained by the Holy Quran in a verse regarding Ila. If a person resorts to *Ila* (a vow of temporary cessation of marital relations) without naming a period, he is bound either to re-establish the normal relations after four months or to divorce his wife. After the lapse of this period, the husband has no right to keep his wife and she is free to marry any man. The Holy Quran says:

Those who forswear their wives must wait four months; then, if they change their minds, Lo! Allah is Forgiving, Merciful. And if they decide upon divorce (let them remember that), Allah is Hearer, Knower. *(2:226-227)*

The husband must have confidence in his wife. He should entrust all the household affairs to her so as to give confidence to her and enhance her prestige and honour. The Messenger of Allah (peace and blessings of Allah be upon him) said: A woman is the custodian of the house of her husband. *(Bukhari)*

The other Ahadith also testify to this fact. It has been said therein that women are custodians of their husband's property. Moreover, confidence in a woman adds to her prestige and honour and she considers herself as in charge of the household affairs. The husband's responsibilities and worries are then decreased with the result that he would lead a peaceful and comfortable life.

One right of a wife on her husband is that the husband should not divulge her secrets to others but must keep it a secret. The Messenger of Allah (peace and blessings of Allah be upon him) has strictly forbidden husbands to divulge the secrets of their wives: The most wicked among the people in the sight of Allah is the man who goes to his wife and she comes to him, and then he divulges her secret. *(Muslim)*

The secrets of conjugal life must not be divulged or discussed publicly. While commenting upon this Hadith, Imam Nawawi has written that it is strictly forbidden to discuss the sexual relations of husband and wife. To explain the detail of the sexual intercourse is an abominable act. According to the above Hadith it is forbidden to expose the secrets of husband and wife, such as sexual intercourse and details thereof and what happened with the woman and (divulgence of), anything said or any act committed by her. *(Sharah Muslim)*

Expenses for Wife : Among the great responsibilities which Islam has put on the husband, his duty is also to provide necessary expenses for the maintenance of the house such as food, clothing, lodging, etc. So that his wife can rear her children without much worry.

It has been mentioned in the Holy Quran:

Let him who hath abundance spend of his abundance, and he whose provision is measured, let him spend of that what Allah hath given him. Allah asketh not of any soul save that which He hath given it. *(65:7)*

None has to bear more burden than he can bear, but the responsibilities placed on him are proportionate to his power and ability. It has been mentioned in another verse of the Holy Quran:

The duty of providing food and clothes to nursing mothers in a seemly manner is upon the father of the child. No one should be charged beyond his capacity. *(2:233)*

The responsibility for providing the means of sustenance has been put on the husband so that the woman can bear and rear her children with full concentration of mind. This helps in the proper development of the personality of the child. We have already quoted a Hadith that among the duties which a husband owes to his wife, one duty is: You should be fair to them in feeding and clothing them.

(Tirmidhi)

The incident of Hinda bint Utba, the wife of Abu Sufyan, is known to everyone. She went to the Messenger of Allah (peace and blessings of Allah be upon him) and complained: My husband is miserly. He does not give sufficient provision to my children of his own accord. After relating her story she asked: If I feed his children out of that held by him, is there any harm to me. The Messenger of Allah (peace and blessings of Allah be upon him) said: Take honestly what is enough for you and your child. *(Bukhari)*

The Messenger of Allah (peace and blessings of Allah be upon him) also made arrangements for household expenses. He had set apart a garden for this purpose. He deposited the income of that garden for defraying his household expenses for the year. The Messenger of Allah (peace and blessings of Allah be upon him) used to sell the trees of Bani Nudair and deposited the amount to provide means of sustenance for the whole year. *(Bukhari)*

The Jurists call Nafqa (household expenses), Wajib (incumbent), on the husband irrespective of whether the wife may be poor or rich. Household expenses mean food, clothing, lodging etc. In the dictionary the word Nafqa means expenses for wife and children and according to the Shariah it implies food, clothing and lodging.

(Durr-ul-Mukhtar)

Other Liberties : Another right of a wife over her husband is that the latter should allow her to see her parents and her near relatives i.e. Mahrams. The Messenger of Allah (peace and blessings of Allah be upon him) used to see his affectionate daughter and Hadrat Abu Bakr and Hadrat Umar (Allah be pleased with them) also used to go to the Prophet's house to see their daughters. A large number of such instances have been mentioned in the Ahadith. The Jurists are of the view that if the wife goes to see her parents once in a week, the husband should not object to it. But this is permissible if the parents are unable to see her for some genuine reason, otherwise, they should themselves go to see her.

If there is a dispute between husband and wife and there is a danger that it would take a serious turn, the husband has been instructed not to take a hasty step. If the situation is not improved even by beating, a judge should be appointed from each side to resolve the dispute. The Holy Quran says:

And if ye fear a breach between them twain (the man and wife), appoint an arbiter from his folk and an arbiter from her folk. *(4:35)*

But it must be kept in mind that the judges should be honest and sincere. It is then that they would be able to resolve the dispute, otherwise they would further aggravate the situation. The Holy Quran testifies to this fact:

If they desire amendment Allah will make them of one mind. Allah is ever Knower, Aware. *(4:35)*

Hadrat Maulana Ashraf Ali Thanvi gives the following comments on this verse:

"And the women who are arrogant in their behaviour should be first admonished. If they do not change their behaviour, do not share their bed. If they still disobey you beat them not causing any injury. If they obey you, do not commit aggression on them on one or another pretext. If the circumstances are such that there is risk of the situation being worsened, a judge who is competent to resolve the dispute may be appointed from either side who should investigate the matter and admonish those at fault, the husband or wife, or both. If the judges are sincere in their mission, they would by Allah's favour succeed in effecting a reconciliation between them. Allah is All Knowing, All Aware. Allah knows how mutual love can be restored between them and when He sees the good intention of the judges, He will guide them on the right lines. The judges must sincerely try to remove the doubts and suspicions existing in the minds of husband and wife and patch up the differences between them. The husband and wife should also cooperate with the judges and act upon the decision arrived at by them."

Rights and Duties of Wife : We have so far discussed in detail the rights of the wife against her husband. Now let us see what instructions have been given to the wife concerning her husband. We can judge from the rights and duties of both what strenuous efforts have been made by Islam to guard modesty and chastity and to ensure stability, love and harmony in conjugal relations. Any rule or law which holds one party responsible, leaving the other free to do as it likes may be apparently nice but it cannot be called perfect or good. Only such rules and laws are complete as are applicable to all and guard the rights of one against the other. There is no denying the fact that woman is a weak and sentimental creature and because of this very reason she deserves our favour, love and regard and it is our duty to overlook her shortcomings. But this does not mean that she is absolved of her duties. Had it been so, the life of both husband and wife would be devoid of any purpose and charm.

Priority of Husband : Islam has kept in view the inherent weaknesses of woman. Due to this reason man has priority over woman. He has been appointed as the leader or president insofar as the family life is concerned, as he has the ability to solve the difficult matters. Allah the Exalted has said in the Holy Quran:

> *Men are in charge of women, because Allah hath made the one of them to excel the other, and because they spend of their property.* *(4:34)*

It means men have been given priority and eminence over women in the matter of knowledge and action. They are responsible for supporting them and providing food, clothing and lodging to his family. Hence he is the leader or president of the house.

There is no denying the fact that man is superior to woman due to his God sent virtues and capabilities. A woman has to go through certain periods in which she is rendered almost unable to do anything and she has to depend upon others, for instance, during pregnancy, suckling, rearing of children, menstruation and during the period of discharge of blood after childbirth. Hadrat Shah Wali Ullah has written:

> *It is necessary and akin to nature that man should have authority over woman as man possesses perfect intellect, he is an expert politician. He defends vehemently and guards respect and honour. He has priority over woman as he provides food, clothing and lodging.*

The modern research has proved that the brain of man is stronger than that of woman. He is more intelligent and wise. His mind is more mature. He possesses a strong body and muscles. We have already quoted the views of some writers. We give below some excerpts from modern research scholars:

> *The famous rationalist scholar and philosopher, Dr. Proudon writes in his book:*

"The perception and intuition of woman is as weak as is her intellect in comparison to man. Her character is also different. Her nature is also different. That is why her criteria of judgement of merits and demerits of a thing also vary. This difference between man and woman is lasting and abiding. It is her inherent nature."

Allama Farid Wajadi gives the following comments:
"The five senses, on which depends the growth of mind and intellect also vary. The scholars Nicholas and Baily have proved that the five senses of women are weaker as compared to men."

He further writes:
"Physiology has proved that there is variation in the weight and dimension of the female and male brain. The average weight of a male brain is 100 grams more in weight than a female."

Allama Wajadi has written:
"Due to the intellectual faculty man has priority over woman. The average weight of a male brain is 49½ ounces and a female brain weighs about 44 ounces. 278 male brains were weighed. The biggest one weighed 65 ounces and the smallest one 34 ounces. But out of 291 female brains, the biggest weighed 54 ounces and the smallest 21 ounces. Is this not sufficient to prove that the intellectual faculties of women are weaker as compared to men?"

The above difference exists everywhere, in the civilized countries as well as in the backward countries. The author of Encyclopaedia writes:

"Just as the difference in the physical strength and intellectual faculty exists in the most civilized city of Paris, in the same way it exists in the savage people of America."

That is to say, modern research has proved beyond doubt that men have more capabilities than women in every respect.

Equal Rights : From the authority given to man it should not be construed that in Islam, a wife is the maidservant of the husband. This view is incorrect. Only a person who is ignorant of Islamic knowledge can hold this view. Sometimes it happens that a husband and wife have different opinions on certain matters. If there is any such dispute between them, the opinion of the husband should be given precedence over the opinion of the wife as he is the head of the family because of his special knowledge and capabilities. Islam desires that all matters may be settled amiably with mutual consent of both husband and wife. There is equality between the two and both husband and wife have rights against each other and they also owe duties to each other. The Holy Quran has mentioned:

> *And they have rights similar to those (of men) over them in kindness, and men are a degree over them.* (2:228)

This brief verse contains a fundamental principle that men and women are equal in all respects and their rights and duties are also equal except that, as explained above, men have power over women. In all other matters concerning conduct and behaviour and 'Ibadat and social dealings they are equal and there is no reason for holding them in contempt. Islam has for the first time given such prestige and honour to womenfolk.

A philosopher has rightly observed:

> *"If Allah wanted to make a woman the head of the family, she would have been born from the portion of the body where the head is set and if He wanted to make the woman a maid-servant, He would have created her from the lowest portion of the body having feet. As it was not Allah's will and He wanted equality, mutual love, harmony and respect and honour for each other, He created her from the side of man."*

Despite the fact that man is the head of the family, he has been asked to consult his wife and settle all matters by mutual consent of each other. Where the Holy Quran has ordained that the mother should suckle her baby for a full two years and the duty of providing food and clothing, etc., to the woman who suckles rests with the father, it has also been ordained that if the woman desires to wean the child, it should be done by mutual consent of the husband and wife. It has been mentioned in the Holy Quran:

> *If they desire to wean the child by mutual consent and consultation, it is no sin for them.* (2:233)

It is obvious that mutual consultation is necessary in all matters. The gist of what we have said above is that Islam has framed rules and regulations for the married couple which if acted upon, would bring mutual love and harmony between them and protect their modesty and chastity.

In these hard times, we came across instances of rifts between husbands and wives of rich families over triflings. Their relations are strained. Both begin to live separately. Years pass on and both persist in their behaviour just to keep their false prestige. This period of separation is full of great hazards for both as no one is without sexual desire. Islam condemns such a way of life, there is no room for it in Islam. We shall discuss this point in detail in the next pages.

A Pious Woman : If the husband and wife had acted upon the excellent principles of Islam, the matter would not have gone from bad to worse. On such a critical occasion, if the husband's view-point, his being the head, were to be accepted, the dispute would surely have come to an end. The Holy Quran says:

"So good women are the obedient, guarding in secret that which Allah has made them guard." *(4:34)*

In the above verse the virtue of a pious woman has been explained and she has been instructed to be loyal to her husband so that if there is any difference of opinion between them, it should not cause separation between them. The Messenger of Allah (peace and blessings of Allah be upon him) has further instructed the women to live amiably with their husbands:

'A woman who asks for divorce from her husband on triflings, is forbidden the smell of paradise.'

In the above Hadith women have been admonished that if any unagreeable thing occurs between the husband and wife, she should not demand divorce from her husband, as such, things do happen in married life due to difference in temperaments.

It is, however, the duty of a pious lady that in the event of a clash with her husband, she should overcome her anger considering her husband to be the head of the family. She should keep in mind that it is her duty to obey him. If she is sure that her husband has given her unjust treatment, she should try to convince him that he is wrong. She should however, be careful and cautious and present her viewpoint in a civilized manner.

God forbid, when any woman takes the law in her hand, the married life is bound to be disturbed and this small kingdom of the husband and wife will be ruined. The one inevitable result of this quarrel would be that both husband and wife would lose their honour and prestige when the people would come to know that they are unable to manage their household affairs.

Due to the husband's love for his wife, the latter must also please him, be solicitous for his ease and comfort and have respect for and honour him. She should always keep in mind that he is the head of the family and it is her duty to pay due respect to him. The Messenger of Allah (peace and blessings of Allah be upon him) has observed:

"If I had ordained any individual to prostrate before the other individual I would have ordained the wife to prostrate before her husband." *(Mishkat)*

A husband who showers all his love and affection on his wife and spends his hard earned money to provide her comforts and amenities, taking her to be the centre of his devotions must be respected and honoured by his wife. A mere show of respect and honour is not sufficient; but there must be sincerity in these sentiments so that she may win his heart. For the wife the necessity for seeking her husband's pleasure exists in this world and also in the Hereafter.

"When a woman whose husband is pleased with her dies, she would enter Paradise." *(Mishkat)*

A wife can win the heart of her husband through love and sacrifice. If the wife obeys him and fulfils his genuine demands, he will sacrifice all for her sake and do all that is in his power to please her. Loyalty and obedience in lawful matters are among the excellent virtues of a wife. The Messenger of Allah (peace and blessings of Allah be upon him) has observed:

"A woman who had offered five times prayers and kept the fasts for the month (of Ramadan), and guarded her modesty and was obedient to her husband would be allowed to enter any of the gates of Paradise." *(Mishkat)*

Along with the duties like prayer, fasting and the guarding of modesty, it is also the duty of a woman to obey her husband. It is evident from the above Hadith that whereas it is necessary to fulfil the rights of Allah it is also the bounden duty of a wife to obey her husband. A woman who fails to fulfil the duties she owes to her husband cannot succeed. Once the Messenger of Allah (peace and blessings of Allah be upon him) was questioned as to who is the best woman, he answered:

"The woman who pleases her husband when he sees her, obeys him when he orders and does not have any bad intention in her heart against his person nor against her husband's wealth." *(Mishkat)*

What more stress can be laid on woman obeying their husband? A woman who is not obedient to her husband is surely not a good woman in the sight of the Messenger of Allah (peace and blessings of Allah be upon him). She may be possessing an exalted worldly position and wealth and riches, but she is unfortunate and wretched, if she is not a good woman in the sight of the Messenger of Allah (peace and blessings of Allah be upon him).

The wife should fulfil her husband's lawful demands only. If he transgresses the limits prescribed by Allah and asks her to commit acts against the Shariah, she is allowed to refuse her husband. An incident has been narrated in the Hadith: Once a woman of Ansar came to the Messenger of Allah (peace and blessings of Allah be upon him) and said: I have got my daughter married. Perchance, the hair of my daughter have fallen down. Now my son-in-law demands that the hair of some other woman should be added to her hair so that she may look beautiful. Thereupon the Messenger of Allah (peace and blessings of Allah be upon him) observed: Curse be upon the woman who adds other's hair to her hair.

The wife must, however, obey her husband in permissible things. An obedient wife has been called the greatest of Allah's favours in Ahadith. The status given by Islam to the obedient wife can be judged from the following Hadith:

The best of the things from which a believer can benefit next to the fear of Allah is a pious wife. If he orders her, she obeys and if he sees her, she pleases him. If she takes a vow before him, she fulfils and if her husband is away she has good intention against her person and property. (Ibn Majah)

It is evident from the above Hadith that the best of Allah's favours, next to fear of Him, is a pious and obedient wife who loves her husband dearly, has a smiling and cheerful fascinating face and amiable disposition. She guards her modesty and chastity. The Messenger of Allah (peace and blessings of Allah be upon him) has said: If the husband asks his wife to go from one mountain to the other and from there to the third, the true wife is one who obeys this command.

Islam wants that the relations between husband and wife should be stable and abiding. It has framed rules and regulations keeping in view the nature and temperaments of both. The duties which the wife owes to her husband must be fulfilled by her wholeheartedly. Once the Messenger of Allah (peace and blessings of Allah be upon him) said: A woman must fulfil the lawful demands of her husband and a woman cannot relish the sweetness of faith unless she fulfils the lawful rights of her husband.

We have already mentioned a Hadith that the husband is the head of the whole family including the wife, then how far is it correct on her part to disobey her husband? As she is the better half of her husband and his friend and life companion, it is the duty of a friend to give sacrifice for a friend. She should do everything cheerfully and of her own accord. She should never consider that she is a maid servant or a captive.

Sexual gratification is apparently a worldly act; but in this matter, too, if the husband calls his wife for sexual intercourse, she should obey him out of love for him. The Messenger of Allah (peace and blessings of Allah be upon him) has observed: "If a person calls his wife for his need, she must go to him at once, although she may be standing near the oven (for baking breads)."

There is an explicit hint in the Hadith that if she fails to comply with the husband's above order, she is guilty of sin. The Messenger of Allah (peace and blessings of Allah be upon him) has further observed:

"If a husband calls his wife to his bed and she refuses to come, the angels hurl curses on her till morning."

(Bukhari)

Once the Messenger of Allah (peace and blessings of Allah be upon him) said: "By Allah! If a husband calls his wife to bed and she refuses, Allah and his angels are displeased with her as long as her husband is not pleased with her."

Basing his argument on the above Ahadith. Imam Nawawi has said that without any reasonable excuse of the Shariah, a woman is not allowed to reject her husband's demand for sexual intercourse. The husband should however, take care of the health of his wife. He should not overlook her health merely for the sake of the gratification of sexual instinct. Jurists are of the opinion that if the health of a woman is so weak that sexual intercourse is injurious, sexual intercourse with her should be avoided. If frequent sexual indulgence is harmful for her, the husband should not have sexual intercourse more than her strength permits.

(Durr-ul-Mukhtar)

The woman is, however, bound to obey her husband. The Messenger of Allah (peace and blessings of Allah be upon him) observed: "If the husband is present, the wife should not keep supererogatory fasts without his permission."

(Bukhari)

The women of the Prophet's and Caliphs' times tried their utmost to please their husbands. An expression of slight anger by their husbands disturbed their peace of mind. They obeyed their husbands even when they held indifferent and discourteous attitude.

Hadrat Aishah (Allah be pleased with her) was once wearing silver rings in her hands. The Messenger of Allah (peace and blessings of Allah be upon him) seeing these rings in her hands asked: What are these, O' Aishah! She said: I have worn these to please you. (Uswa Sahaba)

Due to these excellent rules of social conduct and behaviour, both husband and wife had great love and affection for each other. How much love and devotion had Hadrat Khadijah (Allah be pleased with her) for the Messenger of Allah (peace and blessings of Allah be upon him). As you know, Hadrat Khadijah (Allah be pleased with her) was a rich lady. When she was married to the Messenger of Allah (peace and blessings of Allah be upon him) she sacrificed all her wealth for her husband's sake. Whenever he was in difficulty, Hadrat Khadijah (Allah be pleased with her) helped him and consoled him.

Hadrat Aishah (Allah be pleased with her) is also well known for her love and devotion for the Messenger of Allah (peace and blessings of Allah be upon him). She washed his clothes with her hands, applied perfume, crushed miswak *(tooth stick) for him and kept it with care. She wove the rope for the sacrificial animal with her hand. Once the Messenger of Allah (peace and blessings of Allah be upon him) covered himself with a blanket and went to the mosque. The Companions pointed out that there was a spot on the blanket. He took off the blanket and sent it into the house. Hadrat Aishah (Allah be pleased with her) took a pot of water and washed the blanket with her own hands. She got it dried and sent it to the Holy Prophet (peace and blessings of Allah be upon him). (Uswa Sahaba)*

The wives of the Companions also possessed the same sentiments of love and devotion for their husbands. They did their utmost to please their husbands. Hadrat Zainab, the loving daughter of the Holy Prophet (peace and blessings of Allah be upon him) was married to Abu Aas. The latter had not yet embraced Islam when the battle of Badr began. In this battle between the infidels and the Muslims, Abul Aas fought from the side of the infidels. The Muslims won the battle by Allah's infinite mercy and grace and a large number of Quraish were made captive by them. Abul Aas was also one among them. When the Holy Prophet (peace and blessings of Allah be upon him) declared that the captives should be set free on payment of ransom, Hadrat Zainab, the Holy Prophet's daughter and the wife of Abul Aas, sent her precious necklace as ransom for Abdul Aas. This necklace belonged to Hadrat Khadijah (Allah be pleased with her) her mother and she had kept it with her in her memory.

Hadrat Hamna bint Jahsh's husband proceeded on Jihad and died as a martyr in the cause of Allah. When this news reached Hadrat Hamna, she was overwhelmed with grief and began to weep loudly.

Hadrat Umar's wife used to kiss the head of his loving husband during fasting out of intense love for him.

When Hadrat Hasan's wife received the dower money, after getting divorce from her husband, she wept saying: This sum is paltry as compared to the separated beloved.

It is the duty of a woman to greet her husband cheerfully when he enters the house. The smile of a woman has such a fascination for the husband that for a moment he forgets all his worries and anxieties. Even if he is totally exhausted and tired, he regains fresh vigour on seeing the smiling face and hearing the sweet words.

> *The woman who cuts a sorry figure before her husband, turns her house into a veritable hell and adds bitterness to the life of her husband. The Holy Prophet (peace and blessings of Allah be upon him) has explained the virtue of the best woman: "When the husband cast a glance at her, it should please him."* *(Mishkat)*

Whenever the wife should come to her husband she should be good looking and in neat and clean dress. All the household goods should be well-dusted and neat and clean.

The wife should not hesitate to serve her husband. The Prophet's wives served him. Hadrat Fatima, the Holy Prophet's daughter used to look to the needs of her husband and did all the household work. In Bukhari there is a separate chapter under the heading: 'The work of a woman in her husband's house' wherein it has been mentioned that blisters were caused on Hadrat Fatima's hands by working the hand-mill.

The Muhaddithin have drawn the conclusion from the above incident that women should themselves do ordinary household work. If Hadrat Fatima (Allah be pleased with her) could work the hand-mill she must also be kneading the flour and baking the bread herself. According to Imam Malik, it is the duty of the wife to do the household work herself if her husband cannot afford a servant, even if she belongs to a rich and wealthy family.

Among the three persons who did not participate in the battle of Tabuk and were boycotted by the people at the Holy Prophet's command, was Hilal bin Umayyah (Allah be pleased with him). After a few days the Holy Prophet (peace and blessings of Allah be upon him) commanded their wives to boycott them till the decision about them was revealed. Thereupon Hilal bin Umayyah's wife went to the Holy Prophet (peace and blessings of Allah be upon him) and reported: My husband is an old man. There is no servant to serve him. Therefore, I may be permitted to serve him. The Holy Prophet (peace and blessings of Allah be upon him) granted permission to Hilal's wife to serve her husband.

Hafiz Ibn Qayyim has narrated the incident of Hadrat Asma, the wife of Hadrat Zubayr. How solicitous was she for the needs of her husband and how hard did she work for him.

A great shortcoming of woman is that they are stubborn and persistent. They must shun from this habit. It is a common experience that whenever anything goes against their whim and desire, they fly into rage and begin to exchange hot words. Thus the relations of husband and wife are strained and the husband is fed up with his wife.

If there is something reasonable, the wife should try to convince her husband. It is not proper to quarrel and wear an angry look. If the husband is in angry mood, she should become polite. If it is quite necessary to express her displeasure, she should do so; but care should be taken that their relations do not become bitter.

If the husband is aggressive and rude, she should show wisdom and not do anything in a hurry. It is better that she should reconcile with him even if it is against her wishes. It has been mentioned in the Holy Quran:

> *If a woman feareth ill treatment from her husband, or desertion, it is no sin for them twain if they make terms of peace between themselves.* *(4:128)*

A careful study of what we have said above makes it amply clear that the rules and regulations promulgated by Islam foster the sentiments of love and harmony among husband and wife so that the real aims and objects of marriage are fulfilled to their fullest possible extent and the people lead a peaceful and comfortable life. By living amicably they can protect their modesty and chastity in the most excellent manner.

Due to this reason, the rights and duties of both against each other have been explicitly determined. If both of them fulfil their rights and duties they owe to each other, there remains no cause of complaint or rancour against anyone.

Rift and Discord : Allah, the Exalted has strictly prohibited all such acts as create hatred and discord between husband and wife. One of the greatest evils of sorcery, according to the Holy Quran, is that it causes separation between husband and wife:

> *And from these two people learn that by which they cause division between man and wife.* (2:102)

The Holy Quran has mentioned the doom of such a person in the following words:

> *And surely they do know that he who trafficketh therein will have no portion in the Hereafter.* (2:102)

It is a great sin to cause rift between husband and wife. A person who is guilty of this act would be deprived of the bounties and rewards of the Paradise. The Allah's Messenger (peace and blessings of Allah be upon him) mentioning the evil tactics of the devil and his team said: The devil sits on his royal throne and sends his disciples among the people for mischief making. He who commits the greatest evil receives the greatest reward. When these mischief mongers come back, they submit their reports to their leader regarding their evil exploits and wrong doings. In the meanwhile, a devil steps forward and standing before the leader submits the following report:

> *'I have performed my duty, I did not take rest until I caused rift between husband and wife.'*
>
> *Allah's Messenger (peace and blessings of Allah be upon him) said: The devil is overjoyed to hear this news and embraces him and extols him saying: Bravo! you have done well. You have excelled all.* (Mishkat)

Mulla Ali Qari writes that the cause of the devil's joy is that he likes large-scale fornication, illegal child-births and spreading of evils and vices on earth.

> *Every one having a grain of sense knows the evil consequences of rift or clash between husband and wife, hence the person who creates hatred and discord between husband and wife deserves to be condemned whole-heartedly. He is the sworn enemy of humanity. Allah's Messenger (peace and blessings of Allah be upon him) said: "He who instigates a woman against her husband is not among us."* (Mishkat)

Islam is a religion of peace and harmony. It puts an end to hatred and enmity among the people and exhorts its followers to live amicably. A person who tries to create hatred and discord among the people by instigating one against the other cannot be called the real follower of Islam. It is a heinous sin to cause hatred between husband and wife due to which the house is turned into a veritable hell. The clash between husband and wife might lead them to evil way of life and moral delinquency which do not behove a true follower of Islam.

HONOUR AND DIGNITY

The sum total of Islamic teachings is to raise human dignity and honour. It relieves mankind from disgrace and provides higher and honourable place in human society. It imparts the lesson of human dignity. Islam directs humanity to prostrate before Allah alone for the achievement of—superiority over other creations. Mankind is the masterpiece creation of Allah. The following verses of the Holy Quran testify this fact :

Verily We have honoured the children of Adam. We carry them on the land and the sea, and have made provision of good things for them, and We have preferred them above many of those whom We created with a marked preferment. *(17 : 70)*

Surely We created man of the best stature. *(95 : 4)*

"When thy Lord said unto the angels : Lo : I am about to create a mortal out of mire. And when I have fashioned him and breathed into him of My spirit, then fall down before him prostrate. The angels fell down prostrate, everyone save Iblis; He was scornful and became one of the disbelievers." *(38 : 72-75)*

In Islam the welfare of mankind depends upon right thinking and right practice. It is sheer ignorance to degrade woman simply because she happens to be a woman, and man is considered a heavenly creature simply because he happens to be a man. Islam has explained it in very clear words that human dignity rests upon piety and virtue. Hence, who is more honourable, man or woman? This question is well answered by the Holy Quran :

"Whosoever doeth right whether male or female, and is a believer, him verily We shall quicken with good life and We shall pay them recompense in proportion to the best of what they used to do." *(16 : 97)*

"Lo! Men who surrender unto Allah, and women who surrender, and men who believe and women who believe, men who obey and women who obey, and men who speak the truth and women who speak the truth, and men who persevere (in righteousness) and women who persevere, and men who are humble, and women who are humble, and

men who give alms, and women who give alms, and men who fast, and women who fast, and men who guard their modesty, and women who guard (their modesty), and men who remember Allah much and women who remember Allah hath prepared for them forgiveness and a vast reward."
(33 : 35)

"And their Lord hath heard them (and He saith): Lo! I suffer not the work of any worker, male or female, to be lost. Ye proceed one from another. So those who migrated and were driven forth from their homes and suffered damage for My cause and fought and were slain, verily I shall remit their evil deeds from them and verily I shall bring them into gardens underneath which rivers—flow a reward from Allah, and with Allah is the fairest of rewards."(3 : 195)

The Holy Quran distinctly explains the characteristics of the Momineen (The faithful followers of Islam) who submitted their lives, property and desires to the Will of Allah:

"(Triumphant) are those who turn repentant (To Allah) ' those who serve (Him), those who praise (Him), those who fast, those who bow down, those who fall prostrate (in worship), those who enjoin the right and who forbid the wrong, and those who keep the limits (Ordained) of Allah, and give glad-tidings to believers! "
(9 : 12)

At another place, the pious wives of the Holy Prophet (S.A.W.) have been 'commanded to develop such qualities in them without which they would not be able to remain in his Nikah. And the Holy Prophet (S.A.W.) would easily find such wives who would possess such virtuous qualities.

"It may happen that his Lord, if he divorces you, will give him in your stead wives better than you, submissive (to Allah) believing, pious, penitent, inclined to fasting, widows and maids."
(66 :5)

Now, it becomes crystal clear that according to the Holy Quran, piety and virtue are the only criteria for the achievement of successful life in the Hereafter. None, whether man or woman can accomplish his or her goal without fulfilling this condition.

The Holy Quran points out that man and woman both have helped and cooperated with each other in the development of human life. Both have equally shared the burden of life. Their union has brought the civilization into existence. No nation or movement of the world can neglect either of them. If man and woman are responsible for the establishment of the authority of Truth and its enforcement, they are equally responsible for the spread of vices in the world, The Holy Quran says:

> *"The hypocrites, both man and woman, are one and the same. They enjoin the evil, and forbid the right; and they withhold their hands from spending in the cause of Allah. They have forgotten Allah and so He hath forgotten them. Indeed, the hypocrites, are the transgressors."* *(9 : 76)*

> *"And the believers, men and women are protecting friends one of another; they enjoin the right and forbid the wrong, and they establish the prayer and they pay the poor-due, and they obey Allah and His Messenger, as for these, Allah will have mercy on them. Lo! Allah is Mighty Wise."* *(9 : 71)*

Since it is admitted that the revolutions in the civilization of the world are brought about by both, man and woman, no logical argument can degrade one and upgrade the other. Besides, it will be foolish to eliminate either of them from the civilization and march forward. No person can play any role in life after having paralysed one half of the body.

Before the advent of Islam, the world had degraded the woman and had almost outcast her. She was thrown in such deep abyss that there seemed no hope of her redemption. Islam boldly remonstrated against this injustice and emphasised that life needed both man and woman. Woman is not created to be derided and cast aside. Like man, woman also has her purpose and right to exist. And the Nature is achieving its aim with the help of man and woman both. As the Holy Quran says:

> *Unto Allah belongeth the Sovereignty of the heavens and the earth. He createth what He wills. He bestoweth female (offsprings) upon whom He will, and bestoweth male (offspring) upon whom He will; or He mingleth them, males and females, and He maketh barren whom He will. Lo ! He is Knower, Powerful.* *(42 : 49-50)*

Islam lifted woman from the abyss of disgrace and granted her rights and facilities. Abdullah-bin-Umar (R.A.A.) relates:

> *During the life time of our Prophet, Muhammad (S.A.W.) we did not talk to 'our woman freely because we feared revelation against us. When the Holy Prophet (S.A.W.) passed away, we became frank with them.*
> *(Bukhari, and Ibn Majah)*

Whereas, all other religions deprived woman of right even to live.' Islam granted her rights almost on a par with man. It also warned that all those who strive to snatch her rights away, will surely be, accountable to Allah on the Day of Judgement.

> *And when the girl-child that was buried alive, is asked For what sin she was slain?* *(19 : 8-9)*

The Holy Prophet (S.A.W.) has issued numerous instructions in favour of woman, the favour which she could not receive even from the so-called modern upholders of the woman's rights. The Holy Prophet (S.A.W.) has said :

> *Allah has forbidden you, disobedience unto your mothers, refusal to sanctioned rights, accumulation of wealth from all sides and burial of living daughters.* *(Bukhari)*

The Prophet of Islam (S.A.W.) has also said:

> *"A man who has a daughter and he neither despises her nor buries her alive nor prefers son to daughter, Allah will admit him in Heaven."* *(Abu Daud)*

Abu Sayeed (R.A.A.) relates that the Holy Prophet (S.A.W.) said:

> *"Whoever brought up three daughters and treated them well, the Heaven is for him."* *(Abu Daud - Tirmidhi)*

The world condemned woman, but Islam honoured her. The Holy Prophet (S.A.W.) raised her status and assigned her respectable place in the human society. He (S.A.W.) said :

> *"In worldly things, I like woman and perfume, but coolness of my eyes lies in salat (Prayers)".*

Once the Holy wives were travelling on camels, the Holy Prophet (S.A.W.) said to the camel driver.

> *"Carry these glasses very carefully."*

About Fatima (R.A.A.) the Messenger of Allah (S.A.W.) has said :

> *"My daughter is my flesh, any trouble to her will cause pain to me."* *(Bukhari, and Muslim)*

Once Hadrat Aishah (R.A.A.) was asked whom did the Holy Prophet (S.A.W.) love most? She replied, Fatima (R.A.A.).

On another occasion, somebody asked the Holy Prophet (S.A.W.), 'Who is your most beloved person?' The Holy Prophet (S.A.W.) replied,' Aishah (R.A.A.).'

Thus we see that the Holy Prophet (S.A.W.) loved his wife Aishah (R.A.A.) and his daughter Fatima (R.A.A.) most. And the sayings of the Holy Prophet (S.A.W.) explicitly explain the aim of Islam with regard to the treatment of fair sex.

The teachings of Islam revolutionized the thinking of those men who buried their daughters alive and felt no shame in doing so. They began to love and nourish their daughters, those who refused to shelter their own daughters, became the guardians of other's daughters. Those who were devoid of love and affection for women, now loved and cared for them.

> *On the occasion of the Battle of Uhud, Jabir's father told Jabir (R.A.A.), "My Son! I may be martyred in the forthcoming battle, so I advise you to look after my daughters." Consequently, Jabir (R.A.A.) who was still young, married a widow owing to the responsibility of his sisters. The Holy Prophet (S.A.W.) asked him, "Why did you not marry a young woman?" He replied, "O Prophet of Allah (S.A.W.) My father was martyred in the Battle of Uhud and he has left behind his nine daughters who are my sisters. Therefore, I chose such woman for my marriage, who could look after them well." The Messenger of Allah (S.A.W.) replied, You did a good deed."* *(Bukhari)*

> *It is related that after the martyrdom of Hadrat Hamzah (R.A.A.), three persons claimed to have the right to look after his daughter. The first was Hadrat Ali (R.A.A.) who claimed his right to look after her because she was his cousin (sister). The second person was Hadrat Jafar (R.A.A.) who said that his claim was better than that of Hadrat Ali (R.A.A.) because she was not only his cousin (sister) but her maternal aunt was his wife.. Hence, she could be brought up in better way. The third man was Hadrat Zaid (R.A.A.) who filed his petition on the ground that she was his brother's daughter and that none else can have better claim than her own uncle.* *(Bukhari, and Muslim)*

These are the examples which the history of other nations cannot present. Islam is the only religion that raised the status of woman to such extent in the world.

According to Islam, society is responsible for the protection of human rights and maintenance of law and order. Its duty is to chop off the hands of the oppressors and unjust. The Quran says:

> *"And there is life for you in retaliation, O men of understanding, that ye may ward off (evil)."* *(2 : 179)*

The law of Shariah awards death penalty to murderer whether he has murdered a man or a woman, because the life of woman is as sacred as that of man. The laws given to the people of Yaman by the Holy Prophet (S.A.W.) included the death penalty to the murderer of woman also.

"Undoubtedly (men) murderer of a woman shall be sentenced to death."

It is stated that a Jew crushed the head of a girl and killed her. The Holy Prophet (S.A.W.) ordered him to be put to death in the same manner *(Bukhari and Muslim)*

Once, all those men who murdered a woman, were put to death by the order of Hadrat Umar Farooq (R.A.A.).
(Al-Ahkam-ul-Quran, Jassas)

If a woman pardons a murderer of her relative, the other relatives have no authority to nullify her consent for forgiveness. Not only this, she can offer protection to an enemy during the emergency of war and this act of her cannot be considered unlawful. The Holy Prophet (S.A.W.) has said:

"Undoubtely, a woman can shelter an enemy for the benefit of Muslims." *(Tirmidhi)*

On the occasion of the conquest of Holy Mecca, Umm Hani said to the Holy Prophet (S.A.W.), "O Messenger of Allah (S.A.W.), I have provided protection to Ibn Hera, but Ali (R.A.A.) says that he will kill him under any circumstance."

The Holy Prophet (S.A.W.) replied, "Umm Hani Whomsoever you have protected, he is under my protection too."
(Bukhari)

Similarly, Islam permits woman, within the limits of Shariah, to participate in the financial affairs and derive benefits.

No man can interfere in this matter. Even her husband has no right to make use of her personal wealth. Likewise, woman has no right to enforce her will for the use of the wealth of her husband. There is a distinct injunction of the Holy Quran :

"And covet not the thing in which Allah hath made some of you excel other. Upto men a fortune from that which they have earned and unto women a fortune from that which they have earned. (Envy not one another). But ask Allah of His bounty. Lo ! Allah is Ever Knower of all things." (4: 32)

According to the Holy Quran the Law of Inheritance is:

"Unto the men (of a family) belongeth a share, of that which parents and near kindred leave, and unto the women a share of that which parents and near kindred leave, whether it be little or much a legal share." *(4 : 7)*

The ancient religions were not prepared to give equal status to man and woman. Therefore, they formulated separate laws for them. But Islam does not make this distinction. In Islam, man and woman both are equal before law. The Holy Quran says:

"Lo ! We offered the trust unto the heavens and the earth and the hills, but they shrunk from bearing it and were afraid of it. And man assumed it. Lo ! He hath proved a tyrant and a fool. So Allah punisheth hypocritical men and hypocritical women, and idolator men and idolator women. But Allah pardoneth believing men and believing women, and Allah is Forgiving, Merciful." (33 : 72- 73)

"And it becometh not a believing man or a believing woman when Allah and His Messenger have decided an affair (for them), that they should (after that) claiming say in their affair, and whoso is rebellious to Allah and His Messenger, he verily goeth astray in error manifest." (33 : 36)

Islam has granted equal rights to both, man and woman. It provides equal opportunity to both of them for the progress and prosperity of life. It guarantees the protection of their lives, property and honour.

The spouses are equally interdependent. Therefore, there is no question of honour for man and dishonour for woman. In Islam both are equally honourable. There is no distinction on the basis of sex. In fact they are created for each other to live in harmony and coexistence. As the Holy Quran says :

"They are raiment for you and ye are raiment for them." (2 : 187)

The relation between man and woman is not of hatred but of love. Man is incomplete without woman and woman is incomplete without man. They are the source of peace and harmony to each other.

According to the Holy Quran:

"And of His signs is this : He created for you help-mates from yourselves that ye might find rest in them, and he ordained between you love and mercy. Lo ! herein indeed are portents for folk who reflect." (30 : 21)

Precautionary Measures

Control of Eyes : Allah Has endowed mankind with charm and beauty. Mankind is also fond of beautiful things. Therefore, man seeks beauty in every thing of the world. He despises ugly and awkward things and he is never tired of seeking beauty in the Nature.

Indeed, it is natural urge of mankind, hence it is essential to fulfil it. But this admiration of beauty is worthwhile so long it is within the limits of Shariah. If it crosses the limits then it opens the door to evil practices which spoil the society. Therefore, Islam restricts the observation of the opposite sex, because, if the sight is not controlled, then it will be difficult to control the sexual desire.

The Holy Quran. says:

"Say to the believing men that they should lower their gaze and guard their modesty that will make far greater purity for them and Allah is well acquainted with all that they do. And say to the believing women that they should also lower their gaze and guard their modesty." (24 : 30-31)

According to the Holy Quran, it is necessary for a man to control his eyes to keep his character blameless. The Holy Prophet (S.A.W.) has said :

"O Ali ! Do. not have a second look-the first glance may be by chance, but the second view is not justified."

(Abu Daud -Tirmidhi)

This Hadith means that the first (casual) sight is pardonable, but the second and deliberate looking is not proper because they are Satanic acts which destroy the human character. , Hadrat Jabir-bin-Abdullah says, "I asked the Holy Prophet (S.A.W.) if I happen to look at the stranger by chance what should be done?" The Holy Prophet (S.A.W.) replied, "Turn your face at once."

(Muslim- Tirmidhi-Abu Daud)

Control on Hearing *:* Hearing also leaves profound impression on human feelings and emotions. This impression can be harmful or beneficial. It is the aim of the good law to clarify the lines of loss and gain. Hence, Islam lays down the rule that a Muslim can hear any beautiful song for the satisfaction of his interest. However, it prohibits the kind of hearing which leads to sexual incitement and immorality, because Islam wants a man to be of finest character. There is nothing wrong in listening to sweet melody but it is a sin to listen to anything that is morally harmful. Therefore, music or musical instruments are not allowed in Islam. The reason for the ban is explained in the best way by Hafiz Ibn Jauzi (R.A.) :

"It should be known that there are two kinds of harms in listening to the music; the one is that it makes man negligent in his duty towards Allah, and secondly it inclines his thinking towards the worldly pleasures only. He strives to satisfy his material wants only particularly the sexual desire which is on the top. And it is not possible to satisfy these wants without having new contact. Such possibilities could not be found in the lawful area of life. Music also incites man for unlawful sexual pleasure. If music is the food of soul, the sexual pleasure is the food of the body. It is related in a Hadith that music leads to sexual pleasure."

(Naqdul-Ilm-wal-Ulama)

Control of the Tongue : The man has been proved very careless in respect of the use of his tongue. Whatever a man utters, it effects the people and the environment. The effects of the tongue are stronger than those of seeing and hearing. The tongue is the means of expression of human thoughts which may be good or bad and accordingly these thoughts leave their impression on the people around. The speaker tries to influence the listener with his power of the tongue. If his speech is liked and appreciated by the listeners then his thoughts grow stronger and this process leads to collective listening and thus his influence grows stronger day by day.

The fact cannot be denied that the power of speech can create chaos if not controlled and allowed to be usẹd wrongly. Hadrat Sohail bin Saad relates that the Holy Prophet (S.A.W.) has said:

"If a person gives me guarantee for the protection of (his or her) tongue and sexual organs, I shall guarantee Heaven for him (or) (her)."

(Bukhari)

On another occasion the Holy Prophet (S.A.W.) said :

"A person who is saved from the evil of the tongue by Allah, shall enter Heaven."

(Tirmidhi)

Dress : Today the greatest evil of the world is the, nudism, which has greatly influenced the human mind and provided the unlimited means of sensuality. The fair sex is already attractive and charming in appearance and if nudity is added, the mischief is greater, making it difficult for the man to control his passions. Therefore, Islam condemns all means and sources of evil which lead to immorality and destroy the human society. The purpose of clothing is to ward off the evil consequences of nudity and maintain decency in the society.

It is the sign of utter ignorance to think that nudity is the call of modernization. In fact, the nudism is the imitation of Western culture. It has nothing to do with the term, 'Modern.' Islam is the most modern 'Deen'. It, not only allows the advancement in modern science and technology but also encourages all efforts intended to attain knowledge from any part of the world.

The concept of dress in Islam is to cover the-body, specially those parts, which must not be exposed to others. It also emphasises decency in dressing. Therefore, Islam has given certain guidelines for the dresses of the man and the woman and both have to follow these instructions strictly. Hadrat Aishah (R.A.A.) says that she has heard the Holy Prophet (S.A.W.) saying:

> *"A woman who removes her clothes in a house other than that of her husband, violates the command of Allah."*
>
> *(Musnad Ahmad)*

It is a very dangerous idea for a woman to meet a stranger in loneliness. Logically speaking there is no sense in meeting a stranger when a woman has no relation with a man. In such circumstances she cannot be sure of protecting her chastity from the attack of the stranger. Therefore '. Islam strictly prohibits woman from meeting a stranger in loneliness. This is done for her own safety and protection of her honour. Hadrat Jabir (R.A.A.) relates that the Holy Prophet (S.A.W.) has said :

> *"The women who have no company of their near relatives, should not visit strangers, because nobody knows when the devil inside man incites him for the commission of sin."*
>
> *(Muslim-Tirmidhi)*

GENDER EQUALITY

Equality is a term which is hard to define. There is a sense in which all human beings are equal, but in actual life, we find that no two human beings are really equal in all respects. There are differences of tastes, temperaments, faculties, powers and outlook, all of which cannot be traced to differences of environment or upbringing. It is apparent that the rights and duties of men and their social position flow from these inborn differences. In spite of the fundamental and essential unity of all human beings, it is impossible in practice to level down all differences and inequalities, because some of them are the outcome of native differences. Inequality leads to injustice and oppression only where artificial impediments, whether in the shape of laws and customs or traditions, are super-added to natural inequalities so as to prevent men and women from developing their native capacities to the full. It is the task of religion, state and law to remove all hindrances to human development and create an environment where only natural inborn differences and inequalities may fix a man's station in life.

The ideal of sex equality should also be studied from, the same angle. If by sex equality is meant that artificial customs, traditions and laws which prevent the female sex from playing its full part in collective life and developing its inherent capacities to the maximum extent should be removed out of the way, there is hardly any individual of sound understanding who would disagree. But if sex equality means that the type of mental and bodily faculties, psychological make-up and temperamental equipment possessed by the two sexes is identically the same and that men and women exist and have their, being not as complements to each other but as competitors and rivals in a common sphere of action, then it is an ideal about which most people would disagree. As we shall discuss later, even modern writers and specialists on sex are not agreed on this point.

As far as the Holy Quran is concerned, it promulgated the doctrine of human equality, including sex equality, in a comprehensive verse which negates all inequalities due to sex, race, colour, nationality, caste or tribe. Says the Quran:

> *O people! be careful of (your duty to) your Lord, Who created you from a single being and created its mate of the same (kind) and spread from these two many men and women.* *(iv. .1)*

This is a declaration in plain terms that, in essential human dignity and fundamental rights, all human beings of whatever sex or race or nationality stand on a footing of equality, because they all ultimately spring from a single source.

When Islam appeared in Arabia, women held a very low position in society. They were treated not only as social inferiors but like slaves and chattel. When a man having many wives died, the latter were inherited by his sons like movable property. It was a mark of dishonour for any man to have a daughter, and many preferred to bury alive their female children rather than face social opprobrium. It was Islam and the teachings of the Holy Prophet which dispelled the prevailing idea that women were inferior to men or that female children deserved any treatment different from that meted out to male issues. The Quran asserted the dignity of women by declaring:

They are an apparel for you and, you are an apparel for them. *(ii. 188).*

Here, again, the Quran lent support to the basic equality of women and men by declaring that each sex complements the other, and neither is inferior in status and dignity. The word 'apparel' may be interpreted to mean either 'protection' or 'dignity and beauty'. The verse would mean, therefore, that men and women protect each other from sin and dishonour or it may mean that woman lends dignity and adds beauty to the existence of man, as, man does to that of woman. Similarly, the Quran heaped scorn on the Arabs' traditional attitude towards the female sex in the following verses:

And when a daughter is announced to one of them his face becomes dark and is full of wrath. He bides himself from the people, because of that which is announced to him. Shall he keep it with disgrace or bury it (alive)- in dust? Now surely evil is what they judge. *(xvi. 58-59).*

With a view to contradicting the notion that women have no rights, the Quran came out with the plain and unambiguous declaration:

They have rights similar to those against them, in a just manner. *(ii. 228)*

In consonance with this spirit of equality the Prophet of Islam constantly reminded his followers that female children should be treated exactly in the same manner as male issues. Prior to Islam, daughters were looked upon with disfavour and as a kind or economic and social burden. The result was that male members of the family enjoyed a respect which was denied to those of the fair sex. There were marked differences, in the treatment and upbringing of sons and daughters. All this was discouraged by the Holy Prophet (peace be on him) who upheld the rights of female children and insisted on their being treated on a footing of equality. For example, according to a report of Ibn Abbas, the Prophet's cousin, he is said to have declared: 'If a daughter is born to a man and he brings her up affectionately, shows her no disrespect and treats her in the same manner as he treats his sons, the Lord will reward him with paradise' (Kanz ul Amal, p. 277). According to another report from Anas b. Malik, the Prophet said: 'Girls are models of affection and sympathy and a blessing to the family. If a person has one daughter, God will screen him from the fire of the hell owing to his daughter; if he has two daughters, God will admit him to paradise, if he has three, God will exempt him from the obligations of charity and Jihad (ibid). Abu Hurrayrah, a revered companion of the Prophet, says: 'The Prophet of God said that if a person has three daughters whom he provides for and, brings up, God will surely reward him with paradise.' According to Abdullah ibn Masud, the Prophet is reported to have said: 'If a daughter is born to a person and he brings her up, gives her a good education and trains her in the arts of life, I shall myself stand between him and hell-fire' (ibid.). Not content with moral exhortations intended to assert the equal rights of free women, the Prophet went so far as to declare. 'A person who has a female slave in his charge and takes steps to give her a sound education and trains her in arts and, culture, and then frees her and marries her, he will be doubly rewarded' (Sahi Bukhari, Kitab al-Nikah).

The Holy Quran has at more than one place made it plain that in regard to moral and spiritual development, men and women stand on a level of perfect equality. There are no limits to the moral progress of a woman as that of a man. For example, the Holy Quran says:

> *Men shall have the benefit of what they achieve and acquire and -women shall have the benefit of that which they similarly achieve and acquire* *(iv. 32).*

And again:

> *And whoever does good deeds, whether male or female, and he or she is a believer, these shall enter the garden and they shall not be dealt with a jolt unjustly.* *(iv. 124)*

In regard to religious duties, the Quran recognises no distinction between men and women. Their obligations towards God and man are similar in many respects, and, therefore, their position and status in the eyes of God are also not dissimilar. Says the Quran:

> *And as for the believing men and the believing women they are guardians of each other; they enjoin good and forbid evil-and keep up prayer and pay the, poor-rate, and obey Allah and, His Apostle; (as for) these, Allah will show mercy to them, surely Allah is Mighty, Wise.*
>
> *Allah has promised to the believing men and the believing women gardens beneath which rivers flow, to abide in them and goodly dwelling in gardens of perpetual abode; and the best of all is Allah's goodly pleasure; that is the grand achievement.* *(ix. 71-71)*

It follows that if men and women have equal, duties in regard to prayers, the payment of Poor-tax and, most of all, in the enjoining of good and the forbidding of evil in all their social, economic and political forms, it is necessary that they should have equal educational opportunities. How can a woman enjoin the good in politics or forbid men from bad politics, how can she raise her voice against ruinous economic policies or advocate, beneficial economic reforms, if she is not mentally and spiritually well equipped for the supreme religious duty? It should also be remembered that Islam makes no distinction between secular duties and religious duties. According to the teachings of Islam all duties, whether they concern politics, economics or social well-being in general, are religious duties, in no way different from prayers, fasts and the organisation of social charity. It is, therefore, a plain deduction from the above verses that men and women should be regarded as equal in the fields of politics and education, etc., and, consistent with the discharge of their special responsibilities in their particular spheres, they should receive equal rights in all these fields of action.

The, Prophet not only enunciated this general doctrine of sex equality involving equal educational opportunities but also practised it. Innumerable are the traditions of the Prophet which show that women like men, used to come freely in the presence of the Prophet for putting questions and addressing inquiries on all sort of social, religious and economic matters. The Prophet used to answer their queries and enlighten them on all live issues. Arabia, in particular and the world in general, was so backward in those days that there were no organised educational institutions even for boys, not to speak of girls. So the Islamic attitude towards female education can be studied only from the casual remarks of the Prophet and his permission to women to approach him freely for inquiries on matters of religious, economic and social importance. There is no doubt that the Prophet encouraged women in the spirit of understanding and inquiry. His wife, Aishah, was herself a very learned woman, and during the reign of the first four Caliphs her advice, even on political matters, was eagerly sought by the rulers of Islam. On Islamic jurisprudence she was and is still regarded as a great authority. In his collection of traditions, Muslim reports that Aishah praised the women of Ansar for their spirit of inquiry and learning, saying, 'How praiseworthy are the women of Ansar that their modesty does not prevent them from attempts at learning and the acquisition of knowledge'; (Muslims, Sahih, Kitab al-Taharat). This statement was occasioned by the fact that the women of Ansar were more eager than others to learn from the Prophet and they used to address frequent inquiries to him. Instead of discouraging them, the wife of the Holy Prophet characterises as highly praiseworthy their eagerness for learning and inquiry.

The Holy Quran further stresses the equality of women, in regard to the possibilities of spiritual progress by quoting from history the examples of women who reached spiritual eminence by their own efforts:

And Allah sets forth an example to those who believe the wife of Pharaoh when she said: My Lord, build for me a house with Thee in the Garden and deliver me from Pharaoh and his doings, and deliver me from the unjust people.

And Mary, the daughter of 'Imran, who guarded her chastity, so we breathed unto her of Our inspiration, and she accepted the truth of the words of her Lord and His Books, and she was of the obedient one. (lxvi. 11-12).

The Holy Quran further declares that women have been the recipient of special gifts from God so that nothing stands in the way of their reaching the highest pinnacle of spiritual progress:

And We revealed to the mother of Moses. (xxviii. 7)

And (remember) when the angels said: O Mary, surely Allah hath chosen thee and purified thee and selected thee (for His special blessing) of all the women of the world. (iii. 41)

Despite the great stress it has laid on the essential and fundamental equality of men and women and their equal rights in all matters, of vital concern, the Holy Quran does not believe in that conception of sex equality which ignores the natural differences, special aptitudes and specific powers and faculties of men and women with the resulting of men for some kinds of work and the equal fitness, of women for other types of activity. On the whole, the Holy Quran regards men and women as complementary to each other, one sex making up what the other lacked. This is evident from the following verses of Holy Quran which underline the purposive nature of sex differences:

He it is Who created you from a single being, and of the same (kind) did He make his mate, that he might incline to her. (vii. 189)

And one of His signs is that He created mates for you from your selves, so that you may find quiet of mind then and He put between you love and compassion. (xxx. 21)

Men are the maintainers of women because of that excellence which Allah has given to some of them over others and because they spend out of their property. (iv. 34)

And they (women) have rights similar to those against them in a just manner and the men are a degree above them. *(ii. 228)*

The main points to be noted here are, first, that the female sex must be a source of comfort and peace of mind to its male counterpart; secondly, that men and women excel each other or are superior to each other in some respects and that in the general affairs of life men are partially, but not absolutely, superior to women. These general statements involve certain indirect conclusions which are of the greatest importance to social happiness. The Quran, it seems, first sets forth a general doctrine of sex equality and then qualifies and defines it with the assertion that this is not a bald and undifferentiated equality but one involving special rights and duties both for men and women, within the framework of their special responsibilities: both sexes are absolutely equal to each other.

Now, what are the conclusions to be drawn from the qualifications mentioned by the Holy Quran? It is emphasised by the Holy Book that the female sex is a source of comfort and quietness of mind to the male sex. This can happen only if men and women are united in a more or less permanent based of interests which finds expression in a life planned and based on some idea of the future which requires them to cooperate and not to compete, and integrates them as complements in an ordered whole. These considerations involve a pattern of life of which Marriage, Family and Children are the most important factors because there can be no other abiding interest to hold together two individuals of different sexes. A mere community of intellectual interests or identity of special aptitudes is an insufficient bond even for that microscopic minority to whom, these things matter most. For the large majority of men and women these can hardly provide any link unless they are supported and strengthened by the desire for family life and children. It is obvious, therefore, that Islam does not envisage any social pattern from which family and children have been excluded, and since these two factors involve special functions for women and special responsibilities for men, equality of rights in Islam means an equality which is adjusted to and qualified by the special duties and responsibilities of each sex.

Again the Quran recognises the superiority of both sexes over each other in some respects. To the extent that men are superior to women and women to men in certain matters, the doctrine of equality must be, qualified with due regard to natural, facts. About the special position of men, the Quran makes two statements. First that men are the supporters or sustainers of women in a sense. But it must be noted that this implies no natural superiority on the part of men, nor any inherent inferiority of women, because it is a purely, economic arrangement dictated by natural necessities. The Quran, however, accords a slight superiority to men, in general by saying that men are a degree superior to women. This superiority of men relates both to the domestic and political fields. In domestic life, final authority must rest with one sex or the other. There cannot be two co-equal authorities here as elsewhere. Similarly, in the political field also final decisions should rest with men in general, because men are by nature gifted with a wider vision and also because their comparative freedom from certain natural limitations, which absorb a considerable amount of female time and energy, enables them to devote more attention to political affairs.

Having stated the Islamic conception of sex equality, we shall examine whether the qualifications made by Islam to the general doctrine of sex equality find any support from modern writers on the subject of sex. The question ultimately resolves itself into one of differences between men and women in regard to their faculties, powers, aptitudes and temperaments. If there are such differences and dividing lines, then the doctrine of perfect sex equality can be true only with the qualifications set forth by the Holy Quran and to the extent of these qualifications there ought to follow a scheme of life in which men and women, apart from general and equal rights and duties, must be assigned special rights and exclusive responsibilities. Many modern writers on sex, would generally agree with the above proposition. For example, Dr. Alexis Carrel, a French Nobel Prize winner, says in his famous book, Man, the Unknown:

> *The differences existing between man and woman are of a mere fundamental nature. They are caused by the very structure of the tissues and by the impregnation of the entire organism with specific chemical substances secreted by the ovary. Ignorance of these fundamental facts has led the promoters of feminism to believe that both sexes should have the same responsibilities. In reality, woman differs profoundly from man. Every one of the cells, of her body bears the mark of her sex. The same is true of her organs and, above all, of her nervous system. Women should develop their aptitudes in males. Their part in the progress of civilization is higher than that of men. They should not abandon their special functions.*

There are a large number of equality enthusiasts among us now who are either unwilling to recognise such radical differences between the two sexes or accepting them grudgingly, insist on their removal and obliteration by conscious efforts. What these people fail to note is that the peace of mind and comfort on which the Quran has laid stress in the relation between the two sexes is the outcome of these very differences. If they could possibly be removed, sex life and marriage would lose much of their charm. On this point we would quote the American writer, Margaret Mead, who says in her book, Male and Female:

> *Our tendency at present is to minimize all these differences in learning, in rhythm, in type and timing of rewards, and at most to try to obliterate particular differences that are seen as handicap on one sex. If boys are harder to train, train, them harder; if girls grow faster than boys, separate them, so the boys would not be damaged; if women have a little less strength than man invent machines so that they can still do the same work. But every adjustment that minimizes a difference, a vulnerability, in one sex, a differential strength in the other, diminishes their possibility of complementing each other, and corresponds symbolically to sealing off the constructive receptivity of the female and the vigorous outgoing constructive activity of the male, muting them both in the end to the duller version of human life, in which each is denied the fulness of humanity that each might have had. Guard each sex in its vulnerable moments; we must protect and cherish them through the crises that sometimes are harder for one sex than for the other. But as we guard, we may also keep the differences. Simply compensating for differences is in the end a form of denial.*

This sound advice of a writer who herself happens to be a woman and belongs to an advanced country of the West must serve as an eye-opener to those extremists who, in their blind enthusiasm for sex equality, are advocating all sorts of ridiculous reforms and denying the beneficial effects of sex differences as well as the complementary position of man and, woman in respect of each other.

This same American writer, commenting on the increasing entry of women in professional field (of course, under a wrong conception of sex equality) further remarks: 'It is of very doubtful value to enlist the gifts of women if bringing women into fields that have been defined as male frightens the men, unsexes the women, muffles and distorts the contribution the women could make, either because their presence excludes men from the occupation or because it changes the quality of the men who enter.'

It would seem, then, that the doctrine of sex equality cannot be pushed to a point where it means that men and women are equally, fit for all fields of employment or that the indiscriminate entry of women in the professional fields would have no undesirable social effects.

In regard to the Quranic statement that men and women excel each other in some respects and are, therefore, unequal to that extent, we shall quote another American woman writer, Mary B. Bread, who gives a very interesting account of the discussions held on this point by American psychologists, in her book, *Woman as Force in History*. She writes:

> *At its ninth spring meet the Eastern branch of the American Psychological Association held-sessions on the attitude of men and women towards men.*

The meeting lasted for two days and nearly one thousand persons were reported attending its session. The main discussion revolved round the results of a questionnaire submitted to an equal number of men and women. By means of this survey designed to explore opinions of men and women about women, the conclusions was reached by its promoters, that both sexes were in a remarkable agreement in favour of equal social rights for both sexes and a wide disagreement in evaluating the emotional stability and originality of women.

In the discussion which followed, a statement of the survey's findings, men and women participated and according to newspaper accounts, 'seven out of every ten men, and an equal proportion of women, believed that men were less influenced by emotion than women in their judgements.' To the statement that 'women are more interested in the trivial things of life than men,' 91.7 per cent of the men and 92.1 per cent of the women gave their assent.

The discovery or assumption that women differ from men governed discussions of the subject by members of the Psychological Association which assembled at Palo Alto a, few years ago, and much importance was attached to glandular differentiations.

'What is the psychological difference between a boy and a girl?' was the question on which they attempted to focus their remarks. The question had been put before the members of the Association for meditation in advance of this meeting. Indeed, a report, framed by two men and one woman of Stanford University, was ready for the guidance of the discussion. Its burden was that the 'original constitutional' equipment of girls and boys differs. And in women, it asserted, the whole glandular system is 'more precarious' than in men. But mental balance is 'superior in the male'. Whys and where-fores of the divergence in mental balance were 'probably' traceable to the basic physical differences, some speakers averred. As the discussion was reported in the Press, its upshot was the consensus that 'women in general have made no relative progress against mental irregularities since they began throwing off conventional restraints at high speed.'

Now, if the above conclusions are true, it means that men, being less amenable to emotional influences and possessing a more stable mental balance, are better fitted for political activity which requires calm reasoning and lesser susceptibility to emotional influences. Similarly, these conclusions also establish the fact that, being mentally more stable, men are bound to remain superior in intellectual pursuits which require persistent and continuous work. These facts make it clear that the ideal of sex equality cannot be accepted without important qualifications and reservations based on the ultimate facts of the psychology and nature of the two sexes.

Let us now see what Havelock Ellis, one of the greatest modern authorities on the, psychology of sex, has to say about the special nature and characteristics of woman. In *Man and Woman*, Havelock Ellis has considered impartially a great amount of available data as to the intellectual and other capacities of the two sexes. He says that abstract though a woman is, on the whole, marked by a certain docility, and receptiveness. Even in trivial matters, he says, the average woman accepts statements and opinions more easily than a man; and in more serious matters, 'she is prepared to die for a statement or an opinion, provided it is uttered with such authority and action that her emotional nature is sufficiently thrilled'. Further, Ellis points out that woman craves more for sympathy than man and that she has not the same sturdy independence like him. This is a statement which leads support to the Quranic view that men are the maintainers of women, because even if it were possible for all women to become economically independent of men, their emotional nature and craving for sympathy would involve most of them in partial dependence on men. In man, on the other hand, there is no such gravitating force to incline him towards the fair sex, unless it, be sexual attraction or the bond of children. Ellis illustrates his statement on this special characteristic of women by giving a list of famous women of genius who have put forth their best efforts only in sympathetic and intimate association with another person of the nude sex. Thus Madame Curie, the most distinguished woman of science in modern times, was the wife of a distinguished scientific man who shared in her investigations. Mrs Browning wrote her finest poems after she knew Robert Browning. The whole of George Eliot's fiction and other imaginative work was written in the company of a man (J.H. Lewis) who shared her scientific as well as literary tastes.

Taken as a whole, Havelock Ellis considers that the qualities of intelligence in men and women are not of identical character or value; but there is no question of superiority or inferiority. Their respective intellectual qualities fairly balance each other. Thus men, he says, are better able to apply what they have learnt; they are much more inclined, to support what they have learnt; by reflection or further investigation. They have a precise knowledge in their own department, are without doubt more apt to supplement the prescribed course of reading by independent scientific research, take more interest in scientific pursuits and have greater power of observation. Women, on, the other hand, dislike the essentially intellectual process of analysis, because, says Ellis, they instinctively feel that 'analysis may possibly destroy the emotional complexes by which they are largely moved and which appeal to them' This is, why women do not favour rigid rules, principles and abstract propositions. They are more impulsive and believe in its rightness. There are not all defects of the feminine mind, says Ellis; they are innate sexual differences pointing to the ineptitude of women for science, however numerous and, brilliant the exceptions.

Those characteristics, in his opinion, are 'probably correlated with instinctive and emotional qualities which may fairly be regarded as organic'. Ellis then proves that emotion is not, as popularly supposed, a purely mental phenommon. It has its reactions upon man's vascular and muscular system, however self-controlled a man may be. 'No amount of self-control on coarser expressions of emotion alters the case, for even to unscientific inspection the passion of the self-controlled man reveals itself by some quiver of muscle, some quickening, of the heartbeat.' Here he lays down an important truth that emotion depends on physical organisation. Woman's heart, is easily excited under the influence of stimuli by which man's heart in a state of health is unaffected. And he gives a proof of the greater, excitability of woman's heart by pointing out that there is a distinctly greater increase in the number of pulsations on awakening from sleep in women. Even the complex phenomenon of hysteria is due to weakness of resistance of the vaso-motor system. And the special tendency of women to be affected by the disease of the eye called 'glaucoma' is, he says, accepted by all authorities to be due to the disturbances which emanate in generative organs.

He then points out that woman is more liable than man to convulsive manifestations. It is based on an abnormal readiness or, in other words, an undue affectability. Frequent appearance of blushing in women is due to the greater affectability of their vaso-motor system. Convulsive tendency of women is testified by the facility with which they yield to tears and laughters. Tears are not produced by pain even when amounting to agony, but occur when 'sympathetic nervous system is most developed and most impressionable'.

Irritability, which Ellis calls 'irascibility,' is another form of affectability which 'has been quite legitimately attributed to women.' How far is this affectability in women, their, greater emotionality, organic and, therefore, ineradicable, and how far is it the product of external circumstances and, therefore, capable of modification? Ellis says that affectability in women may be decreased to some extent, but that 'there is, however, a limit to this sexual equalisation of affectability, remains extremely probable.' And he further emphasises that the comparatively large extent of the sexual sphere in women and of the visceral regions generally, the physiological tendency to anaemia, the existence of inevitable periodicity of function in women, conspire to famish a broader basis for the play of emotion, which no change in environment or habit could remove. And he quotes Hymen that-all the most characteristic features of women's nature are correlated with emotionality, and half of women's psychic nature would remain unexplained if we struck out this factor.' Affectability in women, therefore, is an innate quality which, according to Havelock Ellis, may be reduced to finer and delicate shades but can scarcely be brought to the male standard.

It is not only Havelock Ellis who holds this opinion on the differences between men and women. There are other psychologists who think almost in the same terms. Thus, Bloch says that 'psychologically also man and woman are different beings;' and Forel expresses a similar opinion. Kisch who has made an elaborate and deep study of woman's sexual life remarks: 'The intellectual changes undergone by the girl at puberty are no less extensive and characteristic than the physical. In brief, the girl is transformed into a young woman endowed with all the attributes, mental and bodily, characteristic of femininity.' Dr. Winge, a Norwegian physician, quoted by Weith-Kundsen, says: 'The difference of sex is fundamental. Both bodily and mentally the difference between the typical woman and the typical man is all-pervading-the difference is by no means confined to sexual organs.' And Weith.-Kundsen himself remarks: 'Man and woman are not equal; they have never been equal and they never will be. On the contrary, the difference of sex is so deep-going that two men of different civilized races are much more nearly similar in their nature than are men and women belonging to the same race.' Dr. Lambrose Gina writes in her book, *The Soul of Woman*, that not only man and woman are different in height, in structure of the bones and in the muscular system, but they are also different in the quality and quantity of air and food that they absorb, that they are subject to different sicknesses, their desires are different and finally they differ in their mental and moral tendencies. She further remarks, 'Progress, evolution and life are possible only through differentiation.'

After quoting these authorities, the author of *Whither Woman* -V.M. Rege writes: 'There is, therefore, no escaping of the fact that there are certain inherent psychological differences which sharply distinguish man and woman. Here there is no question of their relative superiority or inferiority. They only point to the fundamental differences of the sex in their function and mission. In their zeal to show equal educable capacity and intelligence, the English and American women are utterly misguided in demanding the same education for girls as for boys. It is now proved beyond doubt that woman has as much intelligence as man in, pursuing the highest possible education. And this is exactly what has misguided the modern woman. She has misunderstood her own nature, needs and functions. She has allowed herself to be exploited by male-like ideals. She has come to conceive in womanliness something inferior and lacking, so that she has held before her as model all that the male is doing. She has become ashamed of her womanliness and wishes it better if she had been born a male. These ideas have created a false standard before her, and consequently she has identified her personality with that of man. She has ignored that she has an independent personality, quite different and entirely equal to man and which, if she developed, would develop into perfect womanliness.'

In the sphere of sexual morality, it has been observed by modern protagonists of sex equality that it is unjust to apply two different standards in respect of men and women; that if sexual laxity in men is not regarded as a very serious offence, there is no reason why it should be so regarded in women. This is true up to a certain limit and Islamic teachings have never made any discrimination in this respect between males and females. Thus adultery, according to Warn, in both men and women, is legally an equal offence punishable with equal penalties. But even in this sphere unalterable facts of nature tilt the balance in favour of men. Discussing this question, Dr. Westermarck says in *The Future of Marriage in Western Civilization:*

> *But even if public opinion would, in the future, grant complete sexual freedom to the unmarried of either sex, the indulgence of it by girls would still be attendant with serious disadvantages already pointed out. There would undoubtedly be exploitation in women by men; girls who remained virgins would still be preferred as wives, and the others would run the risk of being used for temporary purposes. Feminists advocating equal freedom for men and women seem to overlook the benefits that the men would derive from it; they would find it easier to gratify their desires in a more agreeable manner than through intercourse with prostitutes, and at the same time to acquire sexual experience is considered useful for their future marriage. When speaking of the 'injustice' of different moral demands on men and women, those advocates also fail to notice that this difference is ultimately due to a difference in the sexual instincts of the two sexes.*

The ideas expressed above are more or less in line with the Islamic conception of sex equality; As we have shown in the beginning of this chapter, Islam upholds the essential human dignity and fundamental equality of the two sexes, but, along with the common rights and duties of men and women in which both are equal, it concedes some separate rights and prescribes some separate duties for men and women, in accordance with its view that each sex has its specific functions in society and is charged with an independent mission for the preservation and advancement of the human race. Within the limits of their special mission and functions in society, both men and women will have different rights and responsibilities and neither sex should feel jealous of the other if this involves lesser rights for one sex against the other in a strictly limited sphere and on easily understandable terms capable of adjudication in law-courts. This is the meaning of the Quranic verse:

And do not covet that by which Allah has made some of you excel others; men should have the benefit of what they earn and women shall have the benefit of what they earn.
(v. 32)

According to Islam, there is a specific sex individuality in man and woman which they must preserve and cherish, because it is this individuality which gives them honour and dignity and enables them to fulfil in an effective manner their specific role in society. Where this specific sex individuality, instead of being regarded as a source of honour and dignity, is sought to be pulled and effaced, as if it involved an inferiority in men or women, it produces a dead and colourless equality which is, in effect, a denial of real equality, as it makes for less differentiation and, therefore, for less progress. There are clear instructions of the Holy Prophet on this point which stress the need for preserving sex individuality. Thus Abu Daud records it on the authority of Abu Hurrayrah, a companion of the Prophet, that the Prophet uttered a curse on men who imitate women in their dress and manners and similarly on women who abhorred their femininity by trying to dress and act like men. Similarly, at another place, Abu Daud has recorded that the Prophet severely condemned those women who tried to appear and behave in the form and likeness of men.

Consistent with the exercise of their specific individuality and of the special functions flowing therefrom and involving special rights and responsibilities, both sexes have equal rights and are looked upon by Islam as distinct legal personalities. A wife, even after having come in partnership with her husband, is a separate legal person in Islamic law capable of suing and being sued in her own individual capacity and entitled to sue her own husband for any infringement of her just rights. This is a position which was not accorded to the female sex in Europe and America until the nineteenth century and this too after a great deal of agitation against the existing legal disabilities of women. Blackstone, who was the greatest exponent of the English Common Law and has profound influence on legal theory and practice both in England and America, maintained that the legal position of a married woman was one of unity with husband. In *The Legal Rights, Liabilities and Duties of Women,* Professor Mansfield summarised the Blackstonian thesis as follows:

The first great principle of Scripture, the unity of husband and wife, is repeated by the law. They are, in law, one person .... Upon it, as observed by Blackstone, depend nearly all legal rights, duties and disabilities acquired by marriage.

Commenting on Blackstone's dictum, Mary B. Beard says in her book, *Woman as Force in History:*

> *When Blackstone spoke of the husband's rights over the real and personal property of his wife and of her disabilities in law, he was technically correct, within fixed limits. On its face, the statement meant that, in case of litigation, the husband asserts certain rights over the real and personal property of his wife, and if the wife contests them or the said rights are drawn in question at Common Law, the Common Law Courts will enforce the husband's Common Law rights, unless the husband and wife have made agreements to the contrary before and after the marriage, or a relative of the wife has safeguarded the wife's rights by the creation of a trust or otherwise, which agreements or trusts made in due form are valid in equity and will be enforced by courts of equity. In other words, in the absence of valid agreements and actions to the contrary, the husband may, if he so desires, or his creditors and other litigants may assert a husband's rights over the wife's property and within the limits set by the specific rules of Common Law, the Common Law Courts will enforce them in case of litigation.*

This was the position of a married woman in Europe and America until about 150 years ago. She could lose her rights on her own property, if the husband wished to deprive her of them because the law did not recognise her as separate legal personality. Islam, on the other hand, from its very inception, gave the married woman a separate Legal status with full property rights. Little wonder that a wrong conception of sex equality and extremist stand in respect of female freedom resulted from the sense of utter frustration generated by such great social and legal disabilities. But how could the Muslim women be justified in going to the same extreme length and preaching a conception of sex equality which lacks all scientific and natural basis as evidenced by latest researches on sex psychology.

JUSTIFYING EQUALITY

In the 6th century the greatest event of the history of mankind which shook the very basic ideals and concepts of man and brought about a complete revolution in his thoughts and views and a total change in his character, was the high-spirited and high-hearted proclamation of the Prophethood of Hadrat Muhammad (peace and blessings of Allah be upon him). The result of this revolution was that it not only took a different turn in man's thought, but also gave a new direction to his life. One significant aspect of this new trend of thinking was the 'concept of woman' which underwent a complete change and thereby established the relationship between man and woman on entirely new grounds.

Before the advent of Islam and the arrival of Prophet Muhammad (peace be upon him) and his proclamation of Prophethood, the history of woman was no doubt the history of subjugation and oppression. She was underestimated and condemned as a low and mean creature and was regarded as the root cause of all evils and disasters. Instructions were given to be careful about her and to avoid her like snakes and scorpions. She was bought and sold like animals. She did not enjoy any absolute or independent position in the society and was made subservient to man. She was denied all rights and had to live on the pity and mercy of man. In such a dark period of the history of woman, Islam raised its voice so vehemently that the whole world reverberated with it. Today no one dares say that her previous position was correct and real. It was loudly proclaimed:

O mankind! Reverence
Your Guardian Lord,
Who created you
From a single soul
Created, of like nature
His mate, and from them twain
Scattered (like seeds) Countless men and women:
Reverence God, through Whom
Ye demand your mutual (rights).
And (reverence) the wombs
(that bore) for God
Ever watches over you. *(4:1)*

It was declared that the discrimination which the world has made between one man and the other is false, absurd and baseless. The whole mankind is the offspring of the single human soul. Originally all have the same descent. No one is noble or mean, or low or high by birth. All are equal and enjoy equal position. Any kind of distinction between them on the grounds of family status, race, colour, tribe, region, language, occupation or nationality is null and void.

It was thus a repudiation of the age-old differences and discrimination between man and woman. It brought into light the fact that the very companion of the first man was not of some other kind but belonged to the same species. No different kind of creature was taken for his companionship, rather she was taken from him alone. This first pair gave birth to numerous men and women and among them some or the other kind of relationship existed and thus the whole human generation got spread far and wide. Hence to differentiate and discriminate between man and woman is in fact to differentiate and discriminate between one side of mankind and the other and is the division of the two parts of a single whole. There can be no better elucidation than this for the expression of the equality of man and woman and their equal status.

It is also stated that all human beings are the servants of one God and the children of one and the same father and mother. Therefore on the one side they should worship and obey God and lead their life in fear of Him and on the other, give due respect to the relationships which exist between them. Here, with the honour of man, the honour of woman is also emphasised.

Islam totally repudiated the notion that man is dignified and honoured merely because he is a man and woman is low and mean simply because she is a woman. Both man and woman are equal in the eyes of Islam. Neither the inferiority of anyone nor superiority of anybody is written down for eternity. Whoever is adorned with faith and fair practice emerged successful here and in the hereafter and whoever is devoid of such qualities fails in this as well as in the eternal world:

Whoever works righteousness,
Man or woman, and has faith,
Verily, to him will We give
A new life, a life
That is good and pure, and We
Will bestow on such their reward
According to the best
Of their actions. *(16:97)*

Islam assigns different spheres of activity for man and woman. The field of work of woman is her own house and of men is the world outside. What the Quran instructs the honourable wives of the Holy Prophet (peace be upon him) holds true for all such women as believe in Allah and His Messenger.

Generally, two objections are raised against the position of woman in Islam. First, that the great responsibility of household affairs which is imposed upon her, would debar her from participating in the economic and social development. For this reason it is assumed that her position in the society would not be definite, but would be weak and unstable.

Regarding this, it needs to be clarified, that Islam has not barred woman from economic activities, rather it has given permission while imposing on her a few appropriate limitations. Although it is doubtless that her involvement in family affairs affects her economic struggle, Islam offers its own solution to it. Islam has held man legally responsible for the maintenance of his wife and children.

The second objection is that since the great responsibility of the house is vested in woman, she is confined to the four walls of the house. It is conceived that since she is completely engrossed in the home affairs, neither the society would be benefited from her abilities nor would she get any opportunity to contribute her potentialities to society.

This objection is also incorrect and without any substance. Islam has not forbidden woman from other activities which stand beyond the household activities. What Islam virtually intends and emphasises in this regard is that a woman is mainly a queen and forerunner of her house. Hence, she should not bear the outward burden of the work at the risk of her indoor work. She is allowed to participate in the economic struggle with man while performing her role in the family affairs. Furthermore, she can take interest and contribute her abilities in different fields of life while keeping into consideration her condition, social environment and her own interest. History bears witness to the fact that the Muslim women have manifested their abilities, skill and talent in different fields of life and have left a tremendous impact on the age.

The most important thing is, Islam has assigned woman a prominent position at social level. Hence, she can lead an honoured and dignified life without becoming a victim of any inferiority complex. She can, in fact, offer her fullest cooperation to man in building up a chaste and virtuous society while contributing her potentialities and abilities which she possesses.

Different Spheres : There are two important reasons for which Islam assigns different spheres of activity to man and woman. First, it helps them guard their chastity. When both of them perform their work in the same sphere, it will become difficult for them to lead a life of chastity and modesty. If man and woman mix with each other in educational institutions to pursue education and participate in sports and games, and other recreations in parks and picnic spots and engage themselves openly in markets and in business centres without any checks and balances and meet each other without any restriction and this process of intermingling continues not for a day or two but for years together and in this way all the stages from childhood to youth and from youth to old age will be crossed, it is certain that their physical urges will get excited and flared up and will become uncontrolled and unchecked and ultimately they will become victims of indecent sexual anarchy.

In the present age, wherever free mixing of man and woman has been granted, it has resulted in a disaster. Chastity and honour are ravaged and modesty and decency are crippled. It gives rise to vulgar and ignoble sexual lapses which like an epidemic disease goes to such an extent that it becomes difficult to cure and correct it. And now it is taken as an inescapable social evil. Also all the evil results of it are willingly or unwillingly tolerated.

Chastity and modesty are apparently moral values, and it is on this basis that the direction of the whole society is determined. In a society where no importance is given to these values, man from every direction is taken to debased and evil acts and adultery. It gives rise to a particular kind of culture, civilisation, association, manners and literature, each element of which ignites fire in the sexual emotions of man. Contrary to it, the society which realises the importance and value of chastity and purity is erected entirely on a different standard. Each act of such a society reflects the purity of character, modesty and decency, and piety and purity fills the whole environment.

Islam is very sensitive to the chastity and purity of a man. It forbids free mixing and unrestricted meeting between man and woman. Islam considers it wrong to let man and woman mix with each other in their fields of work and let themselves involve in a severe test from where it is difficult to return. Islam not only forbids the acts of adultery but also prohibits man and woman to go near it.

The Quran says:

Nor come nigh to adultery:
For it is a shameful (deed)
And an evil, opening the road,
(to other evils). *(17:32)*

The second reason to assign different fields of work for man and woman is that their abilities and potentialities differ with each other. It is a fact that a woman is physically weaker than a man. She cannot bear hardship and strains.

Woman passes through such stages of life which restrict her from performing heavy work constantly. Her menstrual period begins from her youth and continues until she steps into the old age. Moreover, she passes through the most difficult and arduous stages like pregnancy and delivery. All these conditions and stages affect her health, strength and manner and stand as obstacles on the way of constant and laborious work. Now, it is the question of justice that she should not be given any tedious and wearisome works. Islam, therefore, assigns the work which requires more strength and valour to man and the work which is not hard and tedious to woman. Islam solves the problem thus that woman should look after the house while man should perform outside duties.

The very nature, interest and the psychology of woman demands the same sort of work. Woman in herself possesses the qualities of grace, love, patience, devotion and sacrifice more than a man. She fills the whole atmosphere of the family with happiness and order, peace and tranquility and love and affection. But to face the hardships and difficulties of life and to march forward firmly on all ups and downs, strong determination, bravery and intrepidity are the qualities which are required. Man possesses all these qualities far more than woman. The home and the family, however, provide a peaceful environment. The abilities of woman distinctively appear more sharply in the house from which full advantage can be derived. Man can face the complications and problems of life. For this reason man should be given such responsibilities as require more courage and valour.

It is no fairness to woman that she should be taken out from her natural field of work and be pushed into an unnatural field of work. It is not advantageous for her, rather a great loss.

The pains of menstrual period, pregnancy and delivery are unavoidable. Man can hardly assist her in all these difficulties and complications. It is, therefore, not a fair play if she is also given the responsibilities of man.

The woman is the queen of the house. She gets all the love and affection from her father, brother and husband and all the members of her family and all her rights are protected in the house. If woman does not bear the responsibility of the house, she cannot claim her rights. Thereafter she will have to work in such a field to pass her life which will not be in fact her own field and where she will have to face such a partner at every step who will be stronger than her. Then, it can be hardly expected that she will surpass man.

The place of honour and dignity of a woman is her own house, not the market. But in the present age, the importance of house and family is not fully recognised. It is the reason that the important role of woman in the house is interpreted as an injustice to her or that it gives her a low and mean position in the society or to deny her rights which she possesses or to condemn her constantly to the lowest position though a family is the basic unit of every society. The importance and significance of the house stands far ahead than of an office or a bazaar.

The service which a woman renders in building the inner environment of her house is more important than the service which she can render outside. Here some aspects of her work are mentioned:

Services of Woman

1. Today, man is engrossed in innumerable political, social, cultural and other problems. Other factors like health, diseases, poverty, difficulties also coincide with these problems. Sometimes for earning and living, man struggles too severely, bears all kinds of pains and faces innumerable difficulties. For maintaining and uplifting his family, he overcomes insurmountable hardships. In such a state of affairs, he deserves mental peace and content. It is the home which can provide him with all this peace and rest. If he does not get peace even at his own home, it becomes too hard for him to live: Islam teaches that a woman should make her home a 'peaceful dwelling' so that man should forget all his tensions and complications after reaching his home and prepare himself for a fresh struggle after breathing an air of gratification.
2. It has become an established fact that there is no better nourishment for a child than the milk of his mother. If a mother does not stay at home and engages herself in outside activities, she cannot set herself for breast-feeding. In this way the proper nourishment of the child for a considerable period even after the age of breast-feeding depends on mother. For the proper bringing up of the child, it is not just enough to give him proper nourishment but the child abundantly needs the love and affection, sympathy and an earnest devotion of his mother. If he is devoid of love and emotions from his nearest environment, his whole personality gets affected and even if his personality blossoms it will develop in a very wrong direction. It is the

heart of mother which is the source of inspiration for the child. Nobody else can take the place of woman for playing a decisive role. If the mother remains outside the home, the child would yearn for the love of his mother and he will not get it.

3. For the basic education and training of the child, mother is most suitable. For the purpose of education of the child, it is necessary that his teachers should be very loving and devoted to him, and should be acquainted with the nature and psychology of the child, and tolerate all his mischiefs and check him with love and patience. The most important thing is that the child should also love the teacher and consider even the bitterest scolding of the teacher to be good and beneficial for his well-being and tolerate even the harshness of the teacher. These sorts of feelings do not prevail between any two persons other than between mother and child. Let us look at another aspect. From educational point of view, it is extremely important that there should prevail an intimate and cordial relationship between the teacher and the child. The stronger this relationship, the better and beneficial it would be for the child. Perhaps, because of this reason, classes of higher standards are not much liked in schools because there the relationship between the teacher and the child is weaker in most of the cases. Comparatively, the classes of the lower standards are liked much because here this relationship is found to be stronger. In this manner the mother can provide basic education for her children which they cannot possibly acquire even at school.

Most of the children do not obtain proper education because they do not get better tutors at home or their parents are not able to afford tutors for them. Furthermore, most of the parents do not get proper tutors for their daughters. If the mother is capable enough to educate her children and even feel that it is her responsibility to give proper education to her children, the expenditure which is incurred on education will also get curtailed and help solve many other problems.

Here, one important point from the Muslim outlook on education is that today little attention is being paid to religious education. Very few children obtain religious education. Consequently, the child is sent to school when he has reached the age of school going. He does not get any opportunity even the preliminary religious instructions. Therefore, even the children of some good and God-fearing people remain ignorant of the basic religious tenets. The reason behind all this is that the father does not get time to give them religious instructions and the mother either herself lacks such education or does not take interest in education. If the mother is thoughtful enough and also capable of giving education to her children, they will not be ignorant of their religion, even after obtaining education in schools.

Even for training the children, the role of the mother is most important and significant. It is the mother who stands as an ideal for a child. The child observes the morals and etiquette of his mother day and night and moulds his behaviour noting the behaviour of his mother. The child maintains the same sort of relationship between himself and others on the mode of the relationship which his mother maintains between herself and others. Mother is his virtual model in this aspect and plays a decisive role in moulding the character of her child.

The fact is that the construction of a society depends upon the construction of a house. This is the reason that Islam has completely relied upon woman to construct her house. Islam does not wish to thrust on her other burdens along with this responsibility. The woman is freed even from the financial responsibilities. In the light of Islam, the construction of their house is no less important than Jihad. Hadrat Anas related that once a group of women asked Prophet Muhammad (peace be upon him) that men perform some acts and attain the reward of Jihad, what we should do to get such reward which men get through Jihad in the way of God? Prophet Muhammad (peace be upon him) replied that woman who sits at home receives the reward of Jihad in the way of God.

SUPREMACY OF MAN

Islam has discussed in detail every aspect of the conjugal life and presented a broad and comprehensive picture of the family. An objection raised against it is that man has been given extraordinary rights and powers, thus curtailing woman's freedom. Man is in authority and rule and can drive her as he is pleased so long as she is shackled through marriage tie. She can in no way take the offensive against him.

This picture of the woman's aggrieved state and helplessness is as far from truth as it is horrible. In painting this dreadful portrait of her, perhaps greater time and effort have been devoted to distortion of Islam than trying to understand its teachings.

Let us take up first of all the religious and moral aspects of this problem which have the basic importance in the Islamic version of familial life. According to Islam the real and basic relationship of the husband and wife is that of affection and love in which both of them in their own spheres and each in his or her own turn tries to please and meet the requirements and provide ease and comfort to the other. The Quran declares this love and affection as one of the Signs of Providence. It says :

And among His Signs is this, that He created for you mates from among yourselves, that ye may dwell in tranquillity with them, and He has put love and mercy between your (hearts) : Verily in that are Signs for those who reflect. [11]
—Al Quran XXX - 21

At another place, the spouses have been likened to garments for one another :

They (the women) are your garments and you (men) are their garments. [12] —Al-Baqarah 2: 187

This characterisation has a deep significance. Dress has certain attributes. The Quran wants, the same attributes to characterise the relationship of husband and wife. One aspect of the dress is that it is next to one's body and nothing intervenes between the dress and the body. Similar is the relationship of husband and wife in a world of materialistic relationships, the closeness found in conjugal relationship is unique. Secondly, dress protects a person from climatic hardships. Husband and wife are also expected to help one another in overcoming various hardships, in achieving peace and solace and in not letting life become uncomfortable. Thirdly, dress covers those parts of body whose exposure is shameful. Similarly, husband and wife should hide each other's weaknesses and drawbacks and not let them be exposed. Fourthly, dress is a means of adornment. Similarly, husband is adornment for wife and wife for husband. The beauty of this world rests on the harmony of this relationship. Otherwise life will become dull and barren. This particular similie of "dress" is pointing towards many such sublime realities.

And in the tradition of the Prophet (S.A.W.), it has been explained from various angles. In one of his sayings :

When the husband looks at her she should gladden his heart; if he suggests something she should accept it cheerfully and whichever item of expenditure trait of behaviour, the husband disapproves of; she should (abstain from it) and not displease him by insisting on it.

Similarly, a polite husband has been called the best person in the tradition. Aishah (R.A.A.) reports the Prophet (S.A.W.) to have said :

> *The better person among you is one who is kindly disposed to his family and I am the best among you in benevolence to my family.*

There are many traditions on this theme. If the moral standards stated therein were adopted by the husband and the wife, the family would become the haven of peace and blessings and an ideal society can on those lines, be easily built.

Taking up now directly the problem of man's guardianship and supervision of the family, we notice that every institution big or small needs the services of a supervisor to run it smoothly and maintain perfect discipline in it. It is his responsibility to keep in view the interests of the institution foremost, recognize the right of its members and treat them with love and kindness. Those associated with the institution should also obey the supervisor cheerfully.

So long as he keeps in view the interest of the institution they should not resort to head strongness and rebellion against him, and in controversial issues his decision should be the last word, to be accepted on all hands. The position of leadership can be the privilege of only one person. In case of more than one person trying to handle its affairs, each one insisting on his or her own opinion, the organisation of the institution will go topsy-turvy.

The family too is an institution and a complicated one at that. Its organisation can be maintained only when only one person is at the helm of affairs to manage it. If the authority is duplicated the organization will cease to function. Rather, its very existence will be in peril. The only question that needs consideration is : who is to be the head of the family, man or woman? The following Quranic verse provides answer to this question:

> *Men are the protectors and maintainers of women because Allah has given the one more (strength) than the other and because they support them from their means. [13]*
>
> *—Al Quran IV: 34*

Here in this verse two reasons have been advanced for appointing man as the head of the family. Firstly he has superiority over woman and secondly that he spends his substance on her. That means that the Quran has selected man as the head of the family not on the basis of any prejudice but in consideration of his capabilities and his financial responsibilities. Let us now ponder over these two arguments seriously.

The Mightier : The physical and mental make-up of man and woman point to the fact that man is better equipped physically and mentally to bear the burden of a family. He is capable of greater effort in seeking the livelihood, his own and that of the family, and can undertake difficult and labour consuming efforts in agriculture, industry and other fields. In the matter of facing the hardships of life and in overcoming them also he manifests better capability. But this marvellous fact can also be witnessed that the jobs that are considered exclusively the woman's fields of activity and she has been at them since the dawn of man's birth, like cooking, tailoring and washing, etc., in these jobs too man exhibits superior skills and powers.

The breast of a woman is the centre of finer sentiments and delicate feelings. Both happy and sad events leave her worse than man. Therefore, it occurs to us at first sight that she should be able to express these impressions much more effectively than man. But it is a historical fact that in literature, poetry, art and fine arts, the height of perfection (in both imagination and skill) the level attained by man, woman could not dream of. Man has presided over all the fine arts through the ages. It can be asserted that man had the monopoly in all these departments and woman had no occasion to exhibit her capabilities in them. But this further raises a question: How did man come to have a monopoly here? And how was woman left behind in this race for perfection and superiority in skills? (And there is hardly any answer to this question). So it will have to be admitted that man can furnish better proof of his capacity for perfection in skills as well as put in greater energy and has done so in every age.

When experience furnishes evidence that man is capable of putting in greater amount of energy and superior capabilities, he must naturally be the head of the family. Not to acknowledge man's superiority and trying to put woman on a par with man in every respect is a sort of reaction or prejudice which may sound logical in discussion and debate, but in the battlefield and bivouac of life it cannot go far enough in our support. Here, the hard facts and realities of life have to be admitted.

Now let us consider the financial responsibilities of man. Under the Islamic Law man must pay the woman her dower, accept the responsibilities of her maintenance and provision of her lodging with all the amenities of life. And along with them he has to arrange for the wife's education and training, looking after the religious and moral supervision and undertaking the responsibility of the protection of her life, property, honour and dignity. Man accepts this burden with the expectation, that under his supervision, his wife shall manage the house, shall provide him peace, shall educate the children and thus cooperate in building up a healthy family.

To meet these different types of financial and administrative responsibilities properly man has been endowed with certain rights, privileges and powers. But they are not absolute and unlimited. There are certain limits beyond which he cannot go in the exercise of those powers and privileges. Undoubtedly in practical life there is a possibility of man's overstepping the prescribed limits and make wrongful use of his powers and woman may become the victim of excesses. Islam does not overlook or disregard this possibility. The woman under these conditions can compel man to abide by the limits through legal action. Under inevitable circumstances she can obtain her freedom through Khula (legal divorce at the request of the wife) or separation from the husband.

Woman as Head : In their zeal to overreach themselves in championing the cause of woman's lib some persons went to the extent of stripping man totally of the rights, privileges and power devolving on him normally in familial life to meet his onerous responsibilities. But obviously enough in course of being deprived of all authority in his own family and home he cannot be expected to meet his financial responsibilities as the head of the family. So the only feasible solution that presents itself under the changed situation is that woman, who is now in saddle, is the new protector and maintainer and all the rights and powers associated with that position have been vested in her, she must also take upon herself all the responsibilities that formerly used to be man's headache. So long as she does not accept and meet those responsibilities, there can be no justification for transferring the important and difficult job of protecting and maintaining the family to her.

It is usually asserted that under the changing social conditions, woman's maintenance is no more a problem since she has already started making economic efforts, doing jobs and rendering utility services to the society which are remunerative, thus attaining economic independence. But apart from the fact that such working and economically independent women are a negligible minority in our society, the problem is not really one of her own maintenance and independence alone.

It also involves bringing up children, their up keep, education and training, liabilities of their marriages and multifarious other problems relating to other members of the family in a wider sense. The question arises weather woman along with her own support can meet fairly and squarely all the other problems devolving on her as the head of her family.

Undoubtedly there have been exceptional women in every age with a sound economic position and, they were also capable of managing family affairs satisfactorily. Such individuals of the female sex are there in our existing society and shall also be there in future. But a gigantic problem is not solved by a microscopic minority, since it concerns along with them the untold millions, each one by herself a problem crying for solution. Apparently enough, notwithstanding the counselling and support of her so-called well-wishers, the champions of the cause of woman's lib, she does not appear to forgo her time-honoured well-recognized right of maintenance, nor is she prepared to shoulder the onerous responsibilities of the familial organization as an independent charge.

2

Social Setup of Islamic World

ISLAMIC SOCIETY

Political themes, either related to leadership, political parties or social control, are essential aspects at communal rituals in Islamic Iran:, along with ethical themes on justice, equality, power and empowerment. A ritual symbol may stand for many things at the same time. By this he means that one must consider the informant's explanation of the socio-structural implication of the treatment and usage of ritual objects in performance, as well as the spatial and hierarchical positioning of ritual objects independent of exegesis and usage. At the women's Quranic meetings, the female preacher often went into great detail to clarify the complexity of various issues and examples. She played an important role, not only in teaching women the correct performance of prayers and Islamic rules, but also in teaching how to understand surrounding political events.

The degrees of political involvement and political rhetoric of preachers were distinguished both symbolically and through actual request. This can be deduced: from the distinctive personal, social, and, political views expressed in the context of sermons and the participant definition. It was not unusual to find that a ritual was performed and interpreted by different preachers in a slightly different manner, depending on the political' and educational background of the preachers.

A woman volunteer started distributing *mehr* (the clay of Karbala) to each participant, and as the reading approached the verses requiring the performance of the two units of *sajdeh*, we laid our foreheads on the assumed clay of Karbala, and repeated the verse read by the preacher loudly. The preacher asked those who were menstruating to leave the meeting and stay outside where they could not hear the sound of the verses. This created an: unpleasant situation, for those women who were obliged to leave the room, and some preferred to leave the meeting altogether.

There are explicit differences in the flexibility of a preacher's interpretations and views regarding women's act of purity and veiling. First it is a matter of social and ritual obedience, and secondly it is a matter of ritual in its cognitive sense, and not a problem of a social nature. In several meetings it became clear that the Hezbullahi preacher was distinguished by the participants as one who made repetitive: and restrictive references to women's rigid veiling and conventional behaviour. This was contrasted, by the modesty of the politically neutral preacher (*bi-taraf*), who took a more moderate view.

Some meetings were conservative, as judged by factors such as the number of women wearing bead-scarves under their chador, the content of the Quranic commentary given by the female preacher, and the repetitive offering of the blessing (*salvat*) to Imam Khomeini; and his successor, and president Rafsanjani. The negative term monafeqin, which means conspiracy, is a strong multivocal symbol conveying various messages and contrasting attributes concerning a series of illegitimate social and political divisions. Monafeqin may refer not only simply to good and evil, but also to state political norms, such as the Iranian case of women who are poorly veiled, as well as to any act of political resistance.

The preacher Zaki usually stopped reciting after every short verse (*ayat*) to offer a commentary. She was one of the preachers who thought it better not to continue before ensuring that the participants had a proper understanding of what was being read. She translated the Quranic meaning into a daily context, thereby making its realisation more practical for the participants, who were from various social categories (the majority being housewives and young schoolgirls). The preacher maintained that the kind of suppressions one could experience varied, and convincingly demonstrated this point by the use of metaphors. The reality of one's experience of 'suppression' was open to interpretation.

According to the preacher Zaki, Islamic suppression may be related both to the lack of juridical teachings concerning the rights of men and women and to being a good Muslim in practical terms according to legitimate Islamic codes. Public lessons in juridical matters were often brief, and in response to complicated questions the preachers might postpone answering to make further inquiries from a more learned religious person, such as a male or female *mujtahid*. The metaphor of suppression continued on another level in another Quranic meeting a few days later. This time it was raised by the preacher Mostafi, who defined suppression as acts of political tyranny, and as something that could be harmful to the whole Muslim community.

The *rowzeh* participants were familiar with the name of Salman Rushdie 94 and the Islamic state's political fight against him. He was understood to have committed an act of blasphemy by denying the existence of God and the legitimacy of Muhammad as his Prophet. The preacher Mostafi wishing him a misfortune, and punishment by hanging. Some of the attendants supported her statement by saying amen. The metaphorical references of suppression and the model of corrupt leadership were two on-going political themes in mass media. They were phrased according to the Islamic state dominant political view.

However, on one occasion it was clear that the preacher lacked accurate knowledge of the international political situation, but was familiar with the Islamic state's political rhetoric. For example, on one occasion the preacher Mostafi referred to both the CIA (American Intelligence Service) and KGB (Soviet Intelligence Service) as the American secret service without anybody making any attempt to correct her. This did not prevent her from conveying the desired political message to her listeners, as she accused these international agencies of 'suppression', in their attempts to undermine the Iranian Revolution and its Islamic virtue.

A Suppressor of Poorly-veiled Women: The identities of 'poorly-veiled' and 'non-veiled' (*bi-hejab*) despite their wearing Islamic suits (*manto*), have emerged in conservative political slogans, condemning the degree of immodesty among women. Posters covering street walls, with slogans such as 'death to bi-hejab and bad-hejab', attach a negative label to women, who neglect to veil themselves fully.

'Poorly-veiled' is a negative term applied to those whose appearance and social manner may be defined as fashionable, tempting and provocative; i.e. to those wearing colourful scarves, light colours, fashionable styles, make-up, transparent stockings, etc. This is considered a political act of *monafeqin*, and is generally applied on those who are believed to oppose and destroy Islamic values, instead invoking perversion. The negative image of a poorly-veiled woman as a suppressor of the Islamic community has developed through religious speeches. This is further illustrated by the case of a widow who had arranged a meeting to mark the annual remembrance ceremony for her husband. Close and distant relatives, as well as friends and local women, gathered for the meeting.

The female preacher Mostafi frequently paused to interpret Quranic recitations, and whenever she came to the term *monafeqin* (conspirators), she explained it in terms of external and internal enemies of Islam. She also included women who wore thin stockings together with Islamic suits, for being 'provocative' and modern in style. Furthermore, she accused women who failed to dress properly of weakening the ideology of the revolution, and repeatedly saluted the martyrs (*shohada*) and prisoners of war (*asiran*) with the verse of *salvat*. She unexpectedly addressed the married daughter of the house, a university lecturer who was serving tea to the attendants, asking her to stop serving to allow the audience to concentrate on the sermon.

After the ceremony some participants believed the preacher had become cross with her on account of the way she was dressed. The initiator of the *rowzeh* complained that she was very disappointed, and that the memorial ceremony for her husband had been used for political ends, which was an insult to his memory. She regretted not having invited another female preacher whom she knew herself, rather than this one who had been recommended by her religiously 'orthodox' sister.

An another example of being an Islamic conspirator, the preacher Zaki cited shopkeepers, who would hoard goods (*ahtekar*) and sell things at inflated prices. Economic gains at the expense of those Muslim customers who are in a financially difficult situation was considered an unmeritful act during their fife of permanent economic well-being. Such undertakings were categorised as illegitimate (*haram*), because the aim was solely to accumulate capital.

Despite hoarding being described in official terms as acts of immorality and corruption, businessmen increasingly adopted it as a new avenue for economic success. These Islamic lessons not only suggest the moral identity of authority at the level of family, community and state, but the way they can be corrupted and distract communal social order. Disagreement was expressed among attendants in private religious meetings either as defenders or against the preacher. Although women seemed reluctant to counter the Islamic state policy directly, they often did so metaphorically. They often felt more free to express themselves outside the religious meetings when talking to a friend, to me, or to relatives.

Once, in the month of Ramadan in 1989, and during a regular lesson concerning the performance of prayer, an older participant interrupted the preacher Mostafi and asked the following question: 'I wonder how it can be an act of *halal* (permission) to perform the prayers of *namaz* on the floor of a house, which has been a forcefully confiscated, property (*qasbi*)?' This was not simply a ritual question, but had numerous connotations for participants, who could clearly explain the political issue the questioner had in mind. This created a funny situation, and some smiled slightly at the preacher who could not give a proper answer, and thus postponed it in order to make further inquiries. On another occasion, also at a meeting held by preacher Mostafi, and following the month of Ramadan, a participant expressed her disagreement on the ethical lesson concerning a Muslim duty, saying: 'I wonder how it can be a sinful act to ask why the price of potatoes has increased so rapidly?' The preacher had repeatedly said that in order not to disturb the ongoing operation of the Islamic state, we should avoid any kind of criticism.

A politically reserved attitude, and a symbolic mode of expression, are more common than ever before in Iranian everyday culture, due to the social and political burden. Thus, in the meeting of *rowzeh*, some of the preachers, either as a matter of personal loyalty to the state, or as a way of avoiding politically sensitive issues, may fail to answer 'improper' questions, and cut them short with a *salvat*. The contradiction between the actual political economy of Islamic states and Quranic notion of *zulm* gives a false representation of ideal religious values. Some middle-class and educated participants were more sensitive to speaking up, and expressing such a distortion.

The political opposition between questioner and preacher could be stated metaphorically. In response to the direct and critical political questions, which a preacher could accept as reasonable, she may excuse herself from answering by giving the impression of not being bothered with such issues. She might request her listeners to recite a salvat so to avoid answering the question before inviting the participants to continue the ritual of reading the Quranic verse for the day or before resuming her *tafsir*.

The political overtone of the male preacher at the mosque was even more direct, and covered broader political and social matters to a larger audience. Some considered that the political link to rituals would reduce the 'true' value of Islam. For this reason some hosts were reluctant to listen to or invite, any preacher.

The Quranic term of *efrat-o-tafrit* (too much and too little), is often used by disappointed religious participants, such as Narges, about situations where local events overlap political and religious commitments. Political intrusion is frequently given as the reason for the loss of one's former religious belief, and the loss of sacred traditional religious symbols in general. Nuzhat, a regular religious participant at private meetings, felt disturbed by the political overload in everyday religious activities. She found the regular Quranic recording from our neighbouring mosque loudspeaker disturbing and tiresome. She telephoned anonymously, asking the authorities to turn down the volume of the loudspeaker because she had a sick relative at home.

The connection between the ethical conduct of women's daily behaviour and the entire order of nature was often an element in the Islamic speeches of the preacher. The negative publicity given to unveiled women in the religious arena by male and female preachers was often the cause of public ideological conflict. In an anthropological study of a Muslim community in Tunisia, the rain ritual: at the time of drought is described as an act of penance and a rite of reconciliation by which the members of the community are 'purified' and reincorporated.

In the context of the urban Shirazi, misfortunes or natural disorder are not only defined as a basis for community solidarity, but also as a metaphor for disagreement and political hostility between social categories, e.g. between the Islamic conservatism and the more liberal middle-class Muslim believers. In day-to-day social situations ideological differences have become aspects of individuals' social identities, frequently leading to conflict, and in extreme cases to public violence such as in 1989. The concept of *mosibat* or *bala* denotes misfortune as a result of too much sin. Sin is destructive to individual well-being and is believed to create social and ecological disorder, with drought as a consequence.

The idea is that God is angered by ingratitude, arrogance, immoral behaviour, and particularly by non-veiling. Heavy rain and drought are both believed to be caused by social disaster (*bala*), bringing negative consequences to the whole community. In March 1989 in daily Ramadan lessons, the preacher Zaki raised the unveiling question as usual. This time an attendant supported her view and defined it as a cause of a recent natural misfortune. Reproduction of Islamic order in ongoing political, social, and economic life has produced a new form of cultural complexity which is acted out in various social arenas such as religious meetings.

Prayer Lessons : In addition to the reciting of the Quran and its commentary, there is also reading from the book of *Tawzih ul-Masail"* (clarifying ritual problems) and the giving of prayer instructions at the religious meetings. The Tawzih ul-Masail, in Persian, is the kind of book which may be found in the home of a student in a Quranic class. The women's lessons of prayers (*masaleh-goi*) is central to each Quranic meeting, and is often performed by a leader of the Quranic seminaries or a preacher.

The preacher will spend approximately 15 minutes out of the 2-4 hour meeting on instructions. The instructions are most often performed in the beginning, but sometimes also at the end. The female preacher, her assistant, or the religiously 'learned' give the instructions to the participants. Some of the participants use the free minutes in the middle or at the end of the rowzeh meeting to put their personal questions to the preacher, being ashamed to speak about some family and sexual matters in the presence of others.

The preacher, or ritual expert, referred a question to the local male preacher, or postponed her answer, as she herself was in doubt about the correct answer. The lessons concerning the performance of prayers deal with questions closely related to the women's need to carry out the ritual as it is generally prescribed, particularly in the month of Ramadan. The dominant themes are the fast, the purification for prayers, alternative and compensation prayers, alms, and various forms of ablution (such as for death, *namaz-e mayet*).

The other themes are compensation for prayers neglected or not performed for physical reasons such as menstruation, of *sigheh*, of *mahram* and non-*mahram*, of *zakat* (religious tax), of abortion, and of illegitimate property. The lessons of prayers are largely concerned with ethical and personal matters. The question of the prayers and the matters which could lead to its break, e.g. praying in a house, or touching objects classified as unlawful property, were dominant themes in the religious lessons. The lesson of prayers is not simply about giving and taking. More importantly it provides an atmosphere for the preacher, ritual experts and audience to expound the prayers and the interpersonal norms of Islam, as well as its theology and sociology, in an informal manner.

In course of the lessons on ritual purity and impurity (*najes* and *taher*), obligatory prayers (*vajeb*), merciful acts (*mostahab*), and illegitimate objects or acts (*haram*), the preacher would often go into detail about the social, sexual and psychological problems women might experience. The aim was to instruct and correct their rituals of prayer. The female preacher often, went into great detail to clarify the complexity of questions, by reading to the participants from the book of *Tawzih al-Masail*, as well as quoting stories, telling a relevant narrative, and citing examples from day-to-day social and political life. The extent of an individual's sin and religious debt is emphasised in social and psychological terms with reference to whether the act could be considered intentional or unintentional. These are two central Islamic juridical concepts that determine performing a correct religious duty.

The quality of an individual's ritual is evaluated in terms of impure and pure objects, and permitted and forbidden acts. Unintentional neglect of obligatory prayers is not considered the fault of person and is thought to be excused by God. For example, failure to comply with the ritual prayer is said to be acceptable if the reason is humanitarian, such as saving a child.

Menstruation, pregnancy and childbirth are considered arbitrary and natural causes, and are thus considered as legitimate reasons for not performing ritual prayers, but the women are still expected to undertake some form of compensation prayers at another time. This debt of prayers may be performed during one's lifetime, or they can remain a personal duty of another family member after a person's death. These are ritual services that may be purchased, that is, a spiritual man is paid to perform prayers on behalf of a dead relative. The living are obliged to perform the neglected ritual in the form of a substitute prayer, or in the form of fasting, when they have recovered.

When water is not available for performing ablution it may be replaced by earth and sand. Dust is substituted for water to allow flexibility and continuity in the praying ritual. In this case the prayer performed is incomplete, or so-called 'half performed', and is made in a sitting position. This also applies for very sick people who remain in bed. Such alternatives are not considered appropriate for a healthy person, but are most common among people who travel a lot and who therefore are unable to perform their prayer in the prescribed form. The religious meetings often place a high priority on women's debt to God and after-life. For example, women who fast are advised not to submit to their husband's sexual demands. Sexual abstinence signifies a purity of one's obligatory prayers over the sexual desires of the husband.

Very often the subject concerning the ritual ethic is raised as an important condition to its performance. For example, the act of praying is said not to gain full merit if the worshipper refrains from wearing 'pure' and proper clothing, or if the ritual is not performed on a lawfully owned property. The interpretation of correct prayers does not ignore the present life-style and economic situation. For example, once a question was raised as to how one could perform the ritual of daily prayer on the airplane, or while travelling from one town to another.

Another example concerns the intentional or unintentional act of consuming food when this is prohibited. The former state applies when one is tempted to eat in secrecy, forgetting that God is a witness; the latter applies when one's health is threatened and requires the breaking of the fast. Those guilty of ignoring such a moral issue and ignoring God as witness not only lose merit, but also perform sin.

In fact, some particularly orthodox women may practise the ritual of fasting to an extent where they begin to suffer physically, and the doctor may suggest that they should avoid fasting. This is considered by the young and more liberal middle-class as 'madness', and by elderly women as a 'true' personal faith. These women believe that fasting reflects the value of hardship. The ideal is that the harder the prayers, the more merit will be gained. Furthermore, fasting to the point of physical suffering is considered as an act of *haram* by the ritual experts.

For religiously oriented women, achievement for after-life depends upon properly performed rituals, and the sanctioning of behaviour considered immoral. For religious companion it is better to enter the world of after-life with 'full hands' (a metaphor for sets of meritorious acts which gave her confidence and reduce the fear of death), rather than to be materially well-off in one's lifetime. Generally, women have more knowledge about the ritual instructions for prayers, as well as about visiting shrines and alms-giving, than the average male. This is largely due to a more regular attendance by women at ritual occasions concerning the family.

Political views were not only expressed in the Quranic language of *hezbullahi* preachers, nor only in the atmosphere of the religious meetings, but were also brought into internal political metaphors, such as in communal religious and poetic songs, and chanting.

In salutations to the Prophet Muhammad and his family (*alla-homa-sale-'ala-muhammad va aleh muhammad*), the Quranic reader not only asks for her own merit, but also for the merit of her parents, or for the happiness of her dead mother's soul and those of other recently dead relatives. Men are seldom the recipients of salutations at women's religious meetings, unless recognised as being highly religious learned, dead or war martyrs. Salutation signifies the women's position with strength and faith, and the reader is honoured as a mediator through whom a salutation is offered to the Prophet Muhammad and his family. The arrival of the preacher, for example, is often highlighted by the offering of a *salvat*, which may be initiated by loyal followers, who then expect others to join in on the chanting of the welcome chant. Any disorder, such as whispering or signs of disagreement among the women, and any interruption to the reading of the Quran, may induce a participant to request a *salvat*. The average participant views the recitation of the blessing verses as an instrument to gain merit.

Preachers and hostesses receive most of the salutations: the former for her religious performance, and the latter because she sponsored the rituals. Salutations may be addressed to the preacher herself, to her mother's soul, or occasionally to her husband. The mother-daughter relation, which is identified with the transmission of religious and ritual knowledge, is very often honoured by offering a salutation to the daughter, and to the soul of her dead or absent mother. Offering salutations to a martyr, or to the mothers or sisters of martyrs, are also important, as the latter represent new and prestigious categories within Islam.

In a particular case a woman expressed her emotion by showing her neighbour her bands, on which her hair stood at end, thus expressing her feeling of excitement. Often one of the women would offer a rousing salutation, which was then taken up by the others, even though the story was known to them. Some also whispered 'God is great' (*allah-o-akbar*) to one another in their excitement. At the end of text the preacher Zaki raised her hand, and wished that the mothers of the sons that had disappeared, or had been taken prisoners of war, would soon be reunited with them as the holy Jacob and his son Joseph had been reunited.

The image of a miracle, and the wish for the return of prisoners of war, raised the voices of the audience in *salvat*. The ability to work miracles is considered a personal quality of the Prophet. However, a person with a given religious status of *nazr-kardeh* (having been chosen: by a holy prophet or holy Imam); or a spiritual person who displays the notion of holiness; or who claims to be able to mediate between worldly reality and spiritual life, or to have met the Prophet or someone of his blessed lineage can claim to have the ability to perform miracles.

Shirazi middle-class women may perform both religious and social visits at a religious house. Such social and religious visits represent important aspects of the free social movement of women, and are taken more seriously by women than by men. Meanwhile, the secular visit of kinfolk is based on mutual visits and gift exchanges according to the type of social relation, age, family events and kin ties. The religious visit to a mosque or a shrine in another town, or even to Mecca, is performed individually or in groups. In contemporary Islamic Iran the religious practices of *ziarat* involve different aspects. Although we agree with Tapper that the above two visiting patterns are an effective way of gaining social mobility among Muslim women, the religious or sacred journey is not limited to traditional or lower-class Iranian women.

Carol Delaney opposes the view that the pilgrimage is merely a spiritual experience and suggests that 'sacred' and 'secular' are two aspects of a single event, and are integrated into the social domains. She also opposes the view that Muslim behaviour in the form of 'sacred' and `secular' are two different phenomena. There are many social situations in which a woman may feel motivated to initiate a vow at a mosque or at a nearby shrine. Women may not only vow to make a pilgrimage, but may also vow to stay there for one or more nights.

Women coming from rural areas, are often with their husbands or other family members as part of their vow of making on *ziarat*. In large shrines, such as the tomb of Imam Khomeini in the Behesht-e Zahra cemetery south of Tehran, the shrine of Imam Raza in the city of Mashhad, or in the Astaneh in the city of Shiraz, there are often places to rest and cook. Urban Shirazi women often travel in twos or threes—for example two sisters, a mother and a daughter, an aunt and a niece, two neighbours, or two fellow religious participants. Two or three who have known each other for years as Quranic students may also travel together.

The holy places, such as the main shrine or the Astaneh, are the kinds of religious places a Shirazi woman on particularly holy nights may stay the night alone, or with other female friends. Sometimes their husbands sit separately in the male section, particularly at the time of *ahya* (all-night watch and praying), or during the month of fasting when religious activity increases both for men and women.

Some women come alone and stay in the shrine the whole night; for example village women, or those who seek to use the shrine as a place of refuge from their restrictive husbands and family problems. This use of the public religious places as a free arena for women contrasts strongly with the highly constrained social mobility of women in secular places where sitting alone in a restaurant, or walking in a park, give rise to the stigmatised identity of being an available woman. This means that the acts of women in the religious sphere can be considered supportive: that is, women can stay away from home, make friends, and move freely, without being constrained by the sanctions that surround them in the secular social spheres.

Many wish to travel to distant shrines where, according to local women, the likelihood of a vow being fulfilled is greater. It is also believed that the longer and harder the *ziarat* is, the more pious it is, and the greater the likelihood of the vow's fulfilment. The degree of difficulty is measured against the hardships experienced by the Imam Hussain and his followers in the city of Karbala. The longer the distance travelled, the higher the prestige, and the greater is the relatives' expectations that she will return with presents. Women may go on pilgrimage individually. Nezhat made her first *hajj* journey in the company of her first Quranic teacher thirty years ago. Her second journey was from London where her son was living at the time.

Half of the way she was guided by her secular sister-in-law, and the rest she managed by contacting one of the Iranian pilgrimage agencies in Mecca. For a journey to the holy city of Mashhad, married women are more likely to persuade their husbands to join them, or ask their concession for travelling alone. Even in the orthodox and strongly segregated families, in which husband and wife seldom travel together on secular holidays, the husband may make a concession and travel with his wife, or pay for her expenses.

A wife planning a religious journey in the company of other women may be away from her household for some time. She will therefore make sure that a close female relative, such as an older daughter, her own sister, or a sister of her husband, can take over her responsibilities in her absence. The pleasure of these journeys can be summarised in the following three points: (1) performing religious duties, (2) bringing merit to the family; and (3) creating an alternative social network. Thus, travelling to the city of Mashhad to visit the shrine of Imam Raza is a journey for women's friends and their family.

Returning from Pilgrimage : A pilgrim expects to receive a special welcome on her return, and may herself bring some small gifts from the holy town to distribute among family and friends. Already the first day after her return she may receive visitors. On her return she will be referred to as a woman of higher religious experience.

The *ziarat* or *hajj* gifts are usually simple items valued for their 'goodness', such as a prayer stone symbolising the clay of Karbala, a prayer rug, prayer beads, or fabrics for sewing clothes. Embarking on a pilgrimage, both within and outside one's place of residence, has become very popular among middle-class and business families, especially to destinations such as ziarat and hajj. These have increasingly become the focal point for Islamic cultural innovation and the Islamic policy of nation-building. Such journeys are now being organised by travel agencies on a large scale, and the programmes may also include visits to new shrines.

Through modem technology, and in the context of the new political economy, the journey to Mecca has been reduced from several months to two or three weeks. Before a restriction was put on Iranian pilgrimages to Mecca in 1981-82 an increasing number of well-to-do women of various ages travelled in small groups, led either by female preachers, male spiritual leaders, or semi-government agencies. Today, as the number of pilgrims has increased considerably due to the use of modern transportation, the state arranges pilgrimages to Mecca twice a year. Due to the political changes after the revolution, travelling to other Muslim countries on pilgrimages has increased. Going on a pilgrimage provides the people with a new political and social alternative.

Meanwhile, the Islamic Iran encourages Islamic journeys of large scale while dismissing some of the customary rituals of visiting holy trees and the like as an incorrect practice of Islam. For example, a local house believed to be spiritually efficacious was closed by the local Islamic guards following the Iranian revolution in order to prevent the blessing of a tree and its mediation. This practice was perceived by the revolutionary regime as a kind of animism, and thus contrary to the Islamic belief in God as a single entity.

The house was a place where female visitors came from near and far to cook a meal in the yard and to tie a piece of fabric as a sign of a vow. The tree was known among the traditional Muslim-oriented women in Shiraz as a blessing tree that produced miracles and mediated one's wishes. Such visits were common among lower middle-class urban women. In contrast, it is possible to travel cheaply to a country such as Syria. Such journeys have been facilitated by both Islamic state and semi-private travel agencies, and must be booked at least one year in advance due to the large number of applicants. The official state policy of purifying Islam from 'popular' and 'false' elements has affected some of the customary practices. Popular Islamic practice has been encouraged more towards the public religious places and mosques, where rituals of worship are in the charge of learned preachers and state authorities.

Some aspects and forms of rituals are distinctively practised by different socio-economic categories. This can be defined in terms of ritual economy, since certain practices such as pilgrimage and distribution of big communal meal on holy days, are more accessible to the better-off than to the poor. Consider, for example, the cases of two religious companions, Shazdeh and Nezhat. The former believed it better to buy a place for hajj this year, rather than to wait for years in the hope that her name might come up in the ordinary waiting list. It cost her three times the normal price. However, since the Iranian revolution of 1979, a new form of identity associated with participation in religious fora has emerged, so religious gatherings and sacred journeys have become a new type of enterprise and social involvement where various categories intermingle. This offers women of different social and class backgrounds an alternative opportunity to meet. The policy of the Iranian state plays an important role in discouraging people from travelling to formerly popular destinations such as Europe, in favour of the less expensive neighbouring countries.

In Islamic Iran women of different social and class categories carry out religion in different forms, endowing it with particular meaning. For example, pilgrimages to Mashhad or Syria are a more common kind of religious activity among members of the middle class and entrepreneurial families, and working women, than the expensive journeys to Mecca. Such religious events (whether initiated by oneself or another), have multiple meanings for the participants, who not only share events of happiness and sadness, but also have a chance to initiate their own vows and fulfil their own duties.

OBLIGATIONS OF SOCIETY

Freedom and equality are concepts which have been very much misused by the modern world. There is no doubt that human progress depends to a large extent on freedom and equality, and a society which creates artificial inequalities and places unnatural obstacles in the way of human freedom slowly degenerates and dies out. But it is equally true that real freedom does not lie in unrestricted license and presupposes as its inevitable corollary certain wholesome natural restrictions. Similarly, equality cannot mean a total obliteration of diversity arising from the natural and inborn differences between man and woman. Real equality can be based only on an inequality of function where each individual and each sex is entrusted with the tasks to which its natural endowments and inherent qualities qualify it most. The Western civilisation has placed undue and exaggerated emphasis on self-assertion and self-expression for the historical reason that its fundamental concepts arose out of a struggle against artificial repressions. The result is that the assertive and expressive tendencies of human beings have brought about internal conflicts which threaten to its foundation the very structure of civilisation. A balance between self-expression and self-repression, freedom and order, uniformity and diversity should be achieved to put human society on a stable basis. If this is true in the large spheres of human relations, it is equally true in the sex relations of men and women. An expert on sex psychology like Havelock Ellis says: 'We have always to remember that the whole art of living lies in a fine balance of expression and repression. For repression - understood in a wide sense and not merely in the special sense sometimes given to it by psychoanalysts - is as central a fact of life as expression. We are constantly at the same time repressing some impulses and expressing other impulses. There is no necessary penalty in the repression, for it is essential to expression.

Islam has placed certain restrictions on men as well as on women in order to regulate their sex and family life both of which it regards as the foundations of a stable and progressive civilisation. The restrictions on men and women differ in accordance with their varying functions in society. To the extent that these functions differ in the case of the two sexes, their rights and responsibilities also differ and the restrictions they are required to observe also differ. The advocates *of a bald and dead equality* who do not believe in the functional differentiation of the sexes will cite them as a proof of unequal treatment. Actually, these restrictions arise out of the different social responsibilities of either sex. If it is true that motherhood is one of the essential responsibilities of women, that sexual aberration in women leads to more complications and more serious consequences than the misconduct of men; if, again, it is true that men and women differ in the types (not degrees) of their natural gifts and that the physical powers of women are attuned to particular types of work only, then it is easy to see that, within the general framework of fundamental sex equality, their rights, duties and the channels of their self-expression and self-repression should also differ.

Saner intellectuals even among the Westerners have always recognised the functional differentiation between the two sexes. They also admit that women are better fitted for particular types of work than men, and ill-suited for other tasks. For example, the American authoress of *Male and Female*, Margaret Mead, discussing this point in connection with her researches into the life of savage tribes, writes: 'Thus if the theorist about men and women's natural work-rhythms had based his theories on *Jatmul*, he would easily have come up with a picture of man as the lineal descendant of a nomadic hunter, capable of strong output of effort, but demanding long periods of recuperation, and a picture of women as better fitted by nature for the routine tasks of everyday life, unresisting and unrebelling against a world in which their work was never done and their hands were hardly ever at rest.' Proceeding further, the same authoress says: 'If research finally demonstrates any genuine difference in the capacity to tolerate monotony, or to benefit by working in irregular spurts of energy, we still have to consider whether the most felicitous results are obtained by constructing a society in which women's work, while more monotonous and demanding, is also keyed up to the cycle of menstruation and pregnancy, and men's work, less monotonous and demanding, is the work that can be depended upon in any emergency, since men are subject to no such periodic rise and fall in capacity as women. Possibly we may find instead that if all work is keyed low enough so that women do not suffer too inappropriate demands during their periodic fluctuations in capacity, but men are not prevented from constructing crises if they find them congenial, the gain in adaptation of rhythm between the sexes may be greater than any loss that comes from not pitching the work-rhythms of each sex as perfectly as possible to their distinctive periodicities.'

Now this periodic rise and fall in the capacity of work, among women is an undeniable physical fact that alters their function in society and excludes them from certain kinds of work. A civilisation which keeps this fact in view in the allocation of rights and duties will naturally suggest different social restrictions for women with a view to preventing them from transgressing their natural sphere of duties.

A more important physical factor which has a decisive bearing on the functions of women and marks out a different path of life for them is the physical periodicity of women arising from menstruation. Menstruation is by no means an ordinary phenomenon of local manifestation. It is but the most obvious symptom of the general monthly waves which periodically flow through a woman's body, affecting to a greater or lesser extent all her organs. The observations of a great many medical authorities have shown that during the process of menstruation most significant physical and mental changes are observed in women. The whole nervous system of women is affected during this period and it is the nervous system upon which depends the normal functioning of the general physiological well-being of women. Vemilow in his

Biological Tragedy of Woman says that women's mental equilibrium is upset during the period of menstruation. He records his observation that a woman street-car conductor pulls out the wrong tickets and is muddled in counting the change. A menstruating moto-woman drives the street-car slowly and with hesitancy, becoming confused at crossings. The lady typist's fingers strike the wrong keys. The woman dentist cannot find the proper instrument. An actress is not in the right mood and makes wrong gestures. Writing in *Man and Woman,* Havelock Ellis observes that there is at this period greater impressionability, greater suggestions and more or less diminished self-control. It is at this time that sudden caprices, fits of ill-temper, moods of depression, impulses of jealousy, outbursts of self-confession are chiefly liable to occur. At times menstruation produces abnormal and diseased conditions. There may be so high a degree of physical pain and disability that the woman is really an invalid for several days every month. On the basis of these facts Havelock Ellis had to utter a note of warning that 'it is no longer possible to regard the physiological periodicity of women and the recurring menstrual function as the purely private concern of the woman whom it affects'. Such a view necessarily leads to the conclusion that the public activities work and employment of women must be conditioned and limited by their physiological peculiarities. It cannot be that men and women are treated as equals in the field of industrial employment or in the matter of political activity. If an attempt is made to create an artificial equality which in fact does not exist, it is likely to break down with serious consequences.

Motherhood is another important factor in the life of women which conditions, limits and particularises their sphere of activity. In the modern world, a large number of well-to-do women, under the influence of a wrong conception of equality, have increasingly turned away from this noble life-vocation. Various theories and suggestions have been propounded to prove that motherhood is not essential to the life and happiness of women and that alternative institutions can be evolved which will free the mothers from the burden of rearing and training their children, thus allowing them greater liberty of movement and enabling them to share with men the larger activities of social and political life. While no sane person will maintain that women should be kept confined to domestic life or should in no case participate in the wider spheres of collective activity, many will agree that the duties of motherhood form the primary concern of a woman's life, and a society which allows its female members to plunge into the wider spheres of life at the cost of their primary avocation is bound to suffer from maladjustment. It is only women who are already past the age of motherhood and can easily spare time and energy for other duties that should be really welcome in the political and industrial fields. But by far the largest number of women cannot escape, *if they ace to fulfil their function in society—the burden of their primary biological and social responsibility.* Of course, the more fortunate among them, by reason of their economic condition or limited family, can do, if they are so minded, part-time work in other fields but not in a way which might disturb their main functions. The saner elements among Western writers and thinkers have not overlooked this aspect of the matter and we shall give a few brief quotations from them.

Writing about the depth of maternal instinct in women, Havelock Ellis says: 'Most people, certainly most women, feel at moments, or at some period in their lives, a desire for children,' and in women the longing for a child may become so urgent and imperative that we may regard it as scarcely less imperative than the sexual impulse. Van de Veide writes: 'To be a woman means to have the desire to become a mother both physically and mentally.' He admits that 'there are women, and presumably always have been women, although their number may be relatively very small, who feel such a strong antagonism to motherhood that they refuse to marry for that reason,' but he adds: 'The absence of the maternal instinct in the modern woman is really nothing but a pose. The maternal instinct exists in spite of this, although there may be only one child .... Where it really is repressed, because some women think it fashionable, or because of decadence or love of pleasure, it will also be, seen that such repression has its revenge sooner or later. A more than temporary repression of the mother instinct is, practically speaking, impossible.'

A prominent American authoress Margaret Mead writes in, *Male and Female*: 'Women may be said to be mothers unless they are taught to deny their child-bearing qualities. Society must distort their sense of themselves, pervert their inherent growth patterns, perpetrate a series of .. outrages upon them, before they will cease to want to provide, at least for a few years, for the child they have already nourished for nine months within the safe circle of their own bodies! The same writer quotes the experience of a psychiatrist working in the United States who said: 'I have never seen a woman who was socially and physically able to have children and who refused to have children, who did not suffer psychologically from that refusal.'

Writing about the nursery and other institutions for the education of children in order to relieve mothers of their educational responsibilities, Havelock Ellis says in his book, *On Life and Sex:* 'The idea has been put forward (first of all by Plato in the famous fifth book of his Republic) that the infant should be removed from its natural parents and placed in the hands of nurses skilfully trained in all the science and art of modern hygiene in general and puericulture in particular. Certainly, it is possible to find innumerable parents who are completely and lamentably ignorant of this science and this art. This may be specially so in those lands of communistic tendency, like Soviet Russia, where the Platonic ideal is most commended. But to be content to leave the mothers in ignorance and to train up in the knowledge of the duties of maternity a body of women who are rot intended to be mothers, except for other women's children, seems a perverted attempt to escape the difficulty. It is not calculated to benefit, and still less to render happy, the real mothers, the artificial mothers or the children. An institution on so unreal a foundation cannot possibly compete with one on a sound biological basis which is just as susceptible to any necessary cultivation and development as the other.... The legitimate method of approaching the problem-as is constantly becoming more widely recognised-lies in training the real mothers and, so far as possible, before they have begun to be mothers.... The establishment of Schools for Mothers, in some countries facilitated by law, constitutes a noble step along this path.'

In regard to the advisability and fitness of woman for work in the wider sphere of social activity, Havelock Ellis expresses an opinion which agrees with our own view which we have given above, namely, that women who have had the experience of motherhood and whose maternal duties are over have more justification as well as ability to take part in such activity than those whom motherhood calls for dedication to domestic duties. Writing in his book, *On Life and Sex,* Ellis says: 'There is nothing that is so much needed as the "maternal in politics," or in all sorts of non-political channels of social service and none can be better fitted for such service than those who have had an actual experience of motherhood and acquired the knowledge that such experience should give. There are numberless other ways besides social service in which mothers who have passed the age of forty, provided they posses the necessary aptitudes, can more profitably apply themselves than in hampering or pampering their adult children. It is by wisely cultivating their activities in a larger sphere that women whose chief duties in the narrower domestic sphere are over may better ensure their own happiness and the welfare of others than either by fretting and obstructing or by worrying over their own children who are no longer children. It is quite true that children may go astray even when they have ceased to be children. But the time to implant seeds of virtue, the time to convey a knowledge of life, was when they were small. If it was well done, it only remains to exercise faith and trust. If it was done ill, nothing done later will compensate, for it is merely foolish for a mother who could not educate her children when they were small to imagine that she is able to educate them when they are big.

Writing about the desirability of close mother-child relations during the period of infancy which is completely non-existent in collective social institutions where women, other than mothers, take care of children, Dr. Westermarck writes: 'According to Havelock Ellis, the mortality of artificially fed infants during the first year of life is seldom less than double, and sometimes as much as three times that of the breast-fed, or even more. He also points out that the advantages for an infant being suckled by its mother are greater than can be accounted for by the mere fact of being suckled rather than hand-fed, bemuse the infant's best food is that elaborated in his mother's body. This has been shown by Vitray, who found from the statistics of Astel-Dien at Lyons that infants suckled by their mothers have a mortality of only twelve per cent, while in the case of infants suckled by strangers the mortality rises to thirty-three per cent.'

It may be said that the progress of science may so lighten the manual burden of women that even after discharging their full responsibilities at home, mothers may be enabled to spend a larger and larger portion of their time outside their homes in social, political and industrial activity. While nobody would grudge such a situation, provided: it means equal facilities for all mothers and not merely for a few born with silver spoons in their mouths, it is after all not so certain that the increasing use of mechanical devices would bring about the desired change. The following quotation from Margaret Mead is worth-reading in this connection: 'There was a time also when in the first fine flush of laundries and bakeries, milk deliveries and canned foods, it did look as if American life was being enormously simplified. A vacuum cleaner was a great addition to a home that kept the standard of a carpet-sweeper and a broom, laundries were a godsend to a household whose routine of sheet-changing was geared to the old-fashioned wash-tub, and bakeries to homes in which the making of bread had dominated one whole day. But just as our new medical palliatives are creating new vulnerabilities and new disease states, so the new equipment has not led to more leisure, more time to play with the baby, more time to curl up and read by an open fire or to help the P.T.A., but has merely combined with other trends in making the life of the American home-maker not easier, but more exacting. Most urban living women do not realise that, as the Bryn Mawr report shows, house-keeping activities consumed 60-65 hours a week in a typical farm family, 78.35 in urban household in, cities of over 100,000. This was in pre-war days, and in a world that has been moving steadily towards a forty-hour week on the job.'

Now, if these facts are true, they show that even the mechanical improvements of an industrial civilisation cannot release mothers for whole time work outside their homes, and a pattern of social life which seeks to make men, and women equal in this respect is bound to produce unpleasant consequences. There remains one final argument to justify the full participation of women, in fields other than the sphere of domestic life. It is said that special gifted women should be given full opportunity to utilise their gifts for social and political service and to that extent they should be absolved of the responsibilities of motherhood and domestic life. This is true. But it should not be overlooked that special gifts can be multiplied and passed on to future generations on a wider scale, if the specially gifted woman undertakes the responsibilities of motherhood. So the argument in favour of exempting such women from the burden of motherhood falls down, because the social service which such women can render may be more effectively rendered if they can become proper mothers. A woman who has borne two gifted children and brought them up under her gifted training really does greater service to society than if she exercise her sifts in other ways. Of course, if she can combine motherhood with social or political service, nothing should be allowed to stand in her way, because then her utility will increase tenfold. But motherhood is the essential vocation of a woman's life which should not be sacrificed for any other consideration.

It is in view of all the facts and considerations we have stated above that Islam has laid down certain social restrictions both on men and women. Some of them are common to either sex, while some are different and arise from a particular conception of womanly duties. On the whole, the Islamic pattern of life is one in which woman has her main functions confined to home life. This does not mean that she is completely debarred from going out or taking part in wider activities, as the old-fashioned Muslims maintain. But there is no doubt that Islam disapproves of a social pattern in which women neglect their primary and essential functions or plunge into wider spheres of activity at the cost of their primary duties. Women who have the time and the ability to do useful service in the social or political field are not prevented by Islam to enter these fields, provided it does not prejudice or impede their functions at home. Let us now examine in more detail what these restrict ions are which Islam places on the liberty of men and women in, the interest of sexual purity and the stability of family life.

Among the common restrictions on men and women, the first relates to the duty of behaving with modesty in public. About this the Quran says: 'Say' to the believing men that they cast down their looks and guard their private parts; that is purer for them. Surely Allah is aware of what they do. And say to the believing women that they cast down their looks and guard their private parts and do not display their ornaments except ... to their husbands, or their fathers, or the fathers of their husbands, or their sons, or sons of their husbands, or their brothers or the sons of their brothers, or their sisters' sons, or their women or those whom their right hands possess, or male servants not having need (of women) or the children who have not what is hidden of women, and let them not strike their feet, so that what they hide of their ornaments may be known' (xxiv. 30-31).

In these verses, apart from the common duty of casting down ones looks in public, where men and women may both be present, the Holy Quran has laid down two special restrictions on women, namely, that they shall not make a display of their elegance and ornamentation or behave in such a way as to draw the attention of men towards their ornaments and beauty. The Prophet said that the first look which is generally involuntary is pardonable, but not the second look, which is cast for further sexual satisfaction.

This is meant both for men and women. Similarly, a tradition quoted by Abu Daud says: 'O 'Ali! do not have a second look after the first one, because the latter is not punishable, but the former is.'

Another restriction which is common to both sexes is the compulsory duty of keeping certain parts of the body covered. These parts which should be kept covered in any case and not exposed to any person, except to the wife or the husband, or when medical or other pressing necessities require exposure, are called

Satr. For men, the portion of the body beginning from the knees and extending to the navel has been fixed as *Sam*. A tradition of Daraqdtni reported by Abu Ayub Ansari says: 'What is above the knees and what is below the navel should be kept covered.' Another tradition reported by Ali states: 'Do not expose your thighs to anyone and do not look at the thighs of a living or dead person.' For women the entire body, excepting hands, feet and face, is included in the Satr. A tradition of Abu Daud says: 'When a woman reaches the age of puberty, no parts of her body should be kept exposed except the face and the hands extending to the joints of the wrist.' Just as men have been forbidden to wear pure silk to prevent luxurious living, women have been forbidden to use thin clothing which, instead of covering and hiding the features of their body, makes them all the more prominent. Asma bint Abu Bakr, the sister of the Prophet's wife, Aishah, once came to the Prophet wearing a thin dress which did not properly cover her body. The prophet at once turned away his look and said: Asma! when a woman has reached the age of puberty, it is not proper that any part of her body should be seen except her face, hand and feet.' Another tradition states: 'God has cursed those women who remain naked era after putting on their dress.' Similarly, the corpus of traditions collected by Muslim contains one which states: 'Women who remain naked even after putting on dress and draw others into temptation or walk and move in an alluring manner shall not enter paradise, nor get even its scent.'

There are some special restrictions on men circumscribing their freedom of action with a view to guarding their chastity and sexual purity. The entry of men in the houses of other persons is forbidden except with the permission of the inmates. The Quran says: 'O men who believe! do not enter the houses of other people until you have asked their permission and when you do enter, salute them' (xxiv. 27). Further, with a view to guarding against the possibility of men finding the female members of their own house without proper covering, it is laid down that no male member should enter his house at night, in the early morning and during midday time of siesta and rest without previous notice. The Quran says: 'And when the children among you have attained to puberty, let them seek, permission as those before them sought permission' (xxiv.59). Strangers of the male sex are required to be circumspect, if they have to ask for something from the female inmates of a house. The Quran says on this point: 'And when you ask of them any article, ask of them from behind a curtain; this is purer for your hearts and for their hearts' (xxxiii. 53). Another restriction is that no man or woman is permitted to remain alone with a member of the opposite sex except his or her partner, but women who have passed the age of child-bearing or those with whom, owing to intimate blood-relationship, marriage cannot be contracted are excepted: for example, brothers, sisters, parents, nephews, nieces, etc. A tradition reported by Aqabah b. Amir states. Do not go near women when they are alone. One of the Ansar asked: What about, the husband's elder and younger brothers? The Prophet said: 'Intimacy with them is to be avoided as death.' Another tradition says: 'Do not go near any woman in the absence of her husband because Satan is circulating as blood in your veins.' Amr b. Aas reports a saying from the Prophet: 'The Prophet of God forbade us to go near women except with the permission of the husband' (Tirmidhi). Tirmidhi gives a further tradition saying: 'No man should from this day go near a woman unless there are one or two persons with, him.' Touching of women is also forbidden, except in cases of grave emergency endangering life or health. A tradition says: 'if a person touches a woman with whom he has no legitimate relations, his hands will be burnt on the Day of Judgement.' Whenever a woman or a party of women came to the Prophet for taking the pledge of Islam, he refused to stretch his hands. Once Umaymah bint Ruqayqah came with a few women to take the pledge and asked the Prophet to give his hand. The Prophet refused saying: 'I do not shake hands with women; verbal declaration, is enough for them.'

All these restrictions on men are intended to guard sexual purity. If chastity is of any real and lasting social value, there is no doubt that such restrictions are justified, as they prevent men and women of various disposition from failing into temptation. For those who have already been corrupted and become used to sexual indecency, these and other restrictions are of no avail. We now come to special restrictions on women. Two of them we have already mentioned, namely, that women should not display their beauty and finery to anyone else except their husbands and a few intimate relations with whom they cannot enter into marriage: for example, brothers, fathers, nephews, etc., and that shall not strike their feet in such a way as to draw the attention of men. Other restrictions are specified by the Quran in the following verses:

> *O wives of the Prophet! you are not like any other women if you fear God, be not soft in speech lest in whose heart is a disease yearns, and speak good word. And stay in your houses and do not display your finery like the ostentation of the days of Ignorance.* *(xxviii. 22)*

O Prophet! say to your wives and your daughters and the women of the believers that they let down on their bosoms their overgarments. *(xxx. 59)*

Say to the believing men that they cast down their looks and guard their private parts; that is purer for them. Surely, Allah is aware of what they do. And say to the believing women that they cast down their looks and guard their private parts and do not display their ornaments except what appears thereof, and let them wear their head-covering over their bosoms and not display their ornaments except to their - husbands, or their... *(xxiv. 30.31)*

In the first verse women are forbidden to indulge in alluringly soft speech which may raise amorous hopes in the person spoken to. This is a necessary and natural safeguard, as speech is one of the primary sources of sexual excitation. In the opinion of Van de Velde, speech has an overpowering, effect on sexual passions. Writing in the second chapter of his *Ideal Marriage*, he observes: 'The tone-colour of a voice, and the intonation of a single word and it may be a word with no special meaning or associations in itself-may excite incredible intensity of desire. The unique and precious significance that a woman's voice can give to "you" or "thou" can suffice to overwhelm a man's powers of endurance and control, or to bring about the climax of erotic expression in the organism.' Women have, therefore, been ordered by Islam not to speak in a soft or sexually sweet tone.

The second verse prescribes a certain mode of dress for women which is designed to guard themselves and the member of the opposite sex from falling into sexual temptation. This injunction has been further clarified in the following verse which says that women should keep all, portions of their body fully covered except such as must necessarily become exposed. Explaining this injunction Maulana Muhammad Ali writes a note (1751) on pages 701-02 of his translation of the Holy Quran (1935 edn.): 'To guard the relations between males and females and to check a too free intermingling of men and women, the Quran now lays down another injunction in addition to that which requires both sexes to go abroad with their looks cast down. One part of the injunction is common to both sexes: both must keep their looks cast down and both must guard their private parts. Both men and women must observe some further directions. The injunction which relates to women in particular is to keep their ornaments concealed. There is a difference of opinion as to what *zinat* or ornament means. According to some it includes the beauty of the body, while according to others it is exclusively applied to external adornments (Razi). The use of the same word in the concluding portion of the verse, let them not strike their feet so that what they hide of their ornaments may be known, clearly supports the latter view. But even according to those who include the beauty of the body in the significance of zinat, it is permissible for a woman, to have her hands and face uncovered (Razi), as being allowed under the exception, what appears thereof, as without uncovering these it would be impossible for women to take part in any business; the rest of the body and the ornaments upon it, whether in the form of tight clothes or of gold and silver ornaments, are to be kept concealed by a long head-covering or, say, an overcoat., According to Kashaf. . . except what appears thereof means. . except that which it is customary and natural to uncover. The customs of different societies, would therefore allow a variation, and one rule cannot be laid down for all. According to Qaffal the meaning of the word is... except that which a person discloses usually, and in the case of women this means the face and the two hands (Razi). Thus, a woman when going out should have herself covered over by an external wrapper or an overcoat, it being permissible to leave the hands and the face uncovered. The exposure of such parts as the neck, the bosom or the arms is forbidden, as also the display of decorations.

The modern 'civilised' society has taken precisely to those forms of dress which expose and do not conceal a woman's beauty. The Quran which regards chastity as one of the basic moral and social values has directed its injunctions against these ultra modern forms of dress which are meant more to reveal than to conceal. The justification for these restrictions lies in the hidden springs of sex psychology. Let us quote Van de Velde again on this point. He says in *Ideal Marriage*:

> *The male costume of modern times is not as a rule specially sexually accentuated.*

The exact contrary is the case with female dress, which of late has followed primitive and tropical patterns, and aims not at concealing but at enhancing physical charms. From the earliest times, and even when it had to serve as covering from intense cold, it has tended to accentuate and follow the lines of secondary sexual characteristics. Examples are numerous: for instance, the low-cut bodice -'decollete' of the seventeenth and eighteenth centuries: take corset, which in its original form literally lifted and pressed forward the bosom, in a dangerously painful fashion; and the wasp-waist, which was constructed in order to emphasize the curves of the bust and the hips. Or, again, the 'Tournure' or 'bustle' of the eighties, which was at first only meant to discreetly indicate the roundness of the feminine posterior-in itself an important sexual attraction, but which became so exaggerated and unwieldy that it ended by giving the ladies of the most fashionable society a deplorable resemblance to Hottentots.

Fashions such as those of the Directoire and contemporary periods, which, instead of uncovering the largest possible amount of epidermis, drape the covered portion in light and clinging fabrics, which suggest rather than conceal outlines and give additional suppleness to movements, have a particularly alluring effect — much more so than that of nudity. Women have always recognized and utilized this form of charm in their veils shawls and shawl-dances, etc.

In view of these facts, it is impossible not to agree that the Quranic restrictions on female dress are not only rational but necessary.

One of the Quranic verses quoted above states that women should stay at home and not wander about displaying their beauty and finery. This verse does not mean that they should never go out and remain in perpetual confinement, since otherwise the Quranic injunctions about dress and movement of women would become meaningless. The injunction emphasises the fact that their home should form the centre of their interest and activity and there should be no unnecessary intermingling of the sexes in daily life. This interpretation is supported by a famous tradition of the Prophet in connection with Umar's objection against the appearance of the Prophet's wives outside their homes. Once Sauda, a wife of the Prophet, came out on some private business. Umar recognised her and complained to the Prophet that she was not observing the Quranic restrictions, whereupon the Prophet replied: 'They are permitted to go out for satisfying their real wants.'

Apart from restrictions on dress and speech, as indicated above, women are also forbidden to use scents or perfumes when going out. A tradition from Tirmidhi's collection states: 'The Prophet of God said that a woman who uses scent or perfume when passing through streets is a profligate woman.' A tradition of Muwatta by Imam Malik says: 'When a woman goes to mosque for offering prayers, she should not use perfume or scent.' Here again Islam has shown great insight into sex psychology. Perfumes and odours play a great role in exciting sexual emotion. The subject has been discussed in detail by Van de Velde in his *Ideal Marriage* in which he explains how women have always known the sexual effects of odours and perfumes and utilised them for different purposes. Van de Velde goes so far as to remark: 'I am of opinion that experts who use perfumes as aphrodisiacs for their own emotions - perhaps without being fully conscious of this aim-are generally women.'

Within the home also men and women are required to observe certain rules of decency. Although the sex relations of husband and wife are not subject to any kind of restrictions, the Prophet has given directions that even in their utmost privacy, husband and wife should conduct themselves with decorum and refrain from acts of mere animality. Thus, according to a tradition of Ibn Majah, the Prophet is reported to have said: 'Whenever one of you goes to his wife, he should not uncover himself completely like asses.' A wife of the Prophet, according to Tirmidhi, reports that she never saw the Prophet completely naked. The same ideal of decency and chastity finds expression in the restrictions placed on men and women in their family life. These are explained in the following Quranic verses:

> *O you who believe! let those whom your right hands possess and those of you who have not attained to puberty ask permission of you three times: before the morning prayer, and when you put off your clothes at midday in the summer, and after the prayer of the nightfall; these are three times of privacy for you; neither is it a sin for you nor for them besides these times, because some of you must go around waiting upon others; thus does Allah make clear to you the communications, and Allah is Knowing, Wise.*

And when the children among you have attained to puberty, let them seek permission as those before them sought permission; thus does Allah make clear to you His communications, and Allah is Knowing, Wise.

> *And as for women advanced in years who do not hope for marriage, it is no sin for them if they put off their clothes without displaying their ornaments; and if they restrain themselves, it is better for them (xxiv. 58-60).*

Here the Quran has laid down three rules for the observance of the male and female members of the house. Women who have attained puberty are usually found half-dressed or lightly dressed at night, during midday in the summer or in the early morning. The male members of the family, with the exceptions already stated, as well as male servants should not enter their rooms or come inside the house without previous notice. Barring these stated periods, they are free to move about as they like. It automatically ,follows from this that the Quran desires that women should keep themselves fully dressed during business hours, so that no opportunity of temptation occurs for males or females. But women who have passed the age of childbirth are exempt from this restriction. Children when they reach the age of puberty are also required to observe these directions.

It is clear from all that has been said above with regard to the Islamic restrictions on the dress, movement and social intercourse of males and females that Islam insists on the segregation of sexes to the utmost extent compatible with individual and collective self-preservation. Its pattern of society is one in which men and women do not intermingle too freely. For each sex a certain sphere of life has been allotted within which it should concentrate its energies, leaving other fields for the opposite sex. If intermixture becomes necessary at any time, even then it is necessary to avoid too much freedom and laxity and observe the minimum requirements of decorum and sexual purity.

Now, the question is whether this Islamic pattern of sex life is compatible with industrial efficiency and military preparedness, two factors on which in the modern world depends the collective self-preservation of a community. We shall discuss each of these factors separately.

In regard to industrial efficiency, it should be borne in mind that all efficiency, interest and dynamic energy in men and women depend, to a very great extent on a healthy and happy private and family life. We have already discussed the question whether it is possible to dispense with the institution of the family and shown that, on the testimony of Western thinkers and sex psychologists themselves, it is very difficult to envisage a time when the family will disappear as an organised unit of collective life. If the family is a permanent feature of human civilised life and cannot be satisfactorily replaced by alternative institutions, it is self-evident that its stability and betterment should have the first claim on a nation's attention. If the family becomes disorganised and is not able to throw out healthy and happy individuals, not only will industrial efficiency disappear, all other spheres of human activity will suffer a setback on account of ill-equipped, unhealthy, irresponsible and unhappy individuals who come to these fields. A pattern of collective life which weakens and disorganises the family, in the interest of increased material and industrial productivity, is certain to suffer on the whole and, keeping all other factors in mind, more than others from social and economic maladjustments, because it undermines the very foundation on which the individual's health and efficiency depend. Unhappy, ill-adjusted and uprooted individuals lacking the drive, initiative and moral idealism, which only a healthy and happy family life can create, will hardly be productive in the full sense of the word, materially or spiritually, in any field of life they enter. Before we form any opinion as to the desirability of bringing women in the industrial field as whole time workers, let us consult the experience of industrialised countries. It would seem that the entry of the female sex in the industrial field has had positively harmful results on the 'family organisation of Western countries. Dr. Sallivan observes in his book *Akoholism*:

> *The employment of women in the ordinary industrial occupations not only involves a disorganization of their domestic duties, if they are married,, but it also interferes with the acquisition of housewifely knowledge during girlhood. The result is that appalling ignorance of everything connected with cookery, with cleanliness, with the management of the children, which makes the average wife and mother in the lower working classes in this country one of the most helpless and thriftless of beings, and which, therefore, impels the workman whose comfort depends on her, not only to spend his free time in the public house, but also tends to make him take to alcohol as a necessary condiment with his tasteless and indigestible diet.*

Both directly and indirectly, therefore, the employments that withdraw women from domestic pursuits are likely to increase alcoholism, and, it may be added, to increase its greatest potency for evil ... namely, its influence on the health of the stock.

Again, Arnold Toynbee, the renowned British historian, says in an article published in March 1949 issue of World Review:

> *Certainly our recent efforts to solve our 'problems in strictly materialist terms have failed and made caricatures of all our brave plans. 'We have made enormous strides,' we say, 'in the development of labour-saving machinery,' and so we have. But one of the odd results of this progress is that women today are overworked as never before. Wives in America can no longer get household help or afford to devote themselves exclusively to the home. As a result the woman of today does two jobs: one as wife and mother in the home, one as employee in the office or factory.*

During the war in England, this double working of women was almost universal. And such a trend is not a hopeful one. In history the ages of disintegration were unusually the ages in which women had left the home. In fifth-century Greece, the high point of classical history, women stayed in the home. But after Alexander's time when the city states were breaking up, there was a feminist movement like our own.

Commenting on the female craze to copy and imitate men and prove themselves equal to their power and capacity, Oswald Schwarz remarks in his *Psychology of Sex*:

> *If women try to compete with men they try the impossible, impossible because it is against their intrinsic nature and against the trend of history. The best they can achieve is equality in action in such superficial strata as, for instance, the economic sphere.*

Sensible Western thinkers have never approved of the existing sex and social patterns in Western countries. Their ideas and opinions are much more akin to the pattern of life advocated by Islam. For an example, we quote Anthony M. Ludovici who writes in his famous book, Women, A Vindication:

> *It seems eminently desirable to emphasize more than we have emphasized in the past the ideal of matrimony for every woman up to a certain age, and bring home to parents that marriage is what they must train them for. . . Anything else that she may do must always be second best to this; and those who, by misrepresentation and appeals to vanity, persuade her while she is quite young that there are callings better than, or at least as good as, motherhood for, her, are enemies not only of women but also of the species.*

The same book also contains the following passage:

> *Immersed as woman obviously is up to her, shoulders in the business of life and its multiplication, let it be said openly and unequivocally that all those who teach her that any other business is her business, although who, in the face of the dilemma of modern problems, confuse her with tales about a true womanhood away from life and its multiplication; all those, in short, who beguile her with promises of happiness, contentedness or even comfort, without her primary adaptation to man and the child, are liars both unscrupulous and criminal.*

It is clear from the above quotations that the promiscuous herding together of men and women in factories, besides disorganising family life, has been productive of other evils such as alcoholism, sexual laxity, etc., which, in their combination, have more than nullified the benefits arising from increased industrial productivity. All this should not be taken, however, to mean that Islam desires women, to be wholly confined to domestic life. There is no such restriction in Islam on the activities of women. They are free, to do any work that benefits themselves or their society either materially or spiritually, provided, first, they do not neglect their primary duties as wives and mothers, and, secondly, observe the rules of decency explained above. In general, this means that part-time activities, other than domestic ones, are most suitable for women, if they can spare time and if such activities do not lead to too much intermingling with men., Cooperative family concerns in which a number of women belonging to different families or to one large family take part, are ideally suited for mothers and wives. If it becomes necessary to engage male workers in such undertakings for supervision, teaching or training, men of advanced age can be selected for the purpose. Part-time work in factories can also be performed by women if there is a separate section exclusively meant for them. Women whose maternal or domestic functions are over and who can do whole time work in other fields are not debarred from outside, activities. Such is, the pattern of Islamic social life and it is one which, without breaking up or disorganising family and home life, gives full scope to the abilities and energies of the female sex.

Let us deal now with the question of military preparedness and Islam's attitude in respect of the participation of women in military service. Individual and national self-preservation in time of crisis and emergency alters the normal course of life and individuals as well as communities are forced to deviate from their principles of life when the threat to their existence becomes too serious. In consequence, they have to do things which they would never like to do in the normal course of their existence. It is the sign of a virile individuality and virile civilisation that even if it has to deviate under the pressure of extreme emergency from the standards of conduct that it holds dear, it does so most unwillingly and only in the measures required by the necessities of the situation-neither more nor less; and when the threat to its existence has passed, it hastens to revert to its original pattern of conduct. Islam, being a practical religion and claiming to be the natural way of life, recognises that situations may arise where things otherwise unlawful may have to be legalised as a temporary measure, but it takes care to ensure that its followers do not develop a liking and relish for illegality under flimsy pretexts. Therefore, while it allows temporary relaxation of normally accepted standards, it enjoins on Muslims not to regard them as more than passing concessions and to make use of them except to the extent made absolutely necessary by the requirements of the situation. Examples of this attitude are found in the Islamic commands with regard to wine and exposure of the private parts of a Muslim male or female. Wine has been absolutely prohibited by Islam, but if a person on the point of death can be saved by being made to drink wine, its use is legally justified. Similarly, Islam has given strict injunctions to its followers not to expose their private parts under any circumstances. As explained above, the Prophet even enjoined on married couples not to become completely naked during sexual intercourse. But if a man or woman is threatened with extreme danger of ill-health or one's life is in peril and the threat to life or health cannot be averted except by exposing one's private parts before a doctor for medical treatment, such an act becomes fully legitimate. Islam has adopted that same attitude with regard to the intermingling of the sexes in times of extreme national emergency or during an actual war. During such times, it relaxes all the restrictions as and when required and to the extent made necessary by the situation. When the emergency has passed, the normal restrictions are again made operative. But even during a war or emergency, Islam requires the Muslim males and females to follow as far as possible the rules of decency and avoid unnecessary intermingling. According to the Islamic attitude of life, the Muslim individuals, male and female, and the Muslim brotherhood exist not for mere self-preservation and self-enjoyment. The primary object of human existence in general and of the Muslim community in particular is to live and act for the preservation and growth of moral values and to uphold the spiritual ideals of social fairplay, justice, decency, cleanliness in thought and action.

> *You are the best of the nations raised up for (the benefit of) men. You enjoin what is right and forbid the wrong and believe in Allah* *(iii. 109).*

> *Those who, should We establish them in the land, will keep up prayer and pay the, poor-rate and enjoin good and forbid evil.* *(xxii. 41)*

> *And thus We have made you a nation of the middle path that you may be bearers of witness to mankind and (that) the Apostle may be a bearer of witness to you.* *(ii. 142)*

Sexual purity and chastity are among the fundamental social values upheld by Islam. In themselves they may appear to be of secondary importance, but they affect one's social conduct, one's ideas of justice, honesty and fairplay and in fact one's whole gamut of action in a thousand and one ways. They are, therefore, regarded by Islam as occupying a position of primary importance in its total scheme of values. How is it possible then for a community which claims to be the guardian of morality and spirituality to sacrifice them for the sake of safeguarding and ensuring a bare carnal existence. Suppose the Muslims ensure their self-preservation at the cost of these or other moral values, would it be a soul-satisfying existence? As Jesus Christ, one of the greatest Prophets of God, remarked: 'What does it avail if a man gains the whole world but loses his own soul?'

In view of these facts, Islam has enjoined, while permitting temporary relaxations, that great care should be taken during an emergency to see that these relaxations are neither misused nor used in a way which is unnecessary for individual and national self-preservation. As far as possible, intermingling of the sexes should be avoided even in times of war and resorted to only to the minimum extent compatible with the needs of collective self-preservation. Keeping in view these safeguards and precautions, let us explain the freedoms granted to women during a national emergency.

During the early period of Islam when the Muslims were engaged in a life-and-death struggle with the forces of disbelief, women used freely to take part, in helping the warriors of Islam. Short of actual fighting which was unnecessary for Muslim women, because the women on the other side too did not join battle, they did everything such as nursing, carrying food and water and looking after other needs of the army. Bukhari quotes a tradition stating that when the Prophet received wounds during the battle of Uhud, his daughter, Fatima, dressed up his wounds and carried water to him. It is clear that, under these conditions, she could not have observed any normal restrictions on the dress and movement of the female sex. Similarly in the chapter on Jihad and Siyar, Bukhari states on the authority of Anas b. Malik, that during the battle of Uhud when the nonbelievers inflicted a crushing defeat on Muslims, Aishah, the wife of the Prophet, and Umm Salim, an other Muslim lady, raised up their gowns to the knees and carried water to the wounded. This shows that the normal restrictions on the dress of the females can be abandoned during a war to the extent made necessary by the exigencies of the situation. Again, a tradition found in the Muslim's collection states: Umm Atiyyah says: 'I took part in seven battles with the Prophet of God, and I used to cook food for the warriors, supply them with medicines and dress up their wounds. Anas also reports that the Prophet usually took with him in war Umm Salim and other women of the Ansar and these women administered medicines to the wounded and kept them supplied with drinking water. That the Prophet saw nothing objectionable and even approved of women fighting for Islam is evident from another tradition also which says that the Prophet used to visit the wife of 'Ibadat b. Samit who was related to him. One day the Prophet slept in her house and on waking up began to laugh. The wife of 'Ibadat asked him as to why he laughed. The Prophet said that he saw in a dream a number of men and women travelling in a ship and heading for a battle with the non-believers. The wife of 'Ibadat requested him to pray that she be one of those warriors. Accordingly, the Prophet prayed for her. During the reign of Muawiyyah, the wife of 'Ibadat actually voyaged to the battlefield, but when she landed on the coast she fell down from her horse and died.

All these reports establish the fact that women are permitted to take part in war with men. There is nothing to prevent women from participating in actual fighting if this becomes necessary. During the Prophet's time the Muslim women did not do actual fighting because it was not necessary, if the other side also did not employ women to fight its battles. But the Muslims may be faced nowadays with enemies who recruit women in regular fighting service. Should this happen, Muslim women can also do actual fighting as Islam does not prohibit it.

Only one question remains to be discussed. Modern war requires intensive training both for actual military service and for auxiliary services. How can Muslim women be trained in the art of war and nursing, etc., if intermingling of the sexes is to be avoided? The obvious solution is to train initially a batch of women advanced in age for military and auxiliary services with the help of male experts. When a sufficient number of women have acquired skill in the different fields of military or medical services, they can train a large number of women without the help of men. Thus, intermingling of the sexes can either be avoided or reduced to the minimum extent possible.

SOCIAL REFORMS

There are certain principles which are to be followed by the individuals in the society. No society can allow the opposition or rejection of the principles, because the non-compliance amounts to rebellion against the society. If any society gives up these principles or fails to enforce them, it will disintegrate.

The Islamic society has its own principles which must be followed by the Muslims. The requirements of these principles are explained by the Holy Quran at various places. At one place it says:

"O mankind ! Be careful of your duty to your Lord who created you from a single soul and from it created its mate and from them twain hath spread abroad a multitude of men and women. Be careful of your duty toward Allah in Whom ye claim (your rights) of one another, and toward the wombs (that base you).

Lo ! Allah hath been a Watcher over you." (4 : 1)

"O Prophet, when believing women come to thee to take oath of fidelity, that they will not associate in worship any other thing whatever, with Allah, that they will not resort to stealing, that they will not commit fornication, that they will not kill their children, that they will not utter slanders intentionally forging falsehood, and that they will not disobey thee in any Just matter, then -do thou receive their fidelity, and pray to Allah for the forgiveness (of their sins) for Allah is Oft-forgiving, Most Merciful." (60 : 12)

The principles are meant for the women because, when the Islamic society was developing in Medina, the Islamic State had entered into a treaty with the people of Mecca, on account of certain diplomatic considerations, undertaking not to give shelter to any of the Quraish against their wish. The Muslims could afford asylum to only such women who wanted it. In this background, the Holy Quran has explained the conditions to be followed by a woman in order to become a part of the Islamic society. However, the Muslim men are no exception to these rules. Hadrat Ubada-bin-Samit (R.A.A.) says:

"The Holy Prophet (S.A.W.) had taken oath from us similar to those of women, that we must not believe in plurality of God, nor steal, nor commit adultery, nor commit infanticide, nor blame each other." (Muslim)

This statement of oath clearly explains the concept of Islamic society. It also explains the aims and objects of Islam in respect of the human society. There is no place for the people other than those who are good and virtuous. It is but natural that a good society cannot permit unhealthy environment within itself.

The Quran says:

"We also sent Lot. He said to His people; Do ye commit lewdness such as no people have so far committed before

you? For ye practise your lusts on men in preference to women : Ye are indeed a people transgressing beyond bounds. And his people gave no answer but this : They said, -Drive them out of your city : These are indeed men who want to be clean and pure." *(7 : 80-82)*

If a man thinks that evil practices are destructive to the mankind, he has to change the present criminal environment and make the society free from evil. One of the most important facts is that though there are rules in all societies for the prevention of evil, the failure of implementation is seen everywhere. It is not possible to have a good society unless the laws are strictly implemented and followed. The distinct characteristics of Islam is that it creates a refined society. It becomes incumbent upon every Muslim to follow the principles of Islam strictly in order to make his own life safe and respectable. It is not possible to lead a peaceful and respectable life without adhering to the principles prescribed by the Shariah.

Force of Ideology **:** For the enforcement of an ideology, a society must have three powers : The force of ideology, the force of collective thinking and feeling and the force of law. The force of Islamic ideology is the only capable force to wipe out the evil from the surface of the earth and establish a pious society all over the world. The other ideologies have failed because they are man-made and devoid of Natural laws. The world has tried all possible laws made by man and achieved nothing. On the contrary there prevails disturbance and uneasiness. Therefore, the world has no other alternative but to adopt Islamic laws for the peace and good of mankind.

The man-made laws demand the obedience to the man in authority. Therefore, the people easily ignore these laws and indulge in evil practices. Besides, these laws fail to punish and change the offenders. Whereas, the laws of Islam demand the obedience to Allah, the Creator of all. It is the fear of Allah that keeps man away from the evil practices. The man, who loves Allah, would never like to displease Almighty Allah. The Holy Quran says:

"Eschew all sins, open or secret : Those who earn sin will get due recompense for their Earnings." *(6 : 120)*

At other place, the Holy Quran says :

"Say : the things that my Lord hath indeed forbidden are shameful deeds, whether open or secret." *(7 : 33)*

Islam does not permit any kind of evil under any circumstances. Moreover, the Islamic law cannot be changed by man because he has no authority to do so. Islam disbands the jungle law and enforces the law of Islamic Shariah for the establishment of good and refined society. Islam makes the man and the woman morally high and cultured. It is a fact that woman can live honourably and peacefully only if the society is good, and good society is possible only- if its members are good. Sulaiman bin Baridah (R.A.A.) relates from his father that the Holy Prophet (S.A.W.) has said

> *"Those men who do not go to the battlefield for Jihad and remain at home, for them the wives of the Mujahidin are as respectable as their own mothers. If a man from amongst the people who have stayed at home happens to be the custodian of a Mujahid and if he misappropriates, he shall be brought before the Mujahidin on the Day of Judgement and he would take away as much good deeds from him as he would like. Just imagine, what would be the condition of that culprit." (Muslim, Abu Daud)*

Zaid-bin-Khalid (R.A.A.) relates that the Holy Prophet (S.A.W.) said:

> *"A man who provided arms to a Mujahid, he got the reward of Jihad. And the man who looked after the family of the Mujahid, too earned the reward of Jihad." (Bukhari, Muslim)*

Moral Values : Undoubtedly, the society which is based on such lofty ideals and piety, gives prime importance to moral values. Such a society is the noblest in the world. The men and the women of such a society bear high moral character, and such is the Muslim society. The moral values help men and women to ward off evil and lead virtuous life. In this Islamic society, the individuals respect each other and never become hurdle in any way. The man, who possesses high moral character, is an asset for the society because he not only himself remains good but also helps in the prevention of evils in the society. He has great regard, specially, for the women. The moral values also make the human conscience strong.

> *"Who so obeyeth Allah and His Messenger, He will make him enter gardens underneath which rivers flow, where such will dwell for ever. That will be the great success." (4: 13)*

> *"And who so disobeyeth Allah and His Messenger, and transgresseth His limits, He will make him enter Fire, where such will dwell for ever; his will be a shameful doom." (4 : 14)*

Imam Ibne Taymiyyah (R.A.) says:

"If a person is forced to commit fornication, It is incumbent upon him or her to resist. If the attacker runs away, then it is well and good. If not, then the attacker's life can be taken which is in accordance with the unanimous view of the jurists." (Mukhtarat-e-Islamiyah)

Islam considers it a human right to protect one's honour. Therefore, it gives no authority to any person to violate the chastity of any woman or dishonour her. It also forbids false accusation against a woman. The Holy Quran says:

"And those who level false allegation of adultery against a chaste woman and fail to produce four witnesses (to support their allegation), flog them with eighty stripes and reject their evidence for ever, for such men are wicked transgressors." (24 : 4)

On the one hand, Islam considers it unlawful to falsely defame an innocent woman; this is done in order to enable her to live honourably. On the other hand, Islam condemns the wicked people specially bad characters. Such bad characters are not accorded a decent position in Islamic society as that of virtuous men and women. They always lead disgraceful life. Only the western society harbours such ruffians but there is no place for them in the Islamic society. In fact, a bad character cannot survive in Islamic society. As the Holy Quran says:

"Let no man guilty of, adultery or fornication marry any but a woman similarly guilty, or an unbeliever. Nor let any but such a man or an unbeliever marry such a woman. To the believers such a thing is forbidden." (24 : 3)

Hadrat Abu Hurrayrah and Zaid-bin-Khalid (R.A.A.) relate that the Holy Prophet (S.A.W.) was asked what should be done with an unmarried slave-girl who commits adultery? The Holy Prophet (S.A.W.) replied, "If she commits adultery, she must be lashed, if she commits adultery again, then lash her again; and if she still commits adultery then lash her and then sell her off even at the cost of a rope." (Bukhari)

Celibacy Forbidden : In Islam there is no place for celibacy. If a person is poor, it is the duty of the other well-to-do Muslims to help that person to get married. This is the only way to save that person from immorality and enable him or her to lead a respectable life in the society. According to the Holy Quran it is the natural right of the person.

"Marry those among you who are single, or the virtuous ones among your slaves, male or female." *(24: 32)*

The demand of this verse is that no one should remain unmarried in the Islamic society so that the sexual desire may not lead one to unlawful means. This command applies to all Muslim men and women whether free or slave. The Islamic Society of the early era made all necessary arrangements for the marriage of deserving persons to fulfil the conditions of the Shariah.

A well-known 'Tabie or companion of the companions, Ahnaf (R.A.) says that there are three matters which cannot be delayed. When he was asked to name those matters, he said, "The performance of good deed, the burial of the dead and the marriage of a virgin." He has also said, "He would prefer to have the presence of a python in a corner of his house than to refuse the proposal of marriage from a man of equal age for an unmarried girl."

(Al Bayan Wat Tibiyan)

Shaddad bin Aus (R.A.A.) said to his relatives, "Make the arrangement for my marriage because the Holy Prophet (S.A.W.) has advised me not to meet my Allah without marriage." *(Al Ahkam-ul-Quran)*

Mujahid (R.A.) relates that Abdullah bin Abbas (R.A.A.) used to tell his slaves, "If Any one of you wants to marry, I can arrange. Remember, there is a possibility of indulgence in adultery if you remain celibate. And Allah takes away the faith (Iman) from the man who commits adultery. Then it is left to Allah whether to return the faith to him or not."

(Al Muhalla Ibn Haim)

Imam Nakhayee says, "The masters used to force their slaves to marry and if they refused, they were locked in the houses." *(Tafseer Qurtubi)*

They were locked up so that they may not be the cause of evil in the society. It is not only an individual who is responsible in the society but it is also the duty of the state to make the necessary arrangement for marriage of the people who cannot afford.

The Holy Prophet (S.A.W.) has said:

"The ruler of the time is the guardian of the woman who is helpless." *(Tirmidhi, Abu Dammed)*

The Holy Prophet (S.A.W.) had asked Hadrat Ali to remember three things:

"Offer the prayers in time; if somebody dies, do not delay the burial; and if an unmarried person finds a suitable match then arrange the marriage immediately."
(Tirmidhi)

In reply to the Governor of Kufa Zaid-bin-Abdur Rahman, Hadrat Umar-bin-Abdul Aziz (R.A.) says, "You have written that there is surplus money even after paying the salaries to the army. Then pay the debts of the debtors and the amount of the dower of those who are unable to pay.
(Seerat Umar bin Abdul Aziz)

Sexual feelings exist in a man upto a certain period of the age but the life of woman repeatedly passes through such stages when her emotions become weak and sometimes this state continues for a long period; therefore she cannot adequately fulfil the sexual demands of her husband. It is for this reason, Islam has allowed man to marry four wives. Thus, Islam prevents him from going astray. However, if he has four wives at a time, he has to do justice and treat them equally because the Holy Quran says:

"Marry women of your choice, two or three or four, but if ye fear that ye shall not be able to deal justly (with them), then only one, or a captive." *(4 : 3)*

"Ye will not be able to deal equally between (your) wives, however much ye wish (to do so). But turn not altogether away (from one), leaving her as in suspense." *(4 : 129)*

Thus it is crystal clear that Islam grants a conditional permission to marry upto four wives and not a licence. Islam is the natural religion hence the Quranic injunctions are also based on human nature.

The Holy Quran claims:

"O ye who believe ! Be ye staunch in justice, witnesses for Allah, even though it be against yourselves or (your) parents or (your) kindred, whether (the case be of) a rich man or a poor man, for Allah is nearer unto both (than ye are). So follow not passion lest ye lapse (from truth) and if he lapse or fall away, then to Allah is ever informed of what ye do." *(4 : 135)*

The Holy Prophet (S.A.W.) remarks,

"When a man has two wives and he does not observe equality and deal unjustly with them, he will come before the Throne of Justice of Allah with only half of his body."
(Bukhari)

Allama Ibn Ilham Hanafi has explained the legality of this verse in these words :

"This proves that a man can marry four wives only if there is no fear of injustice to them and if there is a fear, then no more than one wife is allowed. It is clear that in case of more than one wife, justice is essential." (Fathul Qadeer)

Allama Badruddin Kashani remarks :

"If a husband has two wives or two captives, then it is essential for him to maintain equality and justice between them as regards clothes, house and passing of the nights."

(Al Badae-was-Sanai)

The physical conditions of the woman are different from those of the man. Therefore, Islam also enjoins strictly the marriage of the woman. And the stress is the same as that of the man. However, Islam does not permit the plurality of husbands for the woman, but has made the provision for the continuity of her conjugal life. It never deprives her of her legitimate right of sexual satisfaction. In case she is separated from her husband owing to his death or divorce, Islam lays stress upon her second marriage after the passage of the requisite period of 'iddat'. The History of Islam shows that the second marriage of the women was performed very easily during the period of the Holy Prophet (S.A.W.) and the Khulafa-i-Rashideen (R.A.A.).

Aatika-bint-Zaid was married to Hadrat Abu Bakr's (R.A.A.) son, Abdullah. Due to some reasons, Hadrat Abu Bakr (R.A.A.) advised his son to divorce his wife. Though, Abdullah divorced his wife to please his father but he was very sad because he loved her very much. When Hadrat Abu Bakr came to know of this fact, he gave his son permission to re-marry her. After the second marriage, Abdullah was martyred in the battle of Taif. It is related that Zaid-bin-Khattab married Aatika after the martyrdom of her husband. When he was also martyred in the battle of Yamama, Hadrat Umar (R.A.A.) married her. And after Hadrat Umar (R.A.A.), Hadrat Zubayr (R.A.A.) married her. After his martyrdom, Hadrat Ali (R.A.A.) offered her to marry but she herself refused.

Sohaila-bint-Sohail married four companions of the Holy Prophet (S.A.W.) one after the other. Similarly, Jamila, the daughter of Abdullah-bin-Ubay was married to Hadrat Hanzla (R.A.A.). When he was martyred in the battle of Uhud, Sabit-bin-Qais married her. After him, Malik-bin-Wakhsham married her and after him she was married to Habib-bin-Liaf.

Asma bint Umais's first marriage was solemnized with Jafar (R.A.A.), the brother of Hadrat Ali (R.A.A.). After his death, Hadrat Abu Bakr (R.A.A.) married her. And after the death of Hadrat Abu Bakr (R.A.A.), Hadrat Ali (R.A.A.) married her.

> *Umme Kulthum daughter of Hadrat Ali (R.A.A.) was married to Hadrat Umar (R.A.A.). When Hadrat Umar (R.A.A.) was martyred, Aun-bin-Jafar (R.A.A.) married her. After the death of Aun, his brother Abdullah married her.* *(Tabaqat, Al Istiyab).*

These examples prove that the second marriage of the woman is not a matter of disgrace in Islam. It is done with respect and honour to keep the society clean and good,

Islam permits divorce but not just like that. Not only that it is discouraged but also considered as the most abhorrent act. It is allowed in a situation when it becomes inevitable owing to the danger of violation of the limits prescribed by Allah.

When the lives of the husband and the wife turn into a hell, the Islamic law would not compel them to bind themselves together for ever. When the confidence between them is shaken, it is better for them to separate.

In case of an extremely difficult situation, the Holy Quran says :

> *"As for those who accuse their wives but have no witnesses except themselves; let the testimony of one of them be four testimonies, (swearing) by Allah that he is of those who speak the truth; And yet a fifth, invoking the curse of Allah on him if he is of those who lie. And it shall avert the punishment from her if she bear witness before Allah four times that the things he saith is indeed false. And fifth (time) that the wrath of Allah be upon her if he speaketh truth."* *(24 : 6-9)*

The Holy Quran is the complete code of life. It deals with every aspect of human, life. And divorce is one of the aspects. The law of divorce provides protection to human modesty and chastity.

The aim of marriage in Islam is to enable a person to lead virtuous life and to create healthy environments in the society. The marriage can be successful only if there is harmony between husband and wife. It is also essential that they must be capable to satisfy the sexual need of each other. Islam gives the full right to the spouses to divorce each other in case the other party lacks the capability for proper discharge of sexual functions. Hadrat Umar (R.A.A.), Hadrat Ali (R.A.A.') and other Companions opine that not only the sexual incapability but also the diseases like blindness, leprosy and lunacy are the valid grounds for divorce. However Imam Ibn Qayyim (R.A.) says:

> *"It is not enough to rely on Two, Six, Seven or Eight defects and neglect the other major or equal defects. The separation can take place on any ground that creates hatred between the spouses and the love is lost which is the sole aim of the marriage."* *(Zad-ul-Muad)*

On the one hand, Islam emphasises the discontinuation of the conjugal relation, which fails to fulfil the requirement of the marriage and on the other hand, it encourages the spouses to adhere to the bonds of marriage which help in leading a virtuous life. Unless there is love between the spouses and they satisfy the sexual wants of each other, the marriage cannot be successful. Besides, the strained relation leads to evil practices. The marriage is considered a firm bond in the Islamic society. It is based on the natural wants of a man and a woman. Hence the sanctity of the Nikah cannot be violated under any circumstances. Though, Islam allows divorce but only on solid grounds. The marriage cannot be dissolved on trivial matters. The Holy Prophet (S.A.W.) has said:

> *"'The women who seek divorce from their husbands without valid reasons are the hypocrites."* *(Nasai)*

He (S.A.W.) has said on another occasion :

> *"The woman who seeks divorce from her husband without any solid ground, even the smell of Heaven is forbidden for her."* *(Tirmidhi)*

Yet on another occasion, the Holy Prophet (S.A.W.) has said :

> *"He is the greatest sinner before Allah who marries a woman and leaves her after satisfying his sexual desire and also swallows her dower."* *(Mustadrak Hakim)*

It is the duty of an individual and also of the society to respect the lawful marriage.' When the illegitimate relation is condemnable in Islam, the legitimate and lawful relation is respected. It is the duty of the whole society to respect the sanctity of solemn marriage. In Islam no one is permitted to violate the sanctity of marriage. According to the Holy Quran the married women are forbidden for the other men. The Holy Prophet (S.A.W.) has said :

> *"That man is not from amongst us who turns a woman rebellious against her husband or the slave against the master."* *(Abu Daud)*

Imam Ibn Taymiyyah (R.A.) has remarked :

If a man with an intention to marry someone's wife himself or get her married to another man, kills her husband, the law of Islam says that such a man must be deprived of the rights to marry her and it is immaterial whether she herself was involved in the conspiracy or not." (Iqama-tul-Daleel)

Social Responsibility : It is but natural that an individual leaves his or her impressions on the society as a whole. The person of a good moral character leaves good impressions on the society and if the person happens to be of bad character he or she leaves bad influence on the society. Thus, a good person helps in the establishment of a good society and a person of bad character spoils the good society. Therefore, it is not possible to have healthy environment and good society in the world unless every individua realises that it is his or her duty to protect the good character of the society.

Islam creates a sense of duty in an individual and reminds that he or she is the real architect of the good society. Moreover, it is not enough for an individual just to be good but it is also his or her duty to correct and improve others. An individual bearing good moral character plays an important role in the building of a good and healthy environment. Such an individual saves others from the moral degeneration. The Holy Prophet (S.A.W.) says:

"Listen, everyone of you is a guardian and everyone of you shall be questioned about the people. The Caliph who is the ruler of the people is a guardian and he shall be questioned about his subjects. The man is the guardian of the members of his family and he shall be questioned about them. The wife is the guardian of her children and the members of her husband's family, and she shall be questioned about them. The slave is the guardian of his master's wealth and he shall be questioned about it. Listen again; Every one of you is a guardian and everyone of you shall be questioned about the (concerned) people."

(Bukhari)

The pressure of the society is always strong. And if it remains strong, no one would dare to disobey its set principles. If overall environment of the society is bad then all sorts of evils would creep in and the situation would go beyond control and the moral values would die.

Islam keeps the sense of morality alive in the society, hence it would not tolerate any kind of immoral act of an individual. Once a woman, who had scented her clothes, was passing through a road. Hadrat Abu Hurrayrah (R.A.A.) saw her and asked, "Are you coming from the mosque?" She replied "Yes". He further asked, "Have you applied this perfume for going to the mosque?" She replied in affirmation. Then Hadrat Abu Hurrayrah (R.A.A.) scolded her and said that he has heard his beloved friend the Holy Prophet (S.A.W.) saying:

> *"A woman who applies perfume and goes to the mosque, Allah accepts not her prayers unless she takes bath as in case of dirtiness."* *(Abu Daud)*

The Holy Prophet (S.A.W.) saw Umme Darda (R.A.A.) coming from the bath and directed her not to go again. He (S.A.W.) told her:

> *"The woman who removes her clothes at the place other than her house, tears the curtain that exists between her and Allah."* *(Musnad Ahmad)*

According to Islam, it is the duty of man to protect moral values of the people who are socially related to him. This responsibility becomes vital if relation is closer. The chastity of the relative and the woman-neighbour must be protected. Any violation in this respect would amount to unpardonable sin.

> *Hadrat Abdullah bin Masood (R.A.A.) says that a man asked the Holy Prophet (S.A.W.), "Which is the greatest sin?" The Holy Prophet (S.A.W.) replied, "The greatest sin is to associate someone with Allah, Who alone created you." He asked, "Which is the lesser sin than this?" The Holy Prophet (S.A.W.) replied, "After that, the greatest sin is to take the life of your baby thinking that it will take away the part of livelihood (and you would starve)." He again asked, "Which is the greatest sin after these two." The Holy Prophet (S.A.W.) replied." The adultery with your neighbour woman (Bukhari, Muslim and Mishkat).*

Once the Holy Prophet (S.A.W.) asked one of his companions, "What is your opinion about adultery?" The companion replied, "Allah and his Messenger (S.A.W.) have forbidden adultery and it shall remain forbidden until the Day of Judgement." The Holy Prophet (S.A.W.) said, "The adultery with ten women is lesser sin than the adultery committed with his neighbour's wife."

Guiding Principles : Woman has to realize her real position in the Islamic society which aims to establish the environment free from all evils. She is the architect of the domestic life. Therefore neither the state should assign her such duties which are injurious to herself, nor she has the right to destroy the domestic life and take part in such activities which may prove harmful to herself, her house and the society. She is not supposed to solve the political problems but look after the affairs which are solely meant for her.

Obedience : Islam is the complete code of life and provides guidelines for every aspect of human behaviour. Its main object is to relieve man from slavery of man and 'establish the sovereignty of Allah over the entire mankind. It leads to peace and tranquillity. For this reason man has been assigned superiority over woman in certain respects.

The Holy Quran says:

"Men are in charge of women, because Allah has made the one of them to excel the other, and because they spend their property (for the support of women)." *(4 : 34)*

Therefore, the husband can restrict his wife to such principles which are necessary for the well being of the conjugal life, and the wife has to obey her husband in all cases except which oppose the principles of Islam. The Holy Prophet (S.A.W.) has said that for a believer, after fear of Allah, a virtuous wife is the best endowment of Allah. About one of the good qualities of a virtuous wife, the Holy Prophet (S.A.W.) said, "If he (husband) orders, she will obey." *(Ibn Majah)*

Once somebody asked the Holy Prophet (S.A.W.) to explain the good qualities of a virtuous wife. The Holy Prophet (S.A.W.) replied:

"One who pleases her husband when he sees her, and obeys when he orders. And she must not oppose him by an act which he does not like." *(Nasai)*

Hadrat Abdullah bin Umar (R.A.A.) relates that the Holy Prophet (S.A.W.) has said:

"There are two types of persons whose prayers (Salat) do not go beyond their heads (that is, not acceptable to Allah); the one is the slave who runs away and returns and the other is a wife who disobeys her husband and approaches not to him for forgiveness and promises not to disobey him in future." *(Tibarani)*

In order to clarify the legal position of husband and wife, the Holy Prophet (S.A.W.) said on the occasion of the Hafiat-ul-Wida.

"Treat your wives nicely because they are under your custody." *(Tirmidhi)*

The wife is under the control of her husband and, therefore, she has to obey him. On another occasion the Holy Prophet (S.A.W.) said about wife.

> *"The wife, who believes in Allah and the Day of Judgement, is not allowed to admit any man whom her husband does not like. She must not got out under the circumstances which he does not approve. And she must not obey anybody else in respect of the affairs of her husband nor she must quarrel or fight with him when he comes."*
>
> *(Mustadrak Hakim)*

Though wife is allowed to offer her prayers in the mosque but it is better for her to get the permission of her husband. In this respect Hadrat Abdullah bin Umar relates the advice of the Holy Prophet (S.A.W.) to a husband :

> *"If your wife asks for permission to go to the mosque to offer her prayers, she should not be stopped (without a valid reason)."* *(Muslim)*

Hence, it is crystal clear that the wife should take the permission of her husband to leave the house not only for offering prayers in the mosque but for any other purpose, as well.

In the light of these Ahadith it is a proven fact that the wife cannot leave her house without permission of her husband. The Islamic Shariah allows the wife to leave her home for any good cause but not without the permission of her husband. This has been done to keep off evil and maintain harmony in the conjugal life.

But there are certain exceptions to this rule, that is, wife is allowed to leave her home without the permission of her husband under certain unavoidable circumstances which are pointed out by the Hanafi jurists thus :

> *"The wife is not allowed to leave her home without the permission of her husband except in certain restricted circumstances. The circumstances are : She can leave the house if it is going to collapse; if she has a juristic problem which her husband cannot solve, she can leave the house and proceed to the juristic school for its solution; If she has to go for Hajj and there is Mahram (A close relative with whom her marriage is forbidden) to accompany her; the husband can allow her to go and that will be no sin for him. Similarly she is not bound to take permission of her husband for visiting her parents or near relatives."*
>
> *(Fatawa Qadi Khan)*

This juristic argument proves that wife is bound by certain principles to obey her husband and it allowed, certain special concessions only under unavoidable circumstances. The husband also can impose certain restriction on her activities in the house.

Allama Ibn Nujaim says:

"The husband has the right to prevent his wife from earning her livelihood because this is the duty of her husband. Similarly the husband can restrict her from performing any other virtuous work which is not obligatory."

(Al Bahr-ur-Raiq- Vol. IV)

The husband has this right because he himself is responsible for the maintenance of his wife and children. However, if the husband is unable to provide the necessities of life for her children, the wife is permitted to look for and earn money for the maintenance of the family. Besides, as Allama Ibn Abedin (R.A.) says, "There are certain expenses of the wife for which the husband is not bound, hence, the wife can work at home and earn money to meet such expenses." He has further said the husband can prevent her from doing such extra hard work which affects her health. It is the right of husband to keep his wife hail and hearty and beautiful."

Allama Ibn Abedin further says:

"A husband can prevent his wife from all such activities which either deprive him of his rights or cause harm, or for which she has to leave her house. But there is no reason to prevent her from any activity -which causes no harm to him." *(Al Durrul Mukhtar)*

The Islamic Shariah imposes restrictions on the movement of the woman in her own interest as well as for the welfare of the whole family. And every good family contributes and helps in the establishment of a good society. Ultimately good societies make a good and disciplined nation.

Islam considers the home as heaven for her faith and morals, whereas there is always a fear of losing them, outside the home. Holy Prophet Muhammad (S.A.W.) has said:

"Women is to be kept in privacy, therefore, keep her confined in the house." *(Tirmidhi)*

Speaking psychologically, Islam wants the conjugal ties to be strong and everlasting, because this relation is very delicate and may be shattered even by a slight misunderstanding. A good husband would never like his wife to go out very often because this creates many problems. Allama Ibn Ilham has said :

"Wife's going out of home very often opens the door for evil, specially when she is young and the husband may be well-bred and courteous, is a gentleman. *(Fath-ul-Qadeer)*

Restrictions : A Muslim lady is allowed by Shariah to leave her ' home with the permission of her husband to perform her religious, educational and social services, but she should keep in mind the fact that she has been restricted from mingling with the male strangers. Islam confines her to home because her presence amongst the men who are strangers gives rise to moral degeneration. If a woman breaks the law of Shariah and enters any field, with however good intentions, her step will be considered against the principles of Islam because it leads to troubles and destruction.

No one, on earth, can be more God-fearing than the Holy Prophet (S.A.W.) and no one else can be compared with him (S.A.W.) so far as the loftiness of character is concerned. Hence, the fact remains that some women of his (S.A.W.) time who came to him to take pledge, to serve the cause of Islam, were not allowed to clasp his (S.A.W.) hand, although the men took the Oath of Allegiance by placing their hands on his (S.A.W.) hand, Hadrat Aishah (R.A.A.) says:

"The Holy Prophet (S.A.W.) took the Oath of Allegiance from women orally according to this Quranic verse." O Prophet ! If believing women come unto thee that they will ascribe nothing as partner unto Allah, and will neither steal nor commit adultery nor kill their children, nor produce any lie that they have devised between their hands and feet, nor disobey thee in what is right, then accept their allegiance and ask Allah to forgive them. Lo! Allah is Forgiving, Merciful." *(60 : 12)*

"His (S.A.W.) hand never touched the hand of any women while taking the Oath of Allegiance, except the hand of his (S.A.W.) wife." *(Bukhari)*

On another occasion she has said:

"No, by Allah ! (The hand of the Holy Prophet (S.A.W.) never touched the hand of any other woman. He (S.A.W.) took woman's Oath of Allegiance orally. Then he (S.A.W.) used to say, "Go, I have taken your Oath of Allegiance orally." *(Muslim)*

Sometimes some women tried to place their hands on his (S.A.W.) hand while taking the Oath of Allegiance, but the Holy Prophet (S.A.W.) said, "I do not shake hand with women, my addressing a group of hundred women is as good as addressing a single woman. Therefore, there is no need to take separate Oath of Allegiance from each woman."

(Nasai)

As it has been said before, Islam aims to establish a society free from all evils and provides peaceful living for the whole mankind. Therefore, it is absolutely essential to keep the men and women separate in all matters whether educational, cultural, martial, social or political. Thus, according to Islamic Shariah, women are not allowed to mingle with other men. As a matter of fact it is not possible to have healthy environment in any society if the intermingling of men and women are allowed. Hence prevention is better than cure. In Islamic society neither co-education nor co-cultural programmes are allowed. A Muslim woman is not permitted to take military training along with other men. Nor she can participate in games or recreation with men. Whether it is a market place or an assembly hall, Islam considers intermingling of the two sexes at any place, as undesirable.

Women attended the sermons of the Holy Prophet (S.A.W.) but separate seating arrangements were made for them. They never sat alongwith the men. Islam is the Deen for all times. Hence even in the modern times women can participate freely in all activities and functions, within the limits of the Shariah provided separate arrangements are made for them. Hadrat Abdullah Ibn Abbas (R.A.A.) describes the Eid prayers in these words:

"First he (the Holy Prophet (S.A.W.) led the (Eid) prayers and delivered the sermon (Khutba). Then along with Hadrat Bilal (R.A.A.) he came towards the women and addressed them." *(Bukhari)*

Interpreting this Hadith Hafiz Ibn Hajar says, "Hadrat Ibn Abbas says that the expression 'the Holy Prophet (S.A.W.) came towards the women' makes it distinctly clear that the women were separate from the men and not intermingled with them." *(Fath-ul-Bari)*

According to another narration, the Holy Prophet (S.A.W.) first led the prayers and then delivered the sermon. Afterwards he felt that the women could not hear him properly, so he came (a bit closer) to them and advised them. *(Bukhari)*

This Hadith clearly shows that the women were quite at a distance and therefore, they could not hear the Holy Prophet (S.A.W.) properly.

Though no regular military training was given to women during the time of the Holy Prophet (S.A.W.), yet they were always found ready and fit for tendering their services during emergencies. But now the Islamic states can train women for active participation in modern warfare. However, the condition of the Islamic Shariah shall ever remain in force. There shall be altogether separate arrangements for their training and participation in wars.

In War **:** War is a big obstacle in the way of human life. It stops progress and brings devastation. In such situation the entire nation is involved and the circumstances take such turn that it becomes impossible to apply the normal laws and principles. The rules that are framed for normal conditions, do not remain effective in an emergency.

The war creates such dangerous and dreadful situation that the set rules become ineffective and every individual has to become active and helpful for the cause of Islam and Muslims. So the participation of women in war also becomes inevitable. This does not mean that the law 'women should not mingle with men' is broken but automatically suspended to some extent for the time being during the emergency. The Holy Prophet (S.A.W.) and his companions had to face very critical situation during wars. In the first place they had not yet attained the political stability in the country and in the second place they were numerically less and had not enough equipment to fight. On the other hand, the enemies were in large number and well equipped. They also brought a large number of women with them who encouraged the men to, fight and also, provided medical aid to the sick and the injured. But the Muslim women remained attached to the domestic duties only, therefore they knew nothing about war. Ultimately the participation of Muslim women in war became inevitable.

Hadrat Aishah (R.A.A.) says, "I was with the Holy Prophet (S.A.W.) during a battle. I was very thin and lean in those days. The Holy Prophet (S.A.W.) asked his companions to go ahead. After that he (S.A.W.) told me to have a race. I won in the race and the Holy Prophet (S.A.W.) just kept quiet.

> *After a long time, when I had already forgotten all about this event and became fat, I accompanied the Holy Prophet (S.A.W.) on a journey. This time also the Holy Prophet (S.A.W.) asked the companions to go ahead and called me to have a race. But this time the Holy Prophet (S.A.W.) won the race and replied smilingly "It is my victory this time."*
>
> *(Durrul Sameen).*

However, the Holy Prophet (S.A.W.) directed the Muslims that women's participation in battles must be restricted to absolute necessity only. Hence the history of Islam shows that women scarcely took part in the important battles. Besides, it was essential for every woman, wishing to take part in the battle, to take prior permission of the Holy Prophet (S.A.W.).

This restriction was to eliminate the fears and doubts from the minds of the Muslims. After taking all factors into consideration, the Holy Prophet (S.A.W.) allowed women to join the battle. He (S.A.W.) always took care while allowing a woman that she was essentially required for the battle and that the necessary arrangements were made for her safety. The Holy Prophet (S.A.W.) never allowed any woman to participate in the battle unless he (S.A.W.) was fully satisfied in this regard.

Once some women for the sake of Jihad joined the army without permission. When the Holy Prophet (S.A.W.) came to know about this, he warned them. Hashraj bin Ziyad relates from his grandmother

> *"I accompanied the Holy Prophet (S.A.W.) for the battle of Khyber. There were five other women also. When the Holy Prophet (S.A.W.) came to know about this fact, he (S.A.W.) summoned us through a man. When we went to him we found him angry. Then angrily he asked us, "With whom have you come and with whose permission have you come ?"*
>
> *(Abu Daud)*

This shows that firstly the women were required to have permission of the Holy Prophet (S.A.W.) for participation in the war and secondly they were to come with their clan or with very reliable persons. The Holy Prophet (S.A.W.) was angry with the grandmother of Hashraj bin Ziyad (R.A.A.) and other women because they evaded these pre-conditions.

Umm Sinan Islamiya (R.A.A.) relates:

> *"When the Holy Prophet (S.A.W.) decided to move towards Khyber, I went to him and said, "I intend to join you in this battle. There, if necessary, I shall sew the leather bags and treat the sick and the injured (May Allah forbid). I shall look after the belongings of the soldiers." The Holy Prophet (S.A.W.) said, "May Allah grant His bounties, you may join us. Some other women of your and other tribes had sought my permission which I have already granted. All these women shall be your companions. You may join your own clan or if you wish you can join us." I said, "I*

shall accompany you." He replied, "Well, then join my wife Umm' Salama (R.A.A.)." So I joined her.

(Tabaqat Ibn Saad)

The study of the Islamic history shows that the ladies accompanied generally their real relations, father, brothers or sons on the war fronts.

The fact cannot be denied that Islamic states may have to face such situation in every age. So the women, within the limits of the Shariah and above mentioned conditions, can serve the cause of Islam and their country directly or indirectly. Islam is the practical Deen and will remain ever dynamic. Its laws are for the entire mankind and for all times. It controls the activities of men and women for the welfare of the entire mankind. Its target is always to uproot the evil.

Women in History : Woman has achieved an important and significant place in the history of Islam. But the West has done a great disservice to the history by distorting and mis-interpreting the facts of the Islamic history.

The freedom that West has given to woman is not the freedom in real sense of the term. In fact, it is a licence and an attempt at exploitation of woman for the satisfaction of man's sensual desires only. This kind of freedom has made the Western society corrupt and evil.

The Western culture teaches woman to rebel against her own home and encourages her to become a plaything for the men in the so-called modern society. Whereas, Islam has given her the freedom of equal rights, honour and dignity. The main place of her activities is her home. Besides, she is allowed to leave her home when the necessity arises. The freedom of women by West brings disgrace to her, whereas the freedom granted by Islam elevates her status and she becomes an honourable member of the society.

The West has painted a very wrong picture of a historical event. After the martyrdom of Hadrat Uthman Ghani (R.A.A.), the administration of the state was greatly disturbed. When it became difficult to bring to book the assassins of Hadrat Uthman Ghani (R.A.A.), Hadrat Aishah (R.A.A.) entered the arena of politics and endeavoured to enforce the laws of Shariah on the culprits. Her struggle for the cause of Islam brought her to the stage of leadership which is the right of man alone. It was an emergency and there was no man to lead the Muslim nation and fight the forces opposing Islam. The situation was so grave that she declared war even against Hadrat Ali (R.A.A.) who tried to confront her.

The West has interpreted this event wrongly and derived very mischievous conclusions from it. The Western historians base their arguments on this particular event of the Islamic history and maintain that Islam has granted equal rights in the field of politics, that is, a woman can become the leader of the nation. Hence, her participation in politics and social activities cannot be prohibited according to Shariah. They say that men and women can intermingle freely in every sphere of human life. But this notion is absolutely false and baseless. It is a fabrication to defame Islam.

It is a fact that Hadrat Aishah played a leading role on account of unavoidable circumstances. That was an exception and does not make a rule. The rule remains the same that woman cannot be assigned the leadership of the Muslim Ummah. Women was never allowed to play this role during the time of the Holy Prophet (S.A.W.) and Khulfa-i-Rashideen (R.A.A.).

The teachings of Islam restrict the activities of woman to her home and allow her to leave it only in inevitable circumstances. The leadership of the nation was never assigned to woman nor she ever claimed it. Though the Holy Prophet (S.A.W.) and Khulfa-i-Rashideen (R.A.A.) faced great difficulties and hurdles, yet woman was never entrusted with any responsibility for their solution.

During the long period of Islamic rule, a number of battles were fought but woman was never made the commander-in-Chief of the Muslim army. Woman was never appointed as a Governor by the Holy Prophet (S.A.W.) or by any of his four Caliphs. She was not assigned any responsible post in the department of finance or the judiciary. After the demise of the Holy Prophet (S.A.W.) the Muslims never elected any woman as their Caliph.

America is the most advanced and prosperous country of the world. If one or two persons are found there poor, it would not make America a poor country. Similarly if Hadrat Aishah (R.A.A.) played a leading role in the politics of her time, it would not mean that Islam allows the leadership of woman. The act of an individual cannot become the rule of the Shariah.

If an individual act of Hadrat Aishah (R.A.A.) can serve as a model for the Muslim Ummah then why not the act of other Ummahatul Momineen and venerable Sahabiyat? If Hadrat Aishah's (R.A.A.) battle against Hadrat Ali (R.A.A.) can serve as a precedent, then why not the action of Hadrat Umm Salama (R.A.A.)? Because, when Hadrat Ali (R.A.A.) left for Basra to fight against Hadrat Aishah (R.A.A,), Hadrat Zubayr (R.A.A.) and Hadrat Talha (R.A.A.) Hadrat Umm Salama said to him :

"Ameerul Momineen : If we accompany you on this occasion, it will amount to disobedience to Allah and you would not approve this act of ours. We would have come with you if these two factors were not there. My cousin (brother) is here. I love him more than my life. He will go with you and take part in the battle." *(Tarikh Kamil)*

On the other hand she wrote to Hadrat Aishah (R.A.A.):

"Your position is like a door between the Holy Prophet (S.A.W.) and the Muslim Ummah. And your modesty is the veil of honour. But you have unveiled yourself. Remember, the Holy Quran has laid certain restrictions on you, so do not step beyond the limits. Allah wants you to be at home, hence do not leave it and do not come to the battlefield. Allah is at the back of the Muslim Ummah. You know how much Holy Prophet (S.A.A.) loved you ! Had he wanted to assign such responsibilities, he would have assigned during his lifetimes, but he did not. And you know that if the pillar of Islam falls, the women cannot re-erect it and if it cracks, the women cannot repair it. Were the women fit for Jihad, the Holy Prophet (S.A.W.) would have allowed you. The Jihad of women is that they should keep their eyes down and protect themselves.

Had the Holy Prophet (S.A.W.) seen you on the back of a camel wandering about the mountains and monds, what would have been your explanation? One day you will have to present yourself before the Holy Prophet (S.A.W.) and you have disregarded the principle of veil and ignored the law of Allah?

"Had I done what you have done, I would have felt ashamed to enter the Heaven. Therefore, I request you to observe Purdah (veil) established by the Holy Prophet (S.A.W.) and make your home your castle. You can be real well-wisher of the Ummah, if you remain at home instead of coming to the battlefield. If I tell you a Hadith of the Holy Prophet (S.A.W.) you would certainly pounce upon me like a snake to bite me." *(Al-Iqdul-Farid)*

This kind of criticism came not only from Hadrat Umm Salama (R.A.A.) but from many other respectable personalities of the Ummah.

When Hadrat Aishah (R.A.A.) reached Basra on her mission, she wrote to Zaid bin Sauban addressing him as son, "Immediately join the mission which has been launched to avenge the blood of Hadrat Uthman (R.A.A.). And if you do not want to joint, at least keep your people away from favouring Hadrat Ali (R.A.A.),," After reading this letter, Zaid bin Sauban said, "May Allah have mercy upon Ummul Momineen. We were commanded to launch Jihad and she had to be at home. She has ignored the restrictions imposed upon her and she wants me to obey. She has taken over the responsibilities assigned to us and she is preventing us from carrying out our duty. Then he replied to Hadrat Aishah (R.A.A.) "Indeed I am like your real son and you are my mother. Unless you give up your struggle and return home I shall be the first person to leave." (Tabari)

Another well known personality of Basra and companion of the Holy Prophet (S.A.W.), Jariah-bin-Qudama says to Hadrat Aishah (R.A.A.), "The martyrdom of Hadrat Uthman Ghani is lighter than your action. , Allah has bestowed upon you the honour and commanded to observe Purdah (Veil) but you have ignored it. One who considers war against you rightful, can consider taking of your life also rightful. Just imagine in what delicate position you have put the people. Therefore, if you have come of your own free will, then go back home and if you have been compelled then gain the favour of the people against him and you reach home.

Hadrat Abu Bakr (R.A.A.) a well known companion of the Holy Prophet (S.A.W.) says, "I would have joined Hadrat Aishah (R.A.A.) in the battle of Jamal. But the saying of the Holy Prophet (S.A.W.) saved me. When he (S.A.W.) received the news of the coronation of the daughter of Kisra, he (S.A.W.) said, "The nation who bands over its reigns to a woman, cannot be successful." (Bukhari)

An eminent companion like Hadrat Abdullah bin Umar (R.A.A.) says, "For Hadrat Aishah (R.A.A.) her home is better. The criticism of these respectable contemporary personalities was not just to oppose Hadrat Aishah (R.A.A.) out of grudge or enmity but to remind her of the commandments and the limitation of Allah imposed upon woman. Even Hadrat Aishah (R.A.A.) had great respect for them who criticised her for participating in the battle instead of remaining at home. Therefore, the main issue was not the criticism but the strict observance of the principles of Islam.

The history of Islam shows that the Muslims had to face numerous difficulties in the early period. But the men themselves were able to solve the problems of the Ummah and never invited the women to participate in their struggle in person. Hadrat Aishah (R.A.A.) herself survived for about fifty years after the demise of the Holy Prophet (S.A.W) and saw ups and downs in the lives of the Muslims and remained aloof. She took no active part to improve the prevalent unfavourable conditions. This proves that she considered the home, the real place of her activities.

Hadrat Aishah (R.A.A.) adhered to the principles of Islam during her whole life. Hence a single incident cannot become the means of denial for the facts of the whole life. The wise thing is to study the circumstances, that led her to the battlefield.

The facts of history prove that dissatisfaction prevailed among the common people against Hadrat Uthman Ghani (R.A.A.) during the last years of his Caliphate. The people had started criticism against him. The situation became so grave that notorious elements attacked Medina and consequently Hadrat Uthman Ghani (R.A.A.) was martyred. Though the elders of the Muslims strived to avert the catastrophe but failed. And the Millat (nation) had to suffer a tremendous loss. It was the first and the peculiar event that shook the whole Ummah. The wise men thought that it was their defeat and the victory of the ruffians, and if immediate action was not taken against them, then Islam would become a plaything in the hands of the wicked. Some of them decided to punish according to Shariah all those who participated in the martyrdom of Hadrat Uthman Ghani (R.A.A.), otherwise the Ummah would lose the honour, and power would slip into the hands of the enemies of Islam. Such mischief-mongers would select a Caliph and kill him when they so desired, and there would be no power to check them. The senior members of the community like Hadrat Zubayr (R.A.A.) and Hadrat Talha (R.A.A.) held this view. Maleh bin Aaf-ul-Salma asked Hadrat Zubayr (R.A.A.). He replied

> *"What do you want?" "We are preparing the people to avenge the blood of Hadrat Uthman Ghani (R.A.A.) so that it may not go waste. If we allow it to go unavenged then the supreme authority among us would become weak. If they are not corrected and made to respect the authority, then they would continue killing the Caliphs at will. By Allah, it is absolutely necessary to avenge the blood of Hadrat Uthman Ghani (R.A.A.). You do not realize the consequences that would follow."* *(Tarikhur Rusul)*

There was yet another group which considered the unity of the Ummah as the most important issue. It observed that dissension and anarchy was spreading fast. As the whole Ummah had taken the form of a rebellious army; as such they considered unwise to raise the question of avenging the blood of Hadrat Uthman Ghani (R.A.A.) as it would create, further trouble. They, therefore, decided to consolidate the Ummah hence with this end in view they elected Hadrat Ali (R.A.A.) as their Caliph. The majority of the inhabitants of Medina supported this group. Consequently the supporters of the other group left Medina and moved to some other cities. Some of them reached Mecca where Ummahatul Momineen lived. The latter had no knowledge of developments in Medina, because they had left Medina long before and had come to Mecca with the intention of performing Hajj. When they enquired from the people coming from Medina about the prevalent conditions in that city, they gave a quite different account of the situation there. According to them, the riffraffs and unruly persons had taken over the city of Medina and have installed there as Caliph.

> *Hadrat Aishah (R.A.A.) enquired from a relative, "What is the situation?" He replied, "The lawlessness prevailing in Medina has hit hard the people there." Hadrat Aishah (R.A.A.) felt sorry and put another question, "Let me know whether the situation is in our favour or against us ?" He replied, "I do not know all this; but the people were left without any caliph for eight days after the martyrdom of Hadrat Uthman Ghani (R.A.A.). After that the Medinities and the ruffians who had overpowered the city gathered around Hadrat Ali (R.A.A.)." (Tabari)*

> *Another relative of Hadrat Aishah (R.A.A.) informed her that "Hadrat Uthman Ghani (R.A.A.) has been martyred and the people have agreed to take the Oath of Allegiance in favour of Hadrat Ali but the real power is in the hands of the rogues." (Tabari)*

Hadrat Zubayr (R.A.A.) and Hadrat Talha (R.A.A.) had reached Mecca. They did not like to take the Oath of Allegiance in favour of Hadrat Ali (R.A.A.). Naturally their feelings were different from other people. When Hadrat Aishah (R.A.A.) asked them about the situation in Medina they replied :

> *"We have left Medina because we were in minority and afraid of the rebels and bedouins. When we left Medina, the people were in a state of confusion, unable to distinguish between right and wrong; so much so that they had to courage even to defend themselves." (Tarikhur Rusul)*

Hadrat Zubayr (R.A.A.) and Hadrat Talha (R.A.A.) and their supporters now started paving the way for the improvement of the conditions. They invited the Muslims to avenge the death of Hadrat Uthman Ghani (R.A.A.). For this purpose they needed the support and sympathy of Ummahatul Momineen who were fortunately available there. They were also very much affected by the developments in Medina and their support could put life in any movement that could be launched.

Hadrat Zubayr and Hadrat Talha (R.A.A.) therefore, approached Ummahatul Momineen, specially, Hadrat Aishah (R.A.A.) and Hadrat Hafsa (R.A.A.) who had great influence over the society and requested them to support their struggle for the reestablishment of Islamic principles. But all of them excepting Hadrat Aishah (R.A.A.) considered it beyond their capacity and refused to lend their support. As such Hadrat Aishah alone, returned to Medina.

Probably Hadrat Aishah (R.A.A.) thought that if the courage and determination of Hadrat Abu Bakr (R.A.A.) could crush the scourge of heresy, this Ummah still could crush the rebellion it faced then, they needed only the guidance and inspiration. Hence she decided to join the movement launched for reformation of the people. With this end in view she reached Basra. The Governor of Basra, Uthman bin Hanif sent Imran-bin-Haseen to ascertain her intentions. Hadrat Aishah (R.A.A.) replied :

> *"The mischief-mongers and defectors from tribes have waged war in the sacred city of the Holy Prophet (S.A.W.); they have been instrumental in spreading heretical innovations and have joined hands with renegades and innovators, and have invited the wrath of Allah and his Prophet (S.A.W.) upon themselves. Moreover they have slaughtered the Caliph of the Muslims without any justification. Thus they have shed blood of an innocent Imam and robbed the money and property of the people over which they had no right. They have polluted the sacred city of Medina and violated the sanctity of the Holy month. I have come out to show the people what the miscreants have done and what is the state of the people left there after we left the place, and how they can be reformed and corrected." Then she recited this verse of the Holy Quran :*
>
> *"There is no good in much of their secret conferences save (in) him who enjoineth alms giving and kindness and peacemaking among the people. Whoso doeth that, seeking the good pleasure of Allah, We shall bestow on him a vast reward."* *(4 : 114)*
>
> *And she said, "Our position is that we are ordering you to do good and abstain from what is evil."*
>
> *(Tabari, Al Kamil, Ibnul Asir)*

Qaaqa asked, Ummul Momineen "What brings you here?" She replied, "O my son, I have come here to reform the people." *(Al-Kamil)*

Her statement proves that neither she had any ambition for power nor had she come to wage war against Hadrat Ali (R.A.A.). She aimed at reforming the Ummah through her good offices. Imam Ibne Taymiyyah (R.A.A.) says:

"Hadrat Aishah (R.A.A.) neither waged war nor she had come with that intention. She had come just to correct the people. She was under the impression that she had to leave home (at that critical time) for the good of the Muslims." *(Minhajul Sunnah, page 295)*

No doubt, she had to fight against Hadrat Ali (R.A.A.) but this was against her intentions and wishes. She was compelled by the circumstances to fight a battle against him.

This is a fact that Hadrat Aishah (R.A.A.) was the leading personality amongst the Ummah. The people considered her their leader and guide. All matters of the community were settled with her consultation and approval. But it cannot be proved by any instance from history that she ever claimed the leadership of the Ummah for herself. She always thought that she was just a guide and the well-wisher of the Muslims.

The people were always ready to sacrifice everything at her instance but they never elected her as their legal Caliph. When the difference of opinion arose amongst the people as to who should lead the prayers, Hadrat Zubayr (R.A.A.) or Hadrat Talha (R.A.A.), the matter was decided with the consultation of Hadrat Aishah (R.A.A.) and ultimately Hadrat Abdullah bin Zubayr was appointed to lead the prayers. But the name of Hadrat Aishah (R.A.A.) was never suggested for this purpose by any one. This was the attitude of the people, who supported Hadrat Aishah (R.A.A.) and according to them her position was higher than those of Hadrat Talha, Hadrat Zubayr and Hadrat Abdullah bin Zubayr (R.A.A.).

It is a self-evident fact that Hadrat Aishah (R.A.A.) had to take such steps owing to an extreme emergency, which she would have never taken in normal circumstances. It was an exceptional event which occurred owing to unavoidable circumstances and it can never become the rule for all times.

3

System of Marriage

MARRIAGE AND INSTITUTION

'There are three essential elements in every normal marriage,' says Dr. Westermarck in his book, *The Future of Marriage in Western Civilization*, 'the gratification of the sexual impulse, the relation between husband and wife apart from it and procreation of children.' Let us see what is the angle of vision from which Islam looks at marriage and what is the central value in it which it stresses more than any other. Let it not also be forgotten that, unlike Christianity, which looked upon marriage as if it were a necessary evil, Islam regards it as a most sacred institution and makes it incumbent on every Muslim man and woman, unless prevented by valid physical or economic incapacity, to lead a married life.

The following traditions of the Holy Prophet stress the importance of marriage:

It is necessary for you to marry, because marriage is the most powerful shield against the allurements of sight, and the protection of your private parts; if one of you cannot afford it, let him fast because fasting weakens the sexual impulse.

The Prophet declared that marriage was one of his most sacred practices and added: 'Whoever dislikes my way of life is not of me' *(Bukhari).*

A tradition reported by Arias says, 'When a man has got married he has made his religion half perfect. Then let him fear Allah for the remaining half.' *(Baihaqi)*

The Quran also exhorts the followers of Islam to enter into marriage with chaste women:

Then marry such women as seem good to you. *(iv. 3)*

> *And lawful for you are all women, besides those mentioned above, provided that you seek them with your property taking them in marriage not committing fornication.*
> *(iv. 24)*
>
> *You are sprung one from the other; so marry them (slavegirls) with the permission of their masters and give them their dowries justly they being chaste, not fornicating, nor forming secret relations.* *(iv. 25)*
>
> *This day all the good things are allowed to you, and the food of those who have been given the Book is lawful for you and your food is lawful for them; and the chaste from among the believing women and the chaste from among those who have been given the Book before you (are lawful for you), when you have given them their dowries, taking them in marriage, not fornicating, nor taking them for paramours in secret.* *(v. 5)*

The Quran has constantly used the word Mohsin for chaste men and Muhsinat for chaste women both of which come from the Arabic root Him meaning 'fort'. The underlying idea is that marriage safeguards and protects chastity in the same manner as a fort protects the garrison within from a besieging army.

From the above quotations it appears that Islamrecommends marriage because, first, it helps men and women to lead a life of chastity, that is, it secures them against promiscuous sexual indulgence; secondly, because it prevents the formation of secret sex relations. These two values are the cornerstone on which the institution of marriage rests and Islam's conception, of woman's rights in marriage flows logically from them.

Let us see what the social importance of chastity and open sex relation is as opposed to secret love. In modern times, the ideal of chastity has lost hold on man and it has been claimed by some, even among men of science and learning, that chastity is by no means a very important social value and that happiness in marriage as well as the proper upbringing of children need not suffer from sexual promiscuity on the part of either partner.

Some would go to the length of abolishing the family system in order to secure the release of men and women from the bonds of conjugal fidelity. It is presumed by these people that alternative methods of bringing up children can be organised more efficiently. It is difficult to bringout the importance of chastity as a social value unless we discuss all such proposals and ideas.

Let us first deal with the importance of conjugal fidelity and its healthy effects on the happiness of the family and the health of society. Islam has made no distinction in this respect between man and woman; both are equally punishable under the law of Islam if they are guilty of sexual laxity. But, in practice, public opinion has always, even in Western countries, taken more alarm at unchastity in women than in men, the reason being that the disturbing social and family effects of a woman's misconduct are deeper and more widespread. Discussing this inequality of treatment as regards men and women, Dr. Westermarck says in the Future of Marriage in Western Civilization.

But there are also more special reasons for that inequality between the sexes. It was a doctrine of the Roman jurists that adultery is a crime in the wife, and in the wife only, on account of the danger of introducing strange children to the husband. . . . It has been argued that the danger of confusion of pregnancy has disappeared with the development of methods for preventing conception, but it is anything but certain that the lovers trouble themselves about contraceptives. Von Krafft-Ebing writes [in his book *The Modern Family*): 'The unfaithfulness of a wife, in comparison with that of a husband, is morally much more weighty, and should be more severely punished legally. The unfaithful wife dishonours not only herself, but also her husband and her family....' 'The man,' says Kisch in [Die Sexuelle Untreue der Frau], 'can make a lapse in this marriage without the consequences of it being necessarily of vital importance; he can at any moment do remorseful penance without the mischief he has caused being irreparable. The infidelity of the wife poisons the soul for ever, shakes the foundations of the harmony between mother and children, makes the legitimacy of the latter uncertain, and leads to an irreparable rupture of the 'domestic life.' Hedwig Wega observes that while the adultery of the husband is in many cases a purely social act, which need not spoil marriage, that of the wife is in no case merely bodily attachment. Stendhal remarks [in his book on Love] that where love is absent, the fidelity of a married woman is something contrary to nature, but that, 'with love there, one has no taste for any mate but that of the beloved fount.' He also writes: 'The difference between infidelity in the two sexes is so real, that a woman of passion may pardon it, while for a man that is impossible!'

These are some of the consequences of female unchastity, but so less grave are the consequences which follow from the sexual irregularities of men. We shall again quote Dr. Westermarck who says:

However useful sexual intercourse may be to the unmarried, it has also its disadvantages. It may give venereal diseases to him who practises it; and it may be fraught with serious consequences for the female partner.... The illegitimacy of birth affects the offspring even more than the mother. The death rate for illegitimate infants is very much higher than for legitimate ones. . . . Another result of them is the comparatively large number of criminals among the children of unmarried parents, who grow up in so unfavourable circumstances. The way in which they have been treated in the Western world is a disgrace to its civilization... It certainly seems both absurd and unjust that the legal rights of any citizens should be influenced by the judgments which society passes upon their mothers; but however much legislation may improve the condition of illegitimate children, it cannot make them equal to those under which most other children develop. Family allowances may be granted, to their mothers where the father is unknown or indigent, founding institutions may provide them with an education that is the best possible in the circumstances, but nothing can compensate them for the lack of an adequate home.

It may of course be argued that all such evils can be avoided through the use of contraceptives. Dr. Ellis maintains that the much smaller rate of illegitimate children in England, compared with the rate of such children in Germany, is due to the wider adoption of methods for preventing conception, but when we hear that their number is rapidly increasing in Germany, in spite of the fact that contraceptives are used on a large scale in all classes we can by no means feel reassured that extra-matrimonial procreation will some day become an anachronism. Strictly speaking, however, the censure to which the unmarried mother is subject refers to something else than the birth of the child; this event is an impressive and conclusive testimony of an act which itself is considered degrading.

The above quotations should suffice to establish the fact that immodesty and unchastity have a serious disturbing effect on married happiness, family ties and the proper development of children. Apart from these effects, conjugal infidelity breeds jealousy, one of the most destructive human passions, both individually and socially. There are people who try to minimise the effects of jealousy, and regarding it as a relic of primitive barbarity foresee its disappearance with the spread of education and enlightenment. Dr Westermarck himself is one of those who believe that with proper education this primitive feeling would disappear, but even he has been forced to admit that there is one kind of sexual and conjugal jealousy which is not traceable to primitive barbarity.

This kind of jealousy, he says, arises from the uniqueness of the relationship between two persons and the endeavour to stamp this uniqueness on the whole relationship, sexual and moral. If this is true, civilisation and culture may be expected to increase this kind of jealousy rather than refuse its proportion. Let us see what Dr. Westermarck himself has to say on this subject. He writes:

> *The jealousy of a man, particularly a civilized man, differs from that of a male animal, apart from any feeling of injured rights ownership or any other right. It is coloured by the nature of his love, It is accompanied with humiliation, because the loss of possession to which jealousy refers or the failure to obtain it, is of such a nature as carries with it a lowering of a man's self valuation. There may also be envy of what the other has obtained by depriving him of it. There may be fear of another man's offspring being born into the family. But there is one characteristic common to sexual jealousy in all its forms, namely, that it is an angry feeling aroused by loss, or fear of the loss, of the exclusive possession of an individual who is the object of one's sexual desire. It is impossible to suppose that the feeling of anger will ever disappear, however ugly and useless it may be. How violent ... it sometimes is among ourselves is illustrated by the fact that in analysing 188 murders committed by some persons in England, a prison commissioner recently found that the highest number, 46, were due to jealousy.*

But even when the infidelity of a husband or wife does not give rise to the angry feeling of jealousy it causes deep sorrow; and I think it can be demanded of a: spouse to consider whether he or she has a right to inflict such suffering upon the other party. Helene Stocker observes that the refined feeling of love implies instinctively an obligation to avoid, as far as possible, making the beloved person feel pain. It is true, as Bertrand Russell said, that love, is a generous emotion. But it is not generous to the person who has to suffer for his generosity towards another.

Communist-minded persons in our country who really desire to maintain their capitalistic way of living under the garb of communism have spread the false idea that Soviet communism does not attach any importance to the ideal of feminine chastity, because all such ideas and values are really the product of outmoded religious teaching. But a writer of the eminence of Havelock Ellis writes: 'There has been an erroneous idea abroad in the world that the Bolsheviks believe in sexual intemperance and promiscuity in sex relations, an idea no doubt based on the chaos which inevitably resulted at first when the new regime was so suddenly inaugurated. That disorder much distressed Lenin himself, who was entirely opposed to promiscuity and all mere physical indulgence, and held that the highest human elements entered the love relationship. It is Lenin's doctrine which now permeates Soviet society.'

The same writer tells us that unchaste women command little respect in Soviet society. It would almost seem that the polyandric woman whom, in the opinion of some Western persons, Soviet conditions favour, is there unduly depreciated.... Blonsky points out that the depreciation of polyandric women is shared by men, even the men who form temporary relationships with them, for men are inclined to look on such women as a convenient means of satisfying sexual needs, simply as substitutes for prostitution, and feel for them no high regard. That, Blonsky considers, is an influence making for the degradation of polyandric woman whose life courses are not usually, happy. It is unnecessary to add that the monoyandric woman, who is peculiarly adapted for motherhood and family life, will not be easily deprived of that career.

It is sometimes argued by those who wish to lead a life of unlimited sexual indulgence that there is no reason why a man's sexual desires should be tied down to one woman, why he should be put under an unnecessary obligation to bring up a family with all its cares and responsibilities. To such persons Havelock Ellis replies: 'It used sometimes to be asked: What has posterity done for me that I should do anything for posterity? The question was wrongly put. "Posterity" is only another name for mankind, and when we pose the question rightly, there can be no dispute about the answer. If we put aside the part that belongs to nature or God we owe everything to mankind. All that we are, all that we possess in civilization, we owe to the everlasting aspiration and struggle of mankind before us, and to the slow accumulation of knowledge and art on the topmost level on which we now stand. Our immense debt to mankind in the past can only be repaid to mankind in future. It is our privilege, if we do not regard it as our duty, to pass on in even finer shapes the great traditions which have been handed to us.'

Such passages enable us to understand why Islam insists on marriage both for men and women. Without married life involving the care and education of children, human personality can never find its full development and the great traditions of religion, culture and civilisation cannot be passed on to the future generation. It should also be remembered that children contribute as much to our education and personal self-development as we contribute to their proper growth and upbringing, so that it can be safely asserted that a childless man is necessarily a half-developed man. Then there is an additional consideration. If human individuality is a value of some importance, then it is not only necessary for every person to develop his individuality to the fullest extent possible but also to transmit it for the future use of mankind by bringing into the world fresh individuals who will retain at least a part of his individual characteristics.

It is possible, however, to admit the necessity of procreation and the importance of chastity as a cementing and healing bond in family life and yet maintain that by abolishing the family and evolving alternative institutions for the training and upbringing of children, we may allow a large amount of sexual latitude to men and women without any serious social disturbance. Such methods were tried in Soviet Russia for some time and, though the Soviet Republic has widely abandoned them, their echoes are still heard even in our backward country. It is true that if once we can get rid of the family and evolve other means for the preservation of human race and the education of children, modesty, chastity and all other such values lose their necessity. But what is the possibility of success in this attempt? Is it possible to abolish the family or is it rooted in our social nature? Let us deal with the question, as it has a very important bearing on the rights of women versus men.

There are three biological tendencies common to men and animals which form the foundation of family life and which cannot be overthrown now or in any conceivable future. They are the impulse of sexual attraction which leads to mating, the tendency to a close and enduring comradeship with the opposite sex and the instinctive impulse of mates to care for their offspring. Even an authority like Havelock Ellis admits that 'it is vain for even the most conservative of human beings to lament the failure of marriage, it is futile for even the most light-hearted of radicals to hope to get beyond it. The family is at the root of our bisexual constitution, and needs no formal institution. Again the same writer says, 'it has too often been forgotten that the family possesses this manysided flexibility and has in different ages and lands shown endless variation of shape in adjustment to varying social conditions.

Those who overlooked this essential fact have frequently cried out in rebellion against the whole conception of the family. Because they themselves have chanced to come out of an unhappy family life. Though the excellent qualities they have, notwithstanding often displaced, so far show that even an unhappy family life may have happy results they impetuously demand the complete abolition of the family. Havelock Ellis also replies to those who believe that the economic independence of woman achieved by her in modern society, her increasing participation in civil and industrial life and the growing use of contraceptives will in the end lead to the disintegration of the family. He does not believe in any such consummation and says in his essay on the 'Renovation of Family' that these factors, instead of abolishing family, may even strengthen and purify it, if they are well handled.

Institutions like the maternity home, the nursery school and the kindergarten which are increasingly taking over the functions of the home have encouraged a large number of people to believe that as this process goes on to its perfection, the family will soon become unnecessary as a social institution. Those who harbour such notions should not turn a blind eye to evils which are likely to arise from the disappearance of personal and intimately affectionate relations between the parents and children. Mechanical instruments involving depersonalisation of human relations are a source of danger to the growth of human personality. This aspect of the matter is well brought out by Margaret Mead in her book *Male and Female*. Writing about American mothers, she says: 'Birth in America is ideally, more and more frequently and actually in a hospital. This means that but for a few exceptional cases, the father is absent and the mother has been given over to the care of professionals, doctors and nurses. For months before the birth she has been preparing to leave her home and her husband, not for the home of her parents or her brothers, as in many primitive societies, but for a strange, segregated spot, where she and many other women unknown to her will live together, giving birth among strangers. When the baby is born, it is against the force of gravity, on a delivery table designed not to let the child's own weight assist the birth but rather to facilitate the ministrations of the obstetrician. Its first cry is often induced by a vigorous slap. The mother, deep under an anaesthetic dose, does not hear this cry, although recent research has suggested that the cry has a function in making her uterus contract. The infant is taken away to a row of cribs; its lips, ready for sucking, are left to press helplessly against each other. The primary bodily capabilities with which the child enters the world are initially unrewarded. It can suck, but no breast is given it; it can cry for help, but no one holds close and feeds it. Its body is wrapped completely in soft cloth, the first lesson in expecting cloth to intervene between one body and the next. The second lesson will come when it is taken to its mother, at the proper hour for its birth weight, neatly laid out on a moving table, and placed against her fully clothed body, with the carefully sterilised breast exposed just a few inches, and persuaded to suck.

This persuasion is often a grim business, the nurse knows how to take the baby, who very often is so exhausted with hunger that it no longer wants to eat, and, holding it by the scruff of the neck, puts it on the mother's breast. Whether it eats or not, it is supposed to be taken away again after the appointed number of minutes. The mother is left sometimes worried and enraged because the baby would not eat, having very doubtfully enjoyed in routinised cloth-developed experience. During the nine or ten days that follow, the mother handles her baby clothed, and only at regular hours. The father does not handle it at all. Breast-feeding is frequently abandoned altogether, and by the time the child goes home, the mother, if not the baby, has learned that contacts between mother and child have a certain form. The failure of milk, the failure of the baby to nurse, the obstetrical and paediatric pressure towards at least supplementary feeding are all natural enough in a setting where the new child is treated as if its health and well-being depended on the machine - like precision with which it is fed and on what it is fed. The mother learns impatience with her milk, which is too rich or too weak, too much or too little, pouring through nipples that are inverted or sore or otherwise unobliging. She can turn with some relief to the bottle and the formula, the reliable rubber nipple with a hole that can be enlarged with a pin, the graduated bottle into which just the right formula at just the right temperature can be measured. No recalcitrant individual unregulated body here, to endanger her baby's gain in weight, the chief criterion of its healthful existence. At once or in a few weeks, most American mothers reject their own bodies as a source of food for their children, and, in accepting the mechanical perfection of a bottle, reaffirm to themselves, and in the way they handle their babies, that the baby too will be much better the more it learns to use that beautifully mechanical bottle accurately on time, in the right amounts, the more it accepts an external rhythm, and abandons its peculiar rhythms that it brought into the world.

'For primary learning experience, that is, the physical prototype of sex relationship, a complementary relation between the body of the mother and the body of the child is substituted by a relation between the child and an object, an object, that imitates the breast but which is not handled as either part of the mother or part of the body. If the mother holds the baby as she gives it the bottle in most instances it becomes an implement, an extension of her hand so that it holds food, rather than an extension of her breast. At what age the child distinguishes the exact difference between a glass bottle and a rubber nipple, loose in space, and a human breast, we do not know, but the mother experiences the difference from the state, and her experience is available to the child, in her voice, in her hands, in the very tempo of her being. She is not giving the child herself; she is faithfully, efficiently providing the child with a bottle, external to both of them substituting for a direct relationship mediated by an object.'

This ironic description of an ideal delivery in an ideal hospital shows how the substitution of mechanical inventions for direct human contacts retards the growth and mars the personality of the child. Evidence is not lacking to prove that institutional care of children is a poor substitute for home life. A White House Conference on Child Health and Protection held in America in 1930 declared that 'institutional care for the most part has produced uninspired individuals poorly adjusted to the outside world.' Dr. Nimkoff writes: 'We can show that normal family life is indispensable to the proper development of the child's personality.' Floyd Dell writes: 'Institutional life at its best has been notoriously drab and barren in comparison with ordinary family life. Institutional life has been found to fail in developing individual powers and in furnishing incentives for growing up. It has characteristically turned out spiritless creatures who do not know how to get along in the outside world. The best modern institutions for children now model themselves upon the parental home and try to give what it should give. Even at their best, however, these institutions, when they replace the private, home entirely, are regarded as makeshifts, as poor substitutes for a real home with real parents. And real home and real parents are known to be so important to the child's development that it is more and more the practice that only as a last resort are homes broken up and children taken from parents.'

After giving an account of the methods tried by Soviet Russia for providing alternate education to children and the results experienced, Dr. Westermarck says in his book, The Failure of Marriage in Western Civilisation:

> *Many facts thus support the general belief that there is no adequate substitute for the beneficial influence which parents as a rule exercise upon their children, that the love*

of the parents towards the child is one of the most essential features, if the child's moral and emotional development is to proceed harmoniously.

In these circumstances I can find no reason to suppose that it could be in the interests of the state in the future to break up the family. The Bolsheviks' suspicious attitude towards it is due to the view that private property has always served as a cementing bond in the family; and to demolish private property is the object of the most feverish efforts of the new society. It is considered to be of great importance that the mentality of the Russian youth should be largely moulded by agencies outside the home, away from the family circle; in the kindergartens and schools it is always made to feel that the supreme aim of life is the promotion of the purposes of the new society. Yet, though the rulers of Russia regard the family as a menace to their ultimate designs, they find it at the present stage of readjustment indispensable to the maintenance of social stability. But they have obviously underrated its vitality. The persistence of the family does not depend upon the preservation of private property. Its safest guarantee is the love of man and woman for each other and for their children, and the Bolsheviks are even said to assure themselves that this bond will gain in firmness when property has passed from private to social control.

In conclusion, Dr. Westermarck says:

So far as I can see, then, there is every reason to believe that the unity of sexual and spiritual elements, in sexual love, leading to a more or less durable community of life in a common home, and the desire for and love of offspring are factors which will remain lasting obstacles to the extinction of marriage and the collapse of the family, because they are too deeply rooted in human nature to fade away, and can find adequate satisfaction only in some form of marriage and the family founded upon it.

We thus find that the family, as the basic unit of social organisation, is likely to outlast the forces tending to destroy it. A stable family life is necessary not only in the interests of society, not only for the happiness and moral development of the husband and the wife, but also for the proper growth and development of future generations. Conditions and forces which tend to shake the stability of the family should be countered and removed in the interests of the society and the individual. If these basic facts are admitted, chastity becomes a value of the highest social importance to be safeguarded at all costs. And from this conception and pattern of family life, the mutual rights and obligations of men and women can be determined with more scientific precision and greater justice than from an abstract conception of equality which does not keep in view the practical requirements of family organisation. Islam has built its system of rights and obligations for men and women not on a vague and abstract conception of sex equality but on a doctrine of basic sex equality qualified by actual biological sex differences and the practical needs of a stable family organisation. With this background in view, we proceed to discuss the rights and obligations of the female sex as defined by Islam.

In order to ensure a happy home and a really stable family life, Islam has assigned to marriage the status of a contract dissoluble if ,either party develops grievances against the other leading to a final and irrevocable break in their mutual relations. It is not as in Christianity, a sacrament indissoluble except by a difficult process and under very extraordinary circumstances. This may appear, at first sight, to be a factor operating against family stability, but in fact it is designed to safeguard it. There is really no virtue in keeping two persons tied together to save appearances, when their relations have deteriorated beyond all hope of reconciliation. An unhappy marriage resulting in interminable quarrels fails to realise the primary object of the union which brought the partners together, besides increasing the probability of illegal sexual relations outside marriage. It also tells upon the health and education of children. It is, therefore better both socially and morally that the husband and the wife should be allowed to part with each other if the breaking point has been reached in their mutual relations. Therefore, marriage in Islam is not indissoluble but a kind of contract in which specific rights and obligations may be undertaken besides those already implied in marriage. These rights are justifiable in a court of law. It is open both to the husband and the wife to enter into agreement prior to marriage on matters which they consider important for the regulation of their future relations. Such agreements shall be parts of the marriage contract and adjudicable in law-courts, provided they are not repugnant to the basic rights and obligations of husband and wife as stated by Islam. Thus, Umar, the Second Caliph, says: 'When a person marries a woman and the woman stipulates that she would not be taken out of the town or city of her residence, it is necessary for the husband to abide by the stipulation' (Tirmidhi, p. 385). Imam Ahmad and Imam Shafii also hold the same opinion. But Ali, the Fourth Caliph, says:,' The conditions laid down by God take precedence over the, conditions set by man,' which means that, in his opinion, such a condition is repugnant to the basic terms of marriage. Sufyan Thabri and other scholars of Kufah also hold the same opinion. Whatever the differences among the scholars on this point, they relate to the point whether this particular stipulation is or is not repugnant to the basic terms of marriage contract as defined by Islam. There is no disagreement on the point whether a woman can insist on inserting terms of her own in the marriage contract. All are unanimous that she holds this right. Thus, the author of *Nail al-Autar* (Pt. VII, p. 64) says: 'The wife can lay down conditions prior to marriage relating to her way of living, her food, house and dress, according to the social status of the husband and that her just rights shall not be whittled. Similarly, the husband can lay down these conditions: that the wife shall not go out from home without his permission, that she shall not refuse sexual intercourse with him and shall not use his property and possessions except by his permission.'

Just as a man can stipulate that his wife shall not go out except by his permission, it is open to the woman to insist that she shall not be prevented from going out of her home on suitable occasions or for her economic or social needs, so long as this action does not disturb the work of her husband or the proper upbringing of the children. All these matters come within the scope of the marriage agreement, but since some of them are not easily justifiable, much depends on the actual relations of the husband and the wife after marriage and their mutual understanding. All these things show that the wife does not lose, under Islam, her separate legal personality, but retains full possession of it. She can sue her husband in a law-court if the implied or express terms of the marriage contract are violated by the husband. This is in direct contrast to the position of woman under Christianity. Professor Mansfield, writing in his book, *The Legal Rights, Liabilities and Duties of Women*, states: 'The first great principle of Scripture, the unity of husband and wife, is repeated by the law. They are, in law, one person. Upon it, as observed by Blackstone, depend nearly all the legal rights, duties and disabilities acquired by marriage.' The English Common Law, as interpreted by Blackstone, whose commentaries governed actual legal decisions both in England and America for a very long period, assigned the same position to a wife in relation to her husband. It was only with the greatest difficulty and by resorting to parliament any legislation or equity courts that the wife was able to secure a few rights over against her husband. From a strictly legal viewpoint, the position of women among the Muslims has been really enviable when compared to that of their counterparts in the Western countries.

In order to safeguard the economic position of women after the marriage, Islam has made it legally obligatory on the husband to pay her a reasonable amount as dower. The amount to be fixed, as dower depends on the agreement between the two parties, but, in any case, the object is to strengthen the financial position of the wife, so that she is not prevented, for lack of money, from defending her rights. The Quran says:

> *And give women their dowries as a free gift, but if they themselves be pleased to give up to you a portion of it, then eat it with enjoyment and with wholesome result. (iv. 4)*
>
> *And if you wish to have (one) wife in the place of another and you have given one of them a heap of gold (as dowry) take not anything from her; would you take it by slandering (her) and (doing her) manifest wrong? (iv. 20)*

No marriage can be regarded as legally valid, according to Islam, for which dowry has not been stipulated. If the amount of dowry is not fixed, the wife is entitled to proper dowry (*mehr-i-mithl*), even if the marriage was contracted on the express condition that she should not claim any dowry. In determining what is 'proper' dowry, regard is to be had to the amount of dower settled upon other female members of her father's family such as her father's sisters. The following tradition of the Prophet stresses the importance attached to dowry in Islam:

> *Ibn Umar reported that the Prophet of, Allah forbade shighar and shighar is a man's giving his daughter in marriage on condition that another would give his daughter in marriage to him and that there should be no dowry between them.*

Another tradition collected by Abu Daud and Nasai says:

> *Alqamah b. Masud reported that he was asked about a man who married a woman but did not fix any dowry for her, nor had he any intercourse with her till he died. Ibn Masud told her: Fix the equivalent dowries of his women, neither less nor more. And there is the period of waiting for her and there is her share of inheritance for her (from her husband's property), then Maqal b. Sinan got up and said: 'The Messenger of Allah decreed in case of Barwaah bint Washiq (a woman belonging to us) just as you have decreed.'*

Regarding the amount of dowry to be fixed, Islam has given a wide, latitude to men and women. It can be as low as possible or as high as the parties may desire. Ibn Majah and Tirmidhi report from Amir ibn Rabia that a woman belonging to the tribe of Banu Fazarah married a man for a pair of shoes. The Prophet asked her whether she was really happy over that much dowry. She replied in the affirmative, whereupon the Prophet made no objection.

> *According to Abu al-Jafar, it was the opinion of Umar, the Second Caliph, that the dowry should not be fixed at a very high rate, for if this had been a point of honour and pleasing in the sight of God, the Prophet too would have acted accordingly, but he did not fix more than a hundred and twenty-five dirhams of dowry for his wives and daughters (Tirmidhi, p. 132). Umar's opinion was, however, challenged by a woman who said: Umar, you have no right to impose such restrictions, because the Holy Quran says that men should not take back anything from their wives if they intend to divorce them, even if they have given them a heap of gold. This shows that God allows even a very high rate of dowry. Umar replied to her saying that she was right and that he had made a mistake himself.*
>
> *(Nafl-al-Autar by Shaukani).*

The amount of dower may be fixed either before or at the time of marriage or after marriage, and can be increased after marriage. A contract of dower can be made by a father on behalf of his son, if the latter is a minor. The wife may remit the whole or part of dower. Such remission is valid though made without consideration. If the dower is not paid, the wife and, after her death, her heirs may sue for it. The wife may refuse to live with her husband and admit him to sexual intercourse so long as the dower remains unpaid. If the husband sues her for the restitution of conjugal rights, before sexual intercourse has taken place, non-payment of dower is a complete defence to the suit, and the suit will be dismissed. If the suit is brought after sexual intercourse has taken place with her free consent, the court can issue a decree for restitution conditional on payment of the dower, to the extent only of a share of the dower debt proportionate to his share of the estate. When a widow is in actual possession of the property of her deceased husband, she is entitled as against the other heirs of her husband and as against the creditors of her husband, to retain possession of the property until her dower is satisfied. The fact that a widow is in possession of her husband's property under a claim for her dower is no bar to a suit against the other heirs of her husband to recover the dower debt, but she must in such a suit offer, to give up possession of the property.

Further, to secure a strong economic position for women, Islam has given them full property rights. A daughter gets half the share of property allotted to the son, half of the entire property of her father if there is no other son or daughter; and if there is more than one daughter but no sons, the daughters share among them equally two-thirds of the entire property. A widow is entitled to one eighth of the property left by her husband, but if there are no children by the marriage, she receives one-sixth. No distinction is made by Islam between movable and immovable property. The whole, including both kinds, is distributed to the heirs in their fixed proportions. It may be said that by giving the daughter half the share of a son, Islam has let down the position of women, but it should not be forgotten that a woman may also receive dower and property from her husband in which case her inequality is more than compensated for. Moreover, there is no obligation on a wife to sustain her husband economically, while the husband is under a legal obligation to provide for his wife. Thus, the inequality of women in the share of inheritance is matched by a corresponding increase in the economic burden of men, which makes the two sexes equal in respect of their economic rights.

One of the most essential factors of a happy marriage is the right of free choice by either party. Islam has given this right both to men and women. The Prophet insisted on a number of occasions that a person wishing to marry a woman should have a look at her before finally consenting to marriage. Thus, Abu Hurairah reports: 'A man came to the Prophet and said, "I intend to marry a woman of the Ansar." He said, "Have a look at her, because sometimes there is something defective in the eyes of the Ansar." Jabir reports that the Prophet said: 'When one of you seeks a woman in marriage and then if he is able to have a look at one he wishes to marry, let him do so' (Abu Daud). Mughira b. Shubah reports: 'I sought a woman in marriage. The Holy Prophet asked if I had seen her. "No," said I. He said: "Then look at her, because it is more proper that love should be cemented between you."

The jurists agree that this right to have a look at the prospective partner is equally eligible for the members of the female sex. According to Imam Abu Hanifah, it is lawful to have a sight of the bride and the bridegroom. Imam Malik holds that it is lawful with the permission of the bride. Imam Shafii and Imam Ahmad are of the opinion that a look at the prospective husband or wife is lawful with or without the permission of the other. Freedom of choosing one's partner for life has been extended both to men and women. No marriage in Islam can be valid without the consent of either partner. According to a report from Abu Hurairah, the Prophet said: 'A previously married woman shall not be married till she gives her consent, nor a virgin be married till her consent is sought.' They asked: 'How shall her permission be known. He said: 'If she remains silent.' A report from Ibn Abbas, collected by Muslim, states that the Prophet said: 'A previously married woman is more a guardian for herself than her guardian and a virgin should be asked permission about herself, and her permission is her silence.' Abu Hurairah further reports that the Prophet said: 'A grown-up girl shall be asked permission about herself. If she is silent, it is her permission; and if she declines, there shall be no compulsion on her.'

The presence of two witnesses is necessary to make a marriage valid, because open declaration of marriage constitutes its soul and essence. According to a tradition of Tirmidhi reported by Ibn Abbas, the Prophet declared: 'Those women are adulteresses who marry themselves without the presence of witnesses! Umar was once told that a certain marriage had been performed with one witness only. He said that such a marriage amounted to clandestine relationship which was illegal. If he had knowledge of it beforehand, he would have dealt stern punishment to either party.

Guardianship is regarded by some as necessary for the marriage of a woman. There are some traditions in which the presence of a guardian has been made an essential condition precedent to the marriage of a girl. Thus, Bukhari gives a tradition stating: 'There is no marriage without a guardian.' This is probably meant only for minor girls. Imam Abu Hanirah, the greatest and the most popular jurist of Islam, holds that a marriage, whether of a widow or a grown-up virgin, is permissible even without a guardian. Imam Shafii's and Imam Malik, however, hold that guardianship is necessary for the marriage of a woman. As marriage depends essentially upon the choice of a woman, the presence of a guardian, even if not required by law, can be regarded necessary only in the sense that he undertakes to watch the interests of the minor or the grownup girl who is to be married and to see that she is not disadvantaged by reason of sex in the settlement of the terms on which marriage is contracted. This interpretation is supported by a tradition contained in Kitab at Nikah of the collection made by Tirmidhi. The tradition states: Aishah said, the Prophet of God declared: 'Marriage of a woman is invalid without there being a guardian.' He repeated this three times and said that if the husband of such a woman had sexual intercourse with her, she should receive her dower and if, after the performance of the marriage, the two quarrel, then the ruler of the Muslims is the guardian of the woman who has no other guardian. The reference here to the recovery of dowry and the possibility of quarrel as well as recognition of the right of the State to take up the functions of a guardian all point to the fact that the Prophet had in mind the necessity of safeguarding the interests of women by making the presence of a guardian essential. In a society which, until the advent of Islam, had been ridden by sex inequality and where women had been treated as mere chattel, it was always possible, despite the teachings of Islam, that a single woman without a guardian or a patron should find herself at a disadvantage in the settlement of marriage terms. So the Prophet deemed it essential that, if there be no guardian for a woman, the State should become her guardian with a view to ensuring equality and justice at the time of marriage contract and thereafter. No other interpretation is possible in view of the fact that the final say in all matters has been accorded to women themselves and not to their guardians, a fact which is attested by the authentic traditions of the Prophet himself.

That the woman who contracts a marriage, and not her father or guardian has the final choice in the matter, is proved by the following traditions which extend to women the right to repudiate a marriage forced on them through pressure, direct or indirect:

> *Ibn Abbas reported that a virgin grown-up girl came to the Prophet of Allah and narrated that her father had given her in marriage to a person whom she disliked. The Prophet gave her option.* *(Abu Daud)*

Again:

> *Khansa b. Khidham reported that her father gave her in marriage, after, she became a widow. She disliked it and came to the Prophet. He annulled the marriage.*
> *(Bukhari)*

A very significant' report which throws a flood of light on the complete liberty of choice and repudiation extended to women by Islam in the matter of their marriage is found in the traditions collected by Nasai. The reporter is no less a person than Aishah, the wife of the Prophet. She says, 'A girl came and stated that her father had given her in marriage to his nephew and she disliked him. I told her to wait till the Prophet arrived. When the Prophet came, I told him the full story of the girl. He at once sent for the father of the girl and inquired of him whether the facts stated were true, after which he told the girl that she was at liberty to choose or repudiate her husband. The girl replied saying that she chose to retain her marriage, And that she wanted only to know whether women had any rights in the matter.' Another tradition from the collection made by Ibn Majah states: 'Ibn' Umar says: Uthman b. Mazun left behind a young daughter. My uncle, Qudamah, married her to me, and did not even consult her. When the girl came to know of this, she disliked this marriage and wished to marry Mughira b. Shubah. So she was married to Mughira.'

All these traditions furnish conclusive proof that a girl is as free in Islam as a boy to choose or repudiate her partner and that the Prophet's insistence on there being a guardian before a woman can be married was intended to safeguard her position and rights in a society which was not yet completely free from the dominance of the male sex and in which a lonely woman ran a chance of being outwitted by clever men and left without the necessary protection.

The legal equality of men and women in Islam is a fact which has never been in dispute among the Muslims. There is no legal right belonging to man for which a corresponding female right cannot be cited. But the ideal of sex equality or any other kind of equality cannot be wholly given effect to by the law. Specially is this true of the relations between husband and wife which in their very nature refuse to be covered and guided wholly by legal injunctions and principles. Real equality between the sexes depends much more on social opinion and national traditions than on legal commands. Even in Western countries where the claim for complete equality between the two sexes has been pressed to extremes, formidable difficulties have been experienced by legislators to translate the ideal into the actual. Mary Beard, after giving a detailed account of the attempts made in America to give equal property rights to men and women, mentions a long list of legislative failures to give effect to the principle of equality. The following extract from her book, *Woman as Force in History*, will give the reader an idea of the intricate and evasive nature of the ideal of sex equality. Writing about the legislative changes made in America with respect to women's property rights, she says:

A Married Women's Property Act was, therefore, simple in principle. But in application the terms of such an Act were difficult to draw. Despite the theory of independence and equality which was supposed to furnish guidance in drafting the Act, law reformers and lawmakers actually confronted a paradox: The wife is to be treated as if she is a single woman in respect of her property, but in marital relations she has obligations not assumed by single women and is no more of a single person than her husband is; for both are entangled in a network of duties not imposed on single persons. Is the wife free to use her property as she pleased while the husband is in straits to support her and their children? In what, if any, circumstances is the wife to be under obligation to support the family in part or whole? Is the owner of the home, whether husband or wife, to be allowed to sell it at will, without the consent of the other party to the marriage contract, and turn the family out of it? These and a hundred other questions taxed the adroitness of law-makers and were answered by men and women in many different ways. No mere declaration of equality could dispose of them in a few words. At no time or place did it prove possible to write one Married Women's Property Bill which could settle all these questions.

The same writer goes on to say:

In their efforts to clear away anachronisms and to bring the law abreast the advance in civilization, legislators did not, indeed could not, treat a man and a woman who had chosen to marry and bring children into the world as if they were perfectly free and entitled to be wholly whimsical with their respective properties and earnings, without regard for obligations due to each other. Nor could legislators overlook the rights of their children, their creditors and their more or less distant relatives. All lawmakers recognized the fact that husband and wife had to surrender some freedom by virtue of their very marriage contract. How much and what kinds of freedom? ... On the point of how to realize the ideal of equality, men differed and women differed and provisions of law running into hundreds of pages reflected their doubts, uncertainties and aspirations.

Furthermore, after statutes were enacted, the application of the principles in them to human controversies which arose in law and equity, led to a positive risk of variations. The more general the principles, the more difficult it was for men and women as litigants and for courts as tribunals of adjudication to agree on the meaning of principles as governing concrete cases. Especially is this true of novel cases not specifically contemplated or provided for in the written laws. And novel cases were and are perennial and striking features of life and law.

How far Married Women's Property Acts and kindred legislation fell short of covering in concrete anticipation the numerous problems that arose under them is indicated by the following types of questions raised and adjudicated in various jurisdictions of the United States after the process of abolishing common-law doctrines had been started. In order that the readers may decide for themselves, if they can, how these questions should have been answered under the theory of separate property rights and equality, the answers given to these questions by the judges in affirmative opinions, negative opinions, and diversities of opinions, are left to the readers' imagination.

Does the Married Women's Property Act relieve a husband of obligation to support his wife, even if he has become bankrupt and she is earning money?

If the wife leaves the husband without good reasons and returns home voluntarily at a later date, is the husband to pay the bills which she had incurred for her support during her absence?

Can the wife lawfully waive the husband's liability to support her with a view to helping him pay his debts to creditors?

If the husband employs his wife at wages otherwise payable to someone else, may she be deprived of the money or the property in which it is invested on the ground that it is actually her husband's?

May the wife take her separate property, enter business, and, without his consent, compete with her husband's who is legally liable for her support?

Where under a new statute the husband is forbidden to use even gentle force to restrain his wife, may he lawfully restrain her from committing a crime?

If the husband carries on a gambling business in his wife's house, may she be liable for his crimes committed therein?

There are a thousand other questions likely to arise in the married state to show the limitations of law in governing husband and wife relations. Even if perfection in legislative acts were possible and the marital relations of men and women could be placed on a footing of full equality, that would not automatically ensure actual equality in day-to-day relations. Human relations in general and marital relations in particular are governed and regulated far more by customs, traditions and the spiritual and moral outlook of human beings than by legal enactments and commands of the sovereign. Law alone is an insufficient guide and measures in gauging the extent to which a civilisation gives effect to the ideal of sex equality. To understand in full the attitude of a community towards the relations between the two sexes, we must look to its general moral teachings, as distinguished from legal provisions. Let us judge Islam from this angle and see how far it adds to the social dignity of women and ensures their equality in its social precepts, moral principles and spiritual directions.

In stating the general principles according to which marital relations should be regulated, the Quran had laid particular emphasis on love and compassion as an essential ingredient of married life:

> *And one of His signs is that He created mates for you from among yourselves that you may find quiet of mind in them and He put between you love and compassion. (xxx. 21)*

With a view to dispelling the false idea that men are inherently superior to women, the Quran emphasises that differences of race, tribe, sex and nationality do not disturb the fundamental equality of mankind:

> *O you men! surely We have created you male and female and made you tribes and families that you may know each other; surely the most honourable of you with Allah is the one among you most careful (of his duty). (xlix. 13)*

The same breadth of outlook is reflected in those verses of the Holy Quran which deal with the more concrete problems arising out of marital life. In regard to the treatment of wives whom their husbands wish to divorce, the Quran says:

> *O believers! it is not lawful for you that you should take women as heritage against their will and do not straiten them in order to take from them a part of what you have given them, unless they are guilty of manifest indecency; and treat them kindly; then if you hate them, it may be that you dislike a thing while Allah has placed abundant good in it. (iv. 19)*

> *But when you divorce women, and the time for sending them away is come, either retain them with generosity, or put them away with generosity, but retain not them by constraint so as to be unjust towards them He who doth so, doth in fact injure himself. (ii. 231)*

Generosity in the relations between husband and wife has been emphasised again and again:

> *But if you divorce them before consummation and have already settled a dowry on them, ye shall give them half of what ye have settled, unless they relinquish or he should relinquish in whose hands is the marriage tie; and it is nearer to piety that you should relinquish; and do not forget to be generous between yourselves: surely Allah sees what you do.* (ii. 237)

After a woman has been divorced, no motive remains for the husband to treat her kindly, but the Quran insists on kindly and generous treatment so long as there subsists the weakest tie among the partners:

> *Lodge them where you lodge according to your, means, and do not injure them in order that you may straiten them; and if they are pregnant, spend on them until they lay down their burden; then if they suckle for you, give them their recompense; and consult among yourselves and act generously, and if you disagree, another woman shall suckle for him.*
>
> *Let him who has abundance spend out of his abundance, and whoever has his means of subsistence straitened to him, let him spend out of that which Allah has given him. Allah does not lay on any soul a burden except to the extent to which He has granted it.* (lxv. 6-7)

The same generosity towards women is enjoined by the Prophet in his traditions. A report from Abu Hurairah says: 'No believer should be angry towards his wife. If some of her qualities are displeasing, there will be many other qualities worth appreciation' (Nail al-Autar, p. 125). Aishah, the wife of the Prophet, reports: The Prophet of God said: 'The best of you is he who is good to his wife' (Tirmidhi). On the occasion of his last pilgrimage, the Prophet advised the Muslims to treat their women kindly and added: 'You have no more rights against them except that if they are guilty of manifest lewdness, you can ask them to leave your beds and strike them softly; if they improve their conduct, do not leave them helpless, because there are some rights for you over against them and some rights for them over against you. The duty of a woman is that she should not allow anyone to enter your house whom you dislike, nor spoil the bed which is your preserve and the duty of a man is that he should feed, clothe and treat his wife generously' (ibid.). According to a report from Abdullah b. Umar, the Prophet declared: 'The whole world is a thing to be made use of and the best thing in the world is a virtuous wife' (Muslim). On his deathbed, the Prophet's last words related to the duty of offering prayers and safeguarding the rights of women and, slaves. About women he said: 'Women are like prisoners in your hands and you have taken them on trust from God and the word of God has made their private parts lawful for you; so be careful towards the treatment of women.' On another occasion the Prophet is reported to have declared: 'The Angel of God advised me so many times about women that I became convinced that it is not lawful for a man to divorce his wife, except when she commits adultery' (Irshad al-Muhtaj, Huquq al-Azwaj). A report from Bahz b. Hakim states: 'I inquired of the Prophet about his teaching in respect of women. He replied: "Feed them as you feed yourselves, clothe them as you clothe yourselves and do not beat or scold them' (Kanz al-Unimal). According to Aishah, the Prophet's wife, he said about women: 'They are like pleasing roses,' meaning thereby that their grace and tenderness deserve special regard from men (ibid.). In regard to domestic duties, Islam has relieved women of all manual drudgery.

According to strict Islamic injunctions, it is not obligatory for a woman to cook the food for her husband or children, or to wash their clothes or even to suckle the infants. A woman may refuse to do any or all of these things without this being made a ground of legal complaint against her. If she undertakes these duties out of her regard for the husband, it is an act of sheer grace. It is reported that a man once came to Umar, the Second Caliph, with the intention of bringing to his notice certain complaints which he had against his wife. When he reached the door of Umar's, house, he heard the Caliph's wife railing against him. Hearing this he went back as he thought that the Caliph was himself in the same predicament and could, therefore, be hardly expected to set matters right for him. Umar, coming out of his house, saw the person going back. So he called him out and inquired as to the purpose which had brought him to his house. He said that he had come to him with some complaints against his wife, but turned back on finding that the Caliph himself was subject to the same treatment from his wife. Umar said to him that he patiently bore the excesses of his wife, because she had certain rights against him. 'Is it not true that she cooks my food, washes my clothes and suckles my children, thus relieving me of the necessity of employing a cook, a washerman and a nurse, although she is not in the slightest degree responsible for any of these duties? Not only that,

I enjoy peace of mind on amount of her and I am protected from committing the sin of adultery. In view of all these advantages, I put up with her excesses. You should also do the same.'

In regard to the authority of men and women in their respective spheres, the following tradition of the Prophet shows the status enjoyed by women under Islam:

> *Man is the ruler in his home. He will be held responsible for the conduct of his dependents, and woman is the ruler in her husband's home. She will also be held responsible for the conduct of her dependents.* *(Bukhari)*

This tradition makes the wife co-equal of her husband in home affairs. She is as much responsible for the conduct of domestic affairs; as the husband. Only in larger matters affecting, the total welfare of the family, the husband is given a degree of superiority, since two coordinate authorities with equal powers are likely to lead to clashes and conflicts such as may destroy the balance and poise of family life.

A Social Bond : Marriage in Islam is regarded as a strong bond and a total commitment to life, to society and to being a respectable human. It is a promise that the married couple make to one another and to God. This undertaking on the part of the married partners would allow them to find mutual fulfilment and self-realisation, love and peace, comfort and hope. This is because marriage in Islam is essentially a righteous act and an act of complete devotion. As such, celibacy is discouraged not only for men, but for women as well. This is in consideration of the fact that their needs are equally legitimate and valid.

Islam views marriage as a natural course for women in the same way as it is for men, and probably even more so, in view of the fact that marriage guarantees women some form of economic security. It must be stressed here that this benefit for women is in no way an indication that marriage in Islam is sheer economic transaction. Indeed, the economic factor is the least aspect of the whole enterprise; the emphasis has been always on the religious qualities of the spouses.

From the collective point of view the most significant benefit is of course procreation, but not just the physical perpetuation of the human race; rather, the institution of marriage ensures that this procreative function will be both sanctified and orderly, not vulgar and chaotic. From the specifically religious point of view, having children entails the following: the realisation of God's desire, the fulfilment of the Prophet's call to marry and increase his followers' number; gaining the fruit of a child's prayer. Muslims believe that when parents die and leave a child, his prayer would benefit the dead parents. However, if the child dies before his parents, he would make intercession on his parents' behalf. Fulfilling one's sexual desire is another important aspect of marriage. Marriage, from the Islamic viewpoint, helps control sexual passion and channel it in the right direction. Also, it functions as a shield against committing adultery and fornication, both of which are forbidden in Islam. Marriage, moreover, brings peace and tranquillity of spirit and implants love and compassion between the married partners. These are great supports for one's worship of God. Intimacy between spouses is viewed as catalyst for the development of their souls.

In other words, the intimate relationship that develops between a husband and wife is crucial for relieving the heart from its burdens and thus enables the mind to better focus on accomplishing the Divine requirements. Al-Ghazzali beautifully explains this point in the following account: 'The third benefit of marriage is that the heart finds ease through intimacy with women, because of sitting and joking with them. This ease then becomes the cause of an increase in desire for worship. For diligence in worship brings weariness, and the heart contracts. But ease acquired in this way brings back the heart's strength. Ali said, 'Do not remove rest and ease completely from the hearts, lest they become blind'. It sometimes happened that the Prophet was overcome by such tremendous unveilings that his bodily frame was not able to tolerate it.

The marital link helps the partners to work together and cooperate amicably in the management of the domestic affairs of their house; hence sufficient time could be spared to meet the Divine commandments. Therefore, the Prophet is reported to have advised his followers to choose the right spouses who would help them attain Divine blessings. Marriage, in addition, is seen as an opportunity to develop for oneself a good and sound character as a result of the added family responsibility which both spouses have to endure during their married life. Hence, success in carrying out family commitments (which are equally regarded as divine duties) would ensure Divine reward. The Prophet said 'A man will be rewarded for what he spends on his wife, even for putting a morsel of food into her mouth'.

Also, 'Whoever performs his prayers correctly, and spends on his children in spite of his modest means, and does not speak ill against others, will be in paradise as close to me as these [two fingers of mine]'. Finally, marriage ensures social stability and a dignified form of living for both partners (the husband and the wife), probably even more for women since it guarantees their rights both as wives as well as mothers (of course alongside their fights as individuals).

Since Islam takes marriage seriously, its concern has been always to ensure that the marriage bond stays relatively stable and durable. To achieve these goals, it has laid down certain rules and regulations to meet these objectives. First, the couple have to be of proper marriageable age; also, there should be no discrepancy between their ages. It must be stressed that the claim by some scholars that the groom has to be always senior in age so as to ensure a healthy marriage relationship has no religious grounds and in practical terms does not make any sense. In fact, it contradicts the practice of the Prophet, two of whose wives (Khadijah and Sauda) happened to be older than him; despite this, the record shows that they lived in peace and harmony.

Second, there should be a degree of compatibility between the two partners in terms of social status, educational standards and physical attraction (again the claim by some scholars that the bride has to be more beautiful and more attractive than her groom is a fallacy). Third, the dowry of the bride should be of a reasonable level: neither too high, which could cause hardship for both of them, nor too low which might give the impression that the bride is of no worth. The dowry which is in its essence a gift from the groom to the bride-should be affordable and manageable so as to ensure satisfaction and happiness on both sides. Fourth, the consent of the couple is crucial for the stability and durability of the marriage. Both have to enter into the wedlock with free will and without coercion.

Compelling the couple (or even just one of them) to contract an unsatisfactory union would be detrimental to the interest of both sides and could lead to a disastrous end. Fifth, the prospective partners have to be pious and of good moral conduct. Both have to be kind, sympathetic, considerate, patient and loving, caring to one another; this encourages peace and harmony in domestic life. Sixth, the two parties have to declare, from the beginning, their intentions to keep the marital bond as permanent as humanly possible. This commitment requires that the marriage contract should be free of any hidden agenda such as casual or temporary unions. Islam is against all marriages that have been described as experimental, casual and temporary. In a clear statement, the Prophet outrightly denounced those men and women who enjoy the frequent change of marital partners and warned against their unacceptable behaviour. Having stated the importance Islam lays on the permanency of marriage, it is essential to stress that in Islam there is no concept of 'indissoluble' marriage.

Although Islam endeavours to keep the marital link stable and intact, this does not mean that the wedlock cannot be brought to an end if there are compelling circumstances. Indeed, Islam recognises that if the marriage is not working, it is in the interest of both sides to terminate it on good terms. Hence, divorce in Islam is a legitimate act, although it is discouraged by the Prophet. Islam, as we know, encourages both men and women to marry. Just like a man, a Muslim woman (virgin or non-virgin) has the freedom to propose to a man of her liking, either orally or in writing (I wonder how many Muslim women these days would dare to initiate an oral proposal, let alone put it in writing!).

The Muslim woman has the freedom of marital choice: she is at liberty to choose her prospective husband, look at him and get to know him without coercion on the part of the father or other relatives. If force or pressure takes place, she has the right to appeal to the court to redress the wrong. Her consent is essential for the validity of the marriage contract. The Prophet is reported to have made the following statements: 'A previously married woman shall not be married till she gives her consent, nor should a virgin be married till her consent is sought'. 'A previously married woman is more a guardian for herself than her guardian, and a virgin should be asked permission about herself, and her permission is her silence'. 'A grown-up girl shall be asked permission about herself. If she is silent, it is her permission; and if she declines, there shall be no compulsion on her'.

According to Islam, a divorced or widowed woman has the right to remarry without any shame or denunciation. In fact, the Quran allows the betrothal of a divorced or widowed woman even during her period of transition (idda). 'It shall be no offence for you openly to propose marriage indirectly to such women or to cherish them in your hearts. Allah knows that you will remember them. Do not arrange to meet them in secret and, if you do, speak to them honourably. But you shall not consummate the marriage before the end of their waiting period. Know that Allah has knowledge of all your thoughts. Therefore take heed and bear in mind that Allah is forgiving and merciful'.

Neither age nor previous marriage would impede a woman from contracting perfect matches. Many are the examples which can be cited from the early Muslim community during which women were, very often, re-married after they were divorced or widowed, and this was done without stigma or discredit. Take, for instance, Umm-Kulthum bint Uqba, an early convert from Mecca. She emigrated to Medina in defiance of her family, who tried to force her to return to Mecca, but to no avail. She stayed in Medina and married her first husband, Zaid bin Harith. When Zaid was killed in one of the battles she contracted a second marriage with Zubayr bin al-Awwam. Zubayr was rough with her, so she decided to part with him. After the separation, she married Abdul Rahman bin Auf, her third husband, and bore him two sons.

Upon Abdul Rahman's death, Umme Kulthum once more contracted herself into marriage, to her fourth and final husband, this time with the conqueror of Egypt, Amr ibn al-As. She stayed with him until she passed away. Atika bint Zaid is another good example. She was a woman of exceptional abilities who had managed to contract four marriages during her lifetime. Her first husband was Abdullah ibn Abu Bakr, son of the first Caliph Abu Bakr. He died, leaving her a fortune on condition that she would not re-marry. For a while she was content with the idea of living a celibate life, but later she decided to go against his wish and not to spend the rest of her life alone; hence her decision to accept Umar ibn al-Khattab, the second Caliph, as her second husband. When Umar was assassinated in 642 she married her third husband, Zubayr ibn al-Awwam. After his death in 656, she took her fourth husband, Hussain ibn Ali, son of the fourth Caliph Ali; by this time she was around forty-five years old.

Marriage in Islam requires a contract between two equal partners. Hence in Islamic terms, the woman is to be a subject rather than an object in the marriage contract. The contract, in sum, is a legal written document between two adults, which entails an offer by one partner and an acceptance by the other in the presence of two witnesses. The Qadi, or official, usually solemnises the marriage in a mosque or court or any other location.

The consent of the prospective wife is crucial for the effectiveness of the marriage contract. Any force or blackmail on the part of the relatives would automatically render the contract invalid. The bride, moreover, has the exclusive right to stipulate her own conditions in the contract. These conditions include mainly (though not exclusively) such issues as marriage terms (the right, for example, to have a monogamous relationship whilst she is still living with her husband) and divorce terms (the right, for instance, to dissolve the marital bond at her own initiative if she deems it necessary). In addition, dowries-one initial and another deferred in case of divorce-must be specified and written down and they should be of substance. The dowry (or Mehr, in Islamic terms) belongs to the wife; it is her exclusive right and it should not be given away, neither to her family nor to her relatives. The Quran says 'Give women their dowry as a free gift; but if they choose to make over to you a part of it, you may regard it as lawfully yours'.

When the marriage is consummated, the couple assume a new relationship: that is, a husband-wife relationship. It is a kind of reciprocal and interdependent relationship. The Quran says 'And of His signs is that He gave you wives from among yourselves, that you might live in tranquillity with them, and put love and kindness in your hearts. Surely there are signs in this for thinking people'. The verse implies that in a marriage bond the two partners are a comfort to each other. They should find and enjoy peace and tranquillity in each other's company and be bound together not only by a sexual relationship but also by love, compassion and mercy. As such, both have to demonstrate mutual care, affection, respect and be prepared to make sacrifices.

There should be no servility on the part of either side, for they are two equal partners in a healthy, loving and caring relationship. The Quran eloquently illustrates this equal partnership in the following statement: 'They are an apparel to you, as you are an apparel to them'. The verse explains that just as a garment covers a person completely and provides him/her with warmth, protection and decency, in the same way a husband and wife provide each other with the necessary warmth, comfort, intimacy and protection. The realisation of these principles in actual life depends, mainly, on the way both partners react to each other.' In this context, the Quran expects them to behave in the best manner toward each other. The husband, on the one hand, is commanded to treat his wife gently and with kindness, affection and consideration. The Prophet said 'The best of you is the best of you to his wife, and I am better than any of you toward my wife'. He is to deal with her with dignity and in an equitable manner, not to hurt or injure her feelings. He is to show her that he loves her, appreciates her good qualities and he is to give her the impression that he needs her and depends on her to attain happiness in life. Also, he is asked to ensure that his tasks as husband and father are fulfilled to the utmost. Besides, the husband has to meet his legal responsibility to provide full maintenance of the wife: a task which he has to accomplish with good cheer and gladness.

The wife, on the other hand, is similarly required to reciprocate in kindness towards her husband, treat him with respect, admire his good qualities and express her love and affection to him. Also, she is called upon to ensure that her duties as wife and mother are performed to the best of her abilities. To maintain a happy conjugal relationship, both partners must be loyal, honest, direct, and trustworthy. They should be thoughtful, sympathetic and sensitive towards each other's feelings; in particular, they must avoid raising each other's suspicions and jealousy and try to maintain their integrity as husband and wife, united together in a matrimonial link. Concerning their sexual intimacy, both must be pleasing and receptive. They should endeavour to attain and give maximum gratification.

Moreover, in order to keep the marital link intact, stable and healthy, both partners have to demonstrate their willingness to share the burden of looking after the welfare of the family. They must share the ups and downs of married life, be prepared to make sacrifices, pay attention to each other's point of view, consult each other and adopt joint decisions on important matters that affect the entire family. These joint decisions have to be delivered or enforced by the husband since, in Islam, he is the head of the family. This is based on the following Quranic verses which give the husband the right to be in charge of the family: 'Women shall with justice have rights similar to those exercised against them, although men have a degree above women. Allah is Mighty and Wise'. 'Men have authority over women because Allah has made the one superior to the other, and because they spend their wealth to maintain them'. These verses were and still are a source of much discussion and debate throughout the Muslim world, generating a host of different interpretations. These interpretations range from liberal to moderate to conservative.

Our view in this context is that the headship of the husband should on no account be a license for dictatorship; it should entail no absolute freedom on the part of the person in charge; if the husband misuses or abuses his status, the wife has ' the right to interfere to rectify the situation. After all, the whole issue of being a chairperson is to ensure the smooth running of the family. Any neglect on the part of the husband to fulfil the task which is designated to him justifies his replacement by the more able person (the wife).

However, God-conscious pairs would always act responsibly because they are aware of their commitments to God as well as to each other. Also, because they are conscious of the fact that if they live up to their promises and act rationally in their married life they would invoke God's pleasure, hence making their lives a perpetual joy and paradise. But, sadly, this kind of paradise, envisaged by the Quran and practised briefly during the Prophet's time, has hardly ever been realised.

In fact, the case has nearly always been the reverse. Slowly but surely, attitudes towards women and marriage changed. The Quranic principles which bestowed honour, dignity, kindness and respect on women were gradually eroded and went into limbo. Customs, rather than Divine laws, shaped and continue to shape the social fabric of society and govern people's attitudes towards women and marriage. The outcome has been a steady deterioration in the status of women as far as their marital rights are concerned. Take, for example, the right to initiate a marriage proposal. This has been completely abandoned: not even in her wildest dreams would a woman dare to propose orally or in writing. The disappearance of this early practice has been so total that most women, even educated ones, are not aware of its existence, let alone practise it. The right to exercise her choice in selecting a marriage partner has, in most cases, been forgotten.

Most marriages that currently take place in Muslim societies are arranged unions, during which force and intimidation are quite often employed to obtain the girl's consent. Moreover, her freedom to sign the marriage contract has been considerably curtailed. The majority of Muslim marriages nowadays are contracted through agents (guardians, especially on the part of the woman), very often a male member of the family (father, brother, or uncle), who formalises and signs the contract on her behalf. In doing so, her opportunity and right to negotiate marriage and divorce terms are deliberately denied.

In most cases, a woman is subjected to considerable pressure to avoid stipulating in her marriage contract a divorce right or any other rights which might be viewed as a constraint on the freedom of the husband. If she did so, the social pressure on her would be so tremendous that in the end she would be obliged to give up, otherwise she would be accused of endangering the whole enterprise. Divorce has become a stigma and women are always regarded as being culpable.

The prospects for a non-virgin (divorcee or widow) getting remarried is dim. Indeed, in many cases they are forced to spend the rest of their lives cherishing the memories of their dead husbands and serving the male members of their own families. Within the context of a husband-wife relationship, authoritarianism and dictatorship have replaced the ideal and equal partnership advocated by the Quran.

The husband assumes the role of ruler, superior, controller, oppressor and master, while the wife, on the other hand, is reduced to a slave, a captive, a low, inferior and submissive creature. Listen to what the so called Council of Ulama (that is, people with knowledge about Islam) of South Africa has to say about the relationship between the two spouses: 'She (the wife) should mould herself to wholeheartedly submit to his whims and fancies. His likes must become her likes and his dislikes, her dislikes. She should step out of her way to comfort him and to console him in his worries and distress. Her wishes and desires are subservient to his wishes and orders.... After all (God) has created her for her husband's comfort and peace'. The Council goes on to say 'The Shariah has accorded the husband the highest degree of authority over his wife. Likewise it will transpire that the wife has to offer the higher degree of submission to her husband... with humility and patience she should tolerate his shortcomings and even his injustice... men are the rulers of women and they have a superior rank... (as such) it is the husband's right and role to dominate and dictate (and) it is the duty of the wife to submit and serve. The wife should understand that she can never conquer her husband by confrontation and seeking to set herself up as his equal or superior'.

Concerning the financial arrangements between them, the Council stresses: 'It is significant that in spite of the wife remaining the sole owner of her wealth... (she is encouraged) to put her wealth at his disposal and pleasure'. What about his money? 'She should not attempt to appoint herself as the controller of his finances. It is none of her business on whom her husband spends his wealth'. What if the husband fails to perform his duties properly?

The Council emphasises: 'She must not adopt a legal stand and a technical attitude, demanding from her husband perfect and total fulfilment of her legal rights.... The wife has to remember that despite her husband's failure to fulfil his duties to her, she is under... obligation to obey her husband.... obedience to the husband will ensure the everlasting happiness... for her'.

The mutual responsibilities on both sides to demonstrate to each other their loyalty, honesty and respect have become exclusively the wife's domain and obligations. The husband has been deliberately left out of the equation. So whether he is honest and loyal or a cheat it does not matter. What matters most (and this is important to him and to the male-dominated society) is the faithfulness and loyalty of the wife. There is no question of reciprocity between them in this matter. The emphasis has always been on the wife, as if she is a creature with no control over her sexuality.

The word 'divorce' 'traces its origin back to the Latin derivative and conjures up the splitting of a unit, the permanent physical separation of the spouses', while the Arabic word '*talaq*' is derived from the verb *itlaq* which means to set loose, set free or to leave. Talaq, therefore, within the context of the marital link means to terminate the bond created by a marriage contract.

In every society there are ways and means which allow the marital link to be dissolved if it fails to fulfil its objective. The reasons for the dissolution of marriage are, generally speaking, common and almost universal. They apply to human society irrespective of time, place or level of civilisation from the unavoidable death of a spouse or involuntary barrenness to the trivial cooking mistake of burning the husband's food or putting too much salt in it, not to mention the man's arbitrary dislike of his spouse or capricious preference for another woman who seems more pleasing to him. So the termination of marriage is sometimes inevitable and no system can afford to ignore this reality, otherwise it is doomed to failure.

Any system which insists on the indissolubility of marriage and overlooks the fact that under exceptional circumstances the dissolution of the family becomes a necessity is static, impractical and does not respond adequately to human needs. A system under which marriage is indissoluble would inevitably lead to the abuse of marriage, because people will always find ways around it, hence defeating the whole purpose which the system stands for in the first place.

In principle, Islam regards marriage as a lifelong commitment. However, sometimes there do arise situations wherein marriage ceases to fulfil its purpose. Hence, divorce can be invoked by either side or both of them in order to accommodate the realities of an unsuccessful marriage. It, must be stressed that divorce can only be exercised as the last resort after all efforts for reconciliation between the spouses are exhausted. Therefore, in Islam divorce is considered a necessity if the married partners are not happy. However, divorce is heavily disapproved of and discouraged.

The Quran discourages divorce in the following verses: 'And (remember) when you (Muhammad) said to the man (Zaid, Muhammad's adopted son) whom Allah and yourself have favoured: keep your wife and have fear of Allah'. In this verse there is an implicit disapproval of divorce.

In other verses the Quran clearly discourages Muslims from having recourse to a hasty divorce, even though they might be dissatisfied with their marriage partners. 'Treat them with kindness; for even if you do dislike them, it may well be that you may dislike a thing which Allah has meant for your own good'.

The Quran not only discourages divorce, but it prohibits the slandering of one's wife in order to take back her dowry 'If you wish to have a wife in the place of a (divorced) one, do not take from her the dowry you have given her even it if be a talent of gold. That would be improper and grossly unjust; for how can you take it back when you have lain with each other and entered into a firm contract?'

Divorce was also discouraged by the Prophet, who is reported to have said: 'Of all things licit, the most hateful to God is divorce,' Also: 'Let not the faithful man hate the faithful woman; if he dislikes some of her habits, he may like others.' Ali, the son-in-law of the Prophet, said, 'Marry and do not divorce your wives, for divorce causes God's throne to tremble.' These disapprovals notwithstanding, Islam concedes the possibility of divorce as the lesser of two evils when the alternative is a disastrously unhappy marriage and it devotes much attention to dealing with it both in the Quran as well as in the Sunnah.

There are many causes for divorce. If the spouses discover that they are incompatible because of their ideas and opinions, their modes of behaviour and their temperaments, then they should resort to divorce. The conflict and tension that would inevitably arise as a result of their incompatibility would certainly give rise to ill feeling and contempt between the spouses. This would adversely affect not only the couple but their children as well as their relatives and closest friends. As a way out of this difficult situation, Islam therefore prescribes divorce.

Furthermore, spouses locked forcibly in an unhappy union would surely be forced themselves—in an attempt to satisfy their sexual urge—to seek sexual intimacy outside the marriage tie, hence falling into the trap of committing adultery, which is forbidden in Islam. To prevent partners from indulging in such indecency, Islam allows the couple to be divorced so that they can go their own separate ways.

Divorce is also granted if the husband is impotent. Divorce, moreover, can take place if both spouses or one of them suffers a serious disease that renders the continuation of the marital relation either impossible or unsafe, or if the husband is put in prison for a long time or fails to support his wife. In order for the divorce to be effective and valid, the person who is performing it has to be adult (*baligh*), sane (*aqil*), free from any confusion or coercion and full of clear and good intentions (*qasid*). In addition, the witnesses have to be reliable, trustworthy and of good conduct.

Divorce in Islam is one of those issues which has generated considerable controversy and debate among Muslims and non-Muslims alike; this is probably because it has been grossly abused by Muslims and certainly misunderstood by both Muslims and non-Muslims.

Islam is against divorce and is strongly in support of the family unit: hence, both spouses have to do their utmost to build up a strong and harmonious marital relationship. If, however, tension arises between them, they should not rush into a hasty divorce. First, they should try and make some serious efforts to save their marriage. For example, they should attempt to stand the causes of their differences and try to solve them in a private and amicable way. If this proves to be unsuccessful, then they are advised to ask representatives, one from each side, to mediate and try to restore peace between them.

The Quran says, 'If you fear a breach between a man and his wife, appoint an, arbiter from his people and another from hers. If they wish to be reconciled, Allah will bring them together again-Allah is Knowing, Wise'. The arbiters have to be close to the parties involved and command their trust and respect. They should conduct their task impartially and discreetly. Also, they should try and settle the differences between the spouses without publicity; they should especially attempt to avoid the embarrassment of revealing such issues that might be regarded (by the married partners) as very private and intimate. The decisions reached by the arbiters are binding on both spouses. However, if one or both of them refuse to abide by them, then the rulings have to be enforced by the court.

The Quran clearly protects the right of the woman in this matter. By insisting here that two arbiters one from the side of each party (the husband as well as the wife) have to be called to investigate the matter between them peacefully and objectively, it has in fact put the interests of the wife on an equal footing with those of her husband, by giving her the opportunity to present her case and viewpoint before the arbiters. This is surely a fair and just way to deal with divorce matters because it takes into consideration the interests of both sides. More importantly, it protects the weak (the wife) from being abused by the strong (the husband), an outcome which all too frequently occurs in our society these days. For example, it prevents the husband from arbitrarily divorcing his wife without any due consideration for her mental or physical well-being, a practice very often used by the husband to punish his wife in contemporary Muslim societies.

In light of the above it would seem sensible to favour and recommend the adoption of this orderly divorce process by the judicial systems of all Muslim countries for it is simple, civilised and, most importantly, authentically Islamic: it has been described and recommended by the Quran. So, it is not something foreign or alien to Islam; on the contrary, it is an integral part of the Islamic tradition. Indeed there are many examples in which divorce cases were judged according to this procedure in early Islamic history.

For instance, it has been reported that during the reign of the fourth Caliph Ali (son-in-law of the Prophet), a man and his wife approached him complaining about each other's behaviour and stating that there were gross differences between them that had made their lives miserable. Ali immediately acted as Judge and asked for representatives from both sides to be despatched to him. Upon their arrival, he commissioned them to look into the matter carefully and decide whether there would be any possibility of making peace between them.

Also, he reminded them of their responsibility and sacred duty to handle the case with tact, due consideration and impartiality. He told them that if they sensed that there was a chance that they could be reconciled then they should spare no effort in doing so, otherwise they had to be separated with honour and in dignity. When the arbiters reached a decision, Ali made it legally effective by forcing the spouses to abide by it.

If the arbiters realise that there is a good chance for patching up things between the spouses, they are encouraged to do so, but if they think otherwise, the partners have to be allowed to go their own separate ways. It is most unfortunate that such a humane understanding of the verse and such a civilised practice of it failed to materialise throughout most of our Islamic history. For one reason or another, both the jurists as well as the rulers decided to ignore and shelve it.

Nevertheless, there were a few scholars who continued to stress the importance of utilising the directions contained in this verse and use them as guidance to promote legal or judicial divorce systems in the Muslim world. One of the most respected Egyptian scholars, Muhammad Abduh, advocated such reform. In his book *Women and Islam*, Abduh explains as follows:

The call in this verse if you fear a breach between a man and his wife, appoint an arbiter from his people and another from hers is a general, not specific, one. It cannot be the responsibility of every person or every group of people in society. Therefore, there are two opinions among the interpreters: one says that the call is directed to the people who are concealed with the general affairs of the Muslim people, namely the rulers or representatives who are responsible for their overall well being. Both opinions are right, for the first one allocates the responsibility of looking after the interest of the people in the bands of the representatives who have to endeavour to do their jobs properly, while the second one assigns the duty to the general public who have to team up and be cooperative with one another.

As far as the representatives are concerned, Abduh explains that there are two different views: one sees that the arbiters as mere mediators with no legal authority, while the other insists on regarding them as judges with legal power to enforce their decisions. Concerning the part which states, 'If they wish to be reconciled, Allah will bring them together again. Allah is, Knowing, Wise', Abduh interprets it thus: this part means that, God favours peace and harmony between spouses and wishes that they would be reconciled, because of the emphasis Islam lays on the family unit in society. As such the arbiters are exhorted to ensure that peace can prevail between them. However, if the arbiters fail to bridge the gap between the couple, they are not to blame.

Abduh then introduces his own version. He says: 'when conflict erupts between husband and wife and proves difficult to solve amicably, the spouses are advised to take the matter to the judge of the county. The judge here has to appoint two mediators-one represents the wife while the other acts for the husband. Both representatives have to be of good character and highly respected people. The judge, after briefing them, has to send them to the spouses in an attempt to solve the dispute. If the arbiters' efforts culminate in success, then it is good news. But if they fail to bring the two spouses together again, then they have the legal power to divorce them. The representatives, after completing their mission, have to report to the judge and the judge has to enforce their decision. It must be stressed here that the mediators—when they decide on separation have to give only one revocable divorce, so that time may be given to the spouses to reflect on their situation before final separation can take place.' Abduh's view on the judicial process of divorce found acceptance among the reformers in some Muslim countries who thought that improvement in this area was badly needed because the unlimited power of tbe husband to repudiate his wife was grossly abused, hence making the lives of many Muslim women unbearable. His view was, therefore, incorporated into their legal systems and helped them to introduce such reform. Tunisia, for example, was one of a few Muslim countries which decided to introduce legal, reform based on Abduh's view on judicial divorce.

The Tunisian reformers argued that; 'In the case of discord between spouses, the Quran orders the appointment of arbitrators-yet what more obvious case of discord between spouses is there than a pronouncement of repudiation by the husband? And who is then better qualified to undertake the necessary function of arbitration than the official tribunals? On this ground, therefore, the right of a husband to repuditate his wife extra judiciously, was abolished.'

Thus, all divorce actions were prohibited, henceforth taking place outside, the domain of the court. The introduction of such reform has heralded two things. Firstly, it has empowered the court with an unrestricted power to compensate the wife for any injury endured as a result of the divorce; secondly, it ensures that both spouses are treated on an equal basis in this regard.

The Quran deals with divorce issues in another verse which states:

> *Divorce may be pronounced twice, and then a woman must be retained in honour or allowed to go with kindness. It is unlawful for husbands to take from them anything they have given them, unless both fear that they may not be able to keep within the bounds set by Allah; in which case it shall be no offence for either of them if the wife ransoms herself.*

In this verse, God explains that divorce may be pronounced twice, during which period reconciliation can take place; hence it is a revocable type of divorce, since the couple can still resume their marital life if they wish to do so.

However, a third pronouncement would lead to irrevocable divorce, after which the spouses cannot remarry, unless the woman marries another person first and that person also divorces her. In this case, she is allowed to remarry her former husband if she desires to do so: 'If a man divorces his wife, he cannot remarry her until she has wedded another man and been divorced by him; in which case it shall be no offence for either of them to return to the other, if they think that they can keep within the limits set by Allah. Such are the bounds of Allah. He makes them plain to men of understanding.'

Divorce must be pronounced when the wife is in a state of purity (*tuhr*), otherwise it is regarded as invalid. The reason for not allowing the husband to divorce his wife during the state of impurity is that the husband is physically separated from her and this might induce him to press ahead with the separation. While if she is in a state of purity, he is physically close to her and in this case he might be persuaded to reconsider his decision.

Anyway, if divorce takes place, the wife has to observe *idda* or the waiting period. This lasts for three months, during which time sexual intercourse is not allowed between the spouses. By the end of this waiting period, the separation becomes final and legally effective. The reason for making the waiting period obligatory is to ensure the achievement of the following: first, to give the spouses more time to reconsider their attitudes and resolve their differences; second, to determine whether or not the wife is pregnant, for if she is expecting a child there is always a good chance that the spouses might be willing to effect a reconciliation.

Both spouses are encouraged to recognise and respect each other's rights, after the separation. In particular, the Quran exhorts the man to be considerate and kind to his former wife. Also, he is enjoined to act with due care and not allow her to be thrown out of her house. He must ensure that she may stay, if she wishes, with respect and dignity. Moreover, he should properly maintain her and give her sufficient support. Here, it must be noted that there are differences of opinion among scholars regarding the maintenance of divorced women. Some recommend that a divorcee is entitled to sustenance, which includes both the dowry as well as a financial allowance, whilst others insist that the payment of her maintenance should only continue for the period of idda, which is not more than three menstrual cycles.

Under Islamic Law, the marriage contract may be dissolved in three ways: first, the death of one of the spouses; second, by act of the husband or the wife or both of them; third, through Judicial process or a decree of court. The dissolution of the marriage contract by the husband is called Talaq (divorce), which is usually translated as repudiation. It can be done unilaterally by the husband without his having to produce any reason. This form of divorce or *talaq* has been classified (by the jurists) into three main types:

Talaq al-Ahsan: This is the most approved form of repudiation. In this kind of Talaq the husband has to pronounce one single divorce during *tuhr* or the period of purity of the wife. Then he must abstain from having physical contact with her during the waiting period. This form of repudiation is revocable. For the husband can, before the end of the idda, revoke the divorce and resume the conjugal relationship. It must be noted here that the approval of the wife is essential in this context.

The husband cannot force her back, even if he regrets divorcing her. She must first give her consent before the couple can resume their matrimonial relations. In order for him to signal his intention to retain her, he may express this desire either explicitly or implicitly. The former is the preferred one, and is usually done by pronouncing the revocation of the repudiation. If, during the waiting period, one of the spouses dies, the other can still inherit the estate. If the husband allows the waiting period to elapse without reclaiming his wife, the repudiation becomes irrevocable or absolute (*bayan*).

Talaq al-Hasan: This is a less approved form of divorce. Here the husband repudiates his wife three successive times over a period of three months, once each month during the period of tuhr. As with Ahsan talaq, the husband can revoke his divorce after the first or second repudiation, but after the third repudiation the divorce becomes absolute (bayan). The only difference is that the wife cannot remarry her former husband until she has first married someone else and then dissolved that marriage. The reason for adding this condition is to prevent a hasty repudiation on the part of the husband.

Talaq al-Bidah: This is the least approved method of divorce in the Muslim world but, unfortunately, it is the most widely used. It is highly condemned by women and civilised men and regarded as sinful. Nonetheless, it is considered legally effective once it is pronounced. This form of divorce is effected by three repudiations, which may be pronounced at any time (not merely in clean periods) and without definite intervals'. It is an irrevocable form of talaq and the husband can only remarry his ex-wife after she has contracted a new marriage with a second man and dissolved that marriage (after proper consummation). Bidah divorce lacks any Quranic support. Also, it was strongly denounced by the Prophet, who is reported to have reacted angrily when he heard that somebody had divorced his wife by the triple pronouncement of talaq in a single sitting and said 'How would you play with the book of Allah while I am alive and amidst you?' He then ordered the man to take back his wife. Nonetheless, this innovative divorce acquired legitimacy under the reign of the second Caliph Umar, who decided to make it legal in an attempt to prevent any careless use of the formula. However, his efforts in this context proved to no avail as his decree eventually produced counterproductive results. Since then it has remained lawful and legally effective among Sunnis (the Shia do not recognise this type of divorce), and men have continued to make use of it to their own advantage. We are therefore strongly in favour of banning it outright. It is a bizarre and odd practice; most importantly, it is very degrading to the dignity of Muslim women.

The great jurist, Ibn Taymiyyah, was against it. He stated that the erratic use of such a practice (triple pronouncement on a single occasion) was invalid and had no impact on the statutory position of a marriage. His aim was to protect women, as he thought that they were victimised by such a ruling (Umar's validation of Bidah divorce). It is a shame that his position has been forgotten and disregarded in contemporary Muslim societies.

The dissolution of marriage by the wife takes two forms:

Talaq al-Tawfid, (or delegated divorce.) In this form of divorce the husband, at the time of marriage, agrees to delegate to his wife the power of pronouncing the talaq, thus allowing her to dissolve the marriage contract. It must be stressed here that once the husband consents to give his wife the right to divorce him, he is no longer in a position to reclaim it. Tawfid divorce is indeed a powerful weapon in the hands of the wife, since she can easily use it if the conditions in the marriage contract are violated by the husband.

Khula, also called ransom by some jurists Here, the wife initiates the divorce, but the husband has to agree to free her in return for repayment of part or all of the dowry or mehr. A woman, seeking khula, however, may lose her right to maintenance during the waiting period. Women's right to khula was acknowledged and respected during the early Islamic era; they were very often allowed to exercise it without fear or intimidation. For a woman to request khula she does not have to quote any specific reason; the fact that she is unhappy with her husband would be enough to grant her separation under khula.

Divorce through mutual consent is usually called *Mubaraah.* This form of divorce centres around an agreement between spouses to release each other from the marital link with no exchange or payment on either side.

The final method of dissolving the marriage contract is through a judicial process, at the instigation of either the wife or husband.

This can be obtained in the case of (a) Lian and (b) annulment.

Lian: It is the divorce by oath and it occurs when the husband accuses his wife of committing adultery without evidence. The court, after studying the case and hearing particular oaths from both spouses, would issue a decree allowing the marriage to be dissolved. This form of separation is irrevocable and the partners cannot remarry each other again.

Annulment: The annulment of the marriage takes place when the wife lodges a complaint against her husband on the basis of the following: impotence, failure to fulfil the marital obligations, maltreatment, insanity and any other causes which might justify the annulment of the marriage.

RIGHT OF SELECTION

Men have been exhorted to marry women of their choice and liking, provided they do not transgress the prescribed limits. There are some women with whom it is unlawful to marry. Some are near relatives and some belong to other religions. Except these women, man has the freedom to select from among other women. The women also enjoy the same right of choice. There is no pressure or compulsion to marry a particular man or woman. Everyone who has a grain of common sense knows that at the time of purchasing a thing costing even only a few pennies, we make sure of our full satisfaction as having made a good bargain. Who can then advise anyone to marry in haste without proper investigation? It is obvious that the thing upon which depend the lives of two people, who are strangers, cannot be taken lightly.

Islam which is a harbinger of justice and peace for the oppressed and downtrodden humanity and their greatest supporter, does not at all tolerate that the rights of the rightful people should not be restored to them. It aims at curbing tyranny and oppression with an iron hand. So the Holy Prophet (peace and blessings of Allah be upon him) declared that all sorts of persecution should be ended. He did not leave any aspect of life untouched and issued reforms in conjugal life as well. He safeguarded the rights of the downtrodden and trampled humanity by holding back the hand of the tyrant so that the husband and wife could lead a happy and fulfilled life, the real purpose of marriage.

It would be better if the rights and obligations of the husband and wife are determined in the light of the teachings of Holy Quran and the Sunnah. Both the husband and wife enjoy full rights. The only restriction on them is that none of them should transgress the limits imposed by Allah.

Islam has, within prescribed limits, given priority to the opinion of the men and women who are going to be married in the matter of the selection of a spouse. Their opinion must be sought. Before the advent of Islam, the parents or guardians wedded their daughters to men whom they did not like, by exerting undue pressure upon them, thus committing tyranny and oppression on them. Especially, the orphan girls were subjected to the worst oppression. History bears ample proof of the fact that in the Days of Ignorance, the condition of women was most miserable. The poor creature was condemned to be a moveable property which had been bought by a man on payment of dower. After the death of her husband, the heirs considered her as their personal property and perpetrated all sorts of tyrannies on her. Islam eradicated this evil.

Just as every wise man and woman are free to decide their worldly matters after attaining puberty, similarly in the matter of marriage, Islam has given them freedom to give their proposals. Parents and other relatives can give them suitable advice, as they should, but they should not pressurise the boy or girl. The men and women going to be married should act upon the advice of their experienced and loving parents and relatives, but according to Islam, their advice is not binding on them.

> *It is far from the truth to say that in Islam women are helpless, dumb creatures. Islam has given them freedom of choice like men. In contracting marriage, the consent of a woman, attaining the age of puberty must always be sought. The Holy Prophet (peace and blessings of Allah be upon him) has said: 'A divorcee or a widow must not be married until she is consulted and a virgin must also not be married until her permission is sought.'* *(Bukhari)*
>
> *In another Tradition the Holy Prophet (peace and blessings of Allah be upon him) said: 'A woman who has been previously married (Thayyiba), has more right to her person than her guardian. And a virgin should also be consulted and her silence implies her consent.'* *(Muslim)*

A further probe into the above Ahadith would affirm the fact that women are not helpless but they have been given the freedom of choice by Islam and without the consultation of a woman, the marriage of a woman with any man is not permissible. Thus, consent of a woman is an essential condition of marriage and it must be obtained in all circumstances.

It is the duty of a guardian that he should first consult the woman, attaining the age of competency, regarding her proposed marriage and then begin the negotiations. Islam ordains that both the parents and guardians of a girl should seek permission from her before marriage.

But where Islam considers the permission and consent of the woman as an essential condition of her marriage, it does not do so at the cost of her sentiments of modesty and chastity. So if she is a virgin her silence implies her consent, but in the case of a woman previously married (divorced or widowed) explicit consent from her is necessary. Some scholars are of the view that it is more appropriate that it should be made clear to a virgin.

A Hadith narrates the incident of a Sahabia, Hadrat Khansa bint Huzam (Allah be pleased with her) that her father married her to a person whom she did not like. She came to the Holy Prophet (peace and blessings of Allah be upon him) and submitted a petition which was accepted by him, and he revoked the marriage.

Hadrat Abdullah bin Abbas (Allah be pleased with him) reported that a woman came to the Holy Prophet (peace and blessings of Allah be upon him) and said: 'My father has married me to a person whom I do not like.' The Holy Prophet (peace and blessings of Allah be upon him) authorised that woman to accept or revoke the marriage.

According to an incident narrated by Buraida (Allah be pleased with him) a young woman came to the Holy Prophet (peace and blessings of Allah be upon him) and said: 'My father has married me to my cousin whom I do not like.' Thereupon the Holy Prophet (peace and blessings of Allah be upon him) gave her permission to adhere to or revoke the marriage contract. Hearing this the woman heaved a sigh of relief saying: 'I have already given my consent to what my father has done, but what I want to impress upon women is that a father has no right to give the hand of his grown up daughter without her consent.'

Abdur Rahman bin Yazid and Majma' bin Yazid (Allah be pleased with them) narrated an incident. A person, namely Khuddam, married his daughter to a person whom she did not like.

She came to the Holy Prophet (peace and blessings of Allah be upon him) and expressed her disgust. He (the Holy Prophet) (peace and blessings of Allah be upon him) revoked the marriage contracted by her father and then she married Abdul Baya bin Abdul Mundhir (Allah be pleased with him).

The above Ahadith bear ample testimony to the fact that it is not permissible to put pressure on a grown-up lady in the matter of marriage, but that she reserves the full right to select her husband. The sum and substance of what we have said above is that the real aims and objects of marriage i.e., morality and chastity, love and affection and multiplication of the human race should always be kept in view.

The guardian and the father possess the right to get a girl, who has not yet attained the age of puberty, married to someone; but the right of the father is more essential as she cannot, in that case, exercise her option or choice on attaining the age of puberty.

However, marriage is an important matter. It should be arranged after thorough investigation. The parents and guardians should satisfy themselves to the possible extent and those who are going to be tied in wedlock should also feel contented.

Another point worth thinking about is that nowadays people do not consider it necessary to consult their parents and guardians. No doubt, the like and dislike of a person proposed for marriage is the primary factor, but the heart and passions should not be allowed to overrule the mind and one should be vigilant and not lose one's sense. Besides, in the gratification of the sexual instinct, marriage entails responsibilities which one owes to one's family, society, country and nation. One should not be concerned with one's present state only, but should also keep the future in view. It is, therefore, quite necessary to consult elderly people as they possess more experience of life. If there arises a dispute, the choice of the woman should be given priority.

Now the question remains of the case of dispute between a guardian or father and a woman going to be married; how should the matter be decided? Certainly, the verdict will be in the favour of the woman, and according to the Shariah, priority will be given to her opinion as it is she who is going to be married and the matter pertains to her modesty and chastity. The guardian is not being married nor is he to shoulder the responsibility of marriage. Then how is it that the opinion of the woman should be overlooked? There are incidents and clear decisions of the time of the Holy Prophet (peace and blessings of Allah be upon him) that he gave preference to the opinion of the woman. He revoked the marriage contracted by the father, but did not decide against the woman. It has been said in the Holy Quran:

> *"When they reach their term, place not difficulties in the way of their marrying the husbands of their choice if it is agreed between them in kindness."* *(2:232)*

In the matter of marriage, the woman has the right to decide according to her sweet will. The woman is also human, she possesses intellect and wisdom. She is not a helpless creature unable to decide any matter of her own accord.

From the above we are bound to arrive at the conclusion that coordination between the guardian and the woman is essential for arranging the marriage smoothly. The views of Hadrat Maulana Kashmiri on this subject are worth reading. Here we shall give only the gist thereof: In the case of the matters concerning the people, the Shariah has given the right to both the parties. One should decide keeping in view all the Ahadith. One-sided decisions can be wrong. For instance, in the case of Zakat, the matter pertains to both the payer and the payee. So far as the payer is concerned, there is a clear Hadith that if any collector of Zakat comes to him for Zakat, he should please him by giving to him what he demands. If he does justice, the reward will be for him and if he commits injustice, he will be liable to punishment. The excellence of Zakat is that the collector should go back cheerfully.

It has been narrated in a Hadith that the people complained to the Holy Prophet (peace and blessings of Allah be upon him) against the collector of Zakat. He said: 'Please him and give him what he asks for.' Thereupon they asked: 'O' Allah's Messenger, even if he commits injustice?' He answered: 'Yes, in that case too!'

On the other hand, the payee has been admonished: 'Beware against taking the best of the wealth of the people. Be afraid of the outpourings of the heart of the oppressed as there is no barrier between him and Allah.'

Now, ponder over both the Ahadith. According to the instructions of the Holy Prophet (peace and blessings of Allah be upon him) the collector of Zakat should be given what he demands even if he commits injustice. On the other hand, the payee has been warned to receive what the payer gives him justly and should not be arrogant. Similar is the case of husband and wife. On the one hand, the wife has been ordained to please her husband and a stern warning of being thrown into the Fire of Hell has been given for misbehaviour on her part. And on the other hand, it has been said that the perfect in Faith among you is the one who is of good manners and who is the best in behaviour towards his wife.

The same is the case of the woman and her guardian. It is impressed on the woman that the guardian possesses the right in respect of her marriage and without his consultation the marriage contract is not complete. On the other hand, it is said to the guardian that the woman has more right to her person than him and he has no right to intervene.

What can be concluded from the above Ahadith is that both are responsible and that the marriage should not be contracted without each other's consultation. The woman should, as far as possible, give due regard to the opinion of the guardian and the latter must seek the former's consent. Neither is the guardian allowed to deprive the woman of her legal right nor should the woman bring disgrace to the fair name of her family and guardian. In any case, the guardian has no right to put pressure. It is, however, preferable that he should give advice. If the girl is a minor, the guardian can exercise his will. As is evident from the Quran and the Sunnah, in the event of a dispute between the woman and the guardian, priority will be given to the opinion of the woman.

The views of Maulana Kashmiri are most reasonable and practicable in so far as social problems are concerned. He is aware of the implication of Allah's Prophet's directives. He is fully conversant with the significance and style of the Ahadith.

While explaining this point, Shah Wali Ullah also supports the above view, though his style is distinct from Maulana Kashmiri's. He says:

> *'Merely the opinion of the woman is not sufficient for the purpose of marriage It is only men who can solve difficult and knotty problems. Moreover, in the matters covering marriage the proposal by a woman is considered as arrogant and as an act of immodesty on her part. The intervention of a guardian is therefore, necessary to make a distinction between love-affair and marriage and to give due publicity to the proposed marriage. The woman, therefore, should consult the guardian, but the latter has no right to get her married to a person without her consent as the matter pertains exclusively to a woman. The benefits or loss occurring out of this marriage will have to be faced by her alone. So her consent must be sought.'*

Imam Nawawi, who belongs to the Shafii school of thought, is also of the view that the opinion of the woman has preference to the opinion of the guardian. He has written:

> *'The right of a woman has priority over the right of a guardian. If a guardian intends to marry a woman to a relative and she is not inclined, she cannot be pressurized. If she desires to marry with a relative and the guardian is not inclined, pressure will be exerted on the guardian. If he is adamant, the Qadi will get her married. This affirms the view that priority is to the right of a woman and this practice is in vogue.'*

It is evident from what we have said above that in Islam a woman is not quite helpless in the matter of marriage but her consent must be obtained before the guardian arranges her marriage. If a woman refuses to marry a person, she should not at all be forced to do so. Peace and harmony, the foremost aims and objects of marriage cannot be achieved in the case of the unwilling marriage of a woman. The rules and regulations pertaining to divorce and Khula have been framed for this purpose.

It has been mentioned in "Masbut" that at the time of Nikah the consent of a woman must be sought. It is just possible that the woman may have some defect or disease due to which sexual intercourse is not possible or the woman may like another man. If she is married to a person whom she dislikes, she will never be able to live amicably with him.

After the woman, comes the question of the opinion of the man. Here too, the consent of the grown-up man, going to be married, must be sought. Since man is not helpless, this matter needs no detailed discussion, rather it is advisable that he should give due weight to the opinion of his elders and should not ignore them saying: 'This is my personal matter in which the elders have no right to intervene.' In the matter of marriage the views of experienced people and those who have deep human insight count much. It is an obvious fact that young men do not possess the wisdom and prudence of elderly people. In the former case sentiments and passions only play a part.

> *Now we come to the point as to what should be the criteria for the selection of a woman. According to the Shariah, the chastity and piety of a woman should be given top priority at the time of selection. A person may marry an ordinary woman or a rich and wealthy lady or a woman of high descent or one for the sake of her beauty, but her piety and*

moral character must always be kept in view. The Holy Prophet (peace and blessings of Allah be upon him) has observed: 'Marriage with a woman is contracted for the sake of four things: for her wealth, for her descent, for her beauty and for her piety, but you should succeed (marry), for piety.' (Bukhari)

A man chooses a woman for the sake of four things. Sometime he chooses for the sake of her wealth only. He thinks that if the woman possesses property or a grand building, he would lead a luxurious and comfortable life and would be relieved of a large number of worries. He does not care to ponder over the virtues of piety and chastity, in his haste. He is not aware that by marrying a rich woman, he would be deprived of the real pleasure and happiness of marriage, as in that case his wife would rule. He would not feel any pleasure in seeing the furniture and other household goods which have not been purchased by his hard earned income nor would he be glad to see his gaily dressed children after losing his respect and honour in the eyes of his wife. His status or position would be that of a manager or organizer, if his wife is of good behaviour. If, God forbids, the wife happens to be arrogant, she would annoy and taunt him at every moment. The children of that wife would also not pay due respect to their father. If the husband intends to admonish his wife for any mistake of hers, it would come to a fight. Under the above circumstances what pleasure and happiness would exist in his life? The Holy Prophet (peace and blessings of Allah be upon him) has observed: 'Do not marry women for the sake of their wealth. Just possible their wealth makes them arrogant.' (Ibn Majah)

Sometime a man chooses a woman of high descent even if she is deprived of any personal ability and virtues. If she is of high descent but lacks piety, she would be proud and arrogant and would not remain within limits. This kind of behaviour is almost intolerable for a man. It does not mean that one should not attach importance to the race and descent of a woman, but it should not be the only consideration. These things have no value if the woman has no personal ability and is not pious and chaste. Islam holds piety and chastity in high esteem and these virtues are far more important in the eyes of Islam than race and descent. The Holy Prophet (peace and blessings of Allah be upon him) said: 'A woman may be married for four reasons: for her property, her status, her beauty and her religion; so try to get who is religious.' *(Sahih Muslim)*

The other Ahadith also support this view. Once the Holy Prophet (peace and blessings of Allah be upon him) said: 'Wherever they may be and whosoever they may be, my followers are pious.'

According to some people, beauty is the only consideration for the selection of a woman. She must have appealing looks, attractive, wide eyes, fair complexion and a proportionate body. She should be of gay disposition and pert and coquettish. She must be aware of the etiquettes of the modern society and way of life.

But they do not take any trouble to think that the above qualities do not count much if she is lacking in ability and good manners. Mere beauty is not everything. If she is deprived of other virtues, the beauty would become an evil. It would make her proud, flirtatious and arrogant. She would become haughty and extravagant. Other people would try to allure her. The holy Prophet (peace and blessings of Allah be upon him) has said about this kind of beautiful woman: 'Do not marry women merely for their beauty. It is most probable that their beauty may prove disastrous.' *(Ibn Majah)*

The Holy Prophet (peace and blessings of Allah be upon him) has, therefore, made piety and chastity the real criteria for the selection of a woman. Wealth, beauty, race and descent of a woman are not the real virtues. The person going to be married must see the personal ability and intelligence of a woman. The Holy Prophet (peace and blessings of Allah be upon him) has said: 'Do not marry a woman merely for the sake of her beauty and wealth.'

In the matter of marriage, preference should be given to chastity and piety. A black but pious woman is better. The Holy Prophet (peace and blessings of Allah be upon him) has said: 'But marry women on the basis of religion and piety.' *(Ibn Majah)*

There is no denying the fact that a religious and pious lady is always solicitous for the welfare and comfort of her husband and discharges her household duties efficiently and carefully. Such a woman is not unduly proud. She takes the utmost care in bringing up and educating her children. She does not pick up quarrels with the neighbours, relatives and other people. The people rely on her and respect and honour her. She enhances the honour and prestige of her husband. The Holy Prophet (peace and blessings of Allah be upon him) has observed: 'Whosoever achieves four things, is successful in this world and in the Hereafter: A heart which is grateful, a tongue which remains busy in Dhikr (commemorating the name of Allah) a body which shows patience, and a wife who abstains from sins and guards her chastity.'

Once the Holy Prophet (peace and blessings of Allah be upon him) said: 'Marry a woman who has excellent faith in Allah and who is helpful in making the life successful on the Day of Resurrection.'

> ***Indifferent Attitude :*** *Should the people adopt an indifferent attitude towards moral conduct and behaviour, devoting their all out attention to worldly pomp and show and exterior beauty, what would become of this world? A storm of evil and wickedness would rage and destroy the peace and harmony of this world. The respect and honour of everyone would be at stake. A large number of women could not get husbands and would be tempted to wickedness and debauchery as someone has rightly remarked: An idle brain is the devil's workshop. While explaining this fact the Holy Prophet (peace and blessings of Allah be upon him) has observed: 'Whenever a person whose moral conduct and behaviour pleases you, comes to you, get him married, otherwise there will be a widespread evil and wickedness on earth.!* *(Tirmidhi)*
>
> *According to the Jurists, it is advised that the following principles should be observed while selecting a woman: 'It is better if the position of a woman is less in respect of her race and descent and wealth and property and influence, but she should be superior to the man in moral conduct, behaviour, personality and beauty.'* *(Dur Mukhtar)*
>
> *The following points should also be kept in view: The woman with whom a man is to marry should not be tall and weak and thin, nor should she be of short stature, ugly and of bad conduct. She should not be of advanced age. She should not be of easy virtue.* *(Shami)*

In short, the woman with whom one is to marry should be suitable in every respect from the worldly point of view as well as from the religious point of view. Without this there can exist no mutual love and harmony between the husband and wife. As is evident from the Ahadith the woman should possess the following virtues:

- She should be religious and pious.

- She should share her husband's joys and sorrows and should be loyal and obedient.
- She should be chaste and honest and should manage the household affairs properly.
- She should be courteous, grateful and patient.
- She should pay attention to the needs of her children and should be kind to them and be healthy.
- She should love her husband and be a bearer of many offsprings.
- She should be of a pious and noble descent and educated.
- She should be virtuous and free from vices and evils.
- While living in this world, she should remember the life in the Hereafter.

SELECTION OF A HUSBAND

While selecting a husband, a woman should also keep in view the above criteria. This should enable her to lead a happy and cheerful life. The Jurists are of this view: A woman should have a husband who should be pious and broad-minded and of appealing manners, and should not marry a wicked person. (Dur Mukhtar)

Similarly, the father should also keep the above instructions in view at the time of giving the hand of his daughter. Nowadays the illiterate and avaricious generally keep in mind the wealth and status of a person and set little value on his personal ability, character and age. We must, therefore, raise a voice against this erroneous outlook and practice. The Jurists say: "The father should not marry his young daughter to an old and ugly man."(Dur Mukhtar)

It is the moral and religious duty of a guardian to see that there is not much difference in the age of the couple. The Holy Prophet (peace and blessings of Allah be upon him) had kept the age factor in view at the time of giving the hand of his daughter. Nasai has written a separate chapter on this subject: "Marriage of a woman with a man of equal age", and has narrated a Hadith on the authority of Hadrat Buraida (Allah be pleased with him):

Hadrat Abu Bakr and Hadrat Umar (Allah be pleased with them) sent messages of marriage for Hadrat Fatima (Allah be pleased with her). The Holy Prophet (peace and blessings of Allah be upon him) said: "She is lesser in age." Then Hadrat Ali (Allah be pleased with him) sent a message for marriage with her. He married her to Ali (Nasai).

The commentators of Ahadith have said that due regard must be given to age as it is an important factor and has many advantages. It is true that the Holy Prophet (peace and blessings of Allah be upon him) married Aishah (Allah be pleased with her) when she was of tender age, but this marriage had an extremely significant purpose. Everyone knows that this marriage proved to be a great blessing for the dissemination of Islamic knowledge and Hadrat Aishah's magnificent contribution in this respect can never be forgotten.

But it should not be construed from what we have said above that a man should not marry a beautiful woman. This is not our aim. What we want to impress upon the reader is that one should not be so deluded by the fair face that he overlooks the good qualities of a woman such as chastity, piety and moral conduct. If she lacks these qualities, her beauty is of no use.

A Hadith narrates an incident regarding a Companion of the Prophet (peace and blessings of Allah be upon him). He came to the Prophet (peace and blessings of Allah be upon him) and said: 'I have married an Ansari woman.' Thereupon the Holy Prophet (peace and blessings of Allah be upon him) observed: 'Have you satisfied yourself as Ansari women have something (defect) in their eyes?' In other words, we must first make proper investigation so that there may not remain any cause of complaint which may straiten the relations between the husband and the wife.

Marrying a Young Lady : An incident of Hadrat Jabir (Allah be pleased with him) has been narrated in a Hadith. He said to the Holy Prophet (peace and blessings of Allah be upon him): 'I have married only recently.' He asked: 'Virgin or a previously married (Thayyiba)?' He answered: 'A previously married woman.' Thereupon the Holy Prophet (peace and blessings of Allah be upon him) said: 'Why not with a virgin with whom you could sport and she could sport with you?'

> *In the Sahih the same words have been repeated, but with the following addition: 'She could amuse you and you could amuse her.'* *(Muslim)*
>
> *He made mention of a virgin lady as she can be easily moulded and is more cooperating. She is contended with a little and is grateful and she loves her husband passionately. Moreover she is more fascinating. The Ahadith support the view that a virgin and beautiful lady has a joyful disposition and a sense of pleasure and amusement for her husband. The Holy Prophet (peace and blessings of Allah be upon him) said in another Hadith: 'You should*

marry virgin ladies as they are sweet in speech and bearer of more children and they feel contented with a little.' *(Mishkat)*

In the above Hadith special emphasis has been laid on marriage with a virgin. The reason for this emphasis is that a virgin lady is more beautiful, charming and buoyant. These virtues should also be kept in view at the time of marrying a lady.

Hadrat Alqama (Allah be pleased with him) reported: 'When I was walking with Abdullah at Mina, Uthman (Allah be pleased with him) happened to meet him. He stopped there and began to talk with him. Uthman (Allah be pleased with him) said to him: "Should we not marry you to a girl who may recall to you some of the past of your begone days?" *(Muslim)*

While commenting upon the above Hadith, Imam Nawawi says: 'It is preferable to marry a young lady as the purposes of marriage can be best achieved through it. She affords pleasure and her fragrance is sweet. She is more exciting and pleasing and beautiful to look at. She is buoyant and jovial, elegant in appearance and delicate in touching. A husband can easily mould her as he desires.'

Hafiz Ibn Qayyim has reported that the Holy Prophet (peace and blessings of Allah be upon him) used to exhort his followers to marry religious and beautiful ladies. *(Zad al-Maad)*

It is clear from what has been said above that there is no harm in marrying a beautiful woman, rather it is preferable; but beauty should not be the only consideration. Along with it due consideration should be given to good conduct and manners.

We must know that beauty does not mean only fair complexion, but the moral conduct of a woman should be spotless and she should be firm in her religious beliefs. Moreover, the criteria of judgement of feminine beauty differs with different people. It depends upon the tastes and aesthetic sense of a person. It is possible that a woman who is ugly in the eyes of other people may be liked by a particular person. Therefore, the likes and dislikes of other people cannot be the criteria for the judgement of beauty.

As a matter of fact, good conduct and behaviour and appealing manners add to beauty and grace. There are numerous instances where passion and wantonness have had the upper hand as compared to a woman's beauty and elegance. So it is not wise to sacrifice everything at the altar of beauty. If, however, one finds a woman who is beautiful and virtuous it is a great boon. Islam has exhorted its followers to marry sweet and beautiful women, but has condemned immorality and debauchery and one should never even think of committing adultery.

Marrying a Widow : But this does not mean that it is not proper to marry widows. No doubt, in the Ahadith the people have been exhorted to marry virgins and there are solid reasons for it; that they can be easily moulded to the tastes and temperaments of men and that they love their husbands passionately and the husbands too have the same sentiments towards them. They are joyous and buoyant. Due to them men are saved from sins and wicked thoughts. But if a person has a wife or is advanced in age, it would be improper if he marries a young lady. An old man should marry a widow so that the husband and wife may live in peace and harmony.

The Holy Prophet (peace and blessings of Allah be upon him) whose life is a practical example for all mankind. A study of the history of the illustrious Caliphs and Companions reveals that a majority of them married widows. The Sahabiyyat also got married after the death of their husbands.

The above events bear out that if the marrying of widows were an abhorable act, no one would have married widows in the Prophet's or Caliphs' time. So it is not a bad thing to marry a widow, it is a good action and has its reward.

> ***Casting a Glance :*** *Islam has, for the sake of piety and chastity, permitted the casting of a glance at a woman before marriage without making any special arrangement. There is a Hadith: Whenever anyone of you sends proposal to a woman and he is in a position to cast a glance at what induced him to marry, he should do so.* *(Mishkat)*

It is clear that it is permissible to cast a glance in a civilized manner within the limits of the Shariah so that there remains no doubt and suspicion in the mind of the person who is to marry. Moreover, this permission has been given so that he should not, after the marriage, give any remarks to his wife which are derogatory or taunting which would prevent the growth of sentiments of love and affection between the couple. It is, however, not necessary that a person going to be married should himself see the woman. Another person can also see her on his behalf. If he has confidence in a person it is better that he should see. It is permissible to gather any information regarding the wealth, property moral conduct, piety, chastity, race, descent, etc., of the proposed woman for his satisfaction.

Hadrat Mughira bin Shuba (Allah be pleased with him) reported: 'I told the Holy Prophet (peace and blessings of Allah be upon him) about my (proposed) marriage. He asked: Have you seen her? Hadrat Mughira (Allah be pleased with him) answered: 'O' Allah's Messenger! No. He (the Holy Prophet) said: Cast a glance at that woman as it is appropriate for mutual love between the two. (Tirmidhi)

This clear commandment of Allah's Messenger (peace and blessings of Allah be upon him) implies that it is preferable to cast a glance at a woman before marriage. It is mentioned in Tirmidhi that some scholars have drawn the conclusion on the authority of this Hadith that there is no harm in casting a glance at a woman before marriage provided that part of her body should not be seen which is unlawful to be seen. Imams Ahmad and Ishaq also hold this view. Imam Tirmidhi further writes that it means "so that lasting love could exist between the two."

Abu Hurrayrah (Allah be pleased with him) reported: Allah's Messenger (peace and blessings of Allah be upon him) asked a man who had contracted to marry a woman of the Ansar: Did you cast a glance at her? He said: No. He said: Go and cast a glance at her, for there is something in the eyes of the Ansar. (Muslim)

Imam Nawawi writes while commenting on this Hadith: 'It is evident from the above Hadith that it is preferable to cast a glance at a woman whom one is going to marry. Imam Abu Hanifa, Imam Shafii and Imam Ahmad and a majority of other scholars hold this view. Imam Nawawi further writes: Moreover, Imam Abu Hanifa, Imam Malik, Imam Ahmad and a majority of the Ummah support the view that in this case the consent of a woman is not necessary. The woman can be seen without informing her or seeking permission from her. Moreover, the woman might feel shame to grant permission as it is not certain that the person who sees her would also marry her. In the case of seeing the woman unaware, she would not be subjected to any mental torture. So it is preferable to see a woman before sending the message, for marriage. If it is not possible to see the woman personally, a most reliable woman should be deputed for this purpose so that she may give the correct information. All this should be arranged before commencing negotiations of marriage. Muhammad bin Muslim (Allah be pleased with him) reported the Holy Prophet (peace and blessings of Allah be upon him) as saying: 'If Allah puts in the heart of man the desire to marry a woman, there is no harm in casting a glance at her.' (Ibn Majah)

It is evident from the above Ahadith that there is no harm in seeing the woman before marriage, rather it is preferable, whether the man sees himself, or appoints some reliable woman for this purpose. This would help to remove the doubts and suspicions in the mind and provide satisfaction as to the suitability of the selection. But the condition is that one must be sincere at heart and his aim should not be simply to annoy and create mischief.

According to Maulana Thana Ullah Panipati as far as he knew, this act is the Sunnah of the Holy Prophet (peace and blessings of Allah be upon him). He said: The Sunnah is that the person who is prepared to marry may cast a glance at the face and palms of the woman before marriage. There is consensus of opinion on this point. (Tafsir Mazhari)

It is preferable that a husband should cast a glance at his (proposed) wife before marriage despite the risk of lust. (Al-Kawakab al -Mashriq)

The above Ahadith are authentic. The worthy Caliphs acted upon them and they used to see a woman before marriage. Hadrat Jabir (Allah be pleased with him) himself says: I sent a message to a woman for marriage and tried to look at her secretly and succeeded in doing so. I saw in her some things that I married her. (Jama al-Fawaid)

Hadrat Muhammad bin Muslim (Allah be pleased with him) reported: I was engaged to a woman. I tried to have a look at her secretly. At last I saw her in my garden. Some people objected to this act of mine, being the Prophet's Companion. I said:

'I have heard the Holy Prophet (peace and blessings of Allah be upon him) as saying: There is no harm in casting a glance at a woman before marriage.'

It has been narrated about Hadrat Umar (Allah be pleased with him) that he sent a message to Hadrat Ali (Allah be pleased with him) that he intended to marry Umm Kulthum (Allah be pleased with her). It has been mentioned at the end of this narrative that Hadrat Umar (Allah be pleased with him) had seen her before sending the message. (Nida Liljins)

But we must not forget that whereas Islam has granted permission to cast a glance at a woman before marriage it does not allow 'courtship', free mixing and premarital sexual relations of men and women. There is no room for these illicit relations in Islam. From the incident of Hadrat Jabir (Allah be pleased with him) which has been narrated above, it can be judged easily how far Islam grants permission to look at a woman. In Islam woman has been ordained not to expose any part of her body except her face, the palms of her hands and at the most her feet. So one can cast a glance to that extent only.

There should not be any deep looks and curious glances. It is also not necessary that a woman should be aware of this fact before hand. What is aimed at is that a man should possess the necessary information about the woman he is going to marry. Imam Nawawi is of the view that it is permissible to cast a glance at a woman's face and palms only. He has written: It is permissible for a person who is going to marry a woman to cast a glance at her face and palms as these are not required to be covered, and the face is a proof of her beauty and the palms reflect whether the body is healthy and fresh or not. *(Sharah Muslim)*

It is an admitted fact that by casting a glance at the face, a man can judge a woman's shape and features. It reflects the elegance and ugliness of a woman. An intelligent person can gather much information about the woman from her face. It would not be out of place to say that the face is an index of the body and soul of a person. We have already mentioned the view of Maulana Thana Ullah Panipati that it is permissible to see the face and palms of a woman before marriage, and this view is also supported by the Ahadith. The Jurists have also added the words 'feet' to the above Hadith on the basis of Shariah.

Although there is difference of opinion among the scholars as to which portion and to what extent a woman's body could be seen; there is however, consensus of opinion on the point that the face and palms can been seen.

You will read in the next pages that the first glance is ,allowed, but a second glance should not be cast. It is not at all permissible for a man to meet and talk with a woman secretly. He can, however, see a woman, in case of need, in front of others. You will read more instructions on the subject. In view thereof it can be concluded that although Islam has permitted a man to see a woman, it has granted permission with certain limitations. One should not go further. One is allowed to cast a glance at a woman in her house, in her usual dress, but the glance should not be lewd and there should be no wickedness in the heart. In casting a glance the intention should be righteous, and the matter should be entrusted to Allah. *(Al-Uraf al-Shadhi)*

The main purpose of these laws is to lend stability and mutual love and cooperation between the couple and to prevent the occurrence of unpleasant happenings which make the lives miserable so that the full benefits of marriage may be derived.

Allama Rashid Raza of Egypt is speaking truly when he says that he has done much research work on the problems of women and on sexual relations of husband and wife and has read much ancient and modern literature, pamphlets and newspapers on the subject and has also written much on this topic. But despite this I do not believe in the wrong notion that the amicability of husband and wife depends upon premarital contacts and love-making between them.

Sometimes passionate love between husband and wife ceases after marriage. The basic principle to maintain amicable relations between husband and wife is that which was told by Hadrat Umar (Allah be pleased with him) to a woman who submitted an application to him saying: I do not love him from the core of my heart, that is, my heart is not affected by him. Thereupon, Hadrat Umar (Allah be pleased with him) observed: Do not tell this thing to your husband as there are many homes where sentiments of passionate love do not exist. The husband and wife ought to pay due regard to their noble descent, to the teachings of Islam and fulfil their duties and obligations which they owe to each other.

He further said: The husband and the wife should express more love than that they have in their hearts so that by and by it should find a place there and enable them to lead a pleasant and comfortable life.

Islam embodies all the important measures which are necessary to guard morality and establish a pious and healthy atmosphere. It has prohibited all things as might lead to evil and wickedness and the ruination of moral character.

Islam has allowed a boy and a girl to marry before he or she attains maturity. In other words, before the passionate age begins, so that they may not be led astray. The greatest advantage of this marriage is that they will never think of developing illicit and unlawful relations.

On attaining puberty, Islam exhorts its followers to marry without delay. It is the prime of youth, the passions run high and sexual urge is at its height. Although man has the capacity to think over the future and about his loss or gain, he is overwhelmed by passions and if the law does not impose restrictions on him, there is every chance of his being led astray. Addressing the young men, the Holy Prophet (peace and blessings of Allah be upon him) has said, 'O group of young men! He who is able to marry among you should marry.' (Bukhari)

Youth starts when a person attains the age of puberty and it lasts upto the age of thirty-two and Nawawi has said that the more authentic view is that youth lasts from puberty to the age of thirty. Then begins middle age which is upto forty. Thereafter begins old age. (Ibn Majah)

There is no age for grey hair. It differs with different people and depends upon their temperaments. What I want to say is that Islam has laid stress on the immediate marriage of a person upon attaining the age of maturity, so that he might not be led astray at that most passionate age.

Responsibility of Parents : *During this period, the sons and daughters are usually under the care of their parents. They do not often possess the means to marry. Moreover, modesty and shyness stand in their way and they cannot convey their feelings and sentiments to their parents. Sometimes they succumb to evil temptations. Islam has, therefore, laid this responsibility (of getting the children married), upon the parents. The Holy Prophet (peace and blessings of Allah be upon him) has said: The person to whom a son is born should give him a good name and teach him ethics and when he attains maturity he should get him married. If he is mature and his father does not get him married, the responsibility of the sin committed by him will rest with his father. This Hadith was narrated by Baihaqi in Shab al-Iman. (Mishkat)*

The above Hadith teaches us two lessons. Firstly, the parents should teach their children good moral conduct and tell them the righteous way of life so that they may fear Allah and abstain from sins and vices. Secondly, the parents should get their children married when they reach the age of maturity. They should not show any indifference or slackness in this matter as in the event of any sin committed by them due to the delay in marriage, the responsibility would devolve on the parents. The other Hadith pertaining to girls is given below:

> *The Holy Prophet (peace and blessings of Allah be upon him) observed: It has been written in the Torah that when a daughter attains the age of twelve and the person does not get her married and she commits any sin, the responsibility of that sin rests with him. This Hadith was narrated by Baihaqi in Shab al Iman.*

It is evident from the above Ahadith that when a son or a daughter attains the age of puberty, their marriage should be arranged immediately by the parents. The boy and the girl should give their consent and not try to put off the matter but the marriage should not be contracted without obtaining the prior approval of the children, an essential condition for a happy and stable home life.

Importance of Marriage : In order to emphasize the significance of marriage, it has been said that if the parents do not fulfil their duty and delay the matter, the responsibility for any moral lapse on the part of the boy or girl or both of them, would rest with the parents as well as the boy or girl who commits the evil deed, for whom there is severe punishment of Hell.

In contracting marriage, Islam aims at ensuring a happy and stable home life and where there should exist perfect harmony between husband and wife so that the relations between them may not grow strained with the passage of time. Due to this reason, the Shariah has stressed that the two strangers who are going to be wedded should profess the same religion and belief, and their way of life should bear similarity. The marriage of the believing men and women with unbelievers and polytheists has, therefore, been prohibited. While commenting upon the verse banning marriage with the polytheists, Maulana Mahmud al Hasan writes: The development of friendship and marital relations with the polytheists, men and women, cools down the sentiments of enmity and hatred towards polytheism and disbelief which may drag one into polytheism. There is the severe punishment of Hell-fire for such people, so marriage with them is strictly prohibited. Hadrat Shah Wali Allah gives the following comments: There is a lesson in the above verse. When the believers augment their friendships and relations with the infidels and polytheists and there is intimacy between them, resulting in intermarriages, it poses a serious hazard to Islam. The polytheistic creeds deliberately or inadvertently affect the minds.

Besides the above religious disadvantages, the worldly loss is that without religious concord there can be no real love and affection between a husband and a wife. The relations between them are bound to be embittered. By and by the gulf of differences between them is widened and the inevitable result thereof is that husband and wife do not remain loyal to each other and resort to evil and sinful lives, thus nullifying the very aim and objective of marriage.

Equality : In order to achieve mutual love and cooperation which is essential for a happy home life, equality in certain things is necessary. For instance, a pious woman should not be married to a wicked man, similarly it is forbidden to marry a wicked man to a pious lady. It has been mentioned in the Holy Quran:

> *"The adulterer/fornicator should not marry save an adulteress/fornicatress or an idolatress, and the adulteress/fornicatress none shall marry save an adulterer/fornicator or an idolator. All that is forbidden unto believers."*
>
> *(24:3)*

It is evident that an adulterer or an adulteress is not equal to a pious woman or a pious man. There is a great difference between the two and there is little hope of their union.

Equality in wealth does not seem to be necessary. Only Imam Shafii believes in the equality of wealth. But experience has shown that wealth is not such a thing as stands in the way of sincere love and affection, rather it can lead to hatred and discord.

Some scholars believe in the equality of descent. Probably they have based their views on intellectual reasoning. It is a common experience that social difference among the various families give rise to many complications, but Ibn Hajar says that in so far as the religious aspect of this matter is concerned there is no authentic tradition stressing on the equality of descent. On the other hand, ample evidences and Ahadith exist which testify that during the Prophet's and the Caliphs' period, no importance was given to race and descent.

Imam Bukhari has narrated two such events in the chapter Al-Ikfa Fiddin from which it is evident that equality in descent was not considered as necessary. The first incident pertaining to Abu Hudaifa (Allah be pleased with him) a Companion of Badr. He married Hadrat Salim (Allah be pleased with him) a freed servant of a woman of Ansar, to his niece, Hind bint Walid (Allah be pleased with her) who was one of Muhajirat.

The other incident pertains to Dabaa bint Zubayr (Allah be pleased with her). She was married to Hadrat Miqdad (Allah be pleased with him) although Dabaa was a very high - ranking woman in the matter of her descent.

Hafiz Ibn Qayyim has written in detail on this subject and has proved that Islam has not laid any stress on descent and its strict observance is against the teachings and spirit of Islam. Allah has made tribes and clans as means of mutual relations and contracts. It has been mentioned in the Holy Quran:

> *"Lo! the noblest of you, in the sight of Allah is best in conduct."* *(49:13)*

It has been mentioned in another verse:

> *"The believers are not else than brothers."* *(49:10)*

> *The above and many other verses are a clear proof of fraternity and brotherhood in Islam. The Holy Prophet (peace and blessings of Allah be upon him) has thrown further light on this subject. I have already quoted above a Hadith of Tirmidhi that if a proposal for marriage comes to you from a person whose religion and conduct you like, marry him, because if you make any other thing, besides religion and conduct, the basis for marriage, it will spread evil and wickedness on earth. Once the Holy Prophet (peace and blessings of Allah be upon him) observed: The children of such and such Prophets are not my Ummah. My Ummah comprises of pious people whosoever they may be and wherever they may be.'* *(Zad al-Maad)*

It is a fact that the Holy Prophet (peace and blessings of Allah be upon him) got Zainab bint Jahsh married to his freed servant, Zaid bin Haritha, Fatima bint Qais Fahriyya to Zaid's son Hadrat Asama and Hadrat Bilal bin Ribah of Habash to Abdur Rahman bin Auf's sister. It is evident from the above events that Islam does not attach any great importance to race and descent. Strictness in this matter is, therefore, not allowed.

Announcement of Marriage : The rules and regulations promulgated by Islam block all the avenues of sin and vice. We must try to adopt all the ways and means, remaining within the limits prescribed by Allah, to curb immorality and lewdness. Islam has, therefore, stressed the announcement of marriage. Secret or hidden marriage is forbidden in Islam as it involves many dangers. There is no room for flirtation, keeping of concubines or premarital sexual relations in Islam. In Islam the announcement of marriage is required to be made publicly and there is a clear distinction between secret and illicit relations and Islamic Nikah. The wisdom behind this is that one should never try to develop secret illicit relations.

Another condition of marriage is that at least two men or one man and two women must be witnesses. They must be present in the gathering and proposal and acceptance of proposal should be so announced that the witnesses should hear them. The gathering should be, as far as possible, large. It has been observed by the Holy Prophet (peace and blessings of Allah be upon him): Make the marriage publicly known, and perform it in mosques and beat the duff.
(Tirmidhi)

The one great advantage of performing the marriage in a mosque is that every one can reach there, and the beating of a drum is for the purpose of announcement. Islam does not allow frivolous merry making. The Holy Prophet (peace and blessings of Allah be upon him) has said: Announcement and beating of duff at marriage, make a distinction between lawful and unlawful. *(Tirmidhi)*

If public announcement of marriage is not considered to be necessary, there would remain hardly any distinction between secret illegal love affairs and legal marriages and thus the way would be paved for illicit love relations, which are strictly forbidden in Islam. The real aim and subject of marriage, according to Islam, is spiritual elevation and the protection of piety and chastity and not mere gratification of sexual desire. The announcement of marriage is, therefore, necessary. It has been mentioned in the Holy Quran:

When ye give them their marriage portions live with them in honour, not in sin, nor taking them as secret concubines.
(5:5)

They being honest not debauched nor of loose conduct.
(4:25)

The true significance of marriage has been explained in a miraculous style of the Holy Quran and emphasis has been laid on the announcement of marriage.

There is another way to give publicity to marriage and one cannot but wonder at this interesting and solemn function. It is appreciable in Islam that after spending a night with the wife, a man should give a marriage feast. The Ahadith lay special stress on it. The Holy Prophet (peace and blessings of Allah be upon him) himself arranged this feast at the time of marrying Hadrat Zainab bint Jahsh (Allah be pleased with her). He slaughtered a goat and served meat to his Companions in the marriage feast. When he married Hadrat Safiah (Allah be pleased with her) he got *Hees* prepared and served it to the guests. Hees is a kind of Arabian dish composed of dates, cheese and ghee. At the time of some marriages he could not, however, get anything and he arranged the marriage feast with two mud of barley.

He exhorted his Companions to give marriage feasts. Hadrat Abdur Rahman bin Auf (Allah be pleased with him) reported that the Holy Prophet (peace and blessings of Allah be upon him), said: Arrange the marriage feast even if with a single goat.

Some consider this feast as an incumbent duty, but the correct view is that the Holy Prophet (peace and blessings of Allah be upon him) recommended it or that it is his Sunnah. However, it is desirable that one should serve to the people whatever is easily available. It does not at all mean that one should borrow in order to make this arrangement.

> *On the one hand, it has been asked of Muslims to arrange the marriage feast and on the other hand, the people have been directed to accept the invitation to a marriage feast. The Holy Prophet (peace and blessings of Allah be upon him) said: When anyone of you is invited to the marriage feast, he should accept it.* *(Ibn Majah)*
>
> *The Holy Prophet (peace and blessings of Allah be upon him) has said that not only the rich should be invited to this feast, but the poor and the destitute should also be invited. The worst of the feasts is the marriage feast to which the rich are invited and the poor and the destitute are not invited.* *(Agreed Upon)*
>
> *He who did not partake of the marriage feast despite invitation, disobeyed Allah and His Prophet.* *(Agreed Upon)*

The importance of the marriage feast can be judged from the above Ahadith. Apart from the expression of joy and happiness, another advantage of this feast is that the marriage receives due publicity and all doubts and suspicions about the marriage are removed.

Another aim and object of the open announcement of marriage is to discourage illicit secret 'love affairs' and to guard chastity and morality which is possible only through a legal marriage.

Lawful Gratification of Sex : After marriage, Islam has imposed no restrictions on the husband and wife in gratifying their sexual desire in the natural course. There is no restriction of time. Sexual intercourse is permissible during the day and the night, during summer and winter and during spring and rains. No one is allowed to intervene in this matter.

Sexual intercourse is forbidden in the days of the month of Ramadan only, in which both husband and wife have been ordained to keep fast. During the fast, indulgence in sexual intercourse is prohibited in Islam. But no restriction is imposed on mutual conversation and things of other interest. This restriction is only during the period of fasting. After breaking the fast there is no ban on sexual intercourse except during the forbidden periods of which everyone is aware. It has been clearly mentioned in the Holy Quran:

> *It is made lawful to you to go unto your wives on the night of the fasts. They are raiment for you and ye are raiment for them.* *(2:187)*

In the above verse, sexual intercourse has been allowed during the nights of Ramadan. In another verse, the gratification of sexual intercourse is permissible from the sunset just as it is permissible to eat and drink after breaking the fast:

> *So hold intercourse with them and seek that which Allah hath ordained for you, and eat and drink until the white thread become the distinct to you from the black thread of the dawn.* *(2:187)*

Besides the fasts of Ramadan, it is forbidden for a woman to keep fast on any day of the year without the permission of her husband as he might feel her need at any time.

There are two occasions on which the woman remains naturally polluted. The first is during menstrual discharge, the maximum period of which extends to ten days and the minimum period of which extends to three days. The second occasion is during the discharge of blood at childbirth which continues for weeks together. Its maximum limit is forty days and there is no minimum limit for it. During these days of pollution, sexual intercourse is prohibited. As we have already said these are the days of pollution of a woman and there is a natural aversion for sexual intercourse. Moreover, there is every risk of contracting infectious diseases. The Holy Quran has mentioned this fact:

> *They question thee (O' Muhammad), concerning menstruation. Say: It is an illness, so let women alone at such times and go not unto them till they are cleansed. And when they have purified themselves, then go unto them as Allah hath enjoined upon you.* *(2:222)*

Besides the above periods there is no restriction on sexual intercourse in Islam. The women regain fresh vim and vigour after these days and their capability to conceive grows after the menstrual period. Apart from the above occasions, if there is no other reason of the Shariah, the husband and wife can have sexual intercourse at any time and Islam has granted them complete freedom in this respect. While explaining the conjugal relations of husband and wife, the Holy Quran has adopted a very pious, elegant and eloquent style. It has been mentioned in the Holy Quran:

They are raiment for you and you are raiment for them. *(2:187)*

In the above verse husband and wife have been called each other's garments, meaning thereby that a woman protects the moral character of a man and the man guards the chastity and modesty of a woman. Similarly, the woman is an adornment for the husband and the man is her garment. Whenever they desire they meet each other. Thus, there exists mutual love and harmony between the two which is the essence of true marriage. The word 'garment' has comprehensive meaning. In another verse, the woman has been resembled to a tilth. It has been mentioned in the Holy Quran:

Your women are a tilth for you so go to your tilth as ye will. *(2:223)*

Marriage: A Legal Bond : In marriage we find it to be that everlasting conduct which engulfs everything and by which all things become good and bear the required fruit for its kind.

The Holy Quran has the following to say:

"And all things We have created by pairs that happily ye may reflect" *(Quran, 51: 49)*

"Glory to Him Who created all the sexual pairs of that which they knew not". *(Quran 36: 36)*

Marriage is the natural tie between the pair (male and female) as the above quoted verse of the Holy Quran says: all things are created in pairs. It is more so true in everything in our dynamic world. You find this even in things like electricity: we have the positive and negative. Neither of the two will function satisfactorily alone without the help of the other.

Lingering on one of the afore quoted verse:

"And of His signs is this: He created helpmates for you from yourselves that you may find in them quiet of mind, and He ordained in you love and mercy. *(Quran, 30: 21)*

We come to know that marriage is not for the sexual urge only as it could appear at the first instance to teenagers and their like. We cannot, deny this. Sexual desire exists, but it is just a small portion out of the secret that mere words fail to express the true feelings between the pair. It is more so true with the elderly people than with the younger ones. That top secret could be what was meant by the Holy Quran as rest and peace of mind, and love and mercy, mutual understanding, building up the home, as well as society in general. To quote, but a very simple example. When one of the pair is away from the other for one reason or another they both feel that there is something very important missing in their life.

The result of such a holy tie is not to bring up children and the satisfaction of sexual desire only, but consolation, quiet of mind, rest of the soul, love, mercy, mutual understanding, taking ones share in building up the society and the world at large and their advancement, etc.

No Monasticism : Islam encourages marriage. There is no monasticism in Islam. The following verse depicts this in a clear cut way:

> *"Then We caused our messenger to follow in their footsteps, and We caused Jesus, son of Mary, to follow, and gave him the Gospel, and placed compassion and mercy in the hearts of those who followed him. But monasticism they invented— We ordained it, not for them, only seeking Allah's pleasure, and they observed it not with right observance ..."*
>
> *(Quran, 57 27)*

The Messenger of, Allah deplored the idea of monasticism forthwith saying: No Monasticism in Islam.

The Prophet (may blessings and peace, of Allah be upon him) told a group of men who tried to do the following; One of them was saying prayers all night long without sleeping, the other used to fast all the time without eating and the third refrained from women, he never married. The Apostle of Allah (peace and blessings of Allah be upon him) told them what it meant: "I heard what you said I am much more pious than you are, but I fast and eat. I say prayers and sleep, and I marry. This is my Sunna (teaching). Anyone who does not follow it is not one of my followers (does not obey me).

The Messenger of Allah (peace and blessings of Allah be upon him) forbids his followers from marrying women solely for their social status or their wealth. There should be a stronger drive than rank and money. He is quoted to have said:

"Do not marry women for the sake of their wealth, because wealth might make them haughty and proud."

He who marries a woman just because of her social status or her rank in society, Allah will not add anything more than deterioration and humiliation before the eyes of others. He urges the marriage of righteous women. He is quoted as saying :

"If you find a pious woman, (bless your stars) you are lucky."

It is reported that a girl came to the Apostle of Allah complaining that her father forced her to marry a man without her consent. The Prophet (peace and blessings of Allah be upon him) gave her the choice between accepting the marriage or invalidating it. The girl responded: ."I accepted this marriage, but I wanted to let women know that .parents (fathers) have no right to force husbands on them." They must be given the choice of either accepting the marriage or vice versa.

Khaddam, Khansa's father forced her to marry a husband. She did not like the idea. Then she went to the Messenger of Allah (may Allah give him peace) who on his turn respected the girl's wish to marry a man of her approval, naturally the first marriage was made invalid.

It is also reported that the Prophet Muhammad (may blessings and, peace of Allah be upon him) said :

"A widow (or a divorced one) is not to be married before her consent is sought."

"No virgin girl is to marry without first consulting her, and her approval is her keeping silent."

A Muslim woman cannot be forced to marry without her approval. If she is forced to do so, then that marriage is invalidated.

Both husband and wife have equal rights and claims on one another, except for one thing or one responsibility (i.e., leadership). Islam regards leadership as a natural course in any collective life and it is more consistent with the nature of man.

Islam emphasized leadership in all human life. When more than one person say prayers; they are supposed to select a leader for prayers, who is called Imam.

Aqqaad says in his book, *al-Mar-'a fil Quran* (Woman in the Holy Quran): ".. . . . We find in the nature of the sex physiological composition that one sex-desires while the other accepts. This is found in all animal species that have needs and have sexual relations from time to time.

"When there is a sexual urge from both the male and female; it is not the female that commences the wish and call, nor does she fight the rival of the same sex. This is not because of shyness or shame or because of religious obligations or morale. We find this habit even in male and female animals which know nothing of shame or morale. A female animal does not ask a male, one to have relations. She just draws his attention by passing in front of him, so as he might follow her, and get her at her own free will. A female animal generally waits the result of a quarrel between male rivals to win her."

Quran has the following rule about the family leadership :
"....And women shall have rights similar to the rights against them, according to what is equitable; but men have a degree of advantage over them. And Allah is Exalted in, Power, Wise." (Quran, 2: 228) (Abdullah).

One might ask, "Is the husband, then, much superior than his wife, as he is given such an advantage before the law?"

Our answer is this, "Nothing of the sort, A man has been given a degree of advantage in maintenance and protection because of the natural differences between the two sexes. The sex that we all agree to be the fair and weaker sex shows by its name that it needs some sort of protection, especially in very tense situations. There should be no dictatorship on the part of the husband over the wife. There should be, counsel, understanding and mutual satisfaction in all matters pertaining to family decisions. 'If mutual understanding does not prevail in a Muslim family, then it is the innocent children who become poor victims of such a disintegrated family, and all the consequences of it fall on the society. Hence we have delinquents.'

Let us quote one example from the Holy Quran on the weaning of a child which will serve as a green light. This is more so after a divorce has taken place :

"Mothers shall suckle their children for two whole years; (that is) for those who wish to complete the suckling. The duty of feeding and clothing nursing mothers in a seemly manner is upon the father of the child. No one should be charged beyond his capacity. A mother should not be made to suffer because of her child, nor should he on whom the child is born be made to suffer because of his child, And on the father's heir is incumbent the like of that (which was incumbent on the father). If they desire to wean the child

by mutual consent and after consultation, it is no sin for them; and if ye wish to give your children out to nurse, it is no sin for you, provided that ye pay what is due for you in kindness, observe your duty to Allah, and know that Allah is seer of what you do." *(Quran, 2 :.233)*

While discussing the status of women in Islam; at the coffee lounge after supper; with some of the fellow teachers from different parts of the world, who attended a. Refresher Course on the Teaching of English as a Foreign Language years ago; I remember someone to have put, the following before us :

"You must be kidding Eh! You pretend to treat women equally as you do with men; and just now you quoted a verse from, your book in which it was mentioned that a woman's share in inheritance is one half of the man's share, and you still want us to believe in your word. Forget it."

This followed an uproar:

"You can say that again, He is just fooling himself," "I can't agree with you more", etc.

I said, "I beseech you to be patient."

After that our discussion was very hot it took us a nearly one hour when I asked them leave to go for Maghrib prayers. The gist of our discussion from my side was:

"It is generally agreed that a man spends one-third of his income on a woman; she, were a wife, mother, daughter or sister or on any other woman. That (a) and (b) man (husband) is fully responsible for the full maintenance of wife and children. This responsibility is not reduced because the wife is either rich or has an access of any personal income.

On the other hand female is not overburdened with any claims or her possessions, so she is far more financially secure and well off. All her possessions before and after marriage remain hers and are not transferred to her husband. Islam does not ask her to spend a penny out of her income on marriage on her family while she is married. It is upon the husband, whether poor or rich, to maintain her. Islam does not forbid her from her sharing in family maintenance on her own freewill, especially if her means of income are much better than her husband's. On and above this Islam requires from a husband to treat his wife kindly and keep a good company of her. Quran puts this in a clear cut way :

"O ye who believe ! You are forbidden to inherit women against their will, nor should you treat them with harshness,

that ye may take away part of the dowry ye have given them ...... On the contrary, live with them on a footing of kindness and equity if ye take a dislike to them it may be that ye dislike a thing Allah brings about through it a great deal of good."

"But if you decide to take one wife in place of another, even if ye had given the latter a whole treasure for dowry, take not the least bit of it back, would you take it by slander and a manifest wrong?"

"And how could you take it (dowry) when ye have gone in unto each other, and they have taken from you a solemn covenant?" *(Quran, 4: 19-21)*

We learn from the above quoted verses that it is advisable for a man who divorces his wife not to ask for what he had given her as a dowry. What a lovely touch to some hard hearted men. In this respect the Messenger of Allah (Allah's peace be upon him) is quoted as saying what it meant:

"The best of you is the one who is the best for his family. I am the best for my family."

"The perfect believers are those who are the best in their dealings, and the best of you are those who are the best for their wives."

It is also quoted that he said that wives of a lot of people come to his wives complaining against their husbands beating them. He said, "... those husbands are not the beat of you." It is permissible to flog a wife, as we shall see, but under certain circumstances beating a wife should be the last resort.

Divorce : Christianity waged war against Islam as to the problem of divorce. It used to criticize Islam as breaking the heavenly tie between husband and wife. Finally we see Christians accept the natural call and agree or rather recognize divorce as a social solution to many a family problem.

Western Europe is divided into three different ways of accepting divorce: (1) Nations agree with the idea of divorce but, without bodily separation; some such nations are: Sweden, Norway, Portugal, Romania, Switzerland, Germany and Russia. (1) Nations that accept bodily separation but not divorce. These countries are Spain and Italy. (1) Nations that accept both: divorce and bodily separation. They are France, Belgium, Great Britain, United States of America and some of Socialist States.

The reader might ask: What do you mean by separation?

It is like this: The husband and wife are separated for ever; while the female is still regarded by the society as his wife.

Each of the two has full right of doing, whatever he/she pleases without any interference from the other.

Islam does not only give the woman the right to decide on marriage, but also the right of divorce. In order to protect the family from rush divorce decisions under temporary emotional stress, especially if the partners are still young; certain steps and waiting periods must be observed. We shall discuss some such steps forthwith.

If the marriage contract states that the woman can, divorce her husband without resorting to court and file a case she may do so; otherwise she is asked to bring a good reason in asking why she has to divorce before the judge.

This is more so because a woman generally discharges two types of hormones monthly. These hormones affect her behaviour very much and they may even have an effect on her decisions.

Islam took into consideration the relatively more emotional nature of the woman. On this the Holy Quran says :

> *"........ When you have divorced women, and they have reached their prescribed term, retain them in kindness or release them in kindness, and retain them not for injury so that ye transgress limits."* *(Quran 2: 231)*

It is reported that the Apostle of Allah (may blessings and peace of Allah be upon him) said something which meant:

> *"What do those people who play with the limits of Allah think? You hear them say: "I have divorced my wife, or I have remarried her? Do they abuse the Book and I am still with you?"*

He said this to people who misused the right of divorce.

Marriage is a sacred tie between the two sexes. It should never be misused. If there is an unsuccessful marriage, then they part from each other in accordance with the Shariah (Islamic Law) and not otherwise. It was customary in Pre-Islamic Arabia that a husband would forswear his wife and decide not to live as husband and wife. He may leave her in such a state of suspense for indefinite period. Sometimes after much consultation he may decide to divorce her. This attitude was still in vogue in the early Islamic period. It was soon suppressed by Islam and reconciliation was recommended, but if both are still determined, then divorce is the only fair solution. The Holy Quran reminds those who divorce :

"And if they decide upon divorce (let them remember that) Allah is Hearer, Knower." *(2: 227)*

He bears the cry of all who suffer and knows the reasons. Steps of divorce are clearly presented in Quran. (See somewhere between verses. 224 to 237 of *Surah al-Baqara.*) The Holy Quran says :

"Women who are divorced shall wait, keeping themselves apart three monthly courses. And it is not lawful for them, that they should conceal that which Allah hath created in their wombs if they are believers in Allah and the Last Day. And their husbands would do better to take them back in that case if they desire a reconciliation. And they (women) have right similar to those (of men) over them in kindness." *(2: 228)*

The wife is to stay after divorce for three months and ten days; and for four months ten days if she is a widow; this is called "Iddat" (legally prescribed period of waiting during which a woman may not remarry after for being widowed or divorced) before she can marry another husband whereas the husband, who divorced her, can marry at the same moment. This is so, because of the would be pregnancy. Generally if a woman is pregnant, it is known within the first hundred days of her pregnancy.

A very good step of divorce is shown in the following verse of the Quran:

"....so good women are the obedient, guarding in secret that which Allah hath guarded and for those whom ye fear rebellion, admonish them and banish them in bed apart, and scourge them. Then if they obey you, seek not a way against them. Lo! Allah is ever High, Exalted,, Great." *(4: 34)*

The family life should be harmonious If anything goes wrong and there is any misunderstanding; four steps are to be taken to deal with such a situation: (1) verbal advice and admonition, (2) then the family relation is to be suspended, (3) after that slight physical correction (beating slightly) may be administered, and the fourth is a family council to settle the differences if there is any.

No one is to lose his/her temper. There should be no nagging or sarcasm, they should speak to each other in other people's presence, nor should they remind each other of their forgotten faults of long ago because such faults have already been forgiven. They must always remember that Allah is always with them.

First the husband; who uses his reasoning more than his emotions; is asked to talk with her gently and explain to her that what she does angers Allah, and nobody can bear it when Allah is angry with anyone. He should find out the reasons of her rebellion and solve the problems if he can. He is to go with his advice to her for some time. He is to deal with her very tactfully. He should never hurry and act angry with her.

This fails, then the family relation (husband/ wife) is to be suspended. He is to banish her in bed apart. He is not to sleep with her in the same bed. He may be with her in the same room. If he can stay with her apart in the same room, that will be much better as a first step.

If he banishes her from bed apart, this will make her feel an infra dig. Feminism is the best and strongest weapon for any woman to attract a man, and make him follow her instructions. If a man banishes his wife, this act will pierce very deeply into the alter of her womanhood; thus the last stronghold of her's will have fallen. Then she might be in a position to listen to what, her husband tells her.

If she still resists, then he is to administer a slight physical correction. He is to scourge her. When he flogs her, he should remember that he is beating his own wife. He should not beat her When he is angry; whatever the cause of his anger could be. The flogging must never leave any marks on her. It should be slight and not very painful.

The maxim: Spare the rod and spoil the child; stands true to the present time. Psychologists and educationists try to give different thoughts, ideas and arguments all discouraging scourging and beating. They have been trying this for the last thirty to fifty years. What are the results? Too many psychological and neurotic cases that need too many psychological clinics with scores of social workers and hundreds of psychologists and psycho-therapists. You see people being massaged, hypnotised or being given very good pieces of advice which the adviser himself will never practice, and the poor victims, confess under the pressure and torture of suggestion. And, worse still you find people indulge themselves into drugs, alcoholism, fornication, treachery, burglary, piracy, hypism, homosexuality and a hundred other evils that cost a society hundreds of billions of pounds trying to reduce such destructions.

Our daily life is full of reward and punishment. If we misuse our health we become sick and the like. So why for goodness sake do we discourage punishment at school at the same time we punish them when the same people do wrong elsewhere.

May I whisper to Muslim educationists? Islam tells us to teach our children till they are ten years of age. If, they do not follow what we have been telling them all these years, then we are to flog them. Coming to our fourth point: family council to settle the differences or disputes, between a married couple.

On this the Quran says:

> *"If ye fear breach between them twain, appoint (two) arbiters, one from his family, and the other from hers. If they wish for peace Allah will cause their reconciliation for Allah hath full knowledge, and is acquainted with all things."*
>
> *(4: 35)*

The arbiters will know the facts and if they are all (arbiters and husband and wife) honest Allah will help them to effect a real reconciliation without any publicity or resorting to courts.

We have previously pointed out that man is much more rational than a woman. The, husband-wife relation is of a more emotional character, so Islam gave the man four different steps to deal with his rebellious wife, before taking the last weapon: Divorce.

A woman is much more emotional than a man, and as we have just discussed, the husband-wife relation is much more emotional than any other relationship between different people. So Islam has not much said about how should a wife deal with her rebellious husband. It left it to her (to deal with the situation). She knows very quickly; by her innate nature; the reasons of her husband's rebellion or ill-conduct and she has all those strong weapons at her disposal to deal with such a situation.

Let us cite a good example of how a wife notices the signs of ill conduct or rebellion from her husband. Hadrat Sawda bint Zamla; one of the wives of the Apostle of Allah (peace be upon him) noticed that her husband (The Prophet) was not so much encouraged to remain with her. Thinking of the problem, she finally came to the conclusion, that it was because of her age. She was very old, or better still; the oldest of all his wives.

She decided on something very serious. She said to the Prophet something like this: "O! Messenger of Allah, I am too old to need a husband. I give my share and nights to Aishah, your youngest and beloved wife. What I want at this stage is to be among your wives in the Hereafter."

4

Family System

FAMILIAL SYSTEM

The importance of the large-scale ideological and economic factors in the everyday life situation of the individual, and the way in which this ideology has opened up the possibility of divergent adaptations and a new household economy. Moreover, the burden that economic changes place on adult males (who still are the main providers in most families), as well as career married women, has increased. This has complicated and intensified the tradition of child-rearing, cooking, washing, cleaning the house, taking care of the family and social networks, as well as the time spent on purchasing goods and supervising children after school. The large-scale economic reforms, and the new household economy, have affected the life of family members in different ways. The form and the rituals of household activities in everyday life are central themes in the following section.

The economic crises of the Islamic state and the new ideological demands have incurred cumulative and overlapping perspectives. This has left a narrow range of options for young and ambitious couples, forcing them to seek opportunities outside the home country, as exemplified by Mahry's extended family. Marriage and higher education has traditionally served as a passage for social and economic independence, although it has often been the case that newly-weds stay in the house of the wife's or husband's father for a while, before establishing an independent household. For ten years Halima, a 44-year-old female school teacher, shared a residence with her sister-in-law before she and her husband could save enough money to buy one of the two-room flats offered to school employees.

Marriage has always been an economic security for the wife, and the husband is traditionally responsible for the economic security of the family. The reality of the current socio-economic situation for the average lower and middle-class category, is such that extra economic support is necessary, either from the wife-particularly in the case of young married couples-or from parents.

A young family's economic independence and higher social status, such as in the case of Mahry and her siblings, depends upon occupation and further education. Mahry and her family had less chance of obtaining higher education because of the increased number of applicants, and also because of new Islamic ideological criteria for the selection of religiously active candidates. A new mode of adaptation, and a new economic niche, has emerged for family members who are able to take on additional roles.

As a result of constant price increases on household goods, the consequences of these economic niches have affected males and females differently. Managing the household economy is difficult in lower and middle-class families, even when the breadwinner (often the man), has previous work experience, or higher education. Families are dependent on a single income from employment in the public sector, such as teacher or office work jobs.

Grown-up children, despite their higher education, are economically dependent on their parents, who returned home from abroad during the Iranian revolution in 1978. This dependency may be permanent for some, thus placing a burden on the parents. In post-revolutionary Iran, large numbers of urban middle and higher-class Iranians left home.

Two distinctive, significant and completely new household structures emerged in post-revolutionary Iran. These were: (a) the extended household composed of parents and married children who shared a residence, and (b) the households consisting of elderly couples who remained in Iran, while their children left home and took permanent residence abroad. The former household composition is common among families where a majority of the members stayed in Iran, and only a few moved abroad. The latter household composition consisted of elderly couples who voluntarily lived alone at home, visiting their children only once in a while abroad. These are often better-off couples, contrasting dramatically with the lower and middle-class extended household, where parents accommodate a married daughter or son and their families.

To maintain the economy of daily life many young educated men started a business of their own, or with other male relatives. The inevitable solution for lower and middle-class families was to have two members of the family in employment. Alternatively the breadwinner of the family would take two jobs, one in the official sector and another in the private sector. In the case of Mahry, close and distant male relatives were employed as civil servants, teachers, low-ranking army officers, social health personnel, etc. Due to the high cost of living they worked in their spare time as independent taxi drivers, as salesmen buying and selling land, as dealers in foreign currencies or rationed goods, or as shop assistants. In comparison, women were either housewives or, as is the case among a few middle-aged women, they were employed as nursery teachers, computer assistants, students, social health workers or, like Mahry, they worked with sewing and embroidery.

Most of the young families in the community, either rented rooms that cost them half of their salary as state employees, or they shared a residence with their parents or a close relative in order to save money. Many were also dependent on others for economic support, directly or indirectly, in the form of cash, household subsistence, and goods. Such socio-economic insecurity along with the poor educational opportunities for themselves and the problems facing their children, as well as the general political harassment, has led many of these middle-class families to join the flow of migrants of the 1980s.

Household work is not only a distinctive personalised domain, but is also a part of the larger economic and post- revolutionary ideological development, as well as being a focus of change. Domestic work in post-revolutionary Iran involved a series of new tasks and more intensive work schedules for women.

Adaptability of household members to changing conditions depended on the availability of facilities and resources. A married woman explained that due to the intensive work schedule and, for example, the lack of communal facilities, she had to do the laundry at night when water was more easily available, and the shopping before sunrise so as to be able to prepare the mid-day meal for the family. This example illustrates how the mode of work among women mainly concerned with 'domestic' tasks has intensified due to broader political and economic conditions. One could hardly escape the daily observation of lower and middle-class women (often mothers), accompanied by small children, waiting impatiently for several hours in queues, in order to purchase hygienic supplies of milk, foods, and other 'domestic' items, at a more reasonable price than in the open market. Commonly they were worried about the daily household routines; for example, one waiting in such a queue told how worried she was at being delayed in preparing the noon meal for her husband and children coming home from work and school. Foreign goods, such as electrical appliances, were very expensive and considered as luxury items by lower middle-class families. Moreover, these items provided a new form of enterprise for well-off families. Being able to sell foreign goods in the home market greatly boosted the income of such well-off families. The extended household has to some extent solved the problem of married children who are not able to establish an independent household without economic support from their parents.

High prices of household equipment and house rent made it impossible for young families with average economic means to establish an economically independent household. However, such an intensive relation and extended household dependency has increased family conflicts dramatically, particularly in already controversial relationships such as between daughter-in-law and mother-in-law.

Career options are limited for young members of lower-class families. Petty trading seems to be an acceptable strategy for boys. Wheeler-dealers, and street vendors, are two forms of economic activity adopted by recent school-leavers. Bazar-e azad activity has opened a series of channels through which household items rationed by the state flow into the black market. Such enterprises, and the extra income earned, are often considered insecure, illegal, not quite respectable and even immoral. Middlemen, such as wheeler-dealers, after spending long hours in queues, buying goods such as cigarettes and eggs from the cooperatives shops, and then selling them at black-market prices. This type of occupation may serve as a source of income for young and middle-aged male members of low-income families. For families with low incomes, daily petty trading is not a permanent enterprise.

Self-employment yields more income than a low-paid permanent job. Establishing a business requires both economic and social capital, without which it is difficult to obtain goods to sell, or to rent a shop. When renting a shop a deposit is paid. The price has increased with inflation from around 50 thousand tomans in 1979 to an average of one million tomans in 1990. This means that it is virtually impossible to establish a permanent business. It also means that large profits can be made from letting shops, houses, flats and rooms. Those who have parents with a large capital may set up a small business.

While the father is still alive, they will be allowed to enter the family business as part of their eventual inheritance. The street-corner traders sell items such as dollars, cigarettes, rationed foods, and stockings. Dast-farosh is an enterprise open to even those with little capital, and is often a second source of income for individuals such as a grown-up son, or a head of a household. Any form of self-employment to supplement the limited household income, is justified on the grounds that multiple sources of income are necessary. Since a single-income job in the public sector cannot meet all of the household's real expenditures, the idea of a second job has become widely accepted.

Resourceful entrepreneurs will be able to provide for family consumption, as well as accumulate considerable wealth. In contrast, permanent business activities are generally open only to better-off middle-class merchants and craftsmen, and other traditionally independent producers and distributors. These are often cooperative family businesses jointly owned by close male relatives, such as a father and his sons, brothers, cousins and in-laws. This contrasts with the petty trader who sets up his business independently. Recently, because of restrictions, male shopkeepers are forbidden to sell female lingerie, or to open female hair-dressing salons.

As a consequence, female shopkeepers and co-partnership with a female relative has increased. The open market makes non-rationed items available to the public, such as electrical appliances, clothing, and domestic goods, as well as scarce medicines. The scarcity and long queues have forced many people to purchase items in the black market.

The rise in prices of local commodities may be explained by: (a) the government extra export policy for earning foreign currencies; (b) the rise in the exchange rate for dollars; and (c) the two devaluations of the rial. Devaluation of Iranian currency has been of particular importance for the family household economy, since family incomes are in the form of riyals. Subsequently they are the hardest hit by inflation, exchange rates, and the black market policy of the state.

Broad structural and economical changes, such as the rationing system for the distribution of goods, has encouraged the development of a new transactional pseudo-occupation niche. Some of these new enterprises are considered immoral, in terms of their transactional and insecure nature. Self-employment and free-enterprise activities are considered to offer greater opportunities for meeting the daily increases of expenditures. Government employees, who are particularly well educated, and with fixed low wages, have become very disappointed with the monthly income of their permanent jobs. It is not adequate to cover their household expenses, such as rent. The difference in the earnings of these well-qualified government employees, and those whose main source of income is selling dollars in the black market, has marginalised the former category both socially and economically.

Wages for average civil servants and employees in official sectors, such as education, have remained relatively the same as they were before the revolution. According to a study by Behdad, in 1980 there had been an increase in the official minimum wage and a change in the rate of income tax to 12 per cent.

Most workers were affected by the new law stipulating minimum wages, the exception being urban workers in large firms. It must be keep in mind that family economic viability in post-revolutionary Iran is a problem for most government employees, hence the interest in free business and double waged jobs.

The most profitable enterprises involve trading in foreign currencies and goods, such as dollars, pounds, gold, household items and land, and money lending. Thus, the families that had invested capital in such commodities as land, houses, cars, gold, shops, etc., prior to the outbreak of the war between Iran and Iraq in 1980 are now in position. Expansion of the black market has an advantage as it further benefited those who have access to foreign currencies, imported goods, and are able to travel abroad frequently.

Land ownership has always been an important source of local identity and power in Iran. After the revolution, long-term investment in land has more than ever become an important form of capital, as well as a strategy for rapidly accumulating wealth. The dramatic rise in land prices since 1980 has applied even to the purchase of the isolated land outside the city limit, which is not even supplied with electricity and water.

An example of rapid social mobility through land ownership is the case of an educated civil engineer. He qualified in England in the 1970s. He and his family returned to Iran shortly after the Iranian revolution in 1980. He started to work for his former employer, where he had previously been employed in a junior position. Due to his high foreign qualification he was soon offered jobs in different cities, including one in a province where he received high wages due to the difficult geographical conditions. Shortly after he returned home from England he bought a piece of land at a low price. The land was on the nonresidential periphery of a town without electricity and water supplies. It cost him 60 tomans per square metre in 1980. However, inflation increased its value to 5,000/6,000 tomans per square metre in 1989.

In the long term ownership of land is highly beneficial, the rapid increase in value making it a secure investment. The demand for land has particularly increased as a result of demographic changes. These can be explained as follows: (a) rapid population growth; (b) the continuous migration from small towns and nearby villages to large towns. The rapid expansion of towns toward the city limits increased the value of cheap and isolated land from 20-60 tomans per square metre in 1979, to 6,000 tomans per square metre in 1989-90. Such land could not, however, be used for building a house until it had been included within the town's official boundaries.

The profit from land ownership was greater than from the ownership of fruit gardens, the latter providing only a small annual income for urban middle-class and business families. This was the common enterprise that led to the serious destruction of the famous orchard land in Shiraz. The grape and apple farms changed into building sites, thereby bringing a high profit to their owners. It would be interesting to evaluate the impact on agricultural production.

Land confiscated during the revolution has been sold cheap to religio-politically privileged community members, such as war veterans, employees of the Islamic institution for rehabilitation, and to families of martyrs or hostages. In recent years government supporters have been favoured for the redistribution of economic and social opportunities, such as obtaining employment, education, rationed goods and land. Special allocations have been given as the rewards for their support. Thus, economic advancement has been possible not only for those who have accumulated capital under the former regime, but also for those who have gained high status as first-class citizens in the Islamic regime, whatever their class background may have been.

Gifts of gold signify sets of kinship relations and are part of large chains of acts distinguishing close relatives, high-ranking guests and close friends. The value of gold is both an objective and a subjective cultural phenomenon, and concerns the relations between people on various levels. Gold has always been associated with prestige and high status and is often exchanged as valuable gifts among Iranians. There is a strong tendency for women to own some gold, receiving and giving in accordance with expectations. The saving and management roles women play within the family in this context is considered to be related to their orientation toward the future. Gold functions for women both as prestigious ornaments, and as a status symbol. Gifts of gold signify a 'proper' bride and provide capital for the family and her husband. While purchasing land has remained the principal investment and economic transaction for men, gold has played a similar role for women. The constant rise in the value of gold, along with inflation, has meant that its importance not only as solid capital, but also as a status symbol, has grown.

The common strategy is to buy as many articles of gold as possible when the prices are low, and then sell or exchange these items when the prices have gone up. Accumulation of gold is considered a wise policy, both from the point of view of the individual and the family.

Gold is a significant gift requested by the bride. The amount to be received is often agreed upon at the time of engagement. Gold jewelry, or a number of gold coins, may be agreed upon as being a part of, or the entire *mahryeh*. The increasing tendency among middle-class brides to have mahryeh in gold coins than riyals is because gold is more stable in price and more likely to rise in value than fall. The quantity of gold received as wedding presents depends on how wealthy the relatives are, and the number of guests. Such gifts may also be given on other significant occasions, such as at the birth of a child, during the first pregnancy, upon obtaining a higher degree, or on the Iranian New Year in March.

The young married women were considered inexperienced, and were constantly advised by their mothers and sisters about future relations with their husbands and their families. Planning a secure future, the mothers advise their daughters to buy gold instead of toys and decorative items, and to be concerned about the future. Such issues have become important lessons given by mothers to their married daughters. The importance of the gift of gold as capital is revealed at times of family crises. It is increasingly common for married women to give their savings to their desperate husbands to start a business or purchase property. Such a form of economic support brings extra recognition and respectability for the wife. The husband is often willing in return to register part, or whole, of the purchased property in her name.

On one occasion Farid, a 30-year-old married housewife, proudly exclaimed how she sold all of her wedding jewelry and the children's gold to give tomans to her husband, so he could purchase a piece of land that was especially offered to him at his place of work. Her husband in return registered the land in her name. Another situation in which a woman's gold reserves may be vitally important to the whole family is exemplified by Mahtab, an elderly mother with a family of ten, who was forced to seek shelter in Shiraz during the Iraqi bombardment of Abadan in 1981. The only property they could bring with them was her gold (one kilogram). Soon she decided to sell it, despite the market rate being low, because she considered it important to provide the necessary clothing and accommodation for her daughters, and to protect the family. The only thing she had been reluctant to sell was a ring that had once belonged to her mother.

A third example is that of a 55-year-old woman, who sold all of her gold jewelry and borrowed money from her oldest daughter, in order to visit two of her children living in Norway. To her the value of the visit was worth more than her gold. She thought, what would be the use of saving when she might never again have the chance to see her children and grandchildren?

The distance, and the high cost of the journey, signified the importance of the visit and, and as she put it, 'it may be the only chance in my lifetime'. She had to insist on the importance of such a visit since her old husband thought that it was more important to take care of the house, and was thus reluctant to give her any financial support. Finally she alone provided the money for her journey to visit her children. She frequently talked about this as an event to gain respect.

A fourth example is that of a couple educated abroad, who had recently returned home and needed to pay for the transport of their household goods from Germany to Iran. The wife, Shahla, decided to sell her own gold, as well as her daughter's, to pay the required sum. She considered the household items to be of equal value to the gold since these were enormously expensive and scarce in Iran. Her mother, Mahtab, proudly returned to this case, telling others how her daughter managed her family life, thus presenting her daughter as a good wife to a good husband.

Contributions to the family economy in times of crises would allow the wife to emphasise her honourable identity and enable her to negotiate with her husband. The latter may, as noted, often agree to reward his supportive wife by registering some property in her name.

Some women insist on keeping some of the gifts of gold received through their own lineage by transferring it to their daughters or daughters-in-law, or to their mother's lineage (sister's daughter). Such a form of gold exchange signifies sets of kinship relations in which the wife competes with the husband's for support. Thus, women often adopt far-sighted perspectives on the value of gold, a view that their husbands may not necessarily share, but from which they often benefit. Dowry consists of household goods that the bride will bring to her husband's house. Mehr is a sum of money or valuable items such as gold and land that the husband pledges to pay the bride upon marriage. This amount will be written as a legal document for the bride's security, and may become a legal debt upon the bride's request. These two forms of payment play important roles in the dynamics of the marital relation, giving a woman a high degree of security and also a deterrent for a divorce.

It is generally assumed that the larger the dowry (i.e. consisting of kitchen utensils, carpets, bedroom furniture, etc.), the greater is the respect shown to the daughter and, thus, the greater is the prestige gained in the eyes of the husband's female relatives. Due to the open market prices of dowry items people purchase presents through the newly established Islamic state marriage institution, which offers a few items for those newly wed. These might include items such as a stove, a machine-made carpet, and an oil heater. Two or three items were sold to each newly married couple in 1989.

The better the daughter's education, job and appearance, the less pressure is placed on the parents to provide an expensive dowry. This point of view was expressed by at least ten of the working women, aged between 30-45, including 4 teachers (1 nursery, 2 school, 1 university), 3 hairdressers, 1 social worker, 1 accountant, 1 office worker. Of these two had resigned, one of whom was Narges, a 40-year-old woman and former accountant, the other being a teacher who had several times taken leave to avoid the political stress associated with her working conditions.

Working women have often purchased household goods either through the cooperative institution where they worked, or when such goods were available at a special price. Six of them had been working before marriage. As part of their dowry they brought these goods to their husband's house without putting economic pressure on their parents. The average parent, with several marriageable children, may find themselves in serious economic difficulties, unable to provide a dowry for their daughters. However, some parents, in order to reduce these expectations, will give a little dowry to the daughter and in return agree for a simple wedding party and a smaller gift of gold.

In order to reduce the expenses of the groom, a one-day celebration for the two phases of the wedding is the most usual form of marriage. The first phase of the wedding party starts with the *aqad* ceremony, in which the Muslim marriage contract will be written. At that time the close relatives of the bride and the groom are invited, and a warm meal will be served at the expense of the bride's family. In the afternoon the second phase of the celebration, known as the wedding party, will be held. Then dinner will be served to a large number of guests, including distant relatives, friends and close neighbours. This part will be held at the expense of the groom. The wedding marks a recognition of the Muslim marriage contract. It is seldom the case that a bride moves to live with her husband before the second phase of the marriage celebration.

Devaluation of the rial brought a series of dramatic changes to families and the household economy. The reduced value of riyals provided grounds for parents of brides to request higher *mehr*, to guarantee more security for women at the time of divorce. The average mehr requested by the bride's family increased from a few hundred thousands before the revolution, to 3 million for the average middle-class family in 1989, and to 10 million in 1994. Knowing the existence of such a threat causes the girl's family to request a higher amount of mehr.

In the past, the mehr was so low that initiating a divorce today has been easy for some husbands, being only a matter of paying an insignificant amount of cash to the wife. The predicament of a woman facing divorce due to low mehr, can be illustrated in the case of Narges. In 1970, when she married, her mehr was 100,000 tomans; (a high sum at that time). When she divorced in 1989 the average mehr was 3-5 million tomans; among the better educated and well-off families. Her husband thought it was an easy matter simply to give her the total amount of 100,000 tomans in cash, thus fulfilling the sole legal condition for a restricted third-degree divorce. For the husband this equalled the price of a pair of car tyres.

The high amount of mehr today makes it impossible for husbands to pay it to their wives in case of divorce. However, to women the sum is more a matter of status, providing them with more power and ability to negotiate with the husband in case of divorce. Family insecurity and the increasing number of divorces on one hand, and the continuous devaluation of riyals on the other, induces parents to increase their demands of mehr, thus hoping to guarantee greater security for their daughters in marriage.

POSITION IN FAMILY

The legal, moral and social status of woman is not affected in any way if she engages herself in the maintenance and upliftment of the home. Islam, on the one hand, safeguards all her rights by law and on the other, instructs society to render her a kind and fair treatment. Islam creates such an environment that whatever position woman assumes, she holds it with all her dignity and honour. As long as such an encouragement prevails, no change can ever occur in her honour and dignity. There are three prominent positions of woman at home — a daughter, a wife and a mother. Islam bestows great rank and position on her in all her three roles. No one can pull her back from this high position while she remains in the fold of Islam.

Mother : Islam assigns the highest rank, after Almighty Allah and His Prophet, to mother. Islam instructs man to give just and fair treatment to both father and mother and commands him for their obedience because both of them confer benevolence on him. But, in the Quran and Hadith, reference to the great benevolence of mother occurs more evidently and prominently. The Quran says:

And We have enjoined on man (to be good) to his parents:
in travail upon travail.
Did his mother bear him,
And in years twain
Was his weaning (hear the command)
'Show gratitude to Me and to your parents:
To Me is (your final) goal. *(31:14)*

At another place Allah Almighty says:

We have enjoined on man
Kindness to his parents:
In pain did his mother
Bear him, and in pain
Did she give him birth
The carrying of the (child)
To his weaning is
(a period of) thirty months. *(46:15)*

In all the works of child upbringing like feeding, nursing, education and training, the father participates with mother. But it is only the mother who bears all the pains and troubles of pregnancy and delivery individually. To bear the burden of pregnancy for nine long months, to give birth to a child after a great struggle of life and death and to feed her child out of her own blood and to lead a life of full care and strict precaution in all these stages is not at all an easy task. Father does not undertake all these hardships and does not bear all this pain. Therefore the benevolence and favours of mother on man are more than those of the father. There are several Hadith which draw our attention towards rendering great service and obedience to mother and to behave politely with her. Some of its precepts are being discussed here.

Prophet Muhammad (peace be upon him) instructed man to give fair and just treatment to both father and mother. But the Prophet stressed the fair treatment more to mother. The Prophet said:

> *'I enjoin man about his mother, I enjoin man about his mother, I enjoin man about his mother, I enjoin man about his mother.*
>
> *Hadrat Aishah reported that she enquired: 'O Messenger of God, who has the greatest right on woman?' The Prophet Muhammad, upon whom be peace, replied, 'Her husband (has the greatest right on her)'. She then asked, 'Who has the greatest right on man?' The Prophet replied, 'His mother (has the greatest right on him).'*

Some of the people are of the opinion that since mother is weaker than father, hence the Prophet (peace be upon him) instructed man to serve and obey the mother much more than the father. Probably it is also true. However, the fact is, mother confers more benevolence on man than father and therefore she deserves more attention and obedience.

In traditions, disobedience to parents is included in Kabair, i.e., great sins.

A separate instruction is also given forbidding disobedience to mother which is condemned as an unlawful act. Prophet Muhammad (peace be upon him) said:

> *Allah has forbidden you to be undutiful to your mothers, to withhold (what you should give) or demand (what you do not deserve), and to bury your daughters alive. Prophet Muhammad (peace be upon him) mentioned sins and said that when his Ummah perpetrates these sins, great difficulties and torment will fall upon them. One of such sins is:*
>
> *'Man would accept the words of his wife and would disobey his mother; would adopt a pleasant behaviour with his friend and the behaviour with his father would be severe.'*

In one of the Hadith, disobedience to parents is regarded as one of the signs of the approaching Dooms Day. The just and fair treatment to mother is regarded as a means of atonement for one's sins and the attainment of Paradise. Hadrat Aishah states that Hadrat Harsa bin Noman behaved with his mother in a most respectable, pleasant and polite manner. Once Prophet Muhammad (peace be upon him) said:

> *I saw heaven in my dream where I heard somebody reciting the Quran. I asked whose voice was that. I was told that it was the voice of Hadrat Harsa bin Noman. Then the Prophet said that it was the reward of fair treatment to mother.*

Hadrat Abdullah bin Amr says that someone confessed to the Prophet that he had committed a great sin. Is there any way of repentance for it? The Prophet asked: Do you have your aunt (maternal)?' The man replied, 'Yes'. The Prophet said: 'Render her just and fair treatment.'

It evidently shows that it is not the service to mother alone but the service to her relatives too, can be one of the means of the expiation for sins.

Service to mother is superior to the service to father. It is next only to the mother that the position of any other person can be determined. Hadrat Abu Hurrayrah relates that a person questioned Prophet Muhammad (upon whom be peace): Who deserves my polite behaviour most? The Prophet replied: 'Your mother'. The man asked: Who (deserves) the next? The Prophet replied: 'Your mother'. The man enquired for the third time that who deserves the next? The Prophet made the same answer: 'Your mother'. When the man repeated the same question for the fourth time, Prophet Muhammad (peace be upon him) said, 'Your father.'

There is one more Hadith according to which a companion of the Prophet asked him who deserved the greatest right for his decent and just treatment. The Prophet replied: 'Your mother'. The man asked who stands next to her? The Prophet replied: 'Your mother'. The man asked the same question for the third time. The Prophet gave him the same answer again. When he put the same question for the fourth time, the Prophet replied: 'Your father', then whoever stands as much nearer to you in relations deserves as much decent treatment.

Qadi Ayaz states that some people say that both mother and father deserve just and fair treatment. But mother deserves more rights for service. Imam Nawawi says that this opinion is the correct one since most authentic Hadith support it. Harith Muhasbi says that consensus seems to be that in matters of service from children mother has more rights than father.

There are different Traditions on the question whether the polite behaviour with mother should be double or triple? Imam Tahawi says that in this connection those Traditions are more authentic in which it is said that a man should offer kind and mild treatment to mother three times more than what he should offer to his father.

Imam Ahmad says that father should be obeyed, but as far as the fair treatment is concerned, out of the four parts, three belong to mother.

Islam does not stress the legal rights of mother and father alone but also prescribes a kind and decent treatment to them. Islam holds that the legal rights of parents should be observed heartily and with love and devotion and should not be regarded as burden. It also unfolds the fact that apart from the legal rights, one should give as noble and humble treatment to parents as possible and in this treatment again, mother deserves more affectionate treatment. Mother should be offered better behaviour than what is offered to father.

Wife : In Islam woman possesses an independent entity of her own. Because of Nikah, neither her personality gets dissolved in the personality of her husband nor does she become his subject or servant. When she holds some new responsibilities after marriage, she becomes the owner of some new rights at the same time. As she cannot refuse these responsibilities, in the same manner her rights cannot be taken away from her.

Now let us see how Islam views the relationship between wife and husband and what legal and moral basis Islam provides for this relationship.

The relation of husband and wife is, in fact, the relation of love, affection and intimacy. The natural love and attraction which God has placed between husband and wife is described in the Holy Quran thus:

And among His Signs
Is this, that He created
For you mates from among
Yourselves, that ye may
Dwell in tranquility with them
And He has put love
And mercy between your (hearts),
Verily in that are Signs
For those who reflect *(30:21)*

What is suggested is that there should be a relation of love, sympathy and affection between husband and wife. It is all their natural urge indeed. If hostility and animosity take the place of love and affection, it is against nature on which Allah Almighty has created them.

There is always a head of any minor or major institution. The structure of the family and the relationship among its members and its problems are more complicated and varied than all the other institutions and their problems. Order and discipline cannot be there in a family in the absence of its head. If there is no head of a family or no one is responsible for a family, it would definitely get disorganised. In Islam, man obtains the position of a head of the family for several reasons. This does not mean that man has acquired unlimited and whole and sole authority on his wife and that she is merely his subject. It actually means that while it is the responsibility of woman to accept her husband as a leader and obey and follow all his 'lawful demands', she also enjoys her rights. It is compulsory and obligatory for a man to perform these rights rather to pay all her dues. Hence the Quran says:

Men are the protectors
And maintainers of women, because God
Has given the one more (strength)
Than the other, and because
They support them
From their means
Therefore the righteous women
Are devoutly obedient and guard
In (the husband's) absence
What God would have them guard *(4:34)*

Again in another place, says the Quran:

And women shall have rights
Similar to the rights against them, according
To what is equitable;
But men have a degree
(of advantage) over them
And God is Exalted in Power, Wise. *(2:228)*

Woman, while accepting the superiority of man in domestic life, gains and enjoys all rights of maintenance allowance, residence, alimony, and education and training and several other rights. If man falls short of performing all these rights of woman, she can secure them through law.

Islam exhorts man not only to discharge the legal rights of his wife but to behave with her decently and justly. Nice treatment with wife is required in every condition. Sometimes man dislikes the face, temperament and habits of his wife, which affects their relationship. In such cases man is instructed to consider the better aspects of his wife because if he dislikes one aspect of hers, there can be then praiseworthy qualities in her. Therefore it is the demand not only of morality and nobility but also of wisdom and sagacity that man should keep far-reaching interests before him and should not spoil the cordial relationship with his wife. Sometimes a certain thing appears unpleasant to man, but in it are hidden unaccountable aspects of goodness. In this connection, Islam lays down such a noble and ideal rule that cannot be found anywhere else. Allah Almighty says in the Quran.

On the contrary live with them.
On a footing of kindness and equity
If ye take a dislike to them.
It may be that ye dislike
A thing, and God brings about
Through it a great deal of good *(4:19)*

A lucid elucidation of such a polite behaviour with wife can be found in the sayings of Prophet Muhammad (peace be upon him).

Hadrat Muawiyyah Qushairi once enquired about the rights of wife of the Prophet (peace be upon him). In reply the Prophet said:

That you should give her food when you eat, clothe her when you clothe yourself, not strike her on the face, and not revile her or turn her out of the house (if separation becomes necessary) but live separately within the house itself (temporarily).

The same Tradition is expressed again in some other words:

Feed her what you feed yourself with, her clothing should be of the same standard as yours, do not beat or abuse and rebuke her.

First, husband should follow the same standard of eating and drinking, clothing and dressing for his wife which he keeps for himself. It is unjustified if he keeps a high standard of life and compels his wife to subsist on a lower standard. Secondly, in association and relationship with her, his performance should be honourable. He should not treat her harshly or cruelly.

If any action of woman looks unpleasant or disagreeable, Prophet Muhammad (peace be upon him) advised man to endure and to have patience because this unpleasantness may prove temporary. Where some act of hers is unpleasant, some other acts may be pleasing to heart. To express lament and to show hatred and to be enraged at the slightest provocation will spoil mutual affectionate relationships for ever. Hadrat Abu Hurrayrah relates that Prophet Muhammad (peace be upon him) said:

A believer must not hate a believing woman; if he dislikes one of her traits, he will be pleased with another.

Sometimes man demonstrates high morals and displays good conduct with others but his behaviour with his wife is reproachable even though his wife who is his life-partner is most deserving of polite and decent behaviour. Hence the man whose behaviour with his wife is just and fair is regarded as the best man. In a Tradition Hadrat Abu Hurrayrah relates that the Prophet said:

The believers with perfect faith are those who have the best disposition and the best of you are those who are best to their wives.

In a Tradition, showing courtesy and love to wife and children is regarded as an attribute which completed faith (Iman). Hadrat Aishah related that Prophet Muhammad (peace be upon him) said:

Among the believers, the man whose moral is best, has the perfect faith and who behave with his wife and children with more love and affection.

In another Tradition Hadrat Aishah relates that Prophet Muhammad, upon whom be peace, said:

The best of you is he who is the best to his family, and I am the best among you to my family.

Islam regards the standard of relationship between husband and wife free from contention and strife as commendable. Wife should try to keep her husband delighted and contended, to obey him in rightful works and to safeguard his honour and dignity and wealth and property. On the other hand, husband should consider such a chaste and virtuous wife to be an excellent asset of life and should offer more decent and polite behaviour to her.

Hadrat Abu Hurrayrah says that Prophet Muhammad (peace be upon him) was asked about the attributes of a virtuous and righteous woman. The Prophet said:

'The one who pleases (her husband) when he looks at her,

obeys him when he gives a command, and does not go against his wishes regarding her person, or property by doing anything of which he disapproves.'

Hadrat Abu Amama relates that Prophet Muhammad (peace be upon him) said:

'After fear of God, a believer gains nothing better for him than a good wife who obeys him if he gives her a command, pleases him if he looks at her, is true to him if he adjures her to do something, and is sincere towards him regarding her person and his property if he is absent.'

Hadrat Abdullah b. Umar b. Aas says that the Prophet said:

'The whole world is to be enjoyed, but the best thing in the world is a good wife.'

Hadrat Umar asked Prophet Muhammad (peace be upon him) that Allah Almighty forbids to store gold and silver, what type of wealth, then, we should keep with us? Prophet Muhammad (peace be upon him) said:

'Each one of you must possess with you, a thankful heart, a God-remembering tongue, a (Muslim) believing wife who assists him in the works for Akhirah (eternal life).'

It is quite evident from the above Traditions what type of relationship Islam wants to promote between husband and wife. If such a type of relationship exists between them, both of them will be assistant and well-wisher of each other, their life will be pleasant and ideal and all the unpleasant problems of rights and demands which cause disturbance and destroy the domestic life would never occur in their life.

Daughter : Before the proclamation of the Prophethood of Prophet Muhammad (peace be upon him), parents were much proud of their sons and they were supposed to be their great asset, because they gave more strength to their tribe and they were assistant in their great exertion in the field of finance. But daughters were considered to be burden on them and they were supposed to be the cause of ignominy or disgrace and on their very mention their heads dropped in shame.

The Quran portrays a very graphic picture of the feelings of a parent on the birth of his daughter at that time.

When news is brought to one of them of the
Birth of a female (child), his face
Darkens, and he is filled

With inward grief!
With shame does he hide
Himself from his people, because of the bad news
He has had Shall he retain it
On (sufferance and) contempt, or bury it
In the dust. *(16:58-59)*

One of the results of these obnoxious feelings for daughter was that some tribes used to bury their daughters alive. The Quran vehemently criticised the murdering of children and regarded it a capital offence and put an end to this abhorrent practice once and for all. The Quran says that on the Last Day, one would have to answer for the hard-heartedness to God. The Quran says:

When the female (infant)
Buried alive, is
Questioned
For what crime
She was killed *(81:8-9)*

Islam inculcated totally different feelings for girls in place of their barbarous and brutal feelings.

The first and foremost that Islam says is that it is the will and wish of God that favoured some with children and to some He debarred and to some He gave only sons and to some He favoured with daughters alone and to some He blessed with both sons and daughters. None of this case is a cause of honour or disgrace or cause of dishonour or ignominy. All this is a natural phenomenon representing as it does the boundless knowledge and wisdom of God. Those who consider it a standard of dignity or ignominy are cavilling at His wisdom. The Quran says:

To God belongs the dominion of the heavens
And the earth. He creates what He wills
(And plans). He bestows (children) male or
Female according to His will (and plan)
Or He bestows both males
And females and He leaves
Barren whom He will
For He is full of knowledge and power. *(42:49-50)*

There is exhortation in Islam for the proper nourishment and sustenance of daughters. It is regarded as a good deed and a means for the attainment of Heaven. Hadrat Aishah relates that Prophet Muhammad (peace be upon him) said:

'Whoever is in charge of (put to test by)
three daughters and treats them generously,
then they will act as a shield for him
from the (Hell) Fire.'

In Traditions, the upbringing and nourishment of two or three daughters or sisters or even one daughter or sister is referred to as a means for entering Heaven. From this the reward or requital to the person who brings up more than three daughters or sisters can be well realised. Hadrat Utba bin Aamir relates that Prophet Muhammad (peace be upon him) said:

'Whoever has three daughters, and bears with the miseries in their connection, feeds and clothes them with the earnings of his labour, they will become a curtain on the fire of hell, for him.'

Hadrat Abu Sayeed Khudri relates that Prophet Muhammad (peace be upon him) said:

'Whoever amongst you has three daughters,
or three sisters, and he treats them gently,
he will surely enter heaven.'

Hadrat Abu Sayeed relates one more Hadith that Prophet Muhammad, upon whom be peace, said:

'Whoever has three daughters or three sisters or two daughters or two sisters and he adopts a good company with them and fears Allah about them, He has (place for him in) Heaven.'

Hadrat Anas relates that Prophet Muhammad (peace be upon him) said:

'If anyone cares for two girls till they grow up, he and I will come on the day of resurrection thus', and he joined his fingers.'

Hadrat Abu Hurrayrah relates that Prophet Muhammad (peace be upon him) said:

Whoever has three daughters and he bears with the difficulties and financial problems, in connection with them, Allah will make him enter Heaven, for courtesy towards them.' Abu Hurrayrah reports that a man enquired if he has two daughters (and bears with the difficulties in connection with them). The Prophet replied, 'Even if he has two daughters (Allah will bless him with Heaven)'. A man asked, if he has one? The Prophet said (He will) even if he has one.'

Hadrat Abdullah bin Abbas relates a similar Hadith that Prophet Muhammad (peace be upon him) said:

> *'If anyone takes care of three girls or the like number of sisters, training them and showing kindness to them till God enriches them, God will guarantee him paradise.'*

Hearing such a great reward, a man humbly enquired Prophet Muhammad (peace be upon him) that if anyone renders the same service to two daughters or sisters in the same way does he get the same reward? The Prophet replied, 'Yes, he would get the same reward'. The one who relates the above Hadith says that if the man would have enquired for one daughter or sister, the Prophet would have given the same reply.

It shows that for providing nourishment and giving proper training to one daughter or sister a man deserves a seat in paradise. If he nourishes and brings up more than one daughter or sister, his rank may be raised accordingly.

It is stated in the Hadith that with the good nourishment of daughters, they should also be given good education and training and should also select a good match for the marriage and should continue fair and just treatment with them. Hadrat Abu Sayeed Khudri relates that Prophet Muhammad (peace be upon him) said:

> *'Whoever nourishes three daughters, educates and trains them, gets them married (and afterwards) offers a gentle behaviour to them, for him there is heaven.'*

Generally more love and affection is showered on sons in feeding, clothing, education, training and in every respect more preference is accorded to them. This is total injustice and oppression. In Hadith such a treatment is forbidden and condemned.

Hadrat Abdullah bin Abbas relates that Prophet Muhammad (peace be upon him) said:

> *'Whoever has a girl, who has neither buried her alive nor gives a mean treatment to her and not even gives preference to his son over his daughter, God will make him enter Heaven.'*

In all these Hadith on the proper nourishment, education training, arrangement of marriage and equal treatment to daughters or sisters, glad tidings is given for liberation from Hell and the attainment of Heaven. One who does not have faith in God and the eternal day and one who gives all importance to the present world alone does not realise the significance of these Traditions. But the very goal of the believer (Momin) is success on the Judgement Day. There is all what he wishes in this goodness for a believer. With the inducement of the proper care for girls, this conception is also laid down that she is not worthless or valueless as the world considers her, but she is the most valuable boon of nature. The love and affection which she possesses in herself, a boy does not have it. Hadrat Uqba bin Amir relates that Prophet Muhammad (peace be upon him) said:

Do not hate girls. They are comforter and much precious.

Such a teaching for a fair and just treatment of girls is an example which is found nowhere. According to Islamic law, if the child does not own any position and does not have any proper means for living, his maintenance is obligatory on his father. In accordance with this rule, the maintenance or allowances for daughters is obligatory on his father till her marriage and in the absence of his father, it is necessary for her nearest relative to ensure her maintenance. After marriage, the responsibility of her maintenance shifts to her husband and on the death of her husband or in case of divorce and if the woman is not self-sufficient in financial matters, the responsibility goes to her children or in case she has no children, the responsibility for her maintenance falls on her nearest relative. This is a legal right and in the Tradition its importance is well emphasised.

Hadrat Suraqua bin Malik relates that Prophet Muhammad (peace be upon him) asked him:

'Shall I not show you what is the greatest charity. He said: Messenger of God, certainly show (it). The Prophet said, 'To be grateful to your daughters who (after becoming widow or being divorced) is sent back to you and there is no one save you, her earning man.'

The Companions of the Prophet were so thoughtful about their widows and daughters that it can be well understood from this example that Hadrat Zubayr endowed some of his houses. In the details of this endowment the following statement was also included.

Whosoever of his daughters (being divorced or by becoming a widow) would come back to her house, she would stay in it.

Neither she would put it in loss nor would she be put in loss. If she is self-sufficient in respect of finance without depending on her husband, she would not have any right in it.

In this way, in the family system of Islam, the legal right of woman are secured; and on the moral ground also she enjoys a place of honour and dignity.

SANCTITY OF THE HOUSE

Whereas Islam has promulgated rules and regulations for all actions and deeds, it has also set some principles for entering the houses in order to maintain the sanctity of home-life. It is not permissible to enter a house without seeking permission of the head of the family.

In the places not used as residences such as schools, guesthouses, monasteries where there is no restriction to go or in the houses where no one resides, one may enter without seeking permission. If, however, restrictions are imposed on the entry of some persons, they should not go therein. It has been mentioned in the Holy Quran:

> *It is no sin for you to enter uninhabited houses wherein is comfort for you. Allah knoweth what ye proclaim and what ye hide.*
> *(24:29)*

Except the above, it is not permissible to enter the houses without prior permission. It has been said in the Holy Quran:

> *O ye who believe! Enter not house other than your own without first announcing your presence and saluting (saying Assalamo Alaikum) to the folk thereof That is better for you that you may be heedful.*
> *(24:27)*

If you want to go in the house of another person, you should first ask permission from the head of the house according to the Islamic principles. He may be the owner of the house or residing in it on rent or without rent and the inmates of house may be mahram or ghair mahram or males or females. He must ask permission under all circumstances from the head of the house or from the member of the family whom he has authorised to do so. If he refuses permission to enter, he should go back at once and should not insist or compel. If no one responds to his call he should call out thrice and if no one responds even at the third call, he should return. It is not permissible to enter a house about which it is not certain whether anyone is living there are not. It has been mentioned in the Holy Quran:

> *If you find no one therein, still enter not until permission hath been given. And if it be said unto you: Go away again, then go away, for it is purer for you. Allah knoweth what ye do.*
> *(24:28)*

Supposing there is none in the house, even then you have no right to enter a house which is not meant for general public use. Moreover, if the permission to enter is not granted, it is futile to insist and to enter forcibly in the house. It is a great sin and offence. It is also against moral and ethical principles. So the Ulama are of the view:

> *If the entry is refused one should neither insist for permission to enter nor ask that purdah should be observed. He should also not wait as all these acts are against good etiquettes. He should not knock at the door. The author of* Kashaf *has explained his view while commenting upon the above verse.*

There are many advantages of seeking permission to enter a house. In the terminology of Hadith it is called Istidhan. It is an obligatory duty in Islam and one must act upon it. No one knows how much harmful it is to himself or to the family if anyone enters the house suddenly. It is just possible that someone may be naked, his glance may suddenly fall on him/her. It is, therefore, proper that no one should enter the house without seeking permission. If a number of married sons and daughters of the same father are residing in a house, it is necessary to seek permission before entering so that the inmates of the house may become alert and recompose themselves. The principle should be observed in entering the female apartment.

The Holy Prophet (peace and blessings of Allah be upon him) instructed his Companions to seek permission before entering a house. Many such events have been mentioned in the Ahadith where the Holy Prophet instructed his Companions to act upon this principle. Hadrat Abu Musa reported that the Holy Prophet (peace and blessings of Allah be upon him) observed:

> *Asking of permission is for three times. If you are permitted, well and good, otherwise, you should return.*
>
> *(Riyad as-Salihin)*

A person who belonged to Bani Amir once went to the Holy Prophet (peace and blessings of Allah be upon him) who was in the house. When he arrived at the door of the house, he said, May I come in? When the Holy Prophet (peace and blessings of Allah be upon him) heard his voice, he said to his servant: Go to the person who is outside and teach him the way to ask permission in accordance with the Shariah. Ask him to say: Assalamo Alaikum! May I come in? That person heard the instructions which the Holy Prophet (peace and blessings of Allah be upon him) was giving to his servant and said: Assalamo Alaikum! May I come in? Thereupon the Holy Prophet (peace and blessings of Allah be upon him) gave him permission and he came in.

Hadrat Kuldah bin Al Hanbal (Allah be pleased with him) said: I went to the Holy Prophet (peace and blessings of Allah be upon him) and entered without saying Assalamo Alaikum. Thereupon he said: Go back and say: Assalamo Alaikum! May I come in?

It is clear from the above Ahadith that the correct way to ask permission is that one should first say Assalamo Alaikum and then ask permission to enter. To seek permission without saying Assalamo Alaikum is not correct. It is also evident from the above Ahadith that one should ask permission thrice and if there is no response even at the third call one should not insist and return.

> *In a Hadith the incident of Hadrat Abu Musa has been narrated. He went to Hadrat Umar and asked permission thrice. No response came and he came back. Hadrat Umar was busy in some work. When he was free he said: Call Hadrat Abu Musa in. When the person went out to call Abu Musa in, the latter had gone. He informed Hadrat Umar accordingly. When Hadrat Abu Musa again came to see him on some other occasion he enquired from him: Why did you return on that day. He said: I asked permission thrice and having no response I returned as I heard the Holy Prophet (peace and blessings of Allah be upon him) saying: Should anyone of you seek permission thrice and has no response he should return.* *(Ibn Kathir)*

There is another incident relating to the Holy Prophet (peace and blessings of Allah be upon him). He went to Said bin Ubada and asked permission thrice after saying Assalamo Alaikum. When he had no response he returned. Meanwhile, Hadrat Said came to him running and took him to the house.

It is necessary for the visitor to ask permission first so that he could not see any one of the inmates of the house all of a sudden. It has been narrated that once the Holy Prophet (peace and blessings of Allah be upon him) was sitting in the house and scratching his head. Someone came and began to peep in. When the Holy Prophet (peace and blessings of Allah be upon him) knew it, he became very angry and said: Had I known it, I would have had his eyes torn out. Is he not aware: The visitor, must therefore not stand in front of the door; he should remain at one side.

Hadrat Abdullah has reported that whenever the Holy Prophet (peace and blessings of Allah be upon him) went to anyone he stood at one side of the door and said: Assalamo Alaikum! In those days curtains were not hung at the doors of the houses. If it is hung, there is no harm in standing in front of the door; but etiquettes demand that one should not ask permission to enter standing just in front as thus there is every possibility of seeing the inmates of the house.

It has been mentioned in a Hadith that a person came at the door of the Holy Prophet (peace and blessings of Allah be upon him) and asked permission standing in front of the door. The Holy Prophet (peace and blessings of Allah be upon him) beckoned him to stand at one side of the door as the law of seeking permission has been made due to gazing in.

It is forbidden to peep in from fissures of the doors or that of the windows as the very purpose of seeking permission is thus violated. According to a Hadith in Sahihain the Holy Prophet (peace and blessings of Allah be upon him) said:

> *If a person peeps in your house without permission, you throw a stone at him so that it hurts out his eye; there is no sin upon you.* *(Ibn Kathir)*

If he seeks permission to enter after saying Assalamo Alaikum and the inmate of the house asks who is he, he should tell his familiar name. It should not be said: 'It is I', as the person cannot be recognized in this way. The Holy Prophet (peace and blessings of Allah be upon him) does not like that an ambiguous reply should be given.

Once Hadrat Jabir went to the Holy Prophet (peace and blessings of Allah be upon him). He (the Holy Prophet) asked: Who are you? He said: It is I. The Holy Prophet (peace and blessings of Allah be upon him) disliked the reply and said: What do you mean by this I, I. The Companions of the Holy Prophet (peace and blessings of Allah be upon him) also taught their followers the way to seek permission and exhorted them to act upon it.

The permission to enter the house should also be asked from the *mahram* such as mother and sister, etc. It has been stated in the verse regarding 'Istidhan' that a woman from Ansar came to the Holy Prophet (peace and blessings of Allah be upon him) and said: I am in such a condition that I do not like any one, even my father to see me; but these persons come and go in this state. Thereupon the verse a particular was revealed. Various instances have been narrated in Ahadith from which it is evident that *mahrams* are also required to ask permission as no body knows about the condition in which the women would be sitting. In my opinion one should not enter without permission even if there is only wife in the house as she might be naked and no body likes to be seen in a state of nudeness. A person asked the Holy Prophet (peace and blessings of Allah be upon him): Is it necessary to seek permission from mother? He said: Yes, permission needs to be sought from mother. He said: I live with her. In other words, she is not required to observe purdah from me then why is it necessary to ask permission? The Holy Prophet (peace and blessings of Allah be upon him) said: Ask permission from her also. He said: Even if you go to your mother you ask permission. Would you like to see your mother naked? He said: No. He (the Holy Prophet) said: That is why I say that you should seek permission before seeing her.

Hadrat Zainab (Allah be pleased with her) says: Whenever Hadrat Abdullah bin Masud (Allah be pleased with him) came in for some need, he first stopped at the door and coughed and then came in. He did not like to come in suddenly. Zainab was the wife of Hadrat Abdullah bin Masud.

Hadrat Abu Ubaidah says: When Hadrat Abdullah arrived he asked permission loudly at the door. Hadrat Imam Ahmad bin Hanbal says: When a person enters the house he should cough loudly or strike his shoe with force so that the inmate of the house may know that some one is coming.

The purpose of Assalamo Alaikum for three times is that the inmates of the house may know about the arrival of the visitor. They may become alert at the second and may grant or refuse permission at the third.

Ibn Al-Arabi is of the view that it is an incumbent act to ask permission before entering the house of others. As regards one's own house, it is not an incumbent duty. If, however, mother and sisters are living there, he should cough and then enter. At the door he should strike his feet so that the women may become aware of his arrival. Sometimes even mother and sister are in a condition that it is not proper to see them.

According to Imam Malik, it is necessary to ask permission before seeing the mother or sister. It was again and again enquired from Hadrat Ibn Masud and Ibn Abbas whether it is necessary for the persons to ask permission from the mother and sister residing with him. He said: No one likes to see his mother naked, then why do you insist on this question. If you ponder over the Islamic rules and regulations you would come to the conclusion that they are not only rules of wisdom and freedom but excellently safeguard modesty.

We are constrained to say that these rules and regulations of entering the houses which have been explained by the Holy Quran and the Ahadith ~ and practically followed by the noble Companions of the Holy Prophet throughout their lives are being overlooked by the Muslims of today. These rules and regulations need to be revived and enforced in our home-life.

It is an admitted fact that the Divine Law is the most effective safeguard against immorality and debauchery. After the commandments relating to grown up and adolescent boys in the Holy Quran the Ahadith have also explained that the children too have the capability to think. So far as *ghair-mahrams* are concerned, it has already been explained that it is necessary to observe strict purdah from them. It is, however, allowed to expose the face and palms of hands in need; but if there is any fear of evil or mischief, these parts should also not be exposed. From mahrams purdah is for the whole body except face, palms of hands, arms, head and shanks, etc., which remain ordinarily exposed but it is not allowed to expose these parts unnecessarily. The servant is also a ghair-mahram and it is necessary to observe purdah from him. An infidel maid-servant also comes under the definition of a mahram.

What we want to tell you is that the young boys and maid servants who fall under the category of mahrams should also ask permission to enter at special times as during these times men and women do not generally exercise proper care and vigilance in observing purdah. Allah the Exalted has said:

> *O ye who believe! let your slaves and those of you who have not come to puberty ask leave of you at three times (before they come into your presence): Before the prayer of dawn and when ye lay aside your raiment for the heat of noon; and after the prayer of night. Three times are of privacy for you. It is no sin for them or for you at other times, when some of you go round attendant upon others (if they come into your presence without leave). Thus Allah maketh clear the revelation for you. Allah is Knower, Wise.* *(24:58)*

In the above verse, three special times have been mentioned. The one is that of the morning prayer. That time is fresh and pleasant and the time to wake after enjoying a sound sleep during which one cannot take proper care of purdah. The second time is that of noon when almost every one has a nap and rest after lunch. On hot days the people generally take rest at noon and during sleep it is not possible to observe purdah. The third is the time after 'Isha'. This is also the time for rest. After the daily hard labour one feels tired and goes to sleep. As all are asleep, one does not care to observe purdah. Moreover, the husband and wife generally make love during these times. It has, therefore, been ordained that even maid-servants and children should ask permission before entering their apartment. If they are busy in kissing and embracing or sexual intercourse, this scene would have a very adverse effect on their minds. They would have nothing but shame and remorse. There is, however, no restriction to enter during the other times. Moreover, it is difficult to forbid the children from coming in as they are used to come and go. The same is the case of a maid-servant. She has to enter so frequently for household work that you cannot put restriction on her.

Some commentators have written that the instructions of Istidhan in the first verses are applicable to the other people and strangers and those contained in this verse pertain to the relatives, that is to say, to the mahrams. According to some scholars the instructions contained in the verse are for the common men and for all times and those contained in the above verse are for specific persons and for specific times and this view is correct.

The word *malik* used in the above verse means a maid-servant as Abd which stands for servant is according to the Shariah a *ghair-mahram*. A servant is permitted to come among men; but he is not allowed to go among women. The mahram on whom there is ordinarily no restriction to come are also not permitted to come during the special times, the detail of which has been given above. These preventive measures are based on prudence and wisdom. Maulana. Ashraf Ali Thanvi has given the following comments:

> *O believers! your maid-servants and those who have not attained the age of puberty should seek permission to come to you at three times. Firstly, before the morning prayer and secondly at noon when you take off some of your clothes in order to take rest or sleep and thirdly, after the 'Isha prayer. During these three times you should not come in. In other words, these three times are for rest and sleep and privacy and one is not very serious in observing purdah therein in the strict sense. So instruct your maid-servants and immature children not to come to you at these times without asking permission. At other times, however, there is no restriction on coming and going as they come to you so frequently. The servants fall under the definition of ghair mahrams and are not allowed to go in the company of women. Maid-servants and immature children are, however, free to come in and go without asking permission except at the three specific times. The other times are not for taking rest and sleeping and it is not difficult to observe* satr. *Man should cover his body from navel to the knee*

before his servants and a woman should observe purdah from an infidel maid-servant except her decoration. A man is not required to conceal any part of his body from the maid-servant who is lawful for him and if she is not lawful for him he should cover his body from navel to the knee. A woman is required to cover her body from navel to the knee from a Muslim maid-servant; so the latter is allowed to come in without asking permission. A man should cover his body from navel to the knee from a child and woman should observe purdah from him, except that of her decoration so he is also allowed to come in without asking permission except at the specific three times or because of some special reason. Allah, the Exalted has revealed, clear verses for you and He is all-knowing, All Aware.

(Bayanul Quran)

The immature children are also required to ask permission to come on reaching puberty. Previously they were required to seek permission if they wanted to come in at specific times. The practice which is in vogue in India and Pakistan that those children who come in without restriction during childhood and before puberty come without asking permission even after attaining puberty and the women do not observe purdah from them is absolutely wrong and against the Shariah and should be put to an end. There is no ambiguity about this rule that the children when they come to puberty must also ask permission as the concession enjoyed by them in childhood now no longer exists. It is mentioned in the Holy Quran:

And when the children among you come to puberty then let them ask leave even as those before them used to ask it. Thus Allah maketh clear this revelation for you. Allah is Knower, Wise. *(24:59)*

Uptil now the children were required to ask permission at three specific hours; but on attaining the age of puberty they are also required to ask permission at all times like the other people as in childhood and in the adolescence period they were neither aware of the implications of purdah nor women had any attraction for them and vice versa; but now there has occurred a change in them; their feelings and sentiments have awakened raging a tumult in them. Women might also feel attracted towards them. Now the rule which is applicable to the grown-up persons is to be applied to them. Maulana Ashraf Ali Thanvi has added the following comments:

And when the children among you reach the age of competency or be nearing this age, they should also ask permission like the grown-up persons. Allah, the Exalted has revealed clear verses. He is all-knowing, All-Aware. The above commandment has been repeated to emphasize the advantages of the rules of seeking permission.

It has been explained above that for women it is necessary to observe purdah of the whole body except her face and the palms of her hands as is evident from the above verse so that no one should have any misconception about the implication of these words. It may be pointed out that although there is no *satr* of face and hands, yet they should not be exposed to a stranger if there is fear of evil and mischief. The aged women may, however, not cover their faces and hands although it is better for them to do so.

As for women past child-bearing, who have no hope of marriage, it is no sin for them if they discard their (outer) clothing in such a way as not to show adornment. But to refrain is better for them and Allah is Hearer, Knower.
(24:60)

It has been ordained even for the aged women not to display their decoration. It is evident that Islam does not allow the parts of the body which come under the given definition be remained uncovered without any reason. Maulana Ashraf Ali Thanvi has written:

One thing we must understand. Although there is no satr of face and hands in the strict sense of the word, but it is not permissible that women should freely display their faces and hands to strangers as there is fear of evil and mischief. The satr of these parts of the body also becomes incumbent except upon the aged women who have lost attraction for men and have no hope for marriage, only such women are permitted to expose their face and hands and according to some their feet but they are not permitted to display their decoration. So far as a young lady is concerned, it is necessary for her to observe satr of these parts if there is fear of evil and mischief, but it is permitted to expose these parts in case of necessity or genuine excuse. It is, however, better that purdah should be observed.

Ibn Al-Arabi says:

The aged women are specifically exempted from it and the rest have been disallowed (this concession) as the heart has

no attraction towards the aged women. But if they observe full satr it is better than discarding the veil.
(Ahkamul Quran)

According to the Fuqaha (Jurists) although face does not come under the definition of satr, it is better that the women should be asked not to expose their face so that there should occur no mischief. Nature has created such an irresistible attraction and fascination in the face of a woman that man is automatically drawn towards it and his natural sexual instinct is excited. Allama Ibn Abidin writes:

A woman should be forbidden to expose her face lest man should see her face as sometimes when the face is exposed the eyes look towards it with lewdness. (Durr-ul-Mukhtar)

In the above verse, particular words have been used which means that the women should not put on such thin clothes as do not help to maintain their satr; but reflect the outlines of their bodies and display their beauty. Ibn Al-Arabi writes:

It is also displaying one's decoration and charms that a woman should wear such a thin dress as reflects her body.
(Ahkamul Quran)

He has mentioned the following Hadith in support of the above view. The Holy Prophet (peace and blessings of Allah be upon him) observed:

Most of the dressed women are practically naked. They attract others or are drawn towards them. Such women should neither enter Paradise nor have its smell.

We have already mentioned the following verse of the Holy Quran:

And stay in your houses. Bedizen not yourself with the bedizenment of the time of ignorance. (33:33)

Umm Alqama has reported that Hadrat Hafsa bint Abdur Rahman came to Hadrat Aishah (Allah be pleased with her) Hadrat Hafsa was wearing a thin dupatta. When Hadrat Aishah saw this, she tore it and threw it out and gave her a thick one. Hadrat Hafsa was the niece of Hadrat Aishah.

Hadrat Aishah has narrated another incident: Asma bint Abu Bakr (her sister) went to the Holy Prophet (peace and blessings of Allah be upon him). She was wearing thin clothes. The Holy Prophet (peace and blessings of Allah be upon him) turned away his face and said:

> *O Asma! It is not permissible to look at a grown up woman except her face and the palms of her hand.* (Mishkat)

There is a Hadith in Sahih Muslim. The Holy Prophet (peace and blessings of Allah be upon him) observed:

> *Don thy garment and you should not walk naked.* (Mishkat)

The above and many other Ahadith on this subject reveal that both man and woman should wear such garments as do not reflect their bodies. Thus their grace and beauty would remain immune from the wicked eyes and there would be no danger to their modesty and chastity.

If you ponder over what we have said about purdah, you would find that there are many advantages of this institution. The wisdom behind this institution becomes all the more manifest when we see the moral turpitude of the West.

Islam attaches utmost importance to chastity and morality and righteous conduct and behaviour. If the rules and regulations governing the moral conduct and behaviour of society are not perfect and right and do not impose any restrictions on adultery and prostitution and on the action and behaviour leading to these vices, the morality is bound to be cast to the forewinds.

Study the chapter on "Ethics" of the History of the World and see what is the basic cause of spoiling the morals and what are the reasons of the downfall of a country and a nation? In our view the root-cause of all the evils was that there existed no balanced rules and regulations for guarding the chastity and morality of the people.

Islam has given no concession in the rules and regulations pertaining to chastity and morality. You have already read the attitude of Islam about unlawful sex. Now we would tell you about the punishment prescribed by Islam for those who level false accusation against pious and chaste men and women in order to disgrace them.

Islam condemns that person who is guilty of spreading false rumours against a pious man or woman. It has been mentioned in the Holy Quran:

> *Lo! as for those who traduce virtuous believing woman (who) know not. Cursed are they in the world and the Hereafter. Theirs will be aweful doom. On the day Allah will pay them their just due and they will know that Allah, He is the Manifest Truth.* (24:23-25)

Study the above verse deeply. A very stern warning has been administered for this offence. A person guilty of this sin is doomed in this world and in the Hereafter.

If any person brings a false accusation of adultery/fornication against a chaste and pious lady and fails to produce four eyewitnesses, he would be liable to beating with eighty stripes. He would be deprived of giving evidence against any person in future it has been mentioned in the Holy Quran:

> *And those who accuse honourable woman but bring not four witnesses, scourge (with) eighty stripes and never (afterward) accept their testimony - they indeed are evil doers.* *(24:4)*

The above verse throws a light on the significance of morality and chastity in Islam. A person who is guilty of levelling a false charge of immorality against a pious man or woman and fails to bring four witnesses in support thereof will be liable to the following punishments: 1. He should be beaten with eighty stripes. 2. In future his witnesses should not be accepted, being the biggest liar. 3. There is no doubt in his wickedness.

BIRTH CONTROL : MEANS AND MEASURES

Birth Control in its modern form was not practised in the early days of Islam. No doubt, infanticide, abortion and other methods of getting rid of unwanted children were prevalent in Arabia, as in other parts of the world, and Islam forbade them completely. The Quran said: 'Do not kill your children for fear of poverty; We will provide for them and for you.' The question is whether this injunction can be applied to modern methods of birth control which do not amount to killing but aim at the prevention of conception. But this is not the only vital issue. There is the further question whether Islam would have approved of artificial methods for limiting population, if such methods had been used in its day. No clear-cut instructions are available either in the Quran or in the traditions of the Prophet. We will have to decide them on the basis of the general tenor and spirit of Islamic teachings, and the moral considerations involved therein. The Quran's own accepted method in deciding such doubtful issues is to weigh the good and the evil of a habit, institution or way of life, and condemn it if its evil is likely to exceed the good and vice versa. For example, in prohibiting the use of alcoholic liquor, the Quran says: 'Its sin and evil far outweigh its benefits.' Thus the Quran recognises that there are some benefits also in the use of wine but condemns it because the evils of it are more numerous and more dangerous. Proceeding on this basis, let us analyse the argument, for and against birth control.

Among the foremost advocates of birth control in modem times Havelock Ellis stands most prominent, apart from Margaret Sanger. In his book on *Life and Sex* he has devoted a whole chapter entitled 'The Individual and the Race' to prove the thesis that birth control is a social necessity and serves the interest of the race. Let us give a few quotations from this book.

Stressing the eugenic aspect of birth control, Ellis says:

> *It is often said— I have said it myself—that birth-control when practised merely as a limitation of the family scarcely suffices to further the eugenic progress of the race. If it is not deliberately directed towards the elimination of the worst stocks or the worst possibilities in the blending of stocks, it may even tend to diminish the better stocks since it is the better stocks that are least likely to propagate at random. This is true if other conditions remain equal. It is evident, however, that the other conditions will not remain equal, for no evidence has yet been brought forward to show that birth-control, even when practised without regard to eugenic considerations-doubtless the usual rule up to the present has produced any degeneration of the race. On the contrary, the evidence seems to show that it has improved the race.*

Examining the effect of birth control on the health of mothers, Havelock Ellis writes in the same chapter.

There will probably be a longer interval between the birth of the children, which has been demonstrated by Ewart and others to be an important factor not only in preserving the health of the mother but in increasing the health and size of the child. The diminution in the number of children renders it possible to bestow a greater amount of care on each child. Moreover, the better economic position of the father, due to the smaller number of individuals he has to support, makes it possible for the family to live under improved conditions as regards nourishment, hygiene and comfort. The observance of birth-control is thus a far more effective lever for raising the state of the social environment and improving the conditions of breeding, than is direct action on the part of the community in its collective capacity to attain the same end.

Developing this argument further with reference to the effects of heredity, Ellis goes on to say:

> *... if, in accordance with the most careful modern investigations, we recognize that heredity is supreme, that the qualities we have inherited from our ancestors count far more in our lives than anything we have acquired by our own personal efforts, then we have to admit that the capable man's wealth is more the community's concern than his own. So that neither the capable nor the incapable are entitled to an unqualified power of freedom, and neither, like-wise, are justly liable to be burdened by an unqualified responsibility.*

Socialists also come in for scathing criticism by Havelock Ellis, because they are opposed to birth control. Put social conditions on a sound basis, the people on this side often say, let all receive an adequate economic return for their work and be recognized as having a claim for an adequate share in the products of society and there is no need to worry about the race or about the need for birth-control; all will go well of itself. There is not the slightest ground for any such comfortable belief. And further the same writer says:

> *This prejudice against birth control is based on the ground that bad economic conditions, and an unwholesome environment are the source of all social evils and that a better distribution of wealth or a vast scheme of social welfare is the one thing necessary. . . . It is certainly impossible to overrate the importance of the economic factor in society or of a good environment. And it is true that eugenics also, like birth-control alone, can effect little if the economic basis of society is unsound. But it is equally certain that the economic factor can never in itself suffice for fine living or even as a cure-all of social and racial diseases. Its value is not that it can effect any of these things but that it furnishes the favourable conditions for effecting them. He would be foolish indeed who went to the rich to find the example of good breeding and, as is well known, it is not with the rich that the future of the race lies. The fact that under any economic system the responsible personal direction of the individual and the family remains equally necessary, and no progress is possible so long as the individual casts all responsibility away from himself on the social group he forms part of.*

In another book, *Psychology of Sex,* Havelock Ellis says: *The necessity of birth-control is now generally recognized, not only by those who do not desire to have children, but by those who do. The reason is that, both for the sake of the mother and for the health and well-being of the off-spring, it is desirable that births should be properly spaced, allowing at least an interval of two years between births, while there are various legitimate reasons, economic or other, why those who marry early do not see their way to become parents immediately. The child, therefore, however much desired, should come at a time when the parents are best able to receive it and to care for it. Moreover the days of large families are over. For the sake of the family and in the interest of the nation and the race, an average of between two or three for each married couple suffices. The hygienic conditions of civilization should be ample to keep up the population. When for any good reason, such as the health of the mother or the existence, in either parent, of a bad heredity which should not be carried on, conception cannot be allowed, then strict birth-control is compulsory.*

So far we have quoted arguments in favour of birth control. Now let us see the other side of the picture. It must be recognized that over-population is not the only evil which has to be fought against and controlled. A falling birth-rate and a diminution of population is at least an equally serious evil. In the decline of civilisations, under-population and not over-population, is a common symptom. This is true of the Roman civilisation which was faced with serious depopulation in its period of decline. Similarly, one factor in the defeat of modern France against Hitlerite Germany was lack of manpower. This was emphasised by Marshal Petain in his speech on the morrow of French defeat. The reason is that love of luxury and comfort among the richer classes and fear of poverty and insecurity among the poor make them unwilling to bring more children in the world, This tendency has been greatly facilitated by the use of birth-control methods. As Margaret Mead has pointed out in her book, *Male and Female:* 'Every human society is faced not with one population problem but with two: How to beget and rear enough children and not to beget and rear too many? The definition of "enough" and "too many" varies enormously.' The same writer, pointing to the growing sterility among men and women, adds: 'There seems to be a deep-seated belief that conception is an almost automatic process, and that unless drastic measures are taken every sexual act will result in a child. The story of the king and the queen who had no children is replaced by jokes based on contraceptive failures. Even in the face of rising sterility rates and the occasional sterility clinic, the popular mind is still focussed on how not to have children rather than how to have them.' On this evidence, in some countries the widespread use of contraceptives is creating a serious danger of depopulation, apart from facilitating and widening the range of extra-matrimonial illicit sexual relations which is undermining the stability of the home and the family. 'Let us quote Dr. Westermarck who says in *Future of Marriage in Western Civilization*: 'While the knowledge of contraceptives may increase the marriage rate, it also facilitates extra-matrimonial intercourse, the great frequency of which is, in our days, regarded as another indication of the doom of marriage.'

The cult of birth control was one of the by-products of the Malthusian theory that the rate of increase of population is far in excess of any increase in the means of subsistence and if it is allowed to go on unchecked, a point will come when most of the human race will have starved out. This false theory has been exploded, since then, but its influence on the minds of people everywhere is still so great that, they overlook the danger of depopulation. As Stefansson said in 1925: 'According to the false Malthusianism of Malthus himself, we should all have starved to death sometime ago .... But here we all are, alive; prosperous and sceptical of the prophets, of doom.' What Malthus and his supporters overlooked was that humanity is infinitely creative, if it does not lose its spiritual moorings or sink into gross and sordid materialism. The productive powers of man have increased at much faster rate than his numbers. If they have failed to make him happier and contented, it is because, in the mad race for power and wealth, they are being put to destructive uses. As science and knowledge increase, the earth will support more and more of human beings, provided man's spirituality and vision also expand in the right direction. There was never really any danger of population increasing faster than human productivity. Even the available space on earth for human habitation is not so limited as many people imagine. Geographical explorations are opening, up new areas with immensely rich resources which can be made fit for human habitation with the help of scientific power at the disposal of man. This theme has been very brilliantly treated by Parker Hanson in his book, *New Worlds Emerging*.

We give here a few quotations from this great book which will show how much habitable space and available resources are still to be tapped by mankind. Discussing the methods which have been and can be used for meeting the threat of over-population, Hanson says: 'Throughout history and prehistory, man has met his ever recurring problem of over-population, not in any one way but by a complex, interrelated application of three distinct lines of effort, namely, migration, change of social and economic organization, and technical invention.' Strikingly enough, Hanson does not mention birth control as one of the methods for meeting the danger of over-population, because no really great and creative civilisation has ever resorted to birth control except in its period of decadence. The three methods referred to by Hanson are still open to humanity. With regard to the first of these, migration, let us study his conclusions. Speaking about the Amazon basin, he says:

> *The Amazon basin, greatest of all the tropical frontiers, is still being discounted or written off at a time when its possibilities for colonization and development need, in view of the world's present-day problems, the most serious considerations .... Is much of the Amazon valley a semi-swamp? Is the climate so terrible that nobody would want to live there? As long as there is no great pressure for developing: the region, such questions are relatively unimportant for all but the few hundred thousand white men and women and the primitive Indians who live there and seem to get along reasonably well.*

Proceeding further, he asks:

> *Today, four centuries after its discovery by white explorers, the Amazon basin is still an almost empty frontier, undeveloped, wild and often turbulent. Does it mean that it must always remain so? Is its present condition ascribable to natural conditions or to the accidents of history? Was its nature always hostile to human occupation and culture? If not, how do the white men differ from the men who once got along well there? Are those differences physical or emotional or do they stem from differing social outlook? ... As long as the white man felt that he could not live in the tropics except as a colonial administrator, with coloured labour doing his work for him, the Amazon basin, lacking manpower, had no chance. If it is to be developed today, the job must be done by men and women who make their homes there. There may be white, brown, black, yellow or any other colour, but modern immigration policies and racial strings prohibit the importation of large racial blocs to be segregated from the overlords as cheap labour. The basin has been described several times in the past two centuries as a potential area of white settlement and it is today again being regarded in that light.*

William Lewis Herndon who was sent to Amazon in 1851 to examine the possibilities of its future expansions summed up his impressions as follows:

> *It is ....sad to think that ....this country has not more than one inhabitant for every ten square miles of land; that it is almost a wilderness; but being capable, as it is, of yielding support and luxury to millions of civilized people... it should be but a dwelling-place of the savage and the wild beast.*

About the riches and resources of this valley, Hanson says:

> *Few laymen have a true conception of the Amazon basin's size, wealth and variety, or of the truly staggering propositions of the river system itself. In length, the Amazon river is exceeded only by the Nile, and very little-by it, in volume of water, by three of the world's rivers combined. There are some eleven hundred tributaries of the Amazon, not counting thousands of brooks. Nine or ten of these tributaries exceed the Rhine in length, and carry more than double its volume of water. Seven of them are over a thousand miles long, and one, the Madeira, is nearly three thousand miles from source to mouth .... The area drained by that lordly river is an empire virtually untapped and unpooled in the heart of Western Hemisphere, some two million seven hundred thousand miles in extent, or almost as large as the continental United States with its three million square miles. It is as varied as the United States, and possibly as rich in the quantity and variety of its natural resources.*

It is after reading such passages that one is reminded of the Quranic promise: 'Do not kill your children for fear of poverty; We shall provide for them and for you.' The Quran assumes, of course, as a precondition, that men will accept its pattern of life and scheme of values, will be creative and cooperative and not fall into worshipping wealth and power so as to engage in mutual self-destruction.

Let us now see the possibilities of development and colonisation in Iceland. Before discussing this question, Parker Hanson delivers a strong attack against the advocates of birth control. He says:

> *One of the most alarming symptoms of today's psychology of hysteria is the astonishing popularity of those prophets of doom who summarily dismiss both north and south as regions of new endeavour, look about at the lands in between, state correctly that our culture has made a mess of its*

utilization of natural resources, and arrive-via the so-called Malthusian law-at the conviction that there is now no real solution to the Western world's problems except the energetic conservation of natural resources going hand in hand with the partial extermination of human resources, through birth-control-imposed by the few on the many.

Regarding the population and resources of Iceland, Hanson remarks:

In the days of emigration to the United States, Iceland had half its present number of people and was over-populated in line with the Smith-Philip's dictum that 'the meagre resources of the polar and sub-polar regions can support only a sparse population'. Today with the number of its inhabitants growing steadily and rapidly, the land is decidedly underpopulated in relation to its aspirations and potentialities. Changes in Icelandic life, both today and in the past, are worth-watching. Several scientists have called it the finest available laboratory and observation post for the life of man. Nowhere else in the white man's world do we find the same purity of conditions as there..

About the wealth and resources of Iceland, the same author writes:

As though to compensate for its lack of fuels, the republic has large stores of potential waterpower available. Its calculated four million horse-power, or 32 per inhabitant, are greater per capita than those known for any other country on earth. Only a small fraction of that power has been developed for lighting, heating and industrial enterprises, but plans for ever-increasing utilization go steadily forward.... The country's volcanic heat is spectacular. Early in the century a number of farmers began to realize that they had hot springs on their land, even if they did lack fuels and means for transporting such fuels from the outside. They then began to pipe those springs into radiators in their homes, as others harnessed small local waterfalls through power plants that were often in part- made at home, and used the electricity for heat, light and cooking. Natural hot water began also to be used for agricultural purposes. In places it is today run over the ground for irrigation or warmth, in others it is run through buried pipes, in still others it is used to warm glass-covered hothouses. Together with an active program of agricultural development, it has resulted in a marked increase of crop production, both in quantity and kind. Many vegetable crops, formerly considered impossible in Iceland, are now produced and reduce the country's import of food by that much.

Here again is a picture of the Arctic regions drawn by Parker Hanson in his memorable book:

In 1935 there was published a geological map showing two hundred and twenty-eight of the two hundred and seventy-three places where valuable minerals had been found in the Soviet Arctic. A compilation of the results of the preceding fifteen years of study of the mineral deposits in the Soviet Arctic was completed by the geological section of the Arctic Institute revealing that one thousand six hundred and thirty-seven points had been located where there was a suggestion of mineral deposits, although only relatively few of them were estimated to have industrial value. In spite of the tempo and extent of the work accomplished up to 1936, however, only about 100,000 square, miles, or less than five per cent of the Arctic land, had been surveyed.

Coal, iron, nickel, lead, zinc, copper, various sulphites, salt, and peat are only a few subsoil resources that have been located in the Soviet Arctic since 1917. As now transportation facilities by water, land, and air make them available, as the Russians build cities and mining camps and get workers to the scene, these are being developed in line with the general northward course of Russia's economy.

Finally, about Alaska, the author of the New Worlds Emerging says:

Geographically, the territory has room for millions of new settlers. The former mental barriers which tended to keep them out are breaking down; no longer is Alaska the 'remote and barbarous region which under ordinary human conditions will never be largely peopled except by savages'. As the climate improves in men's thinking, the physical resources of Alaska are being studied and are duly proving richer and more abundant. The most significant aspect of the problem is the economy. It is economic Alaska, within which there is little room for new settlers; it must expand before newcomers make place for themselves in the Territory and thereby add to its and our material prosperity.

The Alaskan delegate (without vote) to the American Congress, in a speech on 21 May 1936, stated:

We find ....that Alaska exceeds in area the combined areas of Norway, Sweden and Finland, which now support in comfort more than 12,000,000 people. We find that Finland has no natural gold reserves of any kind; has very little of copper; that its iron reserves are much less than those of Alaska; that its fisheries are only a fraction of the value of the Alaska fisheries; that its agricultural and grazing lands are approximately one-sixth of the area of the farming and grazing lands of Alaska; that it has no coal reserves, no petroleum reserves; in reindeer pasture Finland has 8,000 square miles, Alaska 240,000 square miles. And yet this country sustains a cultural as well as a rugged population of 3,500,000.

A comparison of Alaska with Sweden, which has a population of 6,000 000 is equally favourable to the Territory. Sweden has an area of 173,550 square miles: its farming and grazing lands do not in area exceed one-half of those of Alaska; and yet its agricultural population comprises approximately 2,700,000 people. Sweden has in reindeer pasture about 40,000 square miles, as against 240,000 square miles in Alaska. Sweden, like Finland, has nothing in the way of natural gold reserves, and its copper reserves are very small indeed as compared with the very large copper reserves of Alaska .... Alaska has large deposits of marble, Sweden little. Alaska apparently has large reserves of petroleum, and Sweden is entirely without this resource. . . The fisheries of Sweden, although extensive, do not amount in value to half of those of Alaska... So when I conclude, as I do, that the territory of Alaska is capable of supporting a population of several millions. I am not drawing at all upon my imagination but basing it upon what has been done in the old world and upon an impartial consideration of geographic and scientific facts.

The report on Alaska's post-war economic development discusses at length the problem of agricultural expansion. It states:

Of the millions of acres of potentially arable land in the Territory, Alaska farms contain only about 11,000 acres now classified as cropland.

The report adds:

It is estimated that South-East Alaskan pulpwood forests could support an industry employing at least 6,000 workers full time in this mill and the woods. Directly and indirectly the industry could be expected to provide year-round economic support for 25,000 persons.

> *'It should be noted,' says Hanson, 'that the statement applies to only a small part of the territory's total forest reserves.'*

Mining expansion is another aspect of the Alaskan development treated in the report:

> *Today gold is the Territory's greatest mineral output. It accounts for ninety-two per cent of the total. There are, however, innumerable possibilities for mining activities on coal, iron, copper, nickel, chromate and limestone, to mention only a few, specially when such activity comes to be combined with the utilisation of part of the Territory's extremely low-cost potential hydroelectric power towards the creation of electro-metallurgical and electrochemical industries.*

The above extracts will show that the available space for human habitation and the untapped resources of the world are sufficient to support the growing population of the earth and those who advocate the use of birth control on the basis that the population of the world will soon outrun the means of subsistence do not take into account the limitless resources which the Creator has placed at the disposal of man. As if to contradict such pessimists, the Holy Quran draws pointed attention to the infinitude of Divine power and asks man to trust His infinite providence: 'And there is not a thing in the world but with us are its treasures, but we do not send it down except in a known measure' (xv. 20). Here is comfort for those who despair of the power of God to provide for His creatures. When we add to this the infinite creative power with which man has been endowed and which finds its visible embodiment in the progress of science and technology, we must dismiss all Malthusian fears as unreal.

Turning to the economic aspect of the question, we must emphasise one factor which the advocates of birth control seem to have lost sight of. It is that every child who comes into the world remains as an economic burden on his parents and society only so long as his creative faculties are undeveloped. As soon as he becomes creative—and all individuals properly educated are creative — he pays back to his family and society more than what they contribute towards his growth and development. If lack of economic resources or a defective and unscientific education does not release his latent creativity, it is not the fault of his maker but of the social system in which he is born. As far as Nature is concerned, it never really brings a fresh individual in society without implanting in him the seeds of creativity and endowing him with capabilities of enriching his society materially, and spiritually. Properly brought up and scientifically educated, every human being is capable of creating more wealth than he can possibly use for his individual needs and of giving back more than what his parents have invested on him. From this point of view the birth of every child is an addition to social wealth for which humanity ought to be thankful to God.

It is not a cursor to be eliminated and fought against. When people begin to prevent the birth of children and are afraid of every new addition to human population, it is a sure sign that the society in which they live has ceased to be creative and the acquisitive spirit has so far acquired ascendancy over the mind of the people as to destroy the economic equilibrium of society. In a nation which enjoys economic health and provides equal opportunities for all its members, nobody should be afraid of having an extra child. It is social and economic injustice and the accumulation of wealth in the hands of an uncreative oligarchy of politicians, officials, traders, industrialists and landlords which reduces the common man to poverty and makes him unwilling to add to his burdens by bringing into the world more mouths to feed.

The advocacy of birth control really springs from a subconscious desire to keep intact the socio-economic organisation of an unjust society. It is always a convenient device of the privileged classes when they feel that they cannot prevent the growth of disaffection among the poor without radical changes in the economic structure of society. In the circumstances they feel that a further deterioration in the economic situation of the poor cannot be arrested without the widespread use of birth control. So, instead of cutting down their own privileges and lowering their own luxurious standards of living, they offer the palliative of birth control to the people low down in the scale of life.

Havelock Ellis has attacked the socialists for opposing the use of birth-control methods. But, apart from eugenic considerations, he produces no convincing arguments as to why, instead of exterminating the human race partially or wholly, society should not be so reorganised economically as to remove the fear of poverty on account of procreation. As regards eugenics what Havelock , Ellis seems to forget is that the application of eugenic principles will lead to much interference in private and family matters.

It is the State, after all, which will decide who shall procreate and to what extent particular stocks shall be encouraged to propagate themselves and what shall be withheld from so doing.

Is there any guarantee that the State will not misuse its authority for political ends or that the sordid interests of a small group, holding power in the State, shall not determine the application of eugenic principles to the prejudice of its opponents. And again, how will the State or any other corporate body enforce its decisions on unwilling persons?—A secret police force to watch the operations of birth control and report to the authorities. — Surely this is an absurd idea!

The most serious evil which is likely to attend the spread of birth-control methods is that once people get used to artificial family limitation; there will be nothing to prevent them from carrying that limitation to its furthermost extent and reducing the population to a dangerously low extent. There is no limit to which love of ease and luxuries may not carry a people when they once become addicted to these things. Is there any real need for providing more incentives towards life of irresponsibility? Human nature is already ballasted with this tendency, and for this very reason procreation in man creates its own natural checks. As soon as a couple feel that more children will mean extra burden, they take necessary precautions, as far as they can, to prevent more births. To provide artificial checks and push human beings on the road to pleasure-loving and irresponsibility is tantamount to committing national suicide. When race extermination has become the rage and unwillingness to suffer and sacrifice for the sake of the family and the nation has become deep-rooted, you can do nothing effective to reverse the process or change the habits of a people within a reasonable distance of time.

To introduce such dangerous methods in a nation without an eye on future consequences and psychological reactions on the mental and spiritual attitudes of men and women is the height of unwisdom. A few fleeting advantages should not blind us against far more effective and permanent national and moral injuries. A people using birth-control methods on a large-scale may have more comforts, better standards of economic prosperity and wider educational opportunities, but they are also likely to be incapable of making big sacrifices or undergoing great hardships for any ideal-social, religious or national. Can such a people survive in a world where these very qualities ultimately determine the chances of survival?

The fear that bigger families will mean more hardships and a tougher economic struggle should be balanced by the consideration that it is through struggle, sacrifice and hardship that great individuals as well as nations have achieved success and glory and left their imprint on the sands of time. Very few among the great men of the world and not one among the great nations of the earth initially had those comforts, luxuries and facilities which the advocates of birth control consider to be necessary for the health, happiness and progress of human beings. A small measure of poverty, provided it is not extreme and such as to freeze and corrode the human soul, provides an ideal incentive to progressive effort for creative individuals and nations than all the wealth and comforts sought after by the friends of race extermination. No great creative spiritual or cultural accomplishment has ever come from the rich who wallow in luxury, waste, extravagance, greed, acquisitiveness and ungodly arrogance. It is the poor individuals and nations that have throughout history lit the lamp of spirituality, culture and high scientific achievements. No great soul was ever afraid of moderate poverty.

Let us not be carried away by the slogans of a decrepit civilisation. A society which does not allow the majority of human beings to be reduced to abject poverty in order to provide wealth and luxury and comfort to a privileged group has little need of birth control. Let all people live a life of simple habits, let them have freedom from the ever-recurring threat of starvation, let them be provided with the necessaries of life, even without its superfluities, and, finally, let them be creative in thought and deed, not acquisitive in spirit and attitude, and every fresh addition to the human population will but increase the wealth, happiness and virtue of mankind.

5

Dissolution of Marriage : Divorce

REVOCATION OF MARRIAGE

The real purpose of marriage is that both husband and wife should be loyal to each other and lead a pious and chaste life; but sometimes the circumstances take such a turn that dissolution of marriage becomes a necessity.

We have already pointed out that before marriage both man and woman are allowed to make complete satisfaction as to the suitability of their marriage. If after proper investigation both are satisfied, the marriage should be held, otherwise not. This would ensure stability, love and cooperation between the couple. But sometimes the circumstances are such as defy the real purpose of marriage. Islam has framed some balanced rules and regulations to meet this situation. By acting upon them the risk to modesty and chastity can be averted and both husband and wife can lead a life of peace and comfort.

Apparently all the control seems to be in the hand of the husband and the wife is a helpless creature; but it is not so. A woman can go to a court of law in sudden difficulty and prosecute against her tyrant husband. The judge can deliver her from the clutches of her husband and resolve her problem.

It is not unusual that sometimes the husband lacks sufficient strength to gratify the sexual urge of his wife. In this case, if the woman desires separation and the husband is not willing to leave her, she can go to the court of law and bring a suit against her husband. The judge would issue a notice to her husband and make an investigation. If he is found impotent, the judge would order him to undergo a treatment for one year. If he becomes all right, so much the better. If, he remains defective, the judge would revoke their marriage. Hadrat Said bin Al-Musaib has said:

A man who marries a woman and lacks strength to gratify her sexual urge, should be given concession for one year. If he is able to have sexual intercourse with her, so much the better, otherwise the marriage will be revoked.
(Muatta)

Imam Malik asked Ibn Shahab as to the time from which the concession given to the impotent husband should be reckoned i.e. from the date of his marriage or from the date of bringing the suit. Ibn Shahab said:

From the date of bringing the suit in the court of law.
(Muatta)

Nevertheless, a wife can have a divorce from her impotent husband and can marry according to Shariah, with another man.

How can a woman have divorce from the husband whose sexual organ is cut off and is unable to gratify her sexual urge? She can get separation from her husband in the above manner except that she would not have to wait for even one year. On receipt of petition, the judge would investigate and decide the case in her favour. Imam Quduri writes:

If her husband is impotent, the judge would give him one year (for treatment). If he had sexual intercourse, well and good, otherwise the judge would order separation between them at the request of the woman. If the husband's sexual organ is cut off the judge would there and then order separation between them without giving him time.
(Quduri)

The same rule which is applicable to an impotent husband also applies here. If any person by castration renders himself unfit for sexual intercourse, his woman is allowed to go to the court of law and submit a petition against him. The judge would institute an enquiry and give him one year for treatment. If he still remains unfit, the judge would order separation between them.

"The castrated husband would be given one year time like the impotent husband." *(Quduri)*

Hafiz Ibn Qayyim has observed while giving his comments on this topic:

'It is akin to reason that every defect which creates hatred and discord between the husband and wife and negates the purpose of marriage, mutual love and harmony, makes the dissolution of marriage a necessity.' *(Zad al-Maad)*

The scholars differ on some points; but Islam does not permit debauchery and adultery in any form.

If the clash between husband and wife becomes serious and there is no hope of reconciliation, Islam has allowed the woman to ask divorce from the husband. Islam has, however, forbidden the use of this concession merely to exploit the other party. Allah's Messenger (peace and blessings of Allah be upon him) has observed:

> *A woman who asks divorce from the husband over triflings would not taste the smell of Paradise.* *(Mishkat)*

Once Allah's Messenger (peace and blessings of Allah be upon him) observed:

> *The women who desire separation and ask divorce from husbands are among the hypocrites.*

It is evident from the above Ahadith that the women should not desire separation from their husbands merely for pleasure's sake. They should abstain from making the marriage a plaything.

If, however, she honestly feels that if divorce was not taken, she would not be able to abide by the Shariah and that their relations are harmful from the worldly point of view as well as from the religious point of view, she can have divorce from her husband. It has been mentioned in the Holy Quran:

> *And if ye fear that they may not be able to keep the limits of Allah, in that case it is no sin for either of them if the woman ransom herself.* *(2:229)*

Although it is permissible to get divorce from the husband if she is afraid that she would not be able to keep Shariah, it is not otherwise permissible to ask for divorce. In Ahadith an incident of "Khula" has been narrated in detail. Habibah hint Sahl Ansari was married to Hadrat Thabit bin Qais bin Shams. At dawn Allah's Messenger (peace and blessings of Allah be upon him) went out for the morning prayer. When he arrived at the door of his house, he saw there a woman who had covered herself up and seemed to be rather frightened. Allah's Messenger (peace and blessings of Allah be upon him) questioned: Who are you? She answered: O Allah's Messenger! I am Habibah, the daughter of Sahl. Allah's Messenger (peace and blessings of Allah be upon him) asked: What is the matter with you? She said: Neither am I with Thabit bin Qais nor is he with me, meaning thereby that they could not pull on with each other as husband and wife. Allah's Messenger (peace and blessings of Allah be upon him) heard her story and went to offer the prayer. When Hadrat Thabit bin Qais came to Allah's Messenger (peace and blessings of Allah be upon him) he said to him: Habibah Bint Sahl has told me what. Allah wills. She has also agreed to pay the dower money and return her husband's gift; take it. Thereupon Hadrat Thabit took the gift from his wife and their marriage was dissoluted.

It has been narrated in Bukhari that Hadrat Thabit's wife said to Allah's Messenger (peace and blessings of Allah be upon him): O Allah's Messenger! I do not accuse him of bad conduct or religion but I do not like joining infidelity and disbelief with Islam.

When Allah's Messenger (peace and blessings of Allah be upon him) heard this he said: Are you willing to return his garden? She gave her assent. He then said to Hadrat Thabit:

Accept the Garden and divorce her. *(Zad al-Maad)*

The above incident which has been narrated in Bukhari no doubt pertains to Hadrat Thabit's wife; but it was not Habibah, it was that of his second wife, Jamila bint Abi Salul. In Ibn Majah, this incident has been mentioned as pertaining to Jamila.

As a matter of fact, Hadrat Thabit bin Qais bin Shams was a short-statured, ugly and hot-tempered man and no woman could love him. According to some Ahadith, his wife used extremely harsh words against him.

Some other incidents of "Khula" have also been mentioned in Ahadith but we need not go into their details.

One of the critical times for a woman is when her husband is absent and his whereabouts are not known; whether he is alive or not. What should be done by the woman in such a case? We doubt this is a disputable point; but the verdict of the renowned scholars is that a woman should wait for her absent husband for four years. If his whereabouts are not known during these four years, their marriage would be dissoluted after the expiry of 'iddah for four months and ten days. She may marry according to her desire with any man in a legal manner after the expiry of this period. Imam Malik has mentioned the view of Hadrat Umar (Allah be pleased with him):

> *The woman whose husband is not traceable and his whereabouts are not known should wait for four years and then after the expiry of 'iddah for four months and ten days, she may re-marry.* *(Muatta)*

Imam Malik also holds this view. The Hanifites have used verdicts basing their arguments on the above saying. In this connection the names of the writers of Jami al Ramuz, al-Dar al-

Muntaqi and Dur Mukhtar along with the Indian scholars, Shah Wali Ullah, Muhaddith Dehlvi and Maulana Abdul Hye, deserve to be specially mentioned. They have supported the above view after giving convincing arguments.

Process of Divorce : The provision of divorce in Islam has a special purpose. If the relations of husband and wife become strained and the efforts to effect reconciliation between them fail so that it is not possible for them to pull on, the husband can divorce his wife.

Before we go into the detail of the rules and regulations of divorce in Islam, it is not out of place to mention here that provision for divorce also exists in other religions. The Jewish law of divorce is extremely flexible. The husband's desire to divorce is considered a sufficient plea to divorce the wife. If the husband wants to have a beautiful wife instead of the one he possesses he can divorce the former. Moreover, divorce can be given for minor defects and shortcomings; there is a defect in the eye, the arm-pit gives an odious smell, there is a limp in the leg or the woman is issueless. The divorce can also be given for defects in conduct and behaviour; if she is hot-tempered, talkative, foul mouthed, avaricious and of rough taste, greedy in eating, etc.

In the Jewish law of divorce men have been given great rights whereas sheer injustice has been done to women as they have been deprived of this right and they cannot demand divorce despite the defects and tyranny and oppression of their husbands.

There was no provision for divorce in the Christian law. Marriage was a permanent relation between the husband and wife; they could not be separated due to any reason. This strictness was based on Christ's teaching:

He whom God unites cannot be disunited. *(Bible)*

Christ's saying was wrongly interpreted by his followers as it implied a moral lesson that divorce should not be given without my genuine reason. It has been mentioned in the next lines:

A person who forsakes his wife, except on account of adultery, and marries a second woman commits sin. *(Bible)*

It is evident from the above that divorce can be given if there is a necessity; but the Christian scholars think that this addition and alteration has been made afterwards and some other scholars are of the view that separation would be made between the husband and wife if they are guilty of adultery but the marriage contract will not be revoked. None of the two is allowed to re-marry.

You will be surprised to know that among the Christians this practice was in vogue for centuries. Those who believed in divorce, lived solitary lives after divorce. Later on, the eastern churches recommended revocation of marriage in certain laws but the western churches refused to act upon this law. The Christians had to bear undescribable tortures due to this unjust and tyrannical law.

Reformation in Law : In the sixteenth century voice against this unjust law was raised; but it did not prove effective.

In England upto 1857, the court of law did no accept the laws of divorce unless the crimes of adultery and oppression were proved. Even if the crimes were proved, the law caused only separation between the husband and wife; but none of them was allowed to re-marry. Only the court could decide the cases of separation and any one, husband or wife, who desired to get divorce was legally bound to substantiate the charge of adultery against the other. Besides the charge of adultery, the woman had also to substantiate the charge of maltreatment or oppression by the husband. It is also surprising to note that the husband enjoyed legal right to receive fine from the friend of his wife having illicit relations with her as compensation money for playing with her modesty.

In the law of 1866, the court was given the right to make the husband responsible for bearing the expenses of food, lodging, etc., of his divorced wife; but in the law of 1907, the word 'guilty' was deleted and the court could now order the husband to pay the expenses of his wife despite complete separation between them.

In the law of 1898, it was decided that if a woman left her house and began to live separately due to the tyranny and oppression of her husband, the court could disallow the husband to go to his wife but it coulf demand subsistence for his wife. There was also a provision in this law that if the woman was guilty of adultery due to her husband's maltreatment or indifferent attitude and the husband demanded divorce, the court would reject the appeal of the husband.

In 1910, a Royal Commission was appointed to ponder over the matters concerning marriage, divorce etc., and submit their report. Besides other things, the Commission recommended: Keeping in view the causes and reasons of divorce, there should be no distinction between the husband and the wife, that is, the reasons due to which the husband can get divorce from his wife should also hold good in case the woman demands divorce.

In the law of 1923, it was added that if the husband was found guilty of adultery even once, the woman has the right to get divorce from him.

Thus, the reform now introduced was not only defective, the law itself was devoid of wisdom and prudence. The people did not accept it. In 1930 it was decided:

We cannot allow a woman to marry when previous husband is alive.

Briefly speaking, if the law of the Jews was liberal, the law of the Christians was stingy with the result that when it gave some relaxation for divorce, there was great rush in the number of divorces.

Once in the civil court of Spain, 294 marriages were revoked in one day. In 1844, when the new law of divorce was passed, 4000 divorces were taken. In 1900, the number of divorces reached 7,500 and in 1913, the number was 16,000 and in 1931 it was 21,000.

In 1922, in the city of Denwar, with each marriage there was also an incident of separation and one suit of divorce was brought in the court of law against two marriages. There was almost the same condition in all other cities of America. Arthur Garfield has written in a treatise: Out of seven marriages contracted forty years ago there occurred only one incident of divorce whereas the recent data shows that out of three marriages in the United Kingdom, one ends in divorce and this number is increasing day by day.

When a court of England opened after vacation, four thousand divorce cases were instituted.

In the Days of Ignorance : Men in the Days of Ignorance gave a number of divorces to their wives and then re-established their marital relations. Thus, they tortured them for ages. Hadrat Aishah (Allah be pleased with her) reported that a husband could give as many divorces to his wife as he liked and resume marital relations within the fixed term ('iddah). A man generally gave more than one hundred divorces.

The results of this transgression were alarming. The extent to which it spoiled the moral conduct and behaviour of people can be read in other books. Millions of men and women lost their honour and chastity and had to bear unspeakable tortures due to unjust tyrannical laws of divorce.

In this all pervading darkness the resplendent sun of Islam rose and it gave to the humanity the most balanced and practicable laws of divorce. The oppressed and down-trodden humanity heaved a sigh of relief. The rights of both men and women were safeguarded and no one was deprived of his/her legal right.

Islam has strictly forbidden to use this right of divorce in haste as the matter pertains to two individuals and two families. Despite the fact that divorce is permissible in the Islamic Shariah in the case of extreme urgency, it is said to be one of the most detestable of all permitted things. Islam does not believe in giving divorce on trifling matters. It has been said by Allah's Messenger (peace and blessings of Allah be upon him):

> *With Allah, the most detestable of all things permitted is divorce.*
>
> *(Mishkat)*
>
> *Allah has not created any thing on earth more detestable than divorce.*
>
> *(Mishkat)*

According to the Fuqaha (experts in Islamic jurisprudence), talaq (divorce) is not allowed except in the case of extreme urgency or when the marital relations of husband and wife are poisoned to such a degree as make peaceful home-life impossible for them or the hatred and enmity are aggravated to an intolerable extent or there exists a real danger to chastity and morality.

If the husband is impotent and lacks sufficient sexual strength to satisfy his wife or is castrated or his sexual organ is defective or cut off, in all such cases it becomes necessary to obtain divorce.

Man, however, reserves the right to divorce. It is an admitted fact that man is more wise, intelligent, farsighted, prudent and tolerant than woman due to the experience gained in the outside world.

Moreover, he has to bear the major expenses of marriage and pay the dower money. He is also responsible to pay for food, lodging, etc., to women during 'Iddah. If he marries for the second time, he would have to incur all the expenses of marriage for the second time. Keeping in view the heavy responsibilities that lie on him and the large expenditure involved, it is not easy for him to divorce his wife.

A study of all the rules and regulations pertaining to divorce would further reveal that there remain only rare chances of divorce and this provision can be used only sparingly and under very exceptional circumstances.

In the Islamic Shariah the Ahsan (most laudible) way of divorce according to the Sunnah provides opportunity for reconciliation and resumption of conjugal relations, thus minimizing the chances of final separation. Although the divorce is confirmed on pronouncement of three divorces, the pronouncement of three divorces at one time is not considered to be an appreciable act, and is irregular.

A woman is not allowed to marry immediately after divorce. She should wait for the prescribed period. If she is a matured lady having menses, she must wait for three months. If she does not have menses or is an Aisa, (past child bearing) she should wait for three months. If she is pregnant, she should wait till delivery. This waiting for the prescribed period is to purify the womb. It is also necessary for the safety of the child. Moreover, it affords time to the man to reconsider all the pros and cons of the matter before the conjugal relations are resumed in the case of revocable divorce.

We do not want here to discuss all the rules and regulations pertaining to divorce. What we want to impress is that in Islam the law of divorce contains all such measures as are beneficial for the people or are helpful in protecting chastity and morality and saving the women from high-handedness, tyranny and oppression.

A statistical review of divorces has revealed that in the Islamic countries the number of divorces is only negligible which affirms the fact that Islamic law of divorce is full of blessing for the humanity.

Some people are of the view that only the courts should possess the right to decide the cases of divorce. But this view is not correct. It lacks sufficient prudence and farsightedness. To bring such cases to the court and prove the charges of adultery in the public is to spoil the lives of men and women. No one can deny the fact that after discussing such cases in the court, the chances of the marriage of women become rare. Islam detests slandering, back-biting and false allegations and their advertisement in public. A further probe into the matter would reveal that Islam has authorized the Qadi Oudge to revoke the marriage only when there is no harm to declare the allegation openly, for instance, when husband is impotent.

The Islamic law of divorce is beneficial for the humanity as a whole and is a means of protecting public chastity and morality.

If any husband accuses his grown up, pious, free Muslim wife of adultery and takes his case to the court, the Qadi Oudge would ask him, to bring four eye-witnesses in support of his allegation. If the husband fails to bring four witnesses, he would be required to take the vow in the name of Allah four times and say that he is right. For the fifth time he should say that curse of Allah be upon him if he brings a false accusation against his wife. If the woman is innocent she would have to say four times: By Allah, my husband is telling a lie against me. For the fifth time she should say: Woe of Allah be upon me if my husband be right. This is called lian (invoking curse) in the Shariah.

After the proceedings of Wan according to the Shariah, the Qadi would order separation between them. It has been mentioned in the Holy Quran:

> *As for those who accuse their wives but have no witnesses except themselves; let the testimony of one of them be four testimonies (swearing) by Allah that he is of those who speak the truth; and yet a fifth, invoking the curse of Allah on him if he is of those who lie. And it shall avert the punishment from her if she bear witness before Allah four times that the thing he saith is indeed false. And a fifth (time) that the wrath of Allah be upon her if he speaketh truth.* *(24:6-9)*

The purpose behind the adoption of this method is that if the lives of both husband and wife are poisoned to a degree that it is not proper to legally bound them to live together as it would further aggravate the situation and turn their lives into a veritable hell, it is better to separate them.

The first incident of Wan occurred in the Holy Prophet's time, the detail of which is given in the Ahadith. Further details can be read in the books on Fiqh.

Islam has promulgated such rules and regulations for protection of modesty and chastity as are applicable to our daily routine life. Every responsible man must keep them in view. A slight lapse on the part of man and woman may result in spoiling their moral conduct and behaviour. Sexual instinct which has been ingrained in the human nature is so savage and uncontrollable that it bursts out at the slightest temptation and ruins the character. Moreover, the Devil has vowed to lead the man astray by all means. He is ever looking for an opportunity to allure him into evil and sin. Islam has therefore, enforced some measures to maintain modesty and chastity before and after marriage.

Shame and modesty are the virtues which save a man from going astray when he is prone to evil. Due to these pious sentiments of shame and modesty, people keep the private parts of their ladies hidden. Nudity is a means of excitement of sexual desire. Many people of the world led a nude life and many tribes and nations of today go about naked. African countries are notorious for their nakedness. There is no concept of purdah in Europe. Their dresses are practically nude or half-nude. The western monthly and weekly journals print naked/half-naked photographs of women.

Nude pictures are being published in the name of art and health while morality and chastity is cast to the winds. How long man can resist this onslaught of temptation. This moral turpitude has not only ruined the character and moral of the people but also shattered their health. We give below an excerpt from the American Journal which we have taken from the book *Purdah* written by Maulana Maudoodi.

> *"There are three devilish powers whose triangle has overwhelmed the whole world. They are causing terrible havoc. Evil literature which is being published at an astonishing speed in an alarming large number, movies which not only excite the sexual passions but also give a practical lesson of love-making, moral degeneration of women which is reflected from their dress, their naked and half-naked bodies, their habit of smoking, and their freely mixing up with strangers. These three evils have become a fashion which would ultimately lead to the ruination of western civilization and culture. If proper restrictions were not imposed, our fate would not be different from that of Rome and the other nations who revelled in wine and woman which became the ultimate cause of their ruin."*

AN SOCIAL EVIL

As has been made clear in the previous chapter, Islam never regarded marriage as a sacrament indissoluble except under extraordinary conditions. In accordance with its view of marriage as a contract, it made provision for the separation of married couples if the terms of the contract were not observed by either party. Divorce is the necessary corollary of the freedom given to men and women to choose their partners. The American authoress of *Male and Female* makes the sensible remark: 'With freedom to choose goes the right to change one's mind. If past mistakes are to be reparable in every other field of human relations, why should marriage be the one exception? If their choice of each other was what made marriage a real marriage, then once either makes another choice, its reality is gone. The spouse who, clings to such a marriage is committing one of the worst acts in the American list of sins, limiting the freedom of another person, exploiting and taking advantage of someone else's past dead impulse, freezing a past mistake into a present prison.' The idea that there is something essentially and inherently immoral in divorce was bequeathed to the world by Christianity and Hinduism. Its impracticability has been proved beyond shadow of all doubt, so much so that there is now a swing in the reverse direction and the danger of frequent and easy separation of married couples threatens the stability of the home and the family.

According to the Roman Catholic doctrine, a consummated Christian marriage is a sacrament and must as such remain valid for ever. It represents the union between Christ and the Church, and is consequently as indissoluble as that union. It is also permanent according to the law of Nature, because only a permanent marriage can fulfil this object. And God made it so at the beginning of our race, when He decreed that a man shall leave his father and his mother and shall cleave to his wife, and they shall be one flesh. In spite of this doctrine, which never could work in practice, the Roman Catholic Church allowed separation of married couples under exceptional circumstances on the ground of the invalidity of marriage. Lord Bryce has pointed out in his book, *Studies in History and Jurisprudence*, that the rules covering these exceptional cases 'were so numerous and so intricate that it was easy, given a sufficient motive, whether political or pecuniary, to discover some ground for declaring almost any marriage invalid'. A man might secure a divorce by swearing that he was his wife's distant cousin, or had loved her sister in his youth, or had before his marriage stood god-father to one of her near spiritual kindred.

For a long time the doctrine of the Western Church was not accepted in full by the legislators. But since the days of Charlemagne, the canonical doctrine of the indissolubility of marriage has increasingly influenced the legislation of Western countries. It was only during the course of nineteenth and twentieth centuries that divorce was made legal in the Roman Catholic countries in the case of the Roman Catholic marriages. In the United States, South Carolina stands alone in granting no divorces whatsoever. It is the only Protestant community which nowadays holds marriage indissoluble.

The Roman Catholic doctrine of the indissolubility of marriage except by death was never accepted by Protestant reformers. They all agreed that adultery should be recognised as a ground for divorce, and most of them regarded malicious desertion a second ground for the dissolution of marriage. The views of the Protestant reformers influenced the course of legislation in various Protestant countries and laws were passed permitting divorce for a number of reasons. Apart from adultery and desertion, an attempt made by one of the couples on the life of the other is specified in the law of many countries as a legitimate ground for divorce. Ill-treatment of some kind has also been laid down in some countries as a sufficient reason for the dissolution of marriage. In the United States, divorce is obtainable for cruelty. The degree of cruelty necessary is usually actual and repeated violence endangering life, limb or health. An extremely frequent ground of divorce is the condemnation of one of the parties to a certain punishment or his or her being convicted of a certain crime. In the United States, a husband who is able to support his wife but for a certain time neglects to do so may be divorced. Similarly, in some states divorce may be obtained on proof of the habitual drunkenness of either party for varying terms. In North Carolina, a husband may obtain a divorce if his wife has without good reason refused sexual intercourse to him for the space of twelve months.

Besides offences of some kind or other committed by either husband or wife and entitling the other party to demand a dissolution of the marriage, there are other circumstances recognised as grounds of divorce, which may or may not involve guilt in one of the parties, but in all cases are supposed to make marriage a burden for the other spouse. Impotence in the husband or the wife, existing at the time of the marriage and afterwards, but unknown to the other party, is recognised as a legitimate ground of divorce in some law books. In England it has long been a ground for pronouncing an otherwise valid marriage invalid; and in the United States also divorce is commonly granted for incurable physical incapacity, if the plaintiff was ignorant of the defendant's condition. Other grounds of divorce, according to many law books, are contagious, venereal and other diseases, and insanity which existed at the time of marriage or prior to it with knowledge of the other party, or insanity which has been pronounced incurable or gives no reasonable hope of recovery after three or sometimes five years' duration.

These are the most general grounds of divorce laid down in modern law books. English law is the only one in Europe that recognises none but sexual reason either for the dissolution or the annulment of marriage. The Majority Report of the Royal Commission of 1909 recommended that divorce should, in the future, be obtainable for the following reasons: adultery; wilful desertion for three years or upwards; cruelty; incurable insanity after five years' confinement; habitual drunkenness found to be incurable from the first order of separation; and imprisonment under commuted sentence of death. Among Western countries, France has made divorce much easier. The 1792 Law of Divorce says that marriage is merely a civil contract, and that the facility in obtaining divorce is the natural consequence of the individual's right of freedom which is lost if engagements are made indissoluble. Divorce is granted on various grounds, among others, on the mutual desire of the two parties, and even at the wish of one party on the ground of incompatibility of temper subject only to a short period of delay and to the necessity of appearing before a family council who are to endeavour to bring about reconciliation. In 1804, however, under the provisions of Napoleon's Code Civil des Francais, divorce was made more difficult. Mere incompatibility of temper is no longer recognised as sufficient cause for divorce. Marriage may still be dissolved on the ground of mutual consent, but on certain conditions only: the husband must be at least twenty-five years of age and the wife twenty-one; they must have been married at least for two years and not more than twenty-five years and the wife must not be over forty-five years of age; the parents or other living ascendants of both parties must give their approval; and the mutual and unwavering comment of the married couple must sufficiently prove that their 'common life is insupportable to them, and that there exists in reference to them a peremptory cause of divorce.'

The Soviet law goes even further than the French law in granting extreme facilities for divorce. It states that 'the ground for divorce may be either the mutual consent of the parties or the desire of one of them. If the union is not entered in the registry of books, man and woman part without formalities. If they have 'inscribed themselves,' all that they have to do is to 'write themselves out,' that is, record their separation in the books. The law steps in only when there are children and then not to hold the family together but to make provision for children.'

We thus find that the Western world which began with the doctrine of the indissolubility of marriage is now swinging to the other extreme by granting divorce on terms which can be regarded only as frivolous. Even in countries like England and America, where the divorce law is more stringent than in France and Soviet Russia, the number of divorces is increasing at an alarming rate. In the opinion of Dr. Westermarck, 'It is a mistake to believe that the fate of divorces is proportionate to the facility with which divorce may be obtained according to law.' Dr. Wilcox even maintains that 'the immediate, direct and measurable influence of legislation is 'subsidiary, unimportant, almost imperceptible'.

With regard to the United States he remarks. It seems that the exceptionally great divorce rates in the United States are largely due to the laxity of procedure that has grown up there. One wife alleges that her husband has never offered to take her "riding" (driving); another, that he does not come till ten o'clock at night, and when he does return he keeps the plaintiff awake talking. In England, according to the same writer, the removal of a legal obstacle has distinctly increased its frequency. Shortly after the Act was passed in 1925, which gave men and women equality as regards grounds for divorce, the divorce rate began to climb, and an estimate of this increase shows that between 1924 and 1930 an addition of about 35% per year was made to the residual divorces as a result of that Act.

We have already seen that Islam recognises the necessity for divorce in cases when marital relations have been poisoned to a degree which makes a peaceful home life impossible. But Islam does not believe in unlimited opportunities for divorce on frivolous and unimportant grounds, because any undue increase in the facilities of divorce would destroy the stability of family life. Therefore, while allowing divorce on genuine grounds, Islam has taken great care to introduce checks and balances designed to limit the use of- available facilities. Let us study in more detail the Islamic law on this point.

While permission has been given both to man and woman to obtain a release from the bond of marriage in cases of absolute necessity, the Prophet has made it clear that Islam does not regard it as desirable. A tradition of the Prophet states: 'The most repugnant of things made lawful in the sight of God is divorce.' Another tradition says: 'Marry but do not divorce, because God does not like men and women who relish variety in sexual pleasure.'

So far as men are concerned, they have been given liberty of divorce on certain conditions. First, as regards the dower they have bestowed on their wives, they are not permitted to withhold it or take back anything from it, if they decide upon divorce. Secondly, a divorce pronounced at a single sitting does not have the effect of final separation. It is laid down as a condition that a divorce, to take legal effect, must be pronounced three times at intervals of one month each. There is some difference of opinion as to whether three pronouncements at a single sitting can have the effect of final separation. Most jurists hold that a divorce takes effect if it is pronounced three times even at a single sitting. But Imam Ahmad ibn Hanbal and Imam Ibn Taymiyyah reject this opinion and regard as one pronouncement three declarations of divorce delivered at a single sitting, so that separation does not come of at the end of three such declarations, but only when they are separated each by an interval of one month. There are strong grounds for supporting the stand taken by Imam Ahmad and Imam Ibn Taymiyyah., In the first place it is obvious that the intention of law in prescribing three pronouncements of divorce separated by fixed intervals of time precedent to final separation was to leave open the opportunity of reconciliation. This intention is defeated by recognising three pronouncements delivered at a single sitting as having the effect of final separation. Secondly, there is evidence to show that the companions of the Prophet regarded this form of divorce as being morally reprehensible and involving the person responsible in a great religious sin. It is recorded that Umar, the Second Caliph, used to punish such persons who pronounced three divorces at a single sitting. Ibn Abbas, another companion of the Prophet, was asked about a person who divorced his wife in a single sitting. He said: 'The man was guilty of disobedience to divine commands.' Ali is reported to have said: 'If the people faithfully observed the conditions of divorce, no one would feel sorry for the separation of his wife.' In the face of this strong evidence, it is strange that the majority of jurists should have recognised the legal validity of an act which has been universally condemned as being highly sinful and which obviously defeats the Law-giver's intention. The law-makers of modern Muslim communities should not be bound by the legal, decisions of old jurists but should boldly carry out the intention of the original Islamic law.

During the period of the first two pronouncements of divorce, the husband and the wife are required to live together as formerly, so that if the husband has acted hurriedly or in a fit of passion, he may revoke his pronouncement and normal relations may be restored. Again, if the husband has sexual intercourse with his wife or indulges in the preliminaries of cohabitation, the pronouncement of divorce lapses automatically without express declaration on his part. But, if no such thing has happened and the two intervals of one month each have elapsed, normal relations cannot be restored except by re-marriage. If, however, the husband makes the third and final pronouncement after this period, marital relations are completely dissolved and the divorce is complete. If the husband repents after this and wishes to have his wife again, he cannot do so, except after his wife has been married to someone else and divorced by him too. This provision has been considered necessary in order that it may act as a deterrent for husbands who are prone to act rashly without considering the consequence of their action.

Another condition laid down for husbands intending to divorce their wives is that they should not pronounce the divorce during the period of their wive's menstruation. This condition has been deemed necessary because a woman is liable to become ill-tempered and easily irascible during the period of menstruation. This physical disability leads her sometimes to act and behave in, a manner which she disapproves herself on becoming clean. Another reason for this stipulation is that normal sexual relations between husband and wife are suspended for the time she undergoes her monthly course and sexual relations are commonly the basis of love and amity between husband and wife. It is possible that a couple may resume their normal attitude to each other and forget their quarrels when their sexual relations are restored after the period of menstruation. There is a tradition that Abdullah b. Umar divorced his wife when she was having her monthly period. His father reported the matter to the Prophet who became very angry and ordered that Abdullah should revoke his divorce and wait until his wife is clean, after which he is free to do as he liked. Another tradition states that the Prophet told Ibn Umar to observe the following procedure in divorcing his wife.

'Ibn 'Umar,' said the Prophet, 'you adopted a wrong method. The right one is that you should wait for tuhr (period of cleanliness), then pronounce a divorce during one tuhr and another during the second. During the third tuhr you should decide finally either to retain your wife or to divorce her.'

So far we have given a brief account of the rights given to husband for securing release from the marriage bond and the conditions he is required to observe. Similar rights have been given by Islam to the female sex. There are two ways in which a woman is allowed to seek separation from her husband: first, through mutual agreement between the husband and the wife which is called Khula; secondly, through a judicial decree by filing a suit against the husband in a law-court. It will be seen that the wife is not at liberty, like the husband, to get herself released by an outright declaration of divorce. In case her husband refuses to release her from the marriage bond, she has to go to a court of law and obtain a decree in her favour. This may seem to place her at a disadvantage in comparison with her husband and it may be asserted that this implies inequality of rights, as between husband and wife. Actually, the intervention of the State in the matter is a device for the fuller protection of her rights. Conditions all over the world, including even Western countries, are such that a woman is not altogether free to exercise her legal rights. The husband can, if he so desires, place many impediments in her way. If the State does not come to her help in order to safeguard her rights, the woman may find herself handicapped in many ways, despite all talks and preachings; of sex equality. It is, therefore, in her own interest to seek the support of authority in defending and exercising her rights. This was all the more necessary in the past when woman's social position exposed her to greater difficulties.

As in the case of divorce by the husband, the legal permission given to woman to seek and obtain separation through mutual agreement or the intervention of the court does not imply moral approval of the act. Islam has unreservedly condemned men and women who use their legal rights of divorce on any except legitimate grounds and in absolutely unbearable conditions. Thus a tradition of the Prophet states: 'God does not like men and women who seek variety of sexual experience! Again, 'God has showered curses on those men and women who make frequent use of divorce for the sake of sexual enjoyment! A third report says: The Prophet of God said: 'A woman who seeks divorce from her husband, without any excess on his part will be cursed by God and His angels.' Yet another tradition says: 'Women who make a play of their divorce rights are hypocrites.' These warnings and moral exhortations are intended to discourage men and women from disturbing the stability of family life and resorting to separation except in cases of unavoidable necessity. Moral dissuasion apart, there is no dispute about a woman's legal right to seek separation from her husband. This she may do either by giving up a part or the whole of the dower given her by the husband or by offering an agreed sum of money to her husband in return for his consent to release her from the marriage bond. Thus, both men and women are required to undergo monetary sacrifice for securing their separation. This is likely to act as a deterrent in both cases. Should the husband refuse to part with his wife on any of these terms, it is open to the latter to seek the protection of law by filing a suit against him and obtaining a legal decree of separation.

Actual legal decisions by the Prophet of Islam show the spirit and principles which the law-courts should apply to cases brought by women against their husbands. The most famous case is that of Thabit b. Qais whose two wives sought divorce from him. One of them, Jamilah bint Abi Salul, disliked his features. She came to the Prophet of God and complained against him, saying: 'O Prophet, nothing can bring him together with me. I lifted my face covering to see him coming along with a few other men and I noticed that he is the blackest, the most short-statured and the ugliest of them.' Another report says: She said, 'By God, I don't dislike his morals or behaviowr, but, I cannot stand his ugliness.' According to Ibn Majah, she is reported to have said: 'By God, if fear of God did not stand in my way, I would have spit him in his face.' According to the author of *Fath al-Bari*, Jamilah said: 'You see, O Prophet, how beautiful I am, but Thabit is an ugly person.' Bukhari reports that she said to the Prophet: 'I don't blame him for his morals or religion, but I am afraid Islam will lose its hold upon me if I am compelled to live with him.' After hearing her complaint, the Prophet said to her: 'Will you give him back the orchard he gave you?' She replied, 'Yes, and also more, if he wants.' The Prophet asked her not to give more and ordered Thabit to accept the orchard and divorce her.

Another wife of Thabit b. Qais, Habibah bint Sahil, according to a report from Imam Malik and Abu Daud, came to the Prophet early one morning. When the Prophet came out, he saw her standing before the door. On the Prophet's inquiring how she happened to be there, she replied: 'I and Thabit cannot pull together.' When Thabit came, the Prophet said to him: 'This is what your wife says about you, so leave her.' According to Ibn Majah. Habibah complained to the Prophet that Thabit had beaten her so badly as to break her bone in any case, the Prophet, on hearing both sides of the matter, ordered dissolution of the marriage.

During the time of Umar, the Second Caliph, a suit of divorce was brought to him. He advised the wife not to leave her husband and try to pull on with him. The woman refused to do so. Umar put her in a dirty room for three days. On the fourth day he asked her how she had fared. She said that she had real peace of mind only for those three days, whereupon Umar ordered dissolution of the marriage.

These three cases show that the mere fact of a woman becoming disgusted with her husband is sufficient ground for legal separation between them. In the case of Thabit b. Qais, the Prophet showed by his action that a woman's disapproval of her husband on physical grounds is a legitimate ground for a decree of separation in her favour. It is enough for the court to satisfy itself, that one of the partners has developed sufficient antipathy against the other to make reconciliation impossible. The court need not inquire into the detailed reasons of this antipathy, because a woman may dislike her husband on many grounds, some of which she may not like to state openly. There may also be reasons for disgust which may not seem valid to the court or any other arbiter, but which may be sufficient to spoil the marital relations of husband and wife. The court has no right to give its verdict on the point whether the reasons for dissatisfaction as expressed by the wife are valid. All it can do is to satisfy itself on the point whether the dissatisfaction is genuine or faked, whether it arises from causes which are temporary and may disappear or it is so deep-rooted as to preclude the possibility of happier relations being restored.

It is also inadvisable for the court to inquire whether a wife seeking divorce is doing so because she is sexually erotic and desires a variety of sexual pleasures or her aversion to her husband springs from genuine causes. The right of a man to divorce is not limited by the condition that he should not use it for satisfying his anarchic sexual desire. If this is so in the case of a man, it applies equally well to women who have got equal rights. Moreover, if a woman is really disposed to be sexually anarchic, the mere fact of being unable to obtain a divorce from a law-court will not prevent her from forming illicit unions, and in such a case the court, by refusing a decree of separation, will be supplying an incentive to illegitimate sexual activity, which is morally and socially more reprehensible than a frequency of divorces. The effect of a court decree in favour of separation is the same as that of the final divorce pronounced by the husband which dissolves the marriage finally and irrevocably. The couple cannot be remarried unless the woman marries another husband and gets a divorce.

As regards monetary sacrifices involved when a woman seeks divorce from her husband, it has already been stated that the husband cannot claim more than he has already given his wife as dower. If the separation comes of as a result of mutual agreement without the intervention of the court, the amount has to be settled between the two partners. But if the dispute is brought to the court, the latter can decide what portion of the dower should be returned by the wife, whether the full amount or half of it or one-fourth, etc. Many jurists agree that if separation takes place as a result of the ill-treatment of the husband or his excesses, and such charges are proved during the process of legal inquiry, the court can totally exempt the wife from repayment of the dower, or it can decide in favour of an amount less than that of the dower, according to the circumstances involved. Some jurists are also of the opinion that if the court is satisfied that the wife has no legitimate grounds for seeking separation and is merely the victim of anarchic sexual impulses it can order her to pay more than her dower.

Apart from cases of ill-treatment and genuine aversion of wife against the husband, Islam recognises other grounds of divorce also. These are: (1) option of puberty; (2) refusal to provide economic sustenance; (3) change of religion; (4) impotence; (5) infectious diseases in either partner; (6) wilful desertion; and (7) disappearance of husband.

The Quran has given some importance to the opinion of the guardians in the case of a woman's marriage, but it has not withheld from her the right of final acceptance or rejection. Actual legal decisions by the Holy Prophet show that while a woman is bound to consult her guardians, she is not under any obligation to abide by their advice. Abu Daud, Nasai, Ibn Majah and Imam Ahmad ibn Hanbal have reported a tradition from the Prophet stating that a girl complained to him saying that her father had given her in marriage against her will, whereupon the Prophet told her that she was at liberty to repudiate it. Nasai has given a report from Khansa' bint Khidhan that her father married her to a man whom she did not like. On hearing her complaint the Prophet gave her option to retain or repudiate the marriage. *Sunan Daraquod*, another collection of traditions, contains a report from Jabir, one of the companions of the Prophet, stating that the Prophet ordered the dissolution of a marriage which was performed against the will of the wife. Nasai further gives a tradition from Aishah, the Prophet's wife, stating that a girl was married by her father against her will, whereupon she complained to the Prophet. The Prophet gave her liberty to repudiate the marriage. On hearing this, the girl declared: 'O Prophet, I accept the decision of my father. I wanted only to show to other women that their fathers' decision is not final.' Muslim, Nasai, Abu Daud and Muwatta also contain the following tradition: 'A woman previously married has a greater right than her guardians to decide her choice in marriage, while permission of a virgin should be sought in regard to her marriage.' Another report from Abu Hurairah says: 'No woman who has been married once should be remarried until she gives her permission; similarly, a virgin should not be married until she declares her consent.'

In the face of these traditions, the question arises: What is the position of minor girls married by their guardians or parents during their minority; are they free to repudiate their marriage on attaining puberty? Most of our old jurists give the option of puberty to the minor girls only in cases where they have been married by guardians other than their fathers or grandfathers. But if the marriage has been arranged by the father or the grandfather during the minority of the girl, they maintain, the girl is not at liberty to repudiate the marriage, except when it has been proved that the father or the grandfather is a man of loose character or that he is reputed to be a man of careless disposition. No precedent or authority has been quoted by the jurists for making an exception in favour of the father and the grandfather as distinguished from other guardians. Their opinion is obviously based on the presumption that the father and the grandfather, being the well-wishers of their family, cannot act against the real interest of the minor. This presumption for which no authority has ever been quoted from the Quran or the traditions of the Prophet is open to the following grave objections.

First, a very authentic tradition of the Prophet states that he gave away the daughter of Hamzah in marriage to Umar b. Abi Salama while she was still a minor and declared that after she reach reached puberty, she was at liberty to repudiate the marriage. Here the Prophet did not make any exception in favour of any guardian, nor did he specify it as a reason that because he was not the father or the grandfather of the girl, therefore she had the option of puberty. He made a general statement covering all cases. This shows that even a minor girl married by her father or grandfather has the option of puberty. Secondly, it does not stand to reason that a girl who has reached puberty should be given the right of final choice, but a minor girl should be refused the same right. If the presumption is that the father and the grandfather cannot act in disregard of the real interests of their lineal descendants, it should apply to both grown-up and minor girls. Thirdly, the presumption itself has a very frail basis. There are innumerable cases where a father or a grandfather has not consulted the best interests of his descendants in deciding their future. Fourthly, even if the presumption be valid, it is quite possible that the husband of the minor girl may prove unworthy after he has grown up or he may develop habits and aptitudes ruinous to the health and happiness of his wife. For all these reasons the stand taken by the old jurists appears untenable and since the Muslims are not bound by the decisions of any person or persons except those of the Prophet, there is no reason why the Muslim law should not be amended in accordance with the spirit and principles made explicit by the Prophet in his own legal decisions.

In case a husband refuses to provide-economic sustenance to his wife, there are two courses open to the court. If the husband is able to make provision for her needs, but does not do so, the court can bring pressure to bear on him and force him to look after the needs of his wife. Should the husband still refuse, the court can issue a decree of separation and the marriage will be dissolved thereafter. In case the husband is absolutely, unable to provide for his wife, dissolution of the marriage should come about instantaneously, according to the school of Imam Ahmad ibn Hanbal. In the opinion of Imam Shafii, three days' time should be given to the husband, while Imam Malik would give him one or two months.

Conversion of either partner to any religion (other than Islam) leads automatically to the dissolution of the marriage, because Islam does not allow a Muslim woman to enter into marriage union with a non-Muslim. The only exception in this case is when a Muslim woman is converted to Christianity or Judaism. In such a case the husband can retain her in marriage because Islam allows Muslim males but not Muslim females to contract marriages with the members of the Jewish and Christian communities.

If the husband is impotent, the wife can obtain a decree of separation from the law-court. But in cases where the impotency is not constitutional and incurable, one year's time may be allowed to the husband for undergoing treatment. If he regains his potency during this period, the marriage cannot be dissolved. The medieval jurists have, however, laid down the following conditions which cannot stand rational scrutiny and do not agree with the spirit and intention of Islamic law: (1) That a decree for separation is eligible only if the wife was ignorant, prior to marriage, of the impotence of her prospective husband. (2) If the, wife was ignorant of the fact but consented to retain her marriage when she came to know of it, she cannot demand separation later on. (3) If the husband, after treatment, is able to have sexual intercourse even once, the wife loses the right to demand separation.

These conditions are very unfair and destroy the intention of the marriage and divorce laws, for the object of marriage in Islam is to provide a stable family life and to prevent the formation of illicit sexual unions. Both these objects are defeated if the conditions laid down by the older jurists are given legal sanction. If a woman foolishly commits herself to marry a man whom she knows to be impotent, it is just possible that she may repent her action somewhat later when she knows by experience what association with such a person means. It is a very heavy punishment to poison her whole life for a single act of misjudgment or folly. It is enough if she has to forgo her dower as a result of her separation. The same is true of a woman who comes to know after the marriage that her husband is impotent but, out of sentiment or natural nobility of mind, consents to live with him. It is quite possible that later experience may render her disconsolate or she may be unable to bear a long period of sexual abstinence. If she is afraid that the continuation of marriage would expose her to sexual temptations which she may not be able to stand, she is perfectly justified in claiming separation. To refuse a legal decree on the ground that she had earlier consented to the continuation of marriage is to drive her to sin. But marriage is intended to safeguard men and women from sin and not to force them into situations where they find no alternative except to disregard their faith and conscience.

In regard to infectious diseases and other noxious ailments, there are three classes of opinions among the older jurists. One class of jurists holds that neither partner can demand separation on the ground of noxious or infectious disease in the other partner. Ali and Abdullah b. Masud among the companions of the Prophet, and Imam Abu Hanifah and Imam Abu Yusuf among the jurists, belong to this school of thought. The other school holds that in all diseases which prevent sexual intercourse between man and woman, such as lunacy, leprosy, venereal diseases, etc., either party has full right to demand separation. This is the opinion of the Maliki school. Imam Shafii says that lunacy and leprosy entitle a husband or a wife to demand separation but not venereal and other diseases. Of these three schools, the opinion of the second school is more in accord with the spirit and principles of the Holy Quran. According to the Quran, the two essential factors in healthy marital relations are: the safeguarding of sex morality and the maintenance of love and compassion between husband and wife. Both these factors become non-existent in cases where the husband and wife develop antipathy against each other owing to physical causes. Where there is the slightest danger of either party failing into sexual aberration due to continuance of marriage, it is much more advisable to dissolve the marriage rather than expose the partner to the risk of sexual promiscuity.

In regard to the right of a wife to demand separation when her husband is missing or has disappeared, there is considerable difference of opinion among the religious scholars. The Quran as well as the traditions of the Prophet are silent on this matter. Among the companions of the Prophet, Umar, Uthman. Ibn Umar and Ibn Abbas are of the opinion that the wife should be ordered to wait for a period of four years., Ali and Ibn Masud, on the other hand, hold the opinion that the wife should wait until the husband returns or the fact of his death is ascertained. Imam Abu Hanifah and Imam Shafii have expressed the same opinion.

Both these opinions seem to err on the side of caution and involve manifest wrong to the wife. They are also opposed to the principles of the Holy Quran.

For example, in permitting conditional polygamy the Holy Quran has stated clearly: 'And you have not in your power to do justice between wives, even though you may covet it, but be not disinclined from one with total disinclination, so that you leave' her as it were, in a suspense' (iv. 129). Again, in enunciating the rules of conduct for the persons intending to divorce their wives, the Quran says: 'And when you divorce women and they reach their prescribed time, then either retain them in good fellowship or set them free with liberality, and do not retain them for injury so that you exceed the limits, and who ever does this is unjust to his own soul' (ii. 231).

Further, in the case of husbands who swear not to go near their wives, the Quran says: For those who swear that they will not go in to their wives should wait for four months, meaning that such sexual abstinence should not last more than four months. If the husband does not break his oath after this period, the wife is entitled to ask for separation. These three verses show that the Quran does not allow a husband to hold his wife in suspense for more than a limited period. How then is it permissible to keep a woman waiting not for months but for years, simply because no trace of her husband could be found? During the caliphate of Umar, there was a very striking incident which throws further light on the spirit in which such cases should be dealt with. It is said that while Umar was carrying out his nocturnal vigil, he heard a woman singing erotic verses in which she gave expression to the unbearable pain of separation from her husband and added: 'If there were no God, this bed would not be empty of a male partner.' Umar found, on making inquiries, that her husband was fighting on the war-front. He came home and asked his widowed daughter how long a woman could bear the pang of sexual abstinence.

After some hesitation she told him that six months was the maximum period. Umar at once ordered that no soldier should be sent on war for a period longer than six months. After six months of active service, every soldier should be given compulsory leave to return home. If it is recognised that a woman cannot forgo sexual enjoyment for a period of more than six months, why should it not be applied to cases of missing husbands? How can the wife be forced to wait for four years or for a longer period if such compulsion is likely to drive her into the quagmire of sin, and who is going to provide for her needs during all this period? Obviously the demands of elementary justice and the principles enunciated by the Holy Quran have been ignored in this respect.

It is for these reasons, probably, that the jurists of all schools have adopted the rules laid down by Imam Malik which are more liberal and involve less hardship to the wives of missing husbands. According to Imam Malik, three situations may arise requiring separate decisions:

(1) If the missing husband has left no property wherewith the wife may provide for her needs, the court shall immediately order dissolution of the marriage and set the wife free for marriage with another man. The Shafii and Hanbali schools also agree to this rule as, in their opinion, failure to provide economic sustenance to the wife is itself a sufficient ground for the dissolution of the marriage.

(2) The husband has left property but the wife is so young that she cannot be expected to bear sexual abstinence without running the risk of sin. In this case the court can fix a period of one year or six months or even a smaller period, within which the wife will have to wait for the return of her husband, after which the marriage will be dissolved. In urgent cases the court may order instantaneous dissolution of marriage. It is not necessary for the court to force from the wife an express declaration of her inability to withstand sexual temptation. It is the duty of the court to come to a judgment on this point after studying the situation.

(3) The husband has left property and there is also no danger of the wife falling a prey to sexual temptation. In this case the following steps have been recommended:

If the missing husband was lost in a Muslim country or in another civilised country having diplomatic relations with Muslim countries, the wife will be asked to wait for four years and the Government will order a search to be made for the man.

If he was lost in a war, a full search should be made, after which the wife should be ordered to wait for one year.

If he was lost during a local civil commotion, a full search should be ordered after the completion of which the marriage will be dissolved without further waiting.

It would appear that even the Maliki law, which is followed now by all schools, leaves room for hardship. Six months is the reasonable maximum period for which the wife can wait. No further delay appears reasonable keeping in view the injunctions of the Holy Quran.

Opinions differ as to what would happen if the missing person is found after or without a search. Umar holds that if the husband returns before the wife is married to another person, the wife should belong to him, but if she is already married.

The former husband loses all rights on her, even though her second marriage may remain unconsummated. Imam Malik has adopted this opinion. Ali, another companion of the Holy Prophet, however, was of opinion that the wife belongs to her first husband, whether she marries and has children or remains unmarried, If the marriage has been consummated, the wife is also entitled to her dower from the second husband. The Hanafi school has adopted the same rule.

According to Uthman, the Third Caliph, the returning husband will have the option to take back his wife or leave her and have his dower repaid to him. If he is willing to take back his dower or remit it to his former wife, the wife will be left with the second husband. Otherwise, she will be separated from her second husband and ordered to wait for a period of four months, after which she will become the wife of her first husband. Moreover, she would be entitled to receive her dower from the second husband.

The above is a general picture of the rights given to women by Islam for demanding separation from their husbands. As will be seen, Islam has maintained more or less absolute equality between man and woman in this regard. There is no doubt that man enjoys a greater degree of freedom in this respect, because he has no need to resort to a court of law. But we have also explained the circumstances which made this restriction necessary in the case of woman. In fact, there are so many ways open to a woman to secure her freedom from an unhappy marriage that if she fails on any one ground to obtain a decree in her favour, some other ground remains available to her and the court can hardly refuse a decree of separation to a wife who has determined to seek separation.

Major Problems : One of the objections raised against the Islamic Law of divorce is that in empowering man to divorce, Islam has been harsh and unjust to the woman. It depends entirely on the will even whims of man to divorce her and whenever he likes he can cut her off from himself on any trivial issue. Thus, the future of a woman becomes dark and she finds herself compelled to spend her days without any support.

The horrible picture of divorce presented, is firstly not to be found anywhere. Secondly, divorce is the only proper and reasonable solution to the many familial disputes and complications. It is an undesirable fact that at times it becomes impossible for man and woman to live together under the marriage tie and they are dead set on getting rid of each other.

There can be many reasons for it. At times the temperaments are in total non-conformity and at heart they are not prepared to accept each other. At others their intellectual and educational levels are not the same and in spite of closeness a feeling of distance keeps them miles apart. In yet other situations the social and economic differences between them are so wide that the gulf cannot be bridged.

They clearly appear even to the casual observer belonging to two different social strata—two definite classes alien to each other. On some occasions such degrading moral weaknesses reveal themselves in either party that there is neither hope of reform nor can one put up with them as a sore in the side. In all such situations it is the demand of common sense that they should part quietly without much ado. If the society like that of Christianity, does not permit peaceful separation and they are compelled to go on living under the same conditions, the purposes for which they had come together under marriage-tie shall never be served.

There are certain detriments associated with this state of affairs: Firstly, the woman shall become a burden to man and he is most likely to mete out the worst treatment, he can, to her. Secondly, after divorce woman can get a match suiting her temperament and other conditions, thus entering a better phase of life. By closing the door upon divorce this possibility will be eliminated. Thirdly, the domestic life of a conflicting pair at loggerheads under the same roof becomes hell for them both and their peace of mind departs. Fourthly, in a state of constant quarrel and tension the progeny cannot receive the attention it deserves. They shall grow up without any social and moral training and become the quarrelsome children of quibbling, quarrelling, intolerant parents.

Let us now take up the question who should be endowed with the right of divorce? There are three alternative answers to this query. The first option is that both should enjoy it. The second is that the husband should be so empowered. And the third option can be that the woman should have this right.

Three Options : In the first instance, if both have the right of divorce, the plethora of divorces shall make family life uncertain and insecure. In the case of both exercising their right there will obviously be a much larger number of "casualties" than with only one armed with this weapon to sever relations. It is an admitted fact that a society with lesser number of divorces has a better and much more secure familial order. With frequent and free use of this right the organization gets disrupted. The West has vested it in both the parties with the result that the wedlock in the Western society has become a joke. Whichever of the parties concerned, whenever it likes can exercise his or her right of severance of conjugal relations and part. The frequency and number of divorces has shaken the foundations of the family and the society as a whole.

The second option is that adopted by Islam. It has vested this power in man for the reason that he enjoys a little more dignified position in the family. He is the supervisor of the family, maintainer of the wife and with that bears the heavy burden of the children's upkeep, education and training. Therefore, it is he who should decide whether it is possible to bear the burden of these responsibilities in collaboration with the wife or not? In the Quranic terminology "in his hands has been placed the power to tie the marriage knot (contract) or untie it." (Al-Quran 11 : 227). It would be harsh and unjust to compel him to go on maintaining a woman as the queen of the mini-realm, home, whom he does not like or whose cooperation has been denied to him. It can hardly be asserted with conviction that armed with this weapon he will make use of it indiscreetly since it is he who will suffer in that case. He cannot demand return of the dower endowed upon her. If not already paid, he will have to pay it now after separation. The ornaments and other gifts given to her, are her property and she will take it with her. And all that he spent on the occasion of marriage and on her while she was with him, he cannot claim. In case of a second marriage he will have to pay the would-be wife her dower, bear the expenses of marriage once again and undertake all the accompanying responsibilities. Moreover, he will be burdened with the upkeep of the children by the first wife (now divorced). Those objecting to man's right to divorce are living in an imaginary world, not one of hard facts. Perhaps they do not have time to give the issue a serious thought. But a person having all these problems before him, will have to think twice before divorcing one wife and bringing in another to embellish his house afresh. Rehabilitation after evacuation is not such an easy job !

Taking the third option in which woman will have the right to divorce, it is apparent that abuse of the right shall not be eliminated. If man through exercise of the right can harass woman, the possibility of its improper use at her hands and putting man in serious trouble by creating critical situations and factual calamities cannot be ruled out at all.

In bestowal of right upon her, there are some evils associated with it also :

1. It would be grave injustice to man to make him bear all the responsibilities of the woman (dower, gifts, maintenance and the like) and to grant the right of divorce to her.
2. Divorce is damaging to man entirely whereas the woman remains immune from any harm. If the right is granted to her, a morally irresponsible woman, whenever she chooses, she shall divorce the husband, and handing over children to him, she will take leave of him with the "booty" of her dower and jewelry and gifts in full triumph, and at the first chance coming her way, she will marry another man getting fresh dower and other paraphernalia.
3. It is an obvious fact that woman is much more sentimental than man and can any time under impulse of the moment sever relations with man. That will go a long way in mounting the ratio of divorce under normal conditions confronting the society with a new crisis.

The way suggested to wriggle out of this difficulty is that whichever party, husband or wife, who wished to loosen the bond and get freedom, should approach the competent court requesting separation. If it is satisfied that the reasons put forth are sufficient cause for it, it may legally separate them. And failing that their request be turned down.

The evil attendant upon it is that whichever of the couple is desirous of divorce, to satisfy the court not content with stating the factual shortcomings and excesses of the opposite party, will overstep to freely (with an easy conscience) charge him or her with false accusations. The rejoinder is sure to result to retaliation in a 'bigger way', which will bring them morally to a very low level in the sight of the society from which degradation, they can hardly recover. The family honour and prestige would have been dragged into mire leaving it, as the laughing stock for people.

Again, our courts in general are notorious for their lethargic pace in handling cases before them. They may take ages in administering justice to the couple that is "up in arms" and heaven only knows how they are going to put up with (suffer) each other under the same roof so long. The other aspect of this issue is that if the court decides against them refusing separation, they must remain tied together under severe compulsion of circumstances, making life most miserable, almost insufferable, for them, without even a distant future promise of pleasant time.

Moral Instructions : The way Islam shapes the mind and temperament of man and educates and trains him, divorce can hardly find room in his life and the lurking fear that merely for sexual enjoyment and gratification of abnormal lust he will go on divorcing women most carelessly is only a remote logical possibility. The moral instructions of Islam in this behalf, a faint idea thereof, is being given below:

> *According to Islam, man and woman through nikah do not come together for a brief span of "good times" but enter a life-long contract of the closest relationship and comradeship. This contract has been termed by the Quran a solemn covenant (Q. IV: 21). The person who seriously enters this trust does not easily commit breach of trust. Only one who does not realize its importance and makes such a serious agreement, can be guilty of playing this joke. The Prophet S.A.W. has declared joking (non-serious attitude) in the matter of nikah unwarranted (most improper), since it negates the seriousness which is the demand of this affair. Abu Hurairah R.A.A. reports the Prophet to have said:*
>
> *There are three things in which seriousness has its own reserved place, but even things said and done in joke shall be taken seriously (to be binding on him). And they are nikah, divorce and turning back upon it.*
>
> Imam Khattabi says :
>
> *The Ulama have consensus on it that a major sane person's divorcing his wife is effective legally as divorce. If he, calling it a joke, wants to nullify this earlier pronouncement of his, it will not be accepted. Some of the Ulama are of the opinion that such a joke (in the serious matter of divorce) is just like playing and joking with the Quranic verses, since if it is condoned it will mean that a person after divorcing his wife or emancipating a slave can take back his earlier declaration saying that he was joking (not divorcing his wife or freeing a slave in real earnest). In this way there is every likelihood that divine injunctions may*

not be obeyed at all. Therefore, all that has been mentioned in this tradition, any statement made about them will make it binding on him to act on them, not willy-nilly but with determination.

Extremely Undesirable : Islam certainly allows divorce in need, but also pointed out that it is not a desirable act, rather, one of the most undesirable acts in the sight of Allah. Therefore, recourse to it should be had only when compelled by circumstances beyond control. Abdullah Ibn-e-Umar reports the Prophet S.A.W. to have said :

In the sight of Allah, the Exalted, among the permitted things, the most undesirable is divorce.

Maharib bin Wasar R.A.A. reports the Prophet S.A.W. to have said :

Allah has not permitted any thing more unwholesome than divorce.

A tradition with a similar import has been reported by Muaz. Although weak in authority but corroborates the two foregoing reports. The Prophet has been reported to have said :

O Muaz ! Allah has not created anything more pleasing to Him than the emancipation of a slave. Similarly, he has not created anything more offensive than divorce.

On the one hand, it was impressed on the mind of man that divorce is a disagreeable act and on the other, instructed the woman not to make demands for divorce unnecessarily. Thauban R.A.A. reports the Prophet S.A.W. to have said :

The woman who makes demands on man to divorce her without offering a compelling reason for it, even the fragrance emanating from heaven shall be denied to her (as unpermitted).

Collective life is not subservient to any individual. One has to sacrifice his will and personal opinion on any issue in the collective interest. In conjugal life too there are occasions when the opinion of the husband and wife conflict. However, it should not be allowed to develop into an issue of an erroneous notion of prestige with either party that they may jump up to a serious decision like separation. There are moments when sentiments and impulses of the moment overwhelm him and he fails to have the least consideration for any opinion other than his own and much greater interests are lost sight of. Islamic teaching in this behalf is that in view of the much wider expediency and important interests relating to the familial life, trifling errors of thought and judgment must be over-looked magnanimously and an attitude of love and benevolence should prevail. The Quran says :

> *Live with them on a footing of kindness and equity. If ye take a dislike to them, it may be that ye dislike a thing and Allah brings about through it a great deal good. [32]— Al Quran IV:19*

Attempt at Reform : Even if the woman is lacking in obedience, is headstrong and not listening to reason, Islam does not allow decision on divorce. Man has been vested with discretionary powers so that he may try his best to improve the worsening situation through an agreeable blend of strictness and allowance (sufferance) so that the domestic affairs are amicably settled inside the sanctum (home) itself and not noised abroad. Divorce should not come for consideration in these petty domestic quarrels. Allah, the Exalted admonishes thus in the Quran:

> *As to the woman on whose part ye fear disloyalty and ill-treatment, admonish them (first), (next) refuse to share their beds, (and last) beat them (lightly) : But if they return to obedience, seek not against them means (of annoyment) : For Allah is Most High, Great (above you all). [33]*
>
> *—Al Quran IV: 34*

To bring a woman, disobedient and headstrong, to terms and to reform, the Quran prescribed in the first stage to try to create in her fear of Allah's displeasure and the retribution of the Hereafter, drawing her attention to the mutual obligations and rights of husband and wife as well as the expediencies of the situation in the family perspective. All this can be achieved with tenderness and polite manners. If the primary measure fails in bringing her round, the Quran goes a step further in stern handling and advises the husband to segregate her from the conjugal bed, meaning cessation of sex activities in various degrees. The companions of the Prophet and those following them or Tabieen, have given these different versions of this stern admonitory step. Let them share your bed but abstain from copulation. Even while sharing your bed, turn your face away from them, keeping mum, to demonstrate your displeasure. And the third and final stage is that you do not allow them to share the bed with you but sleep in a separate bed.

This is a psychological measure and a person can adopt it only in case he has sufficient control over his passion. However, if he is capable of that much self-control it is mostly to bring the woman to see reason and behave properly. Sex is a very headstrong passion and if man has a strong will-power of self-restraint, the woman cannot go far in keeping herself in check.

There may, however, be some whom this course of treatment may fail to cure. In such a situation man has been allowed to resort to corporal punishment also. Now, this measure appears rather too harsh and uncivil to adopt in dealing with the fair sex. But it has been allowed only after the first two have proved totally ineffective and the woman persists with her churlish behavior and disobedience.

This is the last resort when nothing appears to avail. Secondly, the Prophet S.A.W. has forbidden hitting hard, not to cause a wound or disfigurement in any way and hitting the face is to be avoided at all costs. Abdullah Ibn-e-Abbas R.A.A. has made it only symbolic, advising to strike with a miswak (tooth stick). Qatadah R.A. and Hasan Basri R.A. advise against causing disability and a strike leaving a scar.

As against this corrective measure, if somebody beats up a woman like a barbarian, the Islamic law shall come to her rescue and duly punish the tyrant. Imam Nawawi says that even if a light corporal chastisement causes her death (it will be deemed murder by mistake) the husband (and his family) shall be liable to pay her blood-money, and the atonement for murder by mistake shall become due from the husband alone.

On the one hand Islam has repeatedly stressed it on man that he should be generous to woman, recognizing her rights and overlooking her mistakes, look to her redeeming features and reform her in the matter of her infirmities and shortcomings. On the other side it advised woman not to make frequent demands for divorce.

If she notices carelessness and neglect on the part of the husband towards herself she should not only give up demands and insistence on her rights but should be prepared to forgo some of them. Instead of confrontation with the husband she should try to live in peace and amity with him as far as possible. In receiving some allowance from the wife the husband's pride is likely to be hurt. So if the wife makes some allowance in her demands on him, he should not feel slighted or insulted. Help in some way from the wife and his benefiting by it is in no way degrading to him. Allah says:

> *If a wife fears cruelty on her husband's part there is no blame on them if they arrange an amicable settlement*

between themselves. And such settlement is best, even though men's souls are swayed by greed. But if ye do good and practice self-restraint, Allah is well acquainted with all that ye do. [34] *—Al Quran, IV: 128*

Hafiz Ibn Katheer says that if a woman fears that man is nursing hatred for her and showing signs of remoteness, she can forgo all the rights of her maintenance, his stay with her during the night, or reduce such days to a minimum. There is no harm in man's agreeing to such an offer and coming to be at peace with her. The wife can spend on her husband and he can accept her offer. The Quran says that their coming to terms of peace and amity is better than separation.

At times differences and conflicts arise out of mere trifles which develop gradually, becoming vehement, creating sort of remoteness and segregation between them. At this stage they are no more in a position that forgetting their quarrels and quibbles they can come to reconciliation by themselves. The Quran directed that in a situation where the principal parties concerned cannot remove their differences, their trustworthy seconds as arbiters, one of either side, should put their heads together and try to sort them out. If they undertake it with sincerity and good will, Allah's help will be there with their efforts and who knows the apparently irreconcilable affairs may somehow be resolved and peace may reign there once again :

If ye fear a breach between the twain, appoint two arbiters one from his family, and the other from hers, if they seek to set things right, Allah will cause their reconciliation. For Allah hath full knowledge, and is acquainted with all things. [35] *—Al Quran IV: 35*

Having failed in all attempts to join and keep joined, divorce presents itself as the only solution to the tangle. Islam took two initiatives by way of reform :

In Arabia of the days of Jahiliyah or pre-Islamic period there was no such check on divorce and revocation. The person intending to harass his wife, divorced her, revoked before the expiry of the term, again divorced and revoked and continued with this nasty joke with her as long as he liked. In this way a woman with a husband and all, was compelled to do existence as a divorcee. The Quran put a ban on indefinite number of divorces and revocations declaring that one can divorce only twice and revocation is allowed with only these two.

A divorce is only permissible twice; after that, the parties should either hold together on equitable terms, or separate with kindness. [36] —*Al Quran 11 : 229*

Repeating it a third time shall deprive man of revocation and wife shall be separated from him automatically.

A person could harass his wife benefiting by the right of even these three divorces, divorcing her for long terms. For example, divorcing and not revoking for a year or two and revoking later if he was so pleased. Similarly after divorcing a second time he used to keep her in suspense for a long time, neither meeting his obligations to her, nor separate her, and finally when fed up with her, he did divorce her a third time to throw her out at last on the dung hill.

To render this mischief ineffective Islam fixed a short term within which man will have to decide about revocation or abstaining from it. This is called 'iddat' in Islamic terminology. Once it is over she is free from the bondage to marry again wherever she is pleased.

The Quran directed that account must be maintained after divorcing. It is nothing to play with, divorcing and forgetting it :

O Prophet ! When ye do divorce women, divorce. them at their prescribed periods. [37] —*All Quran LXV : 1*

Divorce is possible after one has gone into the wife and before that stage also. In case of divorce after consummation her term of waiting shall be the period taken by three menstrual cycles. Allah says :

Divorced women shall wait concerning themselves for three monthly periods. [38] —*Al Quran II : 228*

This term is fixed for a young (menstruating) woman. Those not menstruating, past this age or in prepuberty stage or diseased, for them the period of waiting is three months. For a woman with a gravid uterus, the term is until she delivers her burden. Allah says :

Such of your women as have passed the age of monthly courses, for them the prescribed period, if ye have any doubts, is three months. For those who have no courses (it is the same). For those who are pregnant their period is until they deliver their burden. [39]—*Al Quran LXV : 4*

If divorced before being touched they have no period of waiting. Allah says :

Oye who believe! When ye marry believing women, and then divorce them before ye have touched them, no period of iddat have ye to count in respect of them. So give them a present and release them in a handsome manner. [40]
—Al Quran XXXIII : 49

Islam has certainly permitted divorce but desires that it should not be exercised without giving it a serious thought. One should decide it sincerely and after due deliberation. It would be reasonably justified when there is no way out of the difficulties experienced by one or both the parties. To safeguard against carelessness in this matter, we will have to adopt the method prescribed in the traditions. We are guided here by two instructions.

Divorce during the period of monthly course of woman has been prohibited in a tradition of the Prophet. The reason is obvious. Although a normal physiological function, the woman is not her carefree, cheerful self during the period, and the husband is not so close to her as in normal days, a stern measure is most likely, for tempers in many cases are short. All the six most authentic compilations of traditions known by the collective name of "Sihah" carry reports to the effect that when Abdullah Ibn-e-Umar R.A.A. divorced his wife during her period, he was ordered by the Prophet to revoke. He was directed to divorce her in a state of cleanliness without going unto her (so that pregnancy can be eliminated in counting , iddat').

The other thing stressed in the Hadith is that man should divorce his wife during the period of cleanliness without cohabitation. This should be a single pronouncement. This, if necessary, may be repeated after the period and also without intercourse. A third repetition under the same conditions and he is finished with her.

The protracted process of divorce mentioned in the Hadith has many aspects of wisdom and expediency. The first discretionary consideration is that the interval between the two periods is a guarantee against pregnancy. But cohabitation during this period can once again create a position of uncertainty and therefore, ban on intercourse if divorce is contemplated. So many other complications would arise if she becomes pregnant under these conditions. The other psychological point is that when she is clean and approachable both are keen for sexual union and patch up their differences, if any, forgetting some and forgiving others. But once the passion is gratified, lack of lust and attraction towards her, her attitude of benevolence and indulgence may change. Hence the stress on abstinence. This is rather a difficult job, a trial, long enough to tire the patience of man, and possible only in case of a firm resolution on separation.

The Hanafite school of jurisprudence is of the opinion that divorcing a menstruating or pregnant woman, at intervals of one month is in keeping with the Sunnah of the Prophet S.A.W. Cohabitation is not barred in their case. But Imam Zaffer of the same school opines that in case of sexual union even with them he will have to wait for another month for divorce.

The woman not consummated may be divorced during her monthly course. The Sunnah does not make demands on divorcing her in a state of cleanliness.

Imam Zaffer differs here too, saying that she should also be divorced during the period of cleanliness.

The Quran has ordained that for the period of her iddat (waiting) she shall stay at the husband's house, barring cases of immodesty which make such stay unpleasant, even impossible. Allah says:

> *And turn them not out of their houses, nor shall they (themselves) leave, except in case they are guilty of some open lewdness. [41]* —*Al Quran LXV : 1*

The underlying wisdom here is that living under the same roof man may be inclined to revise his decision and the woman to change her attitude, and who knows they may become indulgent to each other and become reconciled to live together as husband and wife after revocation.

Acting on all these instructions together is likely to reduce possibilities of undue haste and heedlessness in divorce. And if even in spite of failure in the first and second stages divorce becomes imminent, man may yet have a chance to review his earlier decision and opt for revocation.

After divorcing once or twice before the expiry of the term the right of revocation can be exercised. If pronounced in unequivocal terms, revocation will take effect, there being unanimity on it. Imam Shafii says that revocation should be verbal. According to the Hanafite school, kissing, embracing and copulation also indicate it (in a practical form). Imam Shafii insists on witnesses to the pronouncement of revocation. But the Hanafites call it only desirable and preferable. Imam Malik too is of the same opinion.

After one or two pronouncements of divorce if man does not revoke within the specified period, parting of husband and wife becomes effective just after the expiry of the iddat. However, if man is desirous of their reunion and the wife too is willing, they can come together through nikah with a fresh mehr. But in case the wife does not consent to such a union, it cannot be thrust upon her.

If a person divorces with a third and final pronouncement following the earlier two, their separation is Complete and remains disallowed unless the woman marries another man and gets divorced or widowed. Then alone she can enter wedlock with the former husband to whom she is now allowed. Allah says :

> *So if a husband divorces his wife (irrevocably) he cannot, after that, remarry her until after she has married another husband and he has divorced her, in that case there is no blame on either of them if they reunite, provided they fee/ that they can keep the limits ordained by Allah. Such are the limits ordained by Allah, which He makes plain to those who know. [42]* —*Al Quran 11 : 230*

This lengthy procedure makes reunion after three pronouncements of divorce a tedious job. Man's unsullied nature too abhors it. This rather severe check has been put on it so that the person intending to indulge in it heedlessly may have a chance to give it a serious thought before a hasty decision. Reunion may not always be possible even after adopting the prescribed course.

At this stage a question arises here that if a person instead of divorcing in three intervals of cleanliness or once every month, pronounces all three in one breath as an outburst, shall he be entitled to the right of revocation or they shall be deemed irrevocable.

According to the generality of the jurists, three at a time make the divorce irrevocable and the person guilty of it shall stand deprived of his right of revoking as under the normal course. The jurists of the Ahl-e-Hadith school take it under the revocable category. Now this is a subject of debate between them and other groups of jurisprudence. However, there is a general consensus on it that this is a serious violation of the Prophet's Sunnah and highly undesirable.

The Hanafite Fiqh has coined a term "The innovative divorce" since it is in direct contravention of the Sunnah. According to them the nice way to do so was to pronounce divorce only once and if the iddat passes off, at least there is a chance of reunion through nikah anew. They say that the companions of the Prophet S.A.W. never divorced more than once. (Those intending to make it final for separation can let the iddat pass and that is the end of the whole affair).

Three divorces in a single sitting are generally the outcome of momentary anger or any other disagreeable incident difficult to put up with. There is no cool calculated decision behind it. The erroneous and accidental step results in serious consequences, and the person concerned witnesses the ruination of his one time happy and peaceful home. His lamentation and grief cannot avail him aught. The remedy lies in the way of the Sunnah which is free from all complications. Divorce at times becomes inevitable. But the Islamic way is the safest way and must be taken to the ignorant masses as the remedy of this social evil. Its general adoption will also remove the objections levelled against the abominable practice.

OPTION OF KHULA

Some people would like the woman also to have the same right, of divorcing the husband which he enjoys. If she wants to get separation from the husband, there should be no restrictions on her and she may go her own way whenever she is pleased. According to them, "Islam has not been unjust to the woman with the right given to man of divorcing a woman, it has granted to her in turn the same right in the form of Khula". They take it for granted that if the woman returning to the husband the dower received by her, takes leave of him the act of Khula' is complete (and she is free). That means they believe Khula' to be the declaration of breaking the marriage tie or nikah on the part of the woman, no matter how the husband takes it (accepts or rejects it). This is a manifestation of their ignorance of the nature of Khula'. Here we would like to clarify its nature under the Islamic jurisprudence.

From the point of view of the Islamic Shariah through the agency of marriage tie or nikah the woman becomes the property of man (known technically as the proprietary right by virtue of nikah). Obviously enough this state of ownership can be used or be nullified only by man and the woman has nothing to do with it. Khula' only means that taking substance from the woman man may give up his ownership. In the well known Arabic compilation on lexicon, Qamus, it has been defined thus :

To nullify the ownership by virtue of nikah in return for the substance offered by the woman, no matter who pays it, she herself or someone else.

Now taking up the opinions of the jurists Allamah Kamal-ud-din Babarti, after its lexicological definition has given its definition in the Islamic Shariah in these words:

In the Islamic Shariah Khula' means to take the substance from the woman in return for ownership rights enjoyed by virtue of nikah, using the word Khula'.

Allamah Ibn-ul-Hummam says:

To bring to an end the proprietary rights in return for something with the word Khula'.

About the word Khula' it has been said :

Absolute use of Khula' will be taken to be divorce for something in return.

These are the expositions in the Hanafite Fiqh. In Maliki Fiqh too Khula' has been interpreted as divorce against something in return for it.

Qadi Baizawi Shafi'i says :

Apparently it is divorce since in separation the man has his say. In this way it becomes divorce for something in return.

This makes evident enough that Khula' is also a form of divorce. It is a fact that Islam has endowed man only with the right to divorce and also exercise Khula'.

Not for Woman's Exploitation : One of the objections raised in this connection is that man in using his right of Khula' can exploit woman. If he wants to get rid of her, he would not divorce but tyrannize her so much that she may, at last, be compelled to pay him her substance for her speedy riddance. But this objection does not hold water since it is the firm principle of the Shariah that nobody can take any one else's substance by force. The woman's substance is her possession and property. If she gives it to her husband it will be permissible to him. But taken away from her by force against her will in the name of Khula' or on some other pretext, will be strictly forbidden to him. Allamah Ibn Jareer Tabri says :

The husband's taking away the substance of his wife by force or to cause her grief and pain, so that she compulsively agrees to part with some of her substance as the return for her freedom from the bondage of the husband's ownership is strictly prohibited to him, be it silver weighing a grain of barley or more than that.

Rather, he also goes on to say that if the man tries to snatch her property by wrongful means, she should try to evade him as much as she can. Succumbing to devilry without resistance will make her guilty.

Allamah Rasheed Raza Misri writes :

To take something from the woman is permissible and in as much as, she gives it to him of her own free will and he on his part has not caused her grief or hurt for its possession.

Now let us take up the expositions of the jurists :

The Hanafite Fiqh says that if the man compels the woman to accept Khula', divorce will be effective, but he will not be allowed the property of woman since the fair deal in this behalf is on the basis of mutual agreement and not under compulsion.

Durrul-Mukhtar says :

If the husband compels the woman, the divorce shall be deemed to be in order without any part of her substance, since payment of anything from her property or nullification of her mehr is conditioned by her willingness.

The same thing has been said in Maliki Fiqh that if the woman were to sue him in a court of Law that she had to agree to Khula' since he was relaxing her, and she was being hurt in a way which justifies obtaining divorce, she can take back her substance given to the husband provided she produces evidence to prove his oppression and tyranny. For evidence it is enough to hear from the people living in the neighbourhood that they constantly heard that she was being tyrannized. If it is the case of an eye-witness two men would bear witness or else the woman would declare on oath her claim, with one man or two women to support it at the court. For eye-witnesses even one observation is deemed enough. Rather, it has been said that even if the man pronounces Khula' on condition that the woman would not furnish proof of his compulsion and tyranny, she can still come up with that proof after Khula'. However, divorce under Khula' is irrevocable.

Imam Shafi'i, Imam Ahmad and others regard such a Khula' false and ineffective. Ibn Qudamah, a Hanbalite writes that if somebody were to tyrannize his wife, beat her and deprive her of her maintenance as well as the night-stay with her, to compel her to consent to Khula', such a Khula' shall be deemed ineffective and her husband will have to return her property. The same is the opinion of Imam Shafii, Ishaq and Rahawaih and others.

Islam has introduced Khula' for the reason that if the man is guilty of excesses or the woman does not like him due to his irremediable faults, she may obtain her freedom in lieu of her property. It is not meant for the tyrannizing of woman at the hands of a despot of a husband. Where such a situation arises she can sue him in a court of law and the Islamic Law will come to her rescue.

Among the multiplicity of opinions on this issue, a section also demands that the powers of enforcing Khula' must be vested in the rulers so that in the presence of reasonable grounds for it, it may be pronounced through a competent court whereas in case of dissatisfaction with them due to their inadequacy it may be refused. This opinion was there among the ancestors also. Hasan Basri R.A. says: Khula' can be pronounced only by one in the seat of authority and rule without which it cannot be permissible. Muhammad bin Sireen R.A. too has quoted it from 'the antiquity.' Later, Abu Ubaid too has adopted it. Their argument rests on the Quranic authority.

> *If ye (judges) do indeed fear that they would be unable to keep the limits ordained by Allah, there is no blame on either of them if she gives something for her freedom. [59]*
>
> *—Al Quran 11 : 229*

At another place it has been said :

> *If ye fear a breach between them twain, appoint two arbiters, one from his family and the other from hers ; [60]*
>
> *—Al Quran IV: 35*

In these Quranic injunctions, apparently the husband and the wife have not been addressed but it is the rulers and the administrators that when they fear violation of the divine limits at the hands of the husband and the wife, they must come forward to bring them to terms or else affect Khula' between them.

But according to the general consensus of opinions on this issue among the jurists, intervention and decisions on the part of the government are not called for. Qadi Shuraih, Imam Malik, Imam Shafi'i, Imam Ahmad bin Hanbal, Ishaq bin Rahawaih and the Hanafites are one on this opinion.

The following arguments have been put forth against the opinion of Hasan Basri R.A. and others :

> *This is an isolated opinion while the great majority is against it. Qatadah says that Hasan Basri has adopted it from the governor of Iraq of the Muawiyyah regime, Ibn*

Ziyad. According to Hafiz Ibn Hajar, Ziyad does not enjoy the status (in religious matters) that his opinion be accepted for pursuit.

This opinion means that Khula' will be in order only in case there is tension and tangle between the husband and the wife, whereas it is not essential. Khula' may be allowed merely on the dissatisfaction and displeasure of the woman against her husband. We find in the reports that the wife of Thabit bin Qais R.A.A. wanted to be separated from her husband due to the extreme disagreeableness of his.

When she brought it to the notice of the Prophet S.A.W., he told her to return the date palm grove given to her by Thabit bin Qais R.A.A. as her mehr, ordering at the same time Thabit bin Qais to divorce her, after taking back that date palm grove. He did not ask him whether he too had any grievance against her.

Like divorce Khula' too is the right of man. Just as he can divorce his wife without the permission of the ruler, he can also exercise his right of Khula'. The right granted to him by Allah, he cannot be divested of it in favour of some one else. It would be wrong to do so.

In a deal of Khula' man takes something in return for the release of woman. The ruler's permission is not required in such deals, return, sale or purchase.

The decision of the general consensus is also supported by the actions taken by Umar and Uthman R.A.A. Imam Bukhari says : 'Umar allowed Khula' without intervention of the authority and rule.

Its details are to be found in the report of Abdullah bin Shahab Khaulani. He reports that during the Caliphate of 'Umar somebody had a deal of Khula' with his wife, he (Umar) allowed it as valid.

Rabi bint Muawwiz and her uncle came to Abdullah bin 'Umar Rabi' told him that during the Caliphate of Uthman R.A.A. she obtained her release from her husband, and when the Caliph Uthman R.A.A came to know about it, he raised no objection. Abdullah bin Umar R.A.A. too did not regard it improper, saying that the iddat for a mukhtaliah (separated by Khula') is the same as that for mutalliqah (divorced).

Urwah bin Zubayr says that some body arranged Khula's with his wife during the Caliphate of Uthman R.A.A., he allowed it as permitted.

That makes it amply manifest that Khula' is a matter between the woman and the man and any intervention in it on the part of the government or inviting it to intervene at any stage would not be proper.

THE MAINTENANCE AND AFTER

One of the objections levelled against the Islamic Law of divorce is that man's mere pronouncement of the word 'divorce' throws the woman out of his house and she finds herself helpless, at the mercy of the society. This objection is very old and carries little weight. But it is repeated again and again as if it were a great challenge to the Islamic Shariah which has nothing to say in its support. Its hollowness has been made evident time and again. But those whose main objective is to hurl stones of objections only at the opponent, without ever listening to what he says, can never own their weakness and no explanation can satisfy them.

They want that accepting their objections, the flaws in the law of the Shariah should be removed and thus it should be set right. According to them, the highest punishment that must be imposed on the person guilty of divorcing his wife is that he should be compelled to go on paying her maintenance charges life-long. However, in case of her second marriage or her own employment and self-support the husband may be released from that imposition. The recent verdict of the Supreme Court, has in a way, declared this objection justified and has given legal sanction to the proposed demand of maintenance for the divorcee to be life long or her second marriage. So we feel obliged to take up this problem in some detail.

If a person were to demand that his economic responsibilities be transferred to an utter stranger will either take it to be a joke or that he has a cracked nut, because for such transfer of one man's burden to another, there must be some basis. There is no such basis to be found between two utter strangers. According to Islam one of the bases on which rest responsibilities is nikah. After entering the tie of wedlock the woman devotes her time to meet the wide-ranging demands of the conjugal life, applying her capabilities and energies to it. In return for this man undertakes the responsibility of her maintenance. The responsibility lasts so long as they are bound together by the marriage tie. Divorce snaps this tie and the man on his part is released from this economic cooperation. A certain remoteness and alienation creep in between the two. If the divorce is irrevocable, the alienation is so vehement that it becomes easier for the woman to wed another man and for the man to wed another woman rather than reunion of these two persons estranged by divorce. In case they want to unite once again, it is the demand of the Islamic Shariah that before that woman should wed another man and he divorces her or dies. Without adopting this tedious course they cannot revert to their former relationship of husband and wife, their wishes notwithstanding. Where divorce generates such alienation and remoteness, taking them farther than utter strangers, who is to impose whose rights on whom and who is to undertake the responsibilities of whom?

It comes to divorce between husband and wife only when they are negligent in the matter of their responsibilities and do not recognize the rights on a mutual basis. When it comes to this there is hardly any cooperation and partisanship in the domestic life. Non-cooperation and conflict come to stay. But divorce is usually talked of as it is an excess, a tyranny on the part of the husband, and the woman has nothing to do with it. Whereas it cannot be ruled out that the woman might have created conditions, compelling man to divorce her. In spite of all that, imposing the maintenance of woman on man for the life time is a grave injustice to him, having no legal or moral justification.

After divorce and separation, the woman may not be prepared to cooperate with the man, likewise man naturally is desirous of throwing away the burden of his responsibilities relating to her. If even after divorce the economic responsibility of the women remains resting on him, abstaining from divorce could be more useful to him. Instead of divorcing and yet remaining burdened with woman's responsibilities, he would prepare to keep her suspended without divorce, depriving her of all her due rights. Some people take it for granted that a suspended woman can also demand her maintenance through legal action. But it has to be borne well in mind that it is not so easy to have one's rights relegated to him through legal procedure. The other consideration should be that man would like to escape from it and there are so many outlets for him. Thirdly, where does the wisdom lie in making divorce so difficult just by imposition of maintenance of the divorce that a person for, fear of payment of the upkeep of the wife may abstain from divorce, keeping her suspended. To perpetuate one mistake, committing another is not at all reasonable.

After divorce both man and woman are at liberty to choose another partner for themselves, thus filling this void created by divorce. But if even after divorcing her he has to bear the burden of the divorcee, the husband can hardly venture on a second experiment in matrimony. Compared with the total expenditure of the divorced woman and the new wife, he would rather think of and decide on a life of celibacy. This is most likely to make him morally corrupt and inclined to a career of dissoluteness.

There is an equal chance of the woman taking to the disagreeable and prohibited paths. If the woman is assured of her maintenance on a regular basis, even after divorce, she may be inclined to play the role of the naughty girl and vexing the husband off and on and prompted to get divorced. That is why we find that one of the promptings to divorce on a large scale is the wife's surety about the regular receipt of her maintenance from the husband all her life. Islam regards the tendency to divorce wrongful. It cannot support any rule or regulation which promotes this tendency in which every minor unpleasantness is sought to be removed through divorce.

There is another aspect also to it. Divorce alienates man and woman. Through continuance of maintenance, this estrangement is mitigated, wounds caused by separation gradually heal, meetings start becoming frequent with time, and display and declaration of familiarity and love are also on the increase. Since there is no bashfulness between them in the matter of sex relations, this recent familiarity and frequent meetings take a wrong direction. Maintaining a situation which is likely to lead to moral turpitude can never be condoned.

A rejoinder to this effect is possible that direct contact between them can be prevented by proper arrangement of intermediation. But in so far as they live in close neighbourhood this will be difficult to ensure. Very untoward consequences have been witnessed. So often they start living together as husband and wife as of old. And the society also is indulgent in this abominable affair. The demand of the temperament of the Islamic Shariah is that such conditions should never be created for any one that help and promote his advances towards dissoluteness, almost oblivious of his direction of approach.

These are some of those social evils and complications that spring from declaration of the compulsive payment of the divorced woman's maintenance. It is not easy to overlook and carelessly brush them off as mere whims.

Some people earnestly desire that life-long maintenance of the divorcee could somehow be traced to the Quran. But the difficulty is that the Book of Allah is not at all prepared to even humour them on this issue. In case of divorce, problems of woman's dower, maintenance and iddat or waiting present themselves. The Quran and the traditions of the Prophet have definite injunctions in this regard. The only thing missing here is the incessant maintenance of the divorced woman.

We have discussed mehr earlier in these pages. There are four different situations relating to payment of mehr :

- Mehr is fixed and consummation also a certainty, full amount of dower falls due to woman.
- Mehr is not fixed but the husband has gone unto her, entitling the woman to a dower rife in her family.
- Mehr fixed but no consummation. The dower due is just half of that payable after consummation.
- And in a case where there is neither fixation of mehr nor proper privacy (copulation), the woman will get mata' or some sort of parting gift from the husband.

The Iddat : Iddat (Idda) has been specified by the Quran.

In case of divorce after consummation iddat is the term of three periods. [43] —Al Quran 11 : 228

It is only three months in all those cases where menses are absent either due to early age, prepuberty, or advancing senility or menopause. [44] —Al Quran LXV: 4

And there is no iddat for a woman who has been divorced before consummation. [45] —Al Quran XXXIII :49

Now taking up the problem of maintenance and lodging :

Divorce is of two types—revocable in which the husband has the right of revocation and irrevocable in which that right of the husband comes to an end. The laws relating to both are in brief like this : In case of revocable divorce, the jurists are unanimous on it that the woman is entitled to both her maintenance and lodging. They are one here also on the issue that when the woman is pregnant, she gets both board and lodge regardless of the nature of divorce-revocable or irrevocable.

The Quran says :

And if they are pregnant then spend (your substance) on them until they deliver their burden. [46]

—Al Quran LXV: 6

If the woman is not pregnant and the divorce is irrevocable Imam Ahmad, Daud Zahiri, and Abu Thaur with some others are of the opinion that neither her maintenance nor lodging is due from the husband. They take their cue from the report about Fatima bint Qais. She says: "My husband divorced me irrevocably. The Prophet S.A.W. pronounced on it, 'you are not entitled to maintenance from your husband now'." In another report the word 'lodging' accompanies 'maintenance'.

Imam Malik, Imam Shafi'i and some others are of the opinion that since the Quran has mentioned 'lodging for her' she will get it but no maintenance.

(Al Quran LXV : 6)

Ibn Rushd, a Malikite, declares it (Maliki opinion) weak and vascilating. The Hanafite school appears to have a strong stand.

The Hanafite school and some other Ulama opine that irrespective of the nature of divorce the woman will get both the maintenance and lodging, their argument being that since the Quran has expressly mentioned lodging the maintenance naturally follows, being an accompaniment of (some body's stay). The Quran has made it binding on the husband to provide lodging for the term of the iddat, her support too naturally falls due on him; lodging makes maintenance inevitable. The diction of the Quranic verse supports the arguments :

Let the woman live (in iddat) in the same style as you live, according to your means : annoy them not so as to restrict them. [47] *—Al Quran LXV: 6*

Jassas says that the words of the Quranic verse are general in nature covering both the revocable and the irrevocable. The words "according to your capacity" point to the fact that lodging in the property of the husband has been made compulsory. This naturally demands the right of maintenance also (equally) compulsory, since lodging is a part of maintenance. And over and above the instruction that "she should not be annoyed to restrict her," means that annoyance and restriction are just as much applicable to maintenance as they have been said about the problem of lodging.

The report about Fatima bint-e-Qais has been rejected on the plea that Umar R.A.A., the second rightly guided Caliph, did not accept it, saying :

"For the sake of a woman's statement we cannot abandon the Quran and the Sunnah of the Prophet S.A.W. Allah alone knows whether she remembers it (right) or has forgotten it, there is lodging as well as maintenance for the divorcee.

That means according to Umar R.A.A., the Book of Allah and the Sunnah of the Prophet both allow lodging and maintenance both to the divorced woman.

It is evident now that on the basis of this authority that the maintenance and lodging of the divorcee is binding on the husband for the term of her iddat, but nothing after that.

The Mata : Those who try to prove the maintenance for the divorcee by the Quran argue with the support of the Quranic verse 11 : 241.

> *For divorced woman is a suitable gift. This is a duty on the righteous. [48]* —*Al Quran II : 241*

It is argued from this verse that it makes payment of *mehr* and *mata'* compulsory. After divorce so long as she lives, she should get this mata' to subsist on. The Quran has mentioned mata' but not specified it, leaving it to popular usage. That means it can be made definite according to the custom of any particular age. According to these advocates, if this mata' is fixed in the form of maintenance for her life-term or until second marriage, it would be according to the dictates of the Quran and not in contravention of it. Its payment may be in a lump sum or in installments (according to the convenience of the parties) but pay he must.

This quaint sense of mata' is neither supported by the Arabic lexicon nor the context of the Quran, nor the companions of the Prophet, their followers (*tabieen*) and the jurists of the Muslim Ummah take it to mean maintenance. To understand fully the sense of this word mata' or mutāah in which it has been used in the foregoing Quranic verse the following questions will have to be considered carefully: 1. What is mata'? 2. Is it moral or legal in nature? 3. If legal, is it so for every divorced woman in general or some particular ones?

Literally mata' means petty personal effects and also things serving some purpose only for a brief span of time. Zahri says :

> *Mata' literally means something that can be utilised beneficially.*

Imam Raghib says:

> *To derive benefit for a short time is mata'.*

He further goes on to say :

> *Every thing from which benefit of any sort whatsoever can be derived is mata' or mutaah.*

Imam Razi says:

Mutaah and mata' is in fact something that serves and benefits but not for long (transient).

The word mata' has been used in the Quran to denote various utility articles—things of daily use in houses, for instance. The strangers have been directed to borrow the articles of daily use in the following manner:

And when ye ask (his ladies) for anything ye want, ask them from before a screen. [49]—Al Quran XXXI 11: 53

Metallic substances such as utensils and implements :

Even so from that (ore) which they heat in the fire to make ornaments or utensils therewith, there is a scum like wise. [50] —Al Quran XIII : 17

In Surah Yusuf (Q. XII : 79) it has been used for a bowl or a measure and at another place it has been used for the hunter's tackle and personal effects and in Surah Maidah (Q. V: 17) it has been used for water game.

Similarly, among with these things of meagre importance, all those useful articles and substances supporting life, have been termed mata'. The Quran says :

"....On earth your dwelling place and your means of livelihood for a time. [51] —Al Quran 11 : 36

The entire world with all its paraphernalia, gold, jewels and articles of luxury and comfort, has been called mata'.

....(and also adornments of gold). But all this was nothing but enjoyment of the present life : The Hereafter in the right of thy Lord is for the Righteous. [52]

—Al Quran XLII : 35

Here, compared with the life Here after, the worldly existence has been termed mata'. What is meant is that in keeping in view the life-eternal. Hereafter, and the bounties of the Benevolent Lord, this world and its riches and luxuries appear 'Mata'-e-Qaleel' (very little or almost nothing).

But the life of the world is but little comfort compared to the Hereafter. [53] —Al Quran XIII :26

At another place it has been said :

But little is the comfort, as compared with the Hereafter. [54]

—Al Quran IX: 38

Now let us see what the mata' of divorce means? The Quran has ordained mata' of divorce as absolute without any conditions.

It has not been specified what is meant by mata'. It evidently means that even if it is regarded compulsory, giving anything of any value whatsoever, after divorce, fulfills this demand.

The scholars who have laboriously investigated the true sense of the words used in the Quran and the traditions of the Prophet, do not for a moment take it to mean that maintenance is to be paid to the divorced wife life-long or she may be supported for a specified period even. According to them it means that she should be presented with some gift to please or console her in her grief.

Imam Raghib who is a linguist of high standing where Quranic terminology is concerned, says about mata-e-Talaq :

> *Whatever the husband confers on his divorced wife to be benefited by, is mata' or mutaah.*

That means he regards the maintenance during the period of iddat mata' and does not consider her entitled to any other mata'. (The opinions of the jurists a little later).

An expert lexicologist of the diction of Hadith, Allamah Ibn Atheer, has given exposition of the term "mata'-e-Talaq" in these words:

> *It is desirable for the person divorcing his wife that at the time of parting of ways he should give her some sort of gift.*

Allamah Suyuti has prepared an abridged edition of Ibn Atheer's book on the lexicon of the Hadith. He says in it :

> *Mata-at-Talaq is simply this that the woman be given something to console her in her grief.*

The context in which the Quran has mentioned it also devotes the purpose behind it. It has said that:

> *The woman divorced before consummation shall be entitled to half her fixed dower, and the one with dower unfixed shall get only mataor a gift. [55]—Al Quran 11 : 236-23*

Now, if the dower does not mean life-long maintenance, how can mata' come to mean life-long support of the divorcee?

The word mata' cannot be taken to mean maintenance for a life-term for two reasons:

1. The Quran has specified that after divorce the maintenance and lodging of the woman shall be the liability of man for the term of the Iddat and there it ends. To make it binding on man after the expiry of the iddat for the life-time of the divorcee or her second marriage would be an addition to the divine injunction which is highly objectionable. The

liability from which he has been declared free by Allah in view of so many considerations to over burden him once again with the same would be a wilful disregard of those considerations.

2. We have discussed earlier in detail that the responsibility of the wife's maintenance in return for her services to the household devoting her time and energy to run it efficiently, and after divorce since she is relieved of that duty and the man has no more claim over them she too cannot claim support any longer, not to say for the duration of her life or her second marriage.

Opinions of Companions and their Followers : Let us now try to find out what was the practice of the companions and their followers in this behalf. Abdullah Ibn Abbas R.A.A. says that the highest standard of the mata' of the divorcee is a slave. Next in the descending order is a (three piece) change of clothes and the last thing that could be conferred on her is some silver (cash or coins). Abdullah Ibn Umar R.A.A. says that it (cash) should be at least thirty dirhams.

Among the tabieen, Qadi Shuraih has fixed mata' at five thousand dirhams. Imam Shabi has declared it to be the woman's clothes used inside her house, a lihaf (a sleeping bag) and jalbab (a sheet). Hasan Basri says that limits can be put on mata' by every one according to his capacity. Ata ibn Abi Ribah has also said more or less the same thing.

There are examples too of some benevolent persons who have gone far, out of their way, in cooperation in the matter of conferment of mata' (parting gift after divorce).

Abdur Rahman bin Auf R.A.A. gave away a black slave girl to a divorced wife of his, Tamazir.

Hasan R.A.A. (Prophet's grandson) also has been reported to have given ten thousand dirhams as mata' to one of his divorced wives.

Many similar examples of generosity and beneficence can be found, but they cannot become law as precepts binding on every one.

Views of the Jurists : The jurists have tried to pronounce upon it according to the circumstances extant then.

The Hanafite school recommends for the divorcee a change of clothes (usually a three piece suit) but left to the prevailing trends of the times. The standard and quality of cloth will depend on the husband's life-style and standard of living. Another group opines that the standard of life of both the husband and the wife shall be taken into consideration. The Hanafites, besides, have consensus on it that mata' cannot exceed half the 'mehr-mithl' since it is in lieu of it, and not less than five dirhams either, since according to the Hanafite school the minimum of dower is ten dirhams. If it is taken to be half of the dower in vogue, it can be more than the cost of a change of clothes.

In Malikite jurisprudence it has been said that after divorce whatever a person gives to his wife in keeping with his financial status is mutaah.

Imam Shafi'i has specified mutaah thus : For a man of substance a servant and for a person of the middle class a change of clothes. The minimum that can be prescribed for it is thirty dirhams or something of that value. And the husband and the wife have the right to any agreement on more or less than that.

More or less the same point has been made by the Hanafite school, that mutaah shall be that which man's status permits. The higher standard of it is a servant and the minimum is a change of clothes that can suffice her for her prayer (a three piece suit including a sheet). The husband can endow her with more than that at will and the woman can accept less than that if she is so pleased.

The Jurists have tried to fix mata' according to the then existing conditions and adjustments can be made under changed conditions in a particular age. The Quran and the Hadith have left mehr and nafqah (maintenance) unfixed, so has mutaah remained unspecified, depending on the conditions through the ages. The difference of opinions among the companions and the tabieen, Allamah Abu Bakr Jassas has opined on it :

> *The quantum of Mutaah stated are the* ijtihadi *opinions of our ancestors. The opinion of one man was not questioned by another since he himself held a. different opinion of his own. That shows they were their own considered opinions (ijtihad).*

According to some jurists, the social and economic status of woman shall not be considered in fixation of mutaah since the Quran has declared that:

> *The moneyed shall endow mutaah according to their means and the poor according to their means. [56]*
>
> *—Al Quran II : 236*

But the more agreeable opinion is that in apportioning mutaah consideration will be given to the status of both. Jassas says that sticking to maroof (pious populär opinion) has been stressed and over-looking the status of woman is against maroof. How can a lady of an affluent family be treated like a poor common woman in the endowment of mutaah?

The foregoing discussion makes it amply evident that mutaah is the outfit gifted to a divorcee as a mark of sympathy and to console her in her grief. Trying to enlarge its scope and stretching it to life-long maintenance is an excess that cannot be expected of any serious and reasonable person.

Let us now take up the question whether mata' enjoys only a moral position or it is legal in nature. The point of view of Imam Malik on this issue is that it is agreeable to give the divorced woman something by way of gift. It is not a compulsory obligation. His argument rests on the Quranic words "This is a duty on the righteous," as the closing phrase of the verse. In the preceding verse 236, mutaah has been pointed out as piety and Ehsan in the closing words. We cannot declare it obligatory for one and all.

Among the tabieen Qadi Shuraih was also of the same opinion. It has been said in a report that a certain person divorced his wife after consummation. She filed a suit at the court of Qadi Shuraih claiming mutaah. The Qadi persuasively remarked during his talk to the husband that he should not deny himself the enviable position of joining the ranks of the righteous and the pious. However, he did not compel him to endow her with mutaah.

According to Imam Malik, the woman divorced before consummation but with dower fixed, shall get half the fixed dower but shall not be entitled to mutaah.

It has also been reported as the opinion of Imam Malik that mutaah is obligatory, but his well-known opinion is that stated above.

The majority of the jurists have regarded mutaah as obligatory. Their argument is that the Quran has used the words; "matt-e-u-hunna" (bestow on them a suitable gift (Q. II : 241) which imperative form indicates that it is obligatory "For the divorced women" also indicates that it will be their property and therefore, they could demand it. That also proves its obligatory nature. The words "this is a duty on the righteous." (Q. II: 241) also suggest that it must be obligatory. To further stress it, it has been said, "is due from those who wish to do the right thing," (Q. II : 236).

Can it possibly mean that it is binding only on those who fear Allah and wish to do the right thing and not others? In response to this query Allamah Abu Bakr Jassas has proved with precepts from the Quran itself that it does not at all mean to eliminate those who are not righteous. It is there just to stress that people may be further persuaded to this righteous deed.

Now the question arises that if Mutaah is obligatory in nature, If it so for every divorced woman. Or that for some it is obligatory and for others it is not so.

The Hanafite Fiqh has opined that mutaah is the due of that woman whose dower was not fixed and she got divorced before consummation. It is she for whom the Quran has ordained it (Q. 11 : 236). Other divorced women get their mehr and maintenance for the entire iddat term. The last mentioned are not entitled to it as a matter of obligatory duty. They may, however, get as a parting gift.

Imam Ahmad too is, of the same opinion.

Imam Shafii's says mutaah must go to all the divorced women save those with fixed mehr and divorced before consummation. The Quran is explicit about it that she will get half her fixed dower. (Q. II : 237). Among the companions Abdullah ibn Umar R.A.A. is reported to have the same opinion.

Saeed bin Zubayr, Abul Aliyah, Hasan Basri, and some others R.A., have said that every divorced woman must get mutaah as a matter of duty since (for the divorced woman is mutaah) is a Quranic injunction, which is general in nature, and there is no justification for any particularisation. The idea that only those divorced women will be endowed with mutaah whose dower had not been fixed is also erroneous since the dower of the Prophet's S.A.W. consorts was fixed and they had been consummated also, but in case of divorce the Quran ordained payment of mutaah to them. It says:

> *O Prophet ! Say to thy consorts that if it be that ye desire the life of this world and its glitter then come, I will provide for you enjoyment and set you free in a handsome manner. [57]*
>
> *—Al Quran XXXIII :28*

This is said to be the opinion of Ali R.A.A., Imam Zahri, Ibrahim Nakhai, Ata bin Abi Ribah and Sufyan Thauri. This is also the opinion of Zahirites. Ibn Hazam Zahiri says that all types of divorced women are entitled to mutaah on a compulsory basis, whether the divorce is revocable or irrevocable, consummation or no consummation, mehr fixed or unfixed, since 'for the divorced woman there is mutaah according to the pious popular usage' is a general ordainment and it would be improper on our part to make it selective.

All these opinions are similar. Those who are in favour of making mutaah or parting gift to the divorced women obligatory, may favour this (immediately foregoing) opinion, but there are several evils in it. Firstly, the woman divorced before consummation, if her dower is fixed, shall get half of her fixed dower and mutaah, and in case of non-fixation of mehr, she shall get only mutaah, which appears to be sort of iniquity. Secondly, declaring mutaah compulsory would mean that like mehr and maintenance, it is also an undeniable right which she can claim legally. Undoubtedly, as stated above, the opinion of the Zahirities and some others is in support of it. The well-known commentator of the Quran, Ibn Jarir Tabri, has subscribed to it, and according to him mutaah like mehr is binding upon the divorcing husband and in case of non-payment, like mehr and other dues, the aggrieved party can sue for it in a court of law.

This opinion appears to be unsounded in view of the fact that the Islamic courts never pronounced such decisions. Imam Shabi says:

> *By Allah! I never saw any one imprison for non-payment of mutaah. By Allah! If it had been obligatory, the Qadis would have put the defaulters behind the bars.*

In the foregoing pages we discussed in detail the meaning of mata' and its legal position presenting the opinions of various jurists in this behalf, which make it amply manifest that it can not be proved on the authority of the Quran and Hadith that there is any responsibility of the support of the divorced wife on the husband, nor from the antiquity to posterity has any one expressed his opinion in its favour. It is a baseless idea that finds support nowhere.

Economic Problems : Lastly, let us take up the question of the economic responsibility of the divorced woman. This question is hurled at the Muslim community in such a way that after divorce the Muslim woman finds herself in such a difficult fix to which solution has to be found anyway. Then they put forth all sorts of suggestions, delving into the Quran for the support of their new tangled ideas where the problems of nikah and divorce have been presenting themselves for the last fourteen hundred years. Divorce is nothing new. There have been cases from the early period of Islam and problems relating to both young and old divorcees have been dealt with. The reasonable course that should have been adopted was to find out whether Islam has presented any solution to this problem. Rather they should have expected that like so many other problems it must have provided guidance here also. And overlooking all the considerations to think and make others believe that Islam has suggested no solution to this serious problem, the Muslim thinkers never cared to give a serious thought to it all this while, is an example of sheer ignorance.

According to Islam the relationship between the husband and wife gets snapped for good, and therefore, it has not at all associated the problem of the financial burden of the woman with the estranged husband but solved in other ways.

1. It is a baseless proposition that if a divorced woman does not receive her maintenance from the husband, there will be no way of providing her subsistence and she is most likely to starve. There are probably some other motives behind this idea rather than any sympathy for the woman. Or else it is a fact known to an ordinary student of Islamic Theology that under the Islamic Law there are various ways down which wealth flows to the woman, including inheritance, mehr, legacy and other sources. And the possibility of her coming into wealth from either of the above mentioned sources, guaranteeing her subsistence satisfactorily can not be overlooked.
2. Earlier we have convincingly proved that though the woman is not under any compulsion to undertake any economic effort for her support, but there is no bar on her taking to a permitted source of earning her subsistence. She can seek employment, undertake agriculture and trade, partake in industry, in short, having a perfect right to undertake any economic endeavour, of course within the Islamic limits set for her here. Success in this field can enable her not only to support herself unaided but extend a helping hand to others in need.
3. Islam regards conjugal life for man essential. It has instructed the entire society to help the individuals in taking to conjugal life.

   Marry those among you who are single and the virtuous ones among your slaves, male or female. [58]

   —Al Quran XXIV : 32

   The word occurring in the Quranic verse above, is 'Ayama', the plural form of Ayyum, covering in its meaning both the unmarried man and woman. It also encompasses along with the virgins that have not yet found a suitor, those also without a husband due to divorce or widowhood. It is a fact that in the present age, the inclination of Muslims towards second marriage of the divorcee and the widow is at a low ebb. But Islam is in favour of giving it a fresh fillip and reasonably so. The Islamic teaching in this behalf is that if due to disharmony in temperament a husband and wife have parted ways or the death of one of them has closed the chapter of his or her conjugal life, a match should be found for their remarriage, since living alone permits corrupting influences on the morals and may blot characters. Acting on this teaching will itself solve the problem of the divorced and widowed women, since in conjugal life she becomes the liability of the husband. That is why we find during the course of Islamic history, so long as they adhered to this teaching, never did any problem of the support of the widow and the divorced woman confront the Muslim society. This is the best solution of this problem and it must be promoted.

4. If the divorced woman and likewise the widow fail to find suitors and have no means of support of their own, Islam has imposed the responsibility of their support on their families.

In this connection what should be kept in view is the principle that under the Islamic law the woman is never under compulsion to endeavour in the economic field for her livelihood. In the Islamic Fiqh it has been said: "To be a woman is enough for incapability, meaning thereby that for various reasons she lacks the capacity to earn her own bread. And that is why others have to shoulder that responsibility. The husband supports her under all circumstances. After divorce if she is not self-sufficient and her progeny is in a position to work and earn their bread, it becomes charged with her support. Here it would be in the fitness of things to make it evident that according to our jurists the maintenance of the parents includes all those facilities that have come for mention under the maintenance of wife.

The substances included in the maintenance of wife, that for the parents shall have all of them, namely board and lodge, so much so that the services of a servant have not been exempted.

If she does not get remarried after divorce and her children too are unable to undertake her support the burden of her maintenance shall be transferred to her parents and she will be treated as she was before marriage. The expositor of the famous book of Hanafite Fiqh, Hidayah, Allamah Ibn-ul-Hammam writes:

> *The maintenance and support of the daughters until such time as they get married, if they are lacking in substance, is the responsibility of the father. He cannot engage them in any work or service, even if they are able to undertake such jobs. If one of them gets divorced after the expiry of the term of iddat the responsibility of her maintenance will once again revert to the father.*

In the absence of father, whoever happens to be her closest mahram (eternally prohibited to her), such as uncle, brother and others (maternal uncle, maternal and paternal grand fathers) shall be held responsible for her support. If none of these relatives is there or is incapable of shouldering this responsibility, the Islamic state steps in to undertake her support. In the absence of an Islamic state the Muslim society should come forward to take her charge. The society of Indian Muslims desirous of solving the problem of such women can easily do so.

Those who go on raising objections for their own sake, jumping from one to the next, it appears they are totally ignorant of the 'Islamic Law of Maintenance'. We have shown just a glimpse of it here. They should try to acquaint themselves with its details.

Bibliography

Abdullah, Muhammad : *Islamic Prayers,* Idara Ishaat-e-Diniyat Pvt. Ltd, New Delhi, 1999.

Adams, C.C. : *Islam and Modernism in Egypt,* Oxford University Press, New York, 1953.

Adil, H. M. : *Letters of Hadrat Usman Ghani (R.A.A.),* Kitab Bhavan, New Delhi, 1992

Ahmad, Imtiaz : *Divorce and Remarriage among Muslims in India,* Manohar Publishers, New Delhi, 2003.

Ahmad, K. N. : *Muslim Law of Divorce,* Kitab Bhavan, New Delhi, 1988.

Ahmad, Khurshid : *Islam : its Meaning and Message,* Islamic Council of Europe, London, 1976.

Ahmad, Manzooruddin : *Pakistan : the Emerging Islamic State,* Allies Book Corporation, Karachi, 1966.

Ahmad, Naseem : *Liberation of Muslim Women,* Gyan Books Pvt., Ltd., New Delhi, 2001.

Akhtar, Wazir : *Economics in Islamic Law,* Kitab Bhavan, New Delhi, 1992.

Ali, Syed Ameer : *Islam,* Kitab Bhavan, New Delhi, 1992.

Amery, Reeves : *The Anatomy of Peace,* Oxford, New York, 2001.

Anwarullah : *The Islamic Law of Evidence,* Kitab Bhavan, New Delhi, 2000.

Arbery : *Sufism,* George Allen & Unwin Ltd., London, 1996.

Arnold and Guillaume : *The Legacy of Islam,* Oxford University Press, London, 1949.

Arnold, Sir Thomas : *The Caliphate,* MacMillan, London, 1965.

Arnold, T. W. : *Preaching of Islam,* Luzac & Co., London, 1913.

Arnold, Thomas : *The Legacy of Islam,* Oxford University Press, New York, 2000.

Arvind, Sharma : *Women in World Religion,* New York Press, New York, 1990.

Atta, Mohiuddin : *Abu Bakr,* Feroz Pub., Lahore, 1999.

Aurobindo, Sri : *The Foundations of Islamic Culture*, New York, 1973.

Azmi, Majaz : *Muslim Wife,* Idara Ishaat-e-Diniyat Pvt. Ltd, New Delhi, 1991.

Baksh, S. K. : *Politics in Islam,* Kitab Bhavan, New Delhi, 2003.

Baloch, N. A. : *Great Books of Islamic Civilization,* Kitab Bhavan, New Delhi, 2001.

Barkatullah, M. : *Khilafat,* MacMillan, London,1924.

Berger, M. : *Islam in Egypt Today : Social and Political Aspects of Popular Religion,* MacMillan, London, 1970.

Boland, B.J. : *The Struggle of Islam in Modern Indonesia,*The Hague, Nijhoff, 1971.

Brett, M. : *Northern Africa : Islam and Modernization,* Allen & Unwin, London, 1973.

Brockelman, C. : *History of the Islamic People,* G.P. Putnam's Sons, New York, 1947.

Browne, G. Edward : *Islamic Medicine,* Goodword Books Pvt. Ltd., New Delhi, 1996.

Bukhsh, S. K. : *Contribution to the History of Islamic Civilization,* Kitab Bhavan, New Delhi, 2000.

Calverley, Edwin Elliot : *Worship in Islam,* University of Madras, Madras, 1925.

Carl, Bockleman : *History of Islamic Peoples,* Oxford, New York, 2003.

Carra, De Vaux : *Penseurs d' Islam,* A. & B. Pub., Paris, 1921.

Carre, Olivier : *Islam and the State in the World Today,* Manohar Publisher, New Delhi, 1989.

Crone, Patricia : *Themes in Islamic History,* Cambridge University Press, New Delhi, 2000.

Dawud, Rahbar : *God of Justice,* Mac & Jac Pub., Leiden, 1960.

Desai, A. : *Hind Islami : Tarz-e-Tameer,* Publication Division, New Delhi, 1993.

Dhaul, Laxmi : *The Sufi Shrine of Ajmer,* Rupa & Co., New Delhi, 1987.

Dinet and Salman : *Life of Muhammad (PBUH),* Feroz Pub., Lahore, 2003.

Durrani, F.K.K. : *Muhammad (PBUH) the Prophet,* Oxford, New York, 2001.

Edward, Mortimer : *Faith and Power, the Politics of Islam,* Oxford, New York, 2002.

Edwards, Beverly Milton : *Islam and Politics in the Contemporary World,* Blackwell, New York, 1987.

Engineer, Asghar Ali : *Islam : Challenge in Twenty-first Century,* Gyan Books Pvt. Ltd., New Delhi, 2004.

Fatima, T. : *Islamic Law and Judiciary,* Deep & Deep Publications, New Delhi, 2001.

Fazal, Abul : *Akbar Namah,* Kitab Bhavan, New Delhi, 1977.

Flynn, V.J.A. : *Fathepur-Sikri,* Popular Prakashan, Bombay, 1975.

Gairdner, W.H. Temple : *Al-Ghazzali's Mishkatul-Anwar : the Niche for Lights,* Oxford, London, 1915.

Gare, Frederic : *Political Islam in the Indian Subcontinent : the Jannat-i-Islam,* Manohar Publishers, New Delhi, 2001.

Gauba, K.L. : *The Prophet of the Desert (PBUH),* Feroz Pub., Lahore, 2000.

Gibb, H.A.R : *Islamic Society and the West,* Luzac & Co., London, 1960.

Gilsenam, Michael : *Recognizing Islam,* MacMillan, London, 2001.

Grunebaum, Gustave Edmund Von : *Modern Islam,* University Press, Los Angeles, 1952.

Guillaume, A. : *The Traditions of Islam,* Khayats, Beirut, 1966.

Hafiz, Ghulam Sarwar : *Muhammad (PBUH) the Holy Prophet,* Dar-ul Ishaat, Karachi, 1997.

Hamid, Enayat : *Islam in the Political Process,* Cambridge University Press, Cambridge, 1993.

Hamidullah, M. : *Battlefields of the Prophet Muhammad,* Kitab Bhavan, New Delhi, 2003.

Haq, M. Anwarul : *The Faith Movement of Mawlana Muhammad Ilyas,* Country Pub., London, 1972.

Harun, Yahya : *Islam : the Religion of Ease,* Goodword Books Pvt. Ltd., New Delhi, 1993.

Hasan, M. : *Hadrat Ali Murtada (R.A.A.),* Kitab Bhavan, New Delhi, 2003.

Hasan, Mushirul : *Islam and Indian Nationalism : Refection on Abdul Kalam Azad,* Manohar Publishers, New Delhi, 1992.

Hassan, M. : *Hadrat Abu Bakr Siddique (R.A.A.),* Kitab Bhavan, New Delhi, 2004.

Herklots G. A. and Jafar Sharif : *Islam in India,* Atlantic Publishers, New Delhi, 1999.

Hourani : *Islam in European Thought,* New Academic Publishing House, New Delhi, 1989.

Houtsma, T. and Others : *Encyclopaedia of Islam*, Macmillan, London, 1934.

Hughes, T.P. : *Dictionary of Islam*, Allen & Co., London, 1935,

Hurgronje, C. Snouck : *Mohammedanism*, Oxford, New York, 1916.

Husaini, H.A. : *The Religious thought of Mir Syed Ali Hamadani*, Al-Hamra Publishers, Srinagar, 1979.

Husaini, Waqar : *Islamic Thought*, Goodword Books Pvt. Ltd., New Delhi, 1999.

Hussain, S. Saukat, : *Human Rights in Islam*, Kitab Bhavan, New Delhi, 2001.

Ibn, Sina : *Al-Qanun fil-Tibb*, University Press, Lukhnow, 1905.

Imamuddin, S. M. : *Arab Muslim Administration*, Kitab Bhavan, New Delhi, 1984.

Jafar, Sharif : *Islam in India*, Oxford, New Delhi, 1972.

Jalbani, G. N. : *Teachings of Hazrat Shah Waliyullah*, Kitab Bhavan, New Delhi, 1997.

Jamil, Jalbi and Qazi A. Qadir : *The Changing World of Islam*, Royal Pub., Lahore, 1992.

Jansen, G.H. : *Militant Islam*, Pan Books, London, 1979.

John, J. Hue and John L. Esposite : *Islam in Transition*, Oxford, New York, 1969.

Kalerji : *From War to Peace*, Oxford, New York, 1991.

Kaur, R. : *Islamic Co-operation and Unity*, Deep & Deep Publications, New Delhi, 1993.

Khaduri, M. : *War and Peace in the Law of Islam*, Hopkins Press, Baltimore, 1955.

Khalifa, Abdul Hakim : *The Prophet (PBUH) and His Message*, Islamic Pub., Lahore, 1996.

Khan, N. M. Yamin : *God Soul and Universe in Science and Islam*, Kitab Bhavan, New Delhi, 1993.

Khan, Qamaruddin : *Political Concepts in the Quran*, Islamic Book Foundation, Lahore, 1982.

Lambton, A.K.S. : *Islam and Russia*, Oxford, New York, 1956.

Lee, Yerhune : *The Indian Muslims*, Rupa & Co., New Delhi, 1990.

Levy, Reuben : *The Social Structure of Islam*, Cambridge University Press, New York, 1993.

Litvak, Strart : *Sufism : The Sufi Path to Seeking Wisdom*, Jaico Publishing House, New Delhi, 1987.

Madhavan, A. : *What is Sufism ?*, Rupa & Co., New Delhi, 1981.

Manzuruddin, Ahmad : *Islamic Political System,* Kitab Bhavan, New Delhi, 1991.

Maudoodi, S.A.A. : *Islami Riyasat,* Islamic Book Foundation, New Delhi, 1999.

Mohaghegh, Mahdi and Landolt, *Collected Papers on Islamic Philosophy and Mysticism,* Tehran, 1971.

Montgomery, Watt : *Muhammad (PBUH) at Medina,* Oxford, New York, 1973.

Muhammad, Asad : *Islam at the Crossroads,* Kitab Bhavan, New Delhi, 2003.

Muhammed, Ataur-Rahim : *Jesus a Prophet of Islam,* Idara Ishaat-e-Diniyat Pvt. Ltd, New Delhi, 1995.

Muir, William : *Early Caliphate,* Oxford, New York, 1970.

Muslehuddin, M. : *Banking and Islamic Law,* Idara Ishaat-e-Diniyat Pvt. Ltd, New Delhi, 1990.

Nasr, Seyyed H. : *An Introduction to Islamic Cosmological Doctrines,* Cambridge, 1964.

Oudha, Abdul Qadir : *Criminal Law of Islam,* Kitab Bhavan, New Delhi, 1999.

Qureshi, A. Iqbal : *Islam and the Theory of Interest,* Kitab Bhavan, New Delhi, 1994.

Rahim, Abdur : *Principles of Islamic Jurisprudence,* Kitab Bhavan, New Delhi, 1994.

Rahman, F.: *Islam,* Weidenfeld and Nicolson, London, 1966.

Rizvi, Hasan Askari : *Islami Reassertion : a Socio Political Study,* Progressive Publishers, Lahore, 1981.

Rodinson, Maxime : *Islam and Capitalism,* Penguin, London, 1974.

Rosenthal, E.I.J. : *Political Thought in Medieval Islam,* Cambridge, New York, 1962.

Schacht, Joseph, and Bosworth, C.E. : *The Legacy of Islam,* Oxford University Press, New York, 1979.

Sergeant : *Constitution of Madina,* Feroz Pub., Lahore, 1992.

Shah, Sirdar Ikbal Ali : *Islamic Sufism,* Idarah-I-Adbiyat-I-Delhi, Delhi, 1979.

Sharif, M. Raihan : *Islamic Social Framework,* Islamic Book Foundation, Dacca, 1980.

Shemesh, A.B. : *Taxation in Islam,* MacMillan & Co., London, 1965.

Siddiqi, M.Z. : *Hadith Literature,* Deepali Pub., Calcutta, 1961.

Smith, W. Cantwell : *Islam in Modern History,* Princeton University Press, New Jersey, 1957.

Som, Tamarci : *A Brief History of Islam,* Blackwell, New York, 1992.

Stobart, J.W. H. : *Islam and its Founders,* Uppal Publishing House, New Dlehi, 1974.

Syed, Amir Ali : *The Spirit of Islam,* Royal Pub.,Lahore, 1979.

Syed, M. H. : *Islamic Terrorism : Myth or Reality,* Gyan Books Pvt. Ltd., New Delhi, 2002.

Tarachand : *Influence of Islam on Indian Culture,* Adam Pub., Allahabad, 1963.

Titus, M. : *Indian Islam,* Milford, New Delhi, 1979.

Trimingham, J.S. : *The Sufi Orders in Islam,* Oxford, New York, 1920.

Ulama, Majlisul : *Islamic Hijaab,* Idara Ishaat-e-Diniyat Pvt. Ltd, New Delhi, 1997.

Ullah, M. : *Administration of Justice in Islam,* Kitab Bhavan, New Delhi, 1990.

Usmani, Taqi Muhammad : *An Introduction to Islamic Finance,* Idara Ishaat-e-Diniyat Pvt. Ltd., New Delhi, 1999.

Walker, Benjamin : *Foundation of Islam : the Making of World Faith,* Rupa & Co., New Delhi, 2001.

Watt, W.M. : *Islamic Surveys,* Edinburgh University Press, Edinburgh, 1999.

Weeramanthy, G. G.: *Islamic Jurisprudence—an International Perspective,* Vishwa Lekha, Culcutta, 1980.

Yusuf, S.M. : *Economic Justice in Islam,* Kitab Bhavan, New Delhi, 1988.

Zafeeruddin, M.M. : *System of Modesty and Chastity in Islam,* Idara Ishaat-e-Diniyat Pvt. Ltd, New Delhi, 1995.

Zaydan, Jurji : *History of Islamic Civilization,* Kitab Bhavan, New Delhi, 1994.

Index

A

B

C

K

L

M

N

O

P

Q

R

S

❑❑❑